AF446765

External Finance for Private Sector Development

Studies in Development Economics and Policy

General Editor: **Anthony Shorrocks**

UNU WORLD INSTITUTE FOR DEVELOPMENT ECONOMICS RESEARCH (UNU/WIDER) was established by the United Nations University as its first research and training centre and started work in Helsinki, Finland, in 1985. The purpose of the Institute is to undertake applied research and policy analysis on structural changes affecting the developing and transitional economies, to provide a forum for the advocacy of policies leading to robust, equitable and environmentally sustainable growth, and to promote capacity strengthening and training in the field of economic and social policy-making. Its work is carried out by staff researchers and visiting scholars in Helsinki and through networks of collaborating scholars and institutions around the world.

UNU World Institute for Development Economics Research (UNU/WIDER)
Katajanokanlaituri 6 B, FIN-00160 Helsinki, Finland

Titles include:

Ricardo Ffrench-Davis and Stephany Griffith-Jones (*editors*)
FROM CAPITAL SURGES TO DROUGHT
Seeking Stability for Emerging Economies

Aiguo Lu and Manuel F. Montes (*editors*)
POVERTY, INCOME DISTRIBUTION AND WELL-BEING IN ASIA DURING THE TRANSITION

Robert J. McIntyre and Bruno Dallago (*editors*)
SMALL AND MEDIUM ENTERPRISES IN TRANSITIONAL ECONOMIES

Vladimir Mikhalev (*editor*)
INEQUALITY AND SOCIAL STRUCTURE DURING THE TRANSITION

E. Wayne Nafziger and Raimo Väyrynen (*editors*)
THE PREVENTION OF HUMANITARIAN EMERGENCIES

Matthew Odedokun (*editor*)
EXTERNAL FINANCE FOR PRIVATE SECTOR DEVELOPMENT
Appraisals and Issues

Laixiang Sun (*editor*)
OWNERSHIP AND GOVERNANCE OF ENTERPRISES
Recent Innovative Developments

Studies in Development Economics and Policy
Series Standing Order ISBN 0–333–96424–1
(outside North America only)

You can receive future titles in this series as they are published by placing a standing order. Please contact your bookseller or, in case of difficulty, write to us at the address below with your name and address, the title of the series and the ISBN quoted above.

Customer Services Department, Macmillan Distribution Ltd, Houndmills, Basingstoke, Hampshire RG21 6XS, England

External Finance for Private Sector Development

Appraisals and Issues

Edited by

Matthew Odedokun
UNU/WIDER

in association with the United Nations University/
World Institute for Development Economics Research

First published 2004 by
PALGRAVE MACMILLAN
Houndmills, Basingstoke, Hampshire RG21 6XS and
175 Fifth Avenue, New York, N.Y. 10010
Companies and representatives throughout the world

PALGRAVE MACMILLAN is the global academic imprint of the Palgrave
Macmillan division of St. Martin's Press, LLC and of Palgrave Macmillan Ltd.
Macmillan® is a registered trademark in the United States, United Kingdom
and other countries. Palgrave is a registered trademark in the European
Union and other countries.

ISBN 1–4039–2091–5

This book is printed on paper suitable for recycling and made from fully
managed and sustained forest sources.

A catalogue record for this book is available from the British Library.

A catalog record for this book is available from the Library of Congress.

10   9   8   7   6   5   4   3   2   1
13 12 11 10 09 08 07 06 05 04

Printed and bound in Great Britain by
Antony Rowe Ltd, Chippenham and Eastbourne

Contents

List of Tables

List of Figures

Preface

1   Concept of private sector development

In the context of general discussion, private sector refers to the totality of the domestic economy outside the government sector, thus including both the business and household sectors. But a narrower meaning is implied in the context of the private sector development (PSD) debate, as private sector refers only to the business sector, excluding the household sector. Therefore, strictly speaking, PSD should be referred to as 'business sector development' (as opposed to private), a term we use in this volume.

And what about 'development'? In economics, development is often accorded a wider meaning than growth. So also in the context of the usage of PSD in this volume, development has a more expansive meaning than growth. It should be construed to refer to the enhancement and promotion, in a self-sustaining manner, of business sector in totality, and not just, say, multinationals or small-scale enterprises alone. Thus, PSD as referred to in the volume, implies the promotion of the business sector in this manner.

2   Problems militating against PSD

Logically, the promotion of PSD simply refers to the removal or reduction of existing hindrances to business sector development. And what are these hindrances? The literature on PSD in developing countries compiles a lengthy catalogue of hindrances. Discussions of factors militating against PSD are sometimes made in the context of the transition economies (i.e. the former communist economies), for example, Hussain 1992; Stern 1997; Sullivan 1998; Han and Baumgarte 2000 and OECD 2001a. Problems identified often include those relating to the underdevelopment of the legal and institutional and capital markets.

But many other studies have also approached the subject in the context of developing economies in general, both transitional and non-transitional (e.g. Paul 1990; Holden and Rajapatirana 1995; World Bank 1995; Cook *et al.* 1998; Ofosu-Amaah 2000). The latter group of studies has identified a wider range of problems working against PSD. These include adverse macroeconomic and institutional environment, inappropriate trade policies, inadequate regulatory and judicial systems (including property rights system), the nature and prevalence of state-owned enterprises, political instability, poor state of financial systems, inadequate human resources and physical infrastructures and so on. But as contended by Paul (1990: abstract) in his analysis of PSD in Ghana, 'the most severe constraint on Ghana's private sector pertains to credit availability and allocation'. This is likely to be true of PSD in many other countries as well.

Given the plethora of obstacles to PSD in developing countries, foreign assistance – instead of being just a mechanical injection of finances – should take many forms (technological and technical assistance, improvements in the external trade environment and so on). The methods adopted in bringing these about are the subject of this volume. But because the provision of external finance is objective and quantifiable as well as central to, and being a vehicle for, all non-financial external assistance, the main focus here is external finance, however, without overlooking non-finance aid in the analysis of financial flows.

3   Why focusing on external finance for PSD?

Theories and policy prescriptions for economic development have gone through a number of paradigms (see Adelman 1999 and Thorbecke 2000 for surveys). One of these is based on the dual gap analysis of Chenery and Strout (1966), which perceives that for a typical developing country the major obstacle to development is either capital or foreign exchange shortage. Another paradigm, focusing specifically on the private sector, contends that private sector entrepreneurial shortage constitutes the major obstacle to development.

The implicit rationale of foreign financial flows targeted to PSD is based on these capital/foreign exchange obstacles to development, particularly the entrepreneurial problem. Foreign direct investments (FDI) not only augment domestic finance, they also enhance domestic entrepreneurship and update technology. In the same vein, official bilateral and multilateral support from abroad concerns not only finance; but also technical assistance, which is a variant of technology transfer and entrepreneurship.

Similar to the foreign official assistance rationale is the development philosophy of the 1980s that considers the private sector to be the engine of growth. Given this premise, the government sector should no longer be the exclusive beneficiary of foreign official assistance. Arising from the current development philosophy of poverty alleviation and gender gap minimization is the increasing focus on small scale- and microenterprises in recipient countries, to which both bilateral and multilateral donors now earmark increasing portions of their foreign transfers. At the bilateral level, greater self-interest could also have induced foreign official sources to be directed to the PSD of recipient countries. These transfers bestow benefits on the private sector of the 'donor' by providing it with more foreign investment opportunities and export markets than if similar volumes were targeted to the public sector. This is particularly true for export-related transactions which seek to promote the exports of the donor country. And the cost of these official transfers to the source countries are small as they rarely are in the form of grants, or the grant element is minimal in most cases. Thus, foreign resource transfers for PSD are mutually beneficial to both the source and destination countries.

Since the late 1990s, the current thinking on international development agenda also perceives the private sector to be the engine of growth. But, in addition, today private foreign finance, as opposed to predominantly official foreign finance is the more favoured approach for accomplishing PSD in the recipient countries. For instance, private foreign finance occupied a central place in the March 2002 United Nations Summit on Finance for Development in Monterrey as well as the UN Summit of September 2002 on Sustainable World Development in Johannesburg. To achieve the objectives outlined in the millennium development goals, PSD is seen to have an important role to play. In turn, it is envisaged that these can be accomplished through foreign private capital flows. Even prior to the summits in Monterrey and Johannesburg, OECD's Development Assistance Committee (DAC) had considered foreign private flows to be the focus of its official assistance to developing countries. For instance, the OECD official magazine, *Development Cooperation* (OECD 2001b: 76) states:

> Looking at the future of development financing, the policy statement, *Partnership for Poverty Reduction: from Commitment to Implementation*, adopted at the DAC High Level Meeting in May 2000, notes that 'it is important that developing countries progressively rely on their own domestic resource mobilization, complemented increasingly by sustained long-term private capital flows. A role of aid is to contribute to this process and to support efforts to diminish aid dependence, particularly in those countries, regions and sectors where access to private capital flows is still elusive or limited'.

In other words, foreign official support would now focus on the *process* of mobilizing domestic resource and *sustained long-term private capital flows*. In the common macroeconomic policy terminology, this means that foreign official support can be regarded as the instrument, foreign private capital flows as the intermediate target, and PSD as the ultimate goal. The general philosophy of the international development policy arena is also evident in the above quotation; namely, the way to diminish aid dependence (and, hence, teach the recipient countries to catch fish on their own instead of perpetually supplying the fish to them) is to promote PSD in these countries.

4 Sources and types of external finance for PSD in developing countries

The aim of this volume is to provide a 'guided tour' and an overview of the sources of external financial flows to the business sector in developing countries, to examine the observed trends and patterns as well as to identify the reasons for the trends, and to discuss policies for promoting these flows. But the question needs to be asked – why not focus on only those flows that are more development-friendly? – and the answer is that there is no unanimity with regard to which type of foreign financial source promotes PSD in the recipient developing economies, nor with regard to their relative effectiveness in doing so. Some studies suggest that official sources (especially foreign aid, see Burnside and Dollar 2000; Hansen and Tarp 2001) promote growth and development in the recipient countries while others report contrary finds. Similar contradictory findings characterize studies on the effects of private sources (particularly FDI) on growth and development. While this line of analysis is important, it is not explored here. Instead, we aim to investigate how the volumes and forms of aid can be improved for promoting development. The assumption taken here is that even if there are incontrovertible historical facts (which may not exist) that in the past a particular form of foreign finance (say, portfolio capital flows) has not been conducive to growth and development, this does not necessarily mean that it should be discouraged. Instead, this constitutes a challenge of how that particular form of foreign finance could be made development-friendly. Thus, conventional and non-conventional foreign financial sources are examined here, which gives the volume a comprehensive, broad and holistic outlook.

The sources of external finance for PSD, surveyed in Chapter 1 by Odedokun, are given in Figure 0.1, which shows that finance to private

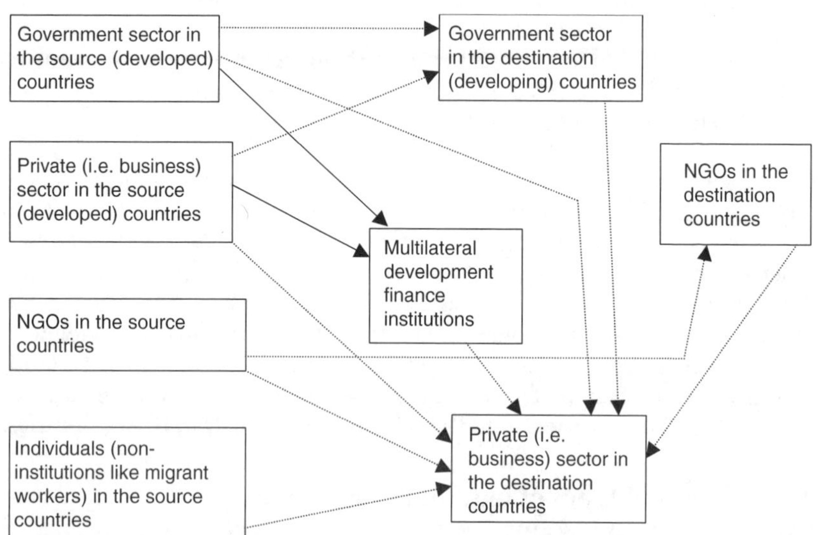

Figure 0.1   Patterns and channels of major flows of foreign development finance for PSD in developing countries

sectors of the developing countries comes either from the public or private sectors of (and also the NGOs and individuals based in) the developed countries. Official foreign sources can be grants, or concessional and non-concessional loans. Non-official sources can be non-commercial (mainly, private remittances and NGO sources) or purely commercial (mainly as foreign direct investment and portfolio capital flows, broadly defined). Official recipients or destinations in developing countries, on the other hand, are the central and lower tiers of government as well as government agencies. These are not the ultimate beneficiaries but are used simply to channel finances to the private sector or for providing an enabling business environment. (See Section 4 of Chapter 1 by Odedokun on the problems associated with the board definition that classifies foreign financial assistance given to a government sector for the promotion of an enabling environment as a form of financial support for PSD.) Non-official or private recipients, within the present context, are the NGOs (for onward transmission to businesses) and the business sector, including large-, medium-, small- and microenterprises.

5 Sustainability of the external finances

A pertinent issue in analysing external financial flows is whether the existing volumes (in relation to source or destination countries' income, population and so on) are adequate. If inadequate, what is the prospect of raising future volumes and at what pace? If adequate, what is the likelihood of sustaining these volumes? If prospects are below what is desirable, what policy measures and interventions are needed to enhance these? This is what sustainability of external finances connotes in the present context.

The sustainability issue thus requires identification of the factors (whether policy or non-policy related) that have in the past determined the volumes of flow, and a likely prognosis of future movements in these factors. To a large extent, the manuscript has tried to identify the determinants of the different types of external financial flows under examination. However, due to space constraint and inherent difficulties, the chapters are unable to explicitly report on the future prospects of sustaining or enhancing aid volumes.

6 Organization of the chapters

Chapter 1 by Odedokun presents a comprehensive survey of the 'shopping list' of sources of external finance that are directly channelled to the business sector of the developing countries. The chapter introduces, complements and provides an overview of the discussions and analyses in the rest of the manuscript. It also reviews other financial flows beyond the scope of the other chapters. Generally, the analytical survey in the chapter covers the 1970–2000 period, and includes the distribution of foreign resources classified according to the different income-based and geographical breakdown of developing countries. The author examines aggregate net resource flows in the form of the saving–investment gap and current account surplus in the balance-of-payments of developed countries, as well as the institutionalized component of this aggregate, encompassing both official and private flows. In addition, he discusses the different components of private flows, including unrequited private transfers (grants by NGOs and workers' remittances) and commercial capital flows (private flows to multilateral institutions and bilateral private capital flows in the form of foreign direct investments and portfolio capital flows) to developing countries.

But what is the rationale behind the emergence of official external support for PSD in developing countries and what are the major instruments of intervention employed in the process? These and other issues are extensively addressed in the chapter by Gibbon and Schulpen. Specifically, the chapter examines the emergence of PSD as a special area of development assistance. It describes the main elements and instruments of PSD policies and provides an overview of the differences and similarities between bilateral and multilateral development agencies with regard to their PSD activities. In doing so, it asks whether agencies' apparent reliance on the same analytical source extends to the use of the same type of instruments. It also examines how far the latter are consistent with donors' broader development objectives and development assistance norms. It then analyses the findings and what they imply for aid coherence, coordination and inter-donor competition. Next, the chapter provides an overview of the discussions on the effectiveness of the numerous PSD instruments. It concludes with a provisional summing-up of the extent to which bilateral and multilateral differ, and why this might be the case.

The next chapter by Jimoh further extends one aspect of the issues addressed in the previous chapter, namely, bilateral donors' current aid practice for PSD. It also examines the role of foreign NGOs in PSD support. In particular, it reviews the donors' major instruments and channels for aid delivery and the extent to which official flows have catalytic effects on private direct foreign capital flows. The major donor instruments for PSD are investment support, an enabling-environment support, privatization and commercialization and business partnership programmes, while the major participants in alternative channels are NGOs, governments of poor countries, firms in the recipient countries and donors' own firms. The chapter concludes that despite the prominent position occupied by NGOs in aid delivery, there is still a pertinent role for the governments of poor countries in the delivery of PSD aid, especially when the provision of public services (or social goods) is involved and free-rider problems prevail. Also, as a result of the decentralized nature of the private sector, the chapter highlights the urgent need for coordination of the donor efforts, requiring either the involvement of recipient governments or/and the creation of a specialized multilateral institution for PSD aid delivery. The study also identifies a number of factors that have limited the effectiveness of PSD aid, one of which is the gap between donor design and local conditions. Further, the chapter finds that official investment-related aid flows are yet to have a catalytic effect on private direct foreign capital flows. Based on these findings, it recommends, among others, that donors should consider new approaches to their investment and partnership programmes so as to encourage technology and knowledge transfers. Finally, the chapter proposes measures to enhance the catalytic and additionality effects of official development finance.

At the multilateral level, many financial institutions have been set up for providing direct support to PSD in developing countries. Multilateral development banks are taking the lead in this regard and one pioneer is the International Financial Corporation (IFC), an arm of the World Bank Group. An understanding of the activities and performance of IFC should therefore provide an indirect insight into the same for multilateral institutions for PSD support in general. This is provided in the chapter by Mavrotas. Specifically, the chapter aims to bring into analytical focus the past activities and operations as well as the problems and prospects of the IFC. Simple econometric analysis is carried out to test a number of hypotheses such as whether IFC finance is an addition to or a substitution for private capital flows as well as the relationship between IFC finance and growth in IFC finance-recipient countries and regions. The central conclusion of the chapter is that the Corporation plays a rather significant role in development financing in many developing countries, although its role as a catalyst in private sector financing needs to be re-examined in view of the mixed findings reported.

One area of much interest in external support for PSD is poverty alleviation and empowerment in the form of microenterprise promotion, usually through microfinance institutions. Donor communities have enthusiastically embraced the microfinance concept as a promising mechanism for achieving poverty reduction and microenterprise development. But high expectations have inadvertently created the myth that microfinance could be the *ultimate* solution to poverty reduction. Are the twin goals of microenterprise development and poverty reduction operationally consistent? What have been the trend and structure in donor support of microfinance institutions in the past? The chapter by Nissanke studies these and other issues relating to donor support of microfinance institutions and microenterprises. In particular, the chapter examines the nature of support rendered by the donor community to microfinance programmes and its effectiveness for microenterprise development and poverty alleviation, as well as its delivery mechanisms. It then assesses empirical evidence on the performance of microfinance institutions and their impact on poverty alleviation and microenterprise development. Against this background, the chapter reviews the main features and trends in donor support and discusses the policy implications of this analysis for the donor community. Given their desire for creating and sustaining microfinance institutions as *social enterprises*, donors provide performance-based support to the microfinance institutions with strong financial incentives to reach the twin targets of financial *sustainability* and *outreach* of the poor. The chapter argues that this might produce unintended negative effects on these very objectives. There is an inherent tension in the two operational targets. Microfinance institutions are expected to be 'subsidy-independent' in an unrealistically short timeframe and to be able to generate substantial surpluses over time to fulfil their social mission on an ever-expanding scale. According to Nissanke, the tension between the two targets at the conceptual level translates directly into incredible pressures on both microfinance institutions and their clients in the field. The author emphasizes the need to improve the design of microfinance programmes with a deeper understanding of the *symbiotic* relationships that have evolved between financial and real sector development. She believes that the performance of microfinance and microcredit programmes reflects – and impacts upon – the development of real economies. Rather than recommend the standardized best practice through financial engineering, there is room for a substantial diversification of financial products and loan portfolio on offer to meet the needs of a wide variety of microenterprise activities.

The previous chapters have mainly focused on foreign official support for PSD, for which the central objective is to catalyse foreign private inflows into PSD. The achievement of this objective would be enhanced by an understanding of the fundamentals that drive these private flows. Identifying the fundamentals that drive FDI, one of the most important components of private capital flows, is the subject of the chapter by Akinkugbe. His analysis shows that the last decade or so has witnessed rather dramatic increases in FDI flows to the developing countries. However, the same statistics unambiguously indicate that the inflow has been uneven. Middle-income developing countries have benefited from this upsurge at the expense of the lower-income ones. Thus, two issues are involved. The first entails identifying the reasons why some developing countries have received practically no FDI inflows while others have fared better. The second, on the other hand, involves the identification of reasons why some countries receive more than others. In an attempt to explore these two complimentary issues, Akinkugbe adapts the two-part econometric approach to the analysis of FDI flows. The first step involves estimating a Probit model in order to examine the binary issue of whether or not to locate FDI in hitherto neglected developing countries. In the second step, a panel regression model is employed to examine the factors that may explain variations in the volume of FDI flows to existing FDI-recipient countries. His findings reveal that a combination of factors, such as high per capita income, outward-orientation to international trade, a high level of infrastructure development and a high rate of return on investment are significant in the decision-making process.

While previous chapters are concerned with external financial inflows, the chapter by Hermes, Lensink and Murinde looks at the finance outflow from the developing countries' private sectors; the nature and magnitudes of the so-called capital flight, the fundamentals driving it and policies for its reversal. First, the authors review the theoretical and empirical literature on the measurement of capital flight. They then provide information on the magnitude as well as the 'burden' of capital flight for a selected group of developing countries in South Asia, East Asia, Sub-Saharan Africa and Latin America. They review the literature to provide an overview of the relevant empirical studies on the determinants of capital flight. In light of these determinants, the authors assess the prospects for flight capital reversal, and conclude with a proposal of policy measures to stem the continuing capital flight and to induce capital flight reversal.

The final chapter by Odedokun is along the same tradition as the chapter by Akinkugbe of pinpointing the fundamentals driving private capital flows except that Odedokun also considers different types of private capital flows, as opposed to FDI alone. In particular, the chapter attempts to rectify some of the modelling problems characterizing earlier studies which have sough to explain private capital flows to developing countries, or at least, to examine the subject from a different and complementary perspective. To accomplish this, the author proposes a model framework which approaches the issue from the per-spective of a capital-exporting developed country and also takes cognizance of developments in other industrialized countries which could compete with the developing world for private capital flows. The model is operationalized and estimated with annual panel data over 1970–2000 for 19 capital-exporting developed countries. Specifically, Odedokun reports estimates of equations for total private flows, FDI, total portfolio capital flows (PCF) and various cate-gories of PCF. He tests for the effects of a number of specific explanatory fac-tors, each of which has its own 'push' or 'pull' components. These are the level of per capita income, interest rate, economic growth, the prevailing phase of the economic cycle, the degree of openness of the economy in the balance-of-payment capital account, macroeconomic imbalances and external debt burden. The empirical findings confirm the posited effects of the 'push' and/or 'pull' components of each of the above factors.

References

Adelman, I. (1999). 'Fallacies in Development Theory and Their Implications for Policy'. Working Paper No. 887. Berkeley, CA: University of California at Berkeley.

Burnside, C. and D. Dollar (2000). 'Aid Policies and Growth'. *American Economic Review*, 90 (4): 846–68.

Chenery, H. and A. Strout (1966). 'Foreign Assistance and Economic Development'. *American Economic Review*, 56 (4): 679–733.

Cook, P., C. Kirkpatrick and F. Nixson (eds) (1998). *Privatization, Enterprise Development and Economic Reform: Experiences of Developing and Transition Economies*. Cheltenham and Northampton, MA: Elgar.

Han, Vo-Xuan and R. Baumgarte (2000). 'Economic Reform, Private Sector Development, and the Business Environment in Viet Nam'. *Comparative Economic Studies*, 42 (3): 1–30.

Hansen, H. and F. Tarp (2001). 'Aid and Growth Regressions'. *Journal of Development Economics*, 64: 547–70.

Holden, P. and S. Rajapatirana (1995). *Unshackling the Private Sector: A Latin American Story*. Directions in Development Series. Washington, DC: World Bank.

Hussain, A. M. (1992). 'Private Sector Development in State-dominated Economies'. IMF Working Paper 92/79. Washington, DC: IMF.

OECD (Organization for Economic Co-operation and Development) (2001a). *Investment Policy Review: Ukraine*. Paris: OECD.

OECD (Organization for Economic Co-operation and Development) (2001b). *Development Co-operation, The DAC Journal, 2000 Report*, 2 (1).

Ofosu-Amaah, W. P. (2000). 'Reforming Business-related Laws to Promote Private Sector Development: The World Bank Experience in Africa'. Washington, DC: World Bank.

Paul, S. (1990). 'Assessment of the Private Sector: A Case Study and its Methodological Implications'. World Bank Discussion Paper No. 93. Washington, DC: World Bank.

Stern, R. E. (1997). *Economic Transition Phase II: Private Sector Development*, Institute for Advanced Studies, East European Series 51, December.

Sullivan, J. D. (1998). 'Institutions and Private Sector Development'. *China Economic Review*, 9 (1): 85–95.

Thorbecke, E. (2000). 'The Evolution of Development Doctrine and the Role of Foreign Aid, 1950–2000', in F. Tarp (ed.), *Foreign Aid and Development: Lessons Learnt and Directions for the Future*. London and New York: Routledge, 423–49.

World Bank (1995). 'Private Sector Development in Low-income Countries'. Development in Practice Series. Washington, DC: World Bank.

Acknowledgements

I am grateful to the participants of the Sustainability of External Development Finance Research Project Meeting held in Helsinki on 23 and 24 August 2002 for their very useful comments on the initial drafts. Special thanks also go to Liisa Roponen (who I fondly call 'Professor Liisa' in recognition of her professional excellence), who doubled as the secretary for the research project and the copyeditor of the draft papers.

UNU/WIDER gratefully acknowledges the financial contribution to this project by the Ministry for Foreign Affairs of Finland.

UNU/WIDER also gratefully acknowledges the financial contributions to the 2002–03 research programme by the governments of Denmark (Royal Ministry of Foreign Affairs), Norway (Royal Ministry of Foreign Affairs), Sweden (Swedish International Development Cooperation Agency – Sida) and the United Kingdom (Department for International Development).

MATTHEW ODEDOKUN

Notes on the Contributors

Dr Oluyele Akinkugbe is Senior Lecturer in the Department of Economics at the University of Botswana and also teaches at universities in Zambia and Swaziland. Formerly he worked with the then Coopers and Lybrand consultancy units in Nigeria.

Dr Peter Gibbon is a senior researcher and research theme and research programme leader at the Institute for International Studies (formally CDR), Copenhagen. He has been a consultant for Danida, the French Ministry of Development Cooperation, Sida, and the Royal Danish Ministry of Foreign Affairs.

Dr Niels Hermes teaches economics at the Faculty of Management and Organization, the University of Groningen, The Netherlands.

Dr Ayodele Jimoh is a Senior Lecturer at the University of Ilorin, Nigeria and was until recently the Director of Research and Training at AFRIBANK further to his holding a senior position at the Nigerian Deposit Insurance Corporation.

Professor Robert Lensink is Professor in Finance and Financial Markets at the Department of Finance, the University of Groningen, The Netherlands.

Dr George Mavrotas is a resident Research Fellow at UNU/WIDER, Helsinki Finland, having previously taught economics at the Universities of Oxford and Manchester. He has been an advisor to, among others, DFID-UK, UNICEF, ILO, UNDP, the World Bank, the Inter-American Development Bank and the EU.

Professor Victor Murinde is Professor of Development Finance at the University of Birmingham. His previous advisory work has included the World Bank, UNCTAD, Kuwait Institute of Scientific Research, the African Development Bank and the Caribbean Development Bank.

Dr Machiko Nissanke is Reader in Economics at the School of Oriental and African Studies, University of London, teaching graduate courses in international economics and financial economics. She has served as consultant/advisor to many international organizations (UNCTAD, UNIDO, UNDP, UNU, World Bank, AfDB, OAU, EEC, AERC) and Japanese government agencies (MITI and MOFA).

Dr Matthew Odedokun is a Research Fellow and Project Director at UNU/WIDER, Helsinki, Finland. Previously a senior university lecturer before working in various research institutions, including the Kuwait Institute for Scientific Research and as an economist with the International Monetary Fund, Washington DC.

Dr Lau Schulpen is head of the Postgraduate Programme at the Centre for International Development Issues, Nijmegen. He has also been a consultant to bilateral aid agencies and has worked with the World Bank and DAC.

List of Abbreviations

ADB	Asian Development Bank (also AsDB)
AfDB	African Development Bank
AMINA	Microfinance Initiative for Africa
ARIA	Assurance de Risque des Investissements en Afrique (France)
AusAID	Australian Agency for International Development
BOP	balance-of-payments
CABBSA	Canadian Association for Black Business in South Africa
CAC	Canada-ASEAN Centre
CAPSSA	Canadian Association for the Private Sector in Southern Africa
CBI	Centre for the promotion of Imports from Developing Countries (The Netherlands)
CDB	Caribbean Development Bank
CDC	Commonwealth Development Corporation
CDG	Carl-Duisburg-Gesellschaft e.V. (Germany)
CEG	Center for Economic Growth (United States)
CFP	Center for Privatization (United States)
CGAP	Consultative Group to Assist the Poorest
CID	Centre for Industrial Development (EU)
CIDA	Canadian International Development Agency
CIM	Centrum für Internationale Migration und Entwicklung (Germany)
COMESA	Common Market for Eastern and Southern African Countries
CRECER	Credito con Educacion Rural
CRPSM	Costa Rica Productive Sector Modernization Programme (Canada)
DAC	Development Assistance Committee
DAFs	Development Assistance Facilities (New Zealand)
Danida	Danish Agency for Development Assistance
DCS	Development programme of Canadian–Senegalese joint ventures
DEG	Deutsche Investions und Entwicklungsgesellschaft (Germany)
DFID	Department for International Development (UK)
DGIS	Directoraat-Generaal Internationale Samenwerking (The Netherlands)
DIPO	Danish Import Promotion Office for Products from Developing Countries
EBA	extreme bound analysis
EBRD	European Bank for Reconstruction and Development

EC	European Commission
ECIP	European Community Investment Partners
EDF	European Development Fund
EDI	Economic Development Institute
EIB	European Investment Bank
ERT	export-related transactions
ETC	Enterprise Thailand Canada
EU	European Union
FAO	Food and Agriculture Organization of the United Nations
FDI	foreign direct investment
FIAS	investment advisory service
FINCA	Foundation for International Community Assistance
FISA	Foreign Investment Advisory Service
FMO	Financiering Maatschappij voor Ontwikkelingslanden (The Netherlands)
FPI	foreign portfolio investment
FY	fiscal year
GIEK	Guarantee Institute for Export Credits (Norway)
GNI	gross national income
GOM	Garantiefaciliteit Opkomende Markten (The Netherlands)
GTZ	Deutsche Gesellschaft für Technische Zusammenarbeit (Germany)
HIPC	highly indebted poor country
IADB	Inter-American Development Bank
IBRD	International Bank for Reconstruction and Development
IBTA	Investment Promotion and Technical Assistance (The Netherlands)
ICDPS	Islamic Corporation for the Development of the Private Sector
ICT	information and communications technology
IDA	International Development Association
IDG	international development goals
IFC	International Finance Corporation
IFOM	Investeringsfaciliteit Opkomende Markten (The Netherlands)
IFU	Industrial Fund for Developing Countries (Denmark)
IIC	Inter-American Investment Corporation
ILO	International Labour Office
IMF	International Monetary Fund
IPG	International Privatization Group (United States)
IRT	investment-related transaction
IsDB	Islamic Development Bank
JFS	Joint Funding Scheme
KfW	Kreditanstalt für Wiederaufbau (Germany)
LDCs	least developed countries

MDBs	multinational development banks
MDF	Mahgreb Development Fund (Canada)
MFI	Microfinance Institutions
MIF	Multilateral Investment Fund
MIGA	Multilateral Investment Guarantee Agency
MNCs	multinational corporations
MOOF	multilateral official flows
MSE	medium- and small enterprises
NCM	Nederlandse Credietverzekerings Maatschappij (The Netherlands)
NEF	Norwegian Enterprises Facility
NGO	non-governmental organization
NIMF	Nederlands Investerings Matching Fonds
NMCP	Netherlands Management Consultancy Programme (The Netherlands)
NORAD	Norwegian International Development Agency
NORFUND	Norwegian Risk Capital Fund for Developing Countries
NZODA	New Zealand Official Development Assistance
OA	official assistance
ODA	Official Development Assistance
ODAEA	ODA bilateral equity acquisition
OECD	Organization for Economic Co-operation and Development
OEG	Operations Evaluation Group
OOF	other official flows
ORET/Miliev	Ontwikkelingsrelevante Export Transacties/Milieu en Economische Verzelfstandiging (The Netherlands)
PCF	Portfolio capital flows
PESP	Programma Economische Samenwerkingsprojecten (The Netherlands)
PIIDS	Pacific Islands Industrial Development Scheme (New Zealand)
POPM	Garantieregeling Particuliere Ontwikkelings Participatie Maatschappijen (The Netherlands)
PPP	purchasing power parity
PROPARCO	Société de Promotion et de Participation pour la Coopération Economique (France)
PSD	private sector development
PSDI Fund	Private Sector Development Initiative Fund (Canada)
PSO	Programma Samenwerking Oost-Europa (The Netherlands)
PSOM	Programma Samenwerking Opkomende Markten (The Netherlands)
PTFSR	Presidential Trust Fund for Self Reliance
PUM	Programma Uitzending Managers (The Netherlands)
PVOs	all non-religious private voluntary organizations
R&D	research and development

RHI	Regeling Herverzekering Investeringen (The Netherlands)
RISPCA	Regional Initiatives Support Programme in Central America (Canada)
RSF CEA	Regional Support Fund Central and Eastern Africa (Canada)
SACU	Southern African Customs Union (SACU)
SAP	Structural Adjustment Policy
SDP	private sector development
SEQUA	Stiftung für wirtschaftliche Entwicklung und berufliche Qualifizierung (Germany)
SES	Senior Experten Service (Germany)
SMEs	small and medium enterprises
SOEs	state-owned enterprises
TOD	total bilateral official disbursements
TOI	total official investment
UNDP	United Nations Development Programme
UNIDO	United Nations Industrial Development Organization
USAID	United States Agency for International Development
VASS	Voluntary Agencies Support Scheme (New Zealand)
WB	World Bank
WDI	World Development Indicators (World Bank)
WIDER	World Institute for Development Economics Research of the United Nations University
WRs	workers remittances
WTO	World Trade Organization

Glossary

ODA   Overseas Development Assistance. It refers to foreign financial flows from donor country governments and official agencies either directly to (conventional) developing countries or indirectly to them via multilateral institutions. Such flows must be for the main objective of promotion of the development and welfare of the recipient countries (so that transfers like military assistance are excluded). Second, the flows must be either pure grants or concessional loans having a grant element of not less than 25 per cent (calculated at a discount rate of 10 per cent).

OOF   Other official flows. It refers to all forms of official flows that do not qualify as ODA. This can be because it is a loan that is not concessional enough. Alternatively, it can be because its *main* purpose is not promotion of development and welfare of the recipient countries – even if it is a grant or a highly concessional loan. Such would be the case if it is a grant for essentially commercial purpose or concessional official export credits.

OA   Official aid. Technically, it has the same definition as ODA except that the recipients are now countries in transition (namely, former communist countries and more advanced developing countries but which are still not developed countries), as opposed to conventional developing countries. By adopting a broad definition of developing countries, countries in transition too would be included.

DAC   The Development Assistance Committee of the OECD. Not all OECD members are DAC members. Membership of DAC is more or less synonymous with attainment of the status of developing country status. It can be viewed as an 'elitist' or 'privileged' club of donors. Presently, there are 22 members: Austria, Australia, Belgium, Canada, Denmark, Finland, France, Germany, Greece, Ireland, Italy, Japan, Luxembourg, Netherlands, New Zealand, Norway, Portugal, Spain, Sweden, Switzerland, the United Kingdom and the United States of America.

1
Foreign Financing of Developing Countries' Private Sectors: Analysis and Description of Structure and Trends

Matthew Odedokun

1 Introduction

Most forms of foreign finance for private sector development (PSD) have gone through peaks and dips over the years. The objective of the chapter is to present not only a comprehensive picture of this pattern but also to describe its movement over the years and to provide likely explanations. While our explanations are at times based on findings reported in existing empirical literature, we also have recourse to some empirical tests, particularly in cases where previous studies have insufficiently reported on factors affecting cross-border flows of the types of finance under consideration.

Conventional balance-of-payments (BOP) accounts do not adequately classify financial flows according to whether these are destined for government or private sector. Thus, with the exception of one or two instances, we have no recourse to the BOP statistics. Nevertheless, we regard the BOP framework a suitable paradigm for describing the various types of financial flows. In particular, the concept of BOP current account surplus in the source countries and the utilization of the surplus in the form of unrequited transfers, capital flows of various categories, monetary or reserve flows and so on is profitably incorporated in our analyses. The next section, accordingly, covers the developed countries' overall resource transfers (in the form of BOP current account surplus) to the rest of the world and the relative shares of selected PSD finance in total. In Section 3, unrequited private transfers by NGOs as well as workers' remittances are discussed. Section 4 is on official sources (loans and grants) for PSD. Section 5 reviews private commercial flows to multilateral institutions, while Section 6 is on FDI (foreign direct investments) and portfolio capital flows. Some cross-border financial flows, by their nature, entail the net transfer of resources from the private sector of developing countries to developed countries. One such cross-border transaction is with the international banks, which is examined in Section 7, while the other is the cross-border flow of foreign currencies and related liabilities. These are discussed in Section 8. Summary and conclusion are given in Section 9.

2   Overall resource transfers from the developed countries

The objective here is to portray the overall picture of total resource transfers of the past decades and to situate the relative position of private sector-to-private sector transfers within this context. While the latter is not the totality of what finances the PSD, it constitutes the bulk of it. As is discussed later, for PSD, the major role of foreign official sources is to act as a catalyst of foreign private sources. In other words, the ultimate concern is still largely foreign private sources.

Background information on the charts and statistical table

The totality of net financial transfers from developed to developing countries is, by definition, the current account surplus (before unrequited transfers) in the consolidated BOP account for the former and, hence, consolidated BOP current account deficit for the latter. In principle, this should also equal the combined excess of domestic saving over investment spending

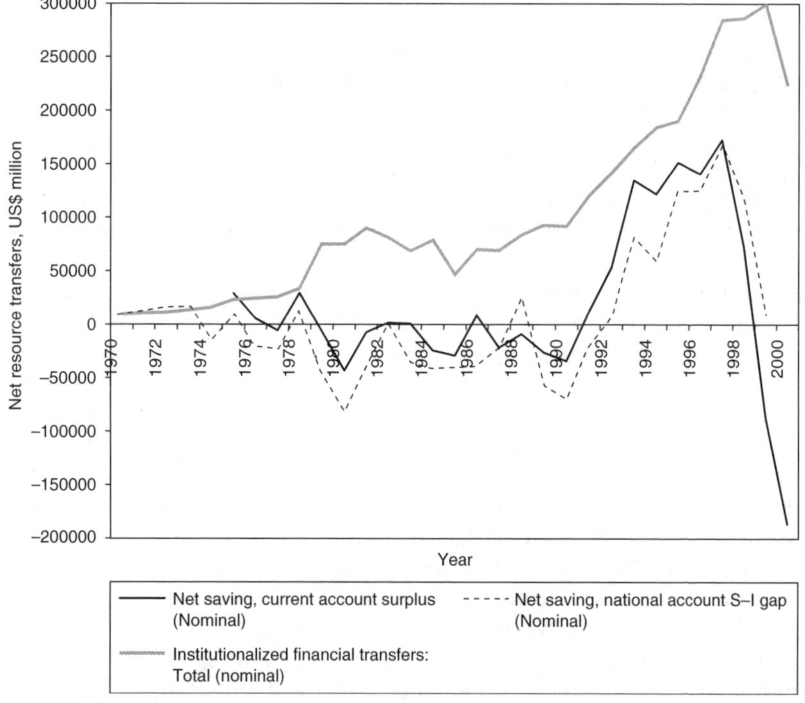

Figure 1.1   Aggregate net resource flows from developed to developing countries, 1970–2000 (US$ million, current values)

Source: OECD/DAC (online) and the World Bank (2001).

(i.e. saving–investment, S–I gap) for developed countries and, hence, the combined excess of investment spending over domestic saving for developing countries.

Figure 1.1 shows the patterns for the years 1970–2000 for the S–I gap (computed as the gross national income [GNI] minus gross national expenditure) and BOP current account balance (computed as the sum of balances in the goods, services and factor incomes) for the high-income OECD members (22 DAC members and Iceland). While the two patterns should in principle be the same, here they differ slightly. This is due to statistical discrepancies, including the 'errors and omissions' item in the BOP. Decade averages are also shown in Table 1.1. The corresponding balances for developing countries, which in principle should be equal and opposite to those for the developed countries, differ substantially. Furthermore, statistics for developing countries' balances are available only for the 1990s. Consequently, it is not possible to plot the trend for these. The decade average for the BOP current account balance, however, is shown in Table 1.1, which indicates that the deficits, instead of being equal to the corresponding surpluses reported for the developed countries, are several multiples off.

Table 1.1 Total resource flows from the north to the south, 1980–99 (US$ billion, unless otherwise indicated)

	US$ billion			
	at current value		1995 constant value	
	1980–89	1990–99	1980–89	1990–99
Current account surplus (balance of payments) OECD countries	−151.6	737.9	−262.7	780.9
Net national saving (national accounts):				
OECD countries	−327.7	605.8	−591.6	628.3
OECD countries (% of GDP)	−0.4	0.3	−0.4	0.3
Developing countries	NA	−4 620.9	NA	−4 949.2
Institutionalized form of resource transfers:				
Total	756.3	1 997.8	1 301.8	2 162.1
Total (% of source countries' GDP)	0.8	0.9	0.8	0.9
Total (% of destination countries' GDP)	2.3	3.6	2.3	3.6
Institutionalized financial transfers:				
Private sources	327.7	1 152.2	579.2	1 235.3
Private sources as % of total	41.8	51.7	41.8	51.7
Private sources, % of source countries' GDP	0.3	0.5	0.3	0.5
Private sources, % of destination countries' GDP	1.0	2.0	1.0	2.0

Source: World Bank (2001) and OECD/DAC (online).

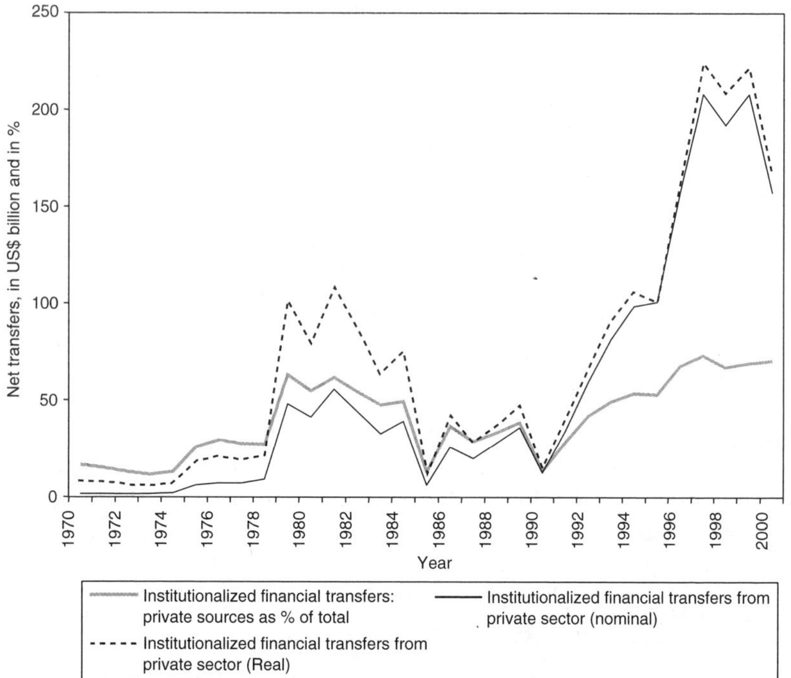

Figure 1.2 Institutionalized private sector-to-private sector net flows to developing countries, 1970–2000 (US$ billion and % of total institutionalized transfers)

Source: OECD/DAC (online).

While it is difficult to know where the 'truth' between the two current account balances lies, it is probable that the balance reported for developed countries has a smaller error margin.

The total institutionalized net financial transfers (official grants and loans and private flows in the form of grants by NGOs, FDI and portfolio capital, broadly defined) are also given in Figure 1.1. It should be noted that these institutionalized forms of financial transfers are not the same as the total transfers being financed by the BOP current account surplus, due to a number of reasons explained in Odedokun (2003: 3). Total institutionalized net transfers from the private sectors of source countries are identified separately. Its development in US dollars and as a percentage of the total institutionalized sources is given in Figure 1.2. See also Table 1.1 for the decade averages.

Overall resource transfers: the picture from the charts and statistical table

Based on the above-mentioned information, we can now examine overall resource transfers in detail. As shown in Figure 1.1, developed countries' current account balance was negative (as was the S–I balance) for most of the 1970s and the 1980s, indicating that net resource flows during the period were actually from the developing to developed countries. This observation is supported by Table 1.1, which shows that the developed-to-developing country net resource transfers, in both nominal and real terms, were negative during 1980–89 decade, with the S–I gap deficit as high as 0.4 per cent of the GDP of developed countries or 0.6 trillion in 1995 US dollars. The figure also shows that during the two decades, net institutionalized transfers, while positive, were also relatively low, more so during the 1970s. Also, according to Table 1.1, the total volume of this in nominal term was US$756 million during the 1980s. This is about 0.8 per cent of developed countries' GDP or 2.3 per cent of the GDP of the developing countries.

But the situation changed suddenly in the early to mid-1990s. The current account and S–I balances turned positive and jumped very fast, attaining an all-time peak between 1997 and 1998. Thereafter, however, the balance fell just as fast as it had risen, to nosedive into an abyss by the end of the 1999–2000 period. Despite this 'southward' movement during the late 1990s, net resource flows were still positive and fairly substantial, or in nominal term, about US$738 billion for cumulative current account surplus (or US$606 billion S–I gap, equivalent to about 0.3 per cent of the developed countries' GDP). This trend is also portrayed by the movement of net institutionalized flows which experienced a fast and steady increase from 1990 to an all-time peak in 1999, declining therefore sharply in 2000. On the whole, net transfers during the decade totalled US$2.2 trillion (in 1995 constant prices), compared with about US$1.3 trillion for the 1980s. However, while this, as a fraction of the GDP of source countries, constituted an increase in terms of the recipient countries' GDP (from 2.3 per cent in the 1980s to 3.6 per cent in the 1990s), the amounts were almost unchanged, or 0.9 per cent in the 1990s vis-à-vis 0.8 per cent in the 1980s. This suggests that the observed upward trend in monetary value has merely kept pace with the source countries' GDP. Nevertheless, the general picture still indicates that overall resource flows from developed to developing countries were broadly on the increase.

Given the ups and downs in the volume of net flows, the question that naturally arises is the explanation or reason for this evolution. To address the issue, we have to examine the fundamentals affecting domestic saving and investment behaviours in the source (developed) countries, as these are the ultimate determinants of net resource flows. Within the life-cycle hypothesis framework, saving rates are generally regarded as being determined partly by the age structure of the population (see Brooks 2000), with a higher proportion of those above working age leading to a reduction in saving rate. In general, this proportion has exhibited a secular increase in the developed countries, which apparently does not explain the post-1990 upsurge in S–I gap in these countries. Another factor often regarded as affecting the savings rate is the income level, with a high level of per capita income raising the fraction of income saved (see Loayza *et al.* 2000 and Browning and Lusardi 1996 for a review). Over time, the level of per capita income has increased in the developed countries. However, rising income can also increase domestic investment through the usual accelerator process, and whether the overall effect on S–I gap is positive is an empirical issue. But even assuming that it is positive, there was no spectacular increase in income during the 1990s to account for the upsurge observed in the S–I gap during that decade. Again, another factor that is often regarded as a determinant of the savings rate is the domestic (real) interest rate (see Browning and Lusardi, for a survey). A high interest rate supposedly increases saving. By also reducing aggregate investment (in line with the received theory), high interest rates should provide a double stimulus to the S–I gap increase. But available evidence does not support domestic interest rates having played a role in the movements observed in the S–I gap. We calculated the (external trade) weighted-average discount rates for all 22 DAC member countries and find that the rate was the lowest during the S–I gap upsurge (1990s), or 6.3 per cent per annum versus 6.8 per cent in the 1970s and 9.2 per cent in the 1980s!

It thus appears that movements in aggregate domestic saving and investment in the developed countries over the past three decades are intriguing, and a more formal empirical explanation based on empirical evidence (which, albeit, is beyond the scope of this chapter) is needed to solve the puzzle. In the meantime, we are inclined to 'speculate' that most of the explanations can probably be found in other factors than those in the developed countries, that is, in investment opportunities and other events in the developing countries. We are forced to this rather startling conclusion because the explanations in the orthodox macroeconomics of saving and investment do not appear adequate.

The pattern of total institutionalized resource transfers over the decades seems to have been dictated and overshadowed by the private sector component, as discussed below.

Private sector-to-private sector portion of the total resource transfers

The pattern in the private sector component of institutionalized resource transfers reflects the movements in total resource transfers, as described above. Starting from a very low level in the early 1970s, the volume attained a peak in the early 1980s and then pummelled in the mid-1980s. Zigzag movements characterized the remainder of the 1980s. Thereafter, it rose to an all-time peak around 1998, after which it started to fall again. But despite this fall, the 1990s recorded the highest volume in three decades, if not in history. Thus, while the cumulative total during the 1980s was only US$579 billion (at 1995 constant US dollar value), it more than doubled during the 1990s, rising to US$1235 billion (see Table 1.1). Movements in nominal and real (1995 US dollar) values indicate a similar pattern and are very close to each other (see Figure 1.2). In relation to the total institutionalized net flows (combined official and private), the private component first rose steadily until 1978, after which it upsurged to a peak in the early 1980s. After a fall, it started another steady upward trend in 1990, reaching again a peak some 20 years later that resembled the magnitude of very early 1980s (see Figure 1.2). Over the decades, the relative size of private sources recorded an overall upward trend, rising from about 42 per cent in the 1980s to about 52 per cent in 1990s (see Table 1.1). An upward trend was also recorded in private source as a fraction of the GDP of both source and destination countries, from 0.3 per cent of the source countries' GDP in 1980s to 0.5 per cent in the 1990s and from 1.0 per cent of the recipient countries' GDP to 2.0 per cent in 1990s.

An insight into the reasons for the rising value and the relative importance of private institutionalized sources can be gained only by examining the components that comprise this aggregate. As already mentioned, these consist of non-governmental organization (NGO) grants (discussed next) as well as FDI and broad category of portfolio capital flows; both are discussed in Section 6.

3   Private unrequited transfers: grants by NGOs and workers' remittances

Private unrequited transfers which have a bearing on PSD are NGO grants and worker remittances. While the former is institutionalized, the latter is not since these are transfers from individuals (the migrant workers, discussed below). By their nature, they both tend to have a unidirectional flow, mainly from developed to developing countries. Reverse flows to developed countries, while possible, are not common.

Grants by NGOs

There are many types of developed country-based NGOs. Some promote religions and cultures, some exist for politics and human rights-related issues, some for social and gender-related missions, some conduct research and so on. But here our interest centres on those that have been established for the promotion of business (often, small-scale and microenterprises development) or PSD. The statistics employed refer to only those that are active in development cooperation.

As can be seen from Figure 1.3, the volume has maintained a more or less log-linear trend over the years in both real and nominal terms. Statistics on the trend are further discussed in Odedokun (2003: 6–9), who concludes that, in general, compared to other financial and economic activities, the amounts involved appear not only insignificant, but they also seem to have maintained a general downward trend, suggesting the need for further

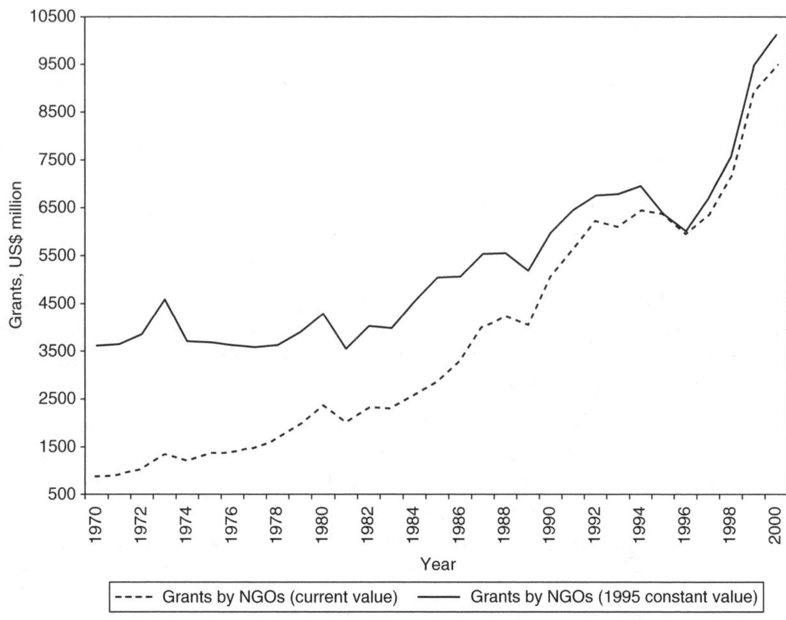

Figure 1.3   Grants by developed country-based NGOs, 1970–2000 (US$ million)
Source: OECD/DAC (online).

efforts at promoting the role and activities of these PSD development agents
so as to keep pace with other economic and financial factors.

Using the usual multi-country panel regression technique, we also try to
provide, in Odedokun (2003), some explanations for the observed movements in foreign grants from the NGOs and to identify their determinants,
broadly along the same line as reported by Jimoh in Chapter 3. The empirical result of our study shows some evidence of a positive effect of a rise in per
capita income in NGO home countries, and much stronger evidence of a negative effect of rising per capita income of recipient countries. It also shows
that a high level of official development assistance (ODA) support from NGO
home governments (whether measured directly or proxied by government
expenditure/GDP ratio) has a decisive positive effect on their transfer volumes. This means that much of the responsibility for rejuvenating the tempo
of NGO activities is on the donor governments. The proposition that rising
hostile external circumstances confronting the developing countries tend to
elicit more assistance from NGOs is also supported. On the other hand, an
increasing degree of openness (and, hence, globalization) in each of the current and capital accounts of the NGOs' home economies is observed to retard
the volume of NGO assistance. This suggests that on the whole, increasing
openness crowds-out financial resources away from NGO transfers.

Workers' remittances

Remittances by migrant workers to their home countries are made for personal (e.g. to relatives) or for business-related purposes, perhaps in preparation of their eventual return (Lopez and Seligson 1991; Ahlburg and Brown 1998). Thus, workers' remittances (WRs) can be a veritable source of financing PSD.

We do not have access to comprehensive and continuous statistics on the volume of WRs being made to each developing country. The only regular statistical sources are the World Bank's *World Development Indicators* and *Global Development Finance* on *gross* (as opposed to *net*) WRs received. These, in addition to having several missing values, do not indicate the source of the remittance. This is a problem because a remittance can be from another developing (as opposed to developed) country. For example, the Gulf countries, which are themselves developing countries, host many migrant workers, and their numbers are probably comparable to those in the developed countries. Also the recorded amounts for each developing country can be questioned since not all WRs go through the official banking channels that provide the basis for the BOP statistics (and, hence, the World Bank sources). Some legitimate migrants, not to mention the illegals, by-pass banks in making remittances, so a gross underestimation by the BOP statistics is likely.

Bearing the foregoing data limitations in mind, the trend of WR volume for the developing countries over the period 1977–2000 is shown in Figure 1.4. These are further analysed into two groups: low- and middle-income. Table 1.2 gives the movements in real terms and in relation to the GDP of the developing countries. As can be seen, an upward and ever-increasing trend in aggregate WRs volumes is noticeable. For the developing countries as a whole, WRs increased from about US$172 billion (or US$17.2 billion per year) in the 1980s to about US$388 billion (US$38.8 billion per annum) in the 1990s. This, in terms of the 1995 US dollar constant value, is an increase from about US$293 billion to about US$421 billion, respectively. The bulk of the amount, however, accrued to middle-income developing countries (i.e. relatively high-income), whose relative share of the total also increased. The share of the low-income developing countries of total volume is low and decreased, notwithstanding the fact that developing countries also recorded increasing volumes of WRs receipts (see Figure 1.4 and Table 1.2).

Table 1.3 summarizes recent surveys on remittances to Latin American and the Caribbean under the auspices of Multilateral Investment Funds (MIF 2002). As can be seen, remittances (with about 80 per cent coming from the US) accounted for over 25 per cent of the GDP of recipient countries like Haiti and Nicaragua.

Some studies have previously analysed factors affecting WRs but these are mostly from a micro-perspective, and are based on microdata for migrants (Nishat and Bilgrami 1993; Funkhouser 1995; Brown 1997; Ahlburg and Brown 1998). Remittance determinants in these studies include factors such

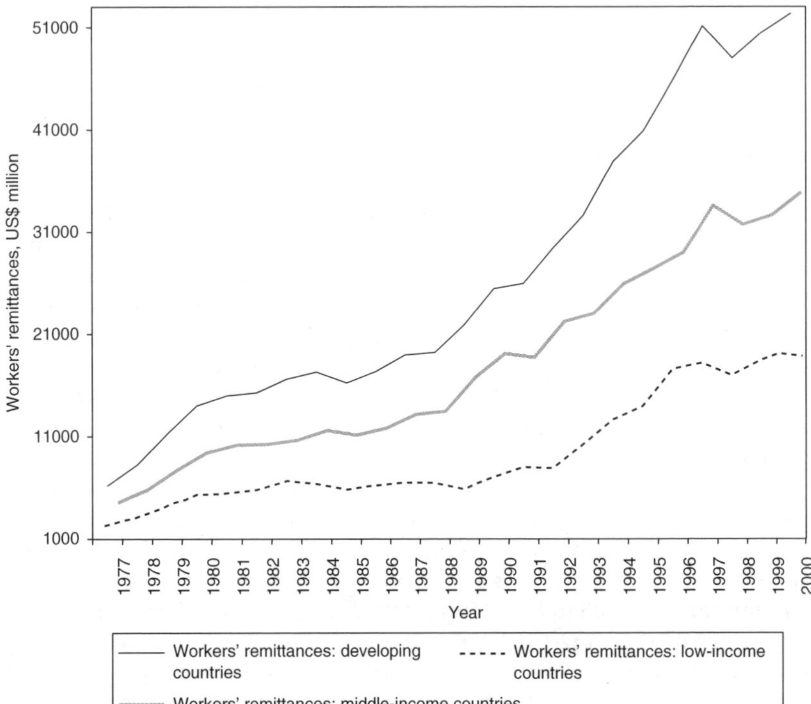

Figure 1.4   Workers' remittances, 1977–2000 (US$ million, current values).
Source: OECD/DAC (online).

Table 1.2   Workers' remittances, 1980–99 (US$ billion, unless otherwise indicated)

	US$ billion			
	current value		1995 constant value	
	1980–89	1990–99	1980–89	1990–99
Low-income developing countries	60.0	130.9	103.7	141.5
Middle-income developing countries	111.7	256.6	189.1	279.0
All developing countries	171.7	387.5	292.7	420.6
All developing countries, % of GDP	2.5	2.9	2.5	2.9

Note: US$ values are decade totals, not decade averages.
Source: The World Bank (2001) (online).

Table 1.3 Remittances to Latin America and the Caribbean, 2001 (US$ million and % of GDP)

	Amount	**%**
Bolivia	103	1.33
Brazil	2 600	0.54
Colombia	670	0.83
Cuba	930	—
Dominican Rep.	1 807	8.99
El Salvador	1 972	14.45
Ecuador	1 400	8.36
Guatemala	584	2.85
Haiti	810	21.42
Honduras	460	7.38
Jamaica	959	13.15
Mexico	9 273	1.53
Nicaragua	610	25.42
Peru	905	1.72

Source: Remittances to Latin America and the Caribbean, Multilateral Investment Fund (2002).

as the intention to eventually return to the home country, family background and so on. Very few studies have used macroeconomic framework and macrodata.[1] Consequently, we have little to fall on in trying to explain the observed trend movements and cross-country variations from a macroeconomic perspective (which we believe to be relevant in the present context) and thus have had to resort to some empirical tests. Again, this is done by running panel regressions for WRs received (scaled by the GDP of receiving countries) over the 1977–2000 period for all developing countries (with one or more non-missing values on WRs), which yielded almost 1000 pooled cross-country and annual data points. The choice of the explanatory factors is based on the assumption that the volume of WRs is determined by the number of migrant workers as well as factors which motivate or deter the decision to send remittances home. Within this context, we postulate the gap between the per capita income of each developing country and the average per capita income of developed countries combined to be a factor. A potential migrant is tempted to travel to seek better opportunities if the per capita income is high in the envisaged destination (developed) country and/or, particularly, if the per capita income in the home country is low. Also, since some degree of literacy is often a requirement for entry, we postulate a high level of illiteracy (an inhibiting factor) to reduce migration and, hence, WRs. Also, opportunities in small countries for gainful employment at one's level of skill are limited and skilled workers are more tempted to migrate to find suitable employment. Hence, outward migration (and WRs) is expected to be higher in relation to GDP for small countries (proxied here by population size). In addition, the degree to which the world is being integrated into a 'global village' can also affect not only migration but also the propensity of migrants to send home remittances in general or to make them through a banking channel (as opposed to hand-to-hand sending of cash). Thus, we posit a rising degree of economic openness in the developed countries as a group, as well as for each individual developing country to exert positive effects on actual WRs (and a stronger impact on the recorded remittances). One measure of economic openness used is the BOP current account, computed as the sum of export and import of goods and services in relation to GDP. Another measure is the openness of the BOP capital account, computed as the ratio of private capital inflows and outflows to GDP. Since home remittances may also be motivated by business-related purposes, migrants are more likely to make remittances during a rising or prosperity phase of the economic cycle in the home country than during economic slumps. Although we have no specific reason to hypothesize a definite direction of the effect of prosperity in the migrant's host country on home remittances, we still test for such an effect all the same, similar to the manner in which a trend variable was included in the equations.

The results are reported in Table 1.4, and the expected effects of all the factors are confirmed. Each of the following factors is found to have a negative effect on the WRs received (in relation to recipient GDP): a high level of illiteracy; narrowing affluence gap defined as the per capita income of each developing country relative to the per capita income level for all developed countries combined; and country (population) size. On the other hand, a positive effect on the WRs is induced by each of the following: high degree of openness in the current and capital accounts in each developing country (just as the corresponding degree of openness for the developed countries as a group, but which do not show a statistically significant effect); and favourable home country conditions such as high economic growth and rising prosperity phase of the economy. Finally, economic indicators such as high economic growth in the migrant's host country and rising phase of economic cycle in the country, are observed to have negative effects on WRs. These, however, are statistically significant for the latter only.

4   Official sources for PSD in recipient countries

Nature of foreign official finance for PSD

There seems to be no consensus as to what constitutes official financial flows for PSD. In a sense, conventional flows to (and for the exclusive use of) the government sector can arguably be described as being targeted for PSD, since what is good for the government sector (and for non-business segments of the society) should also be good for the business sector. Viewed from this perspective, all forms of official foreign inflows, including military

Table 1.4   Factors affecting WRs: some estimates

Trend variable	0.002	0.003
	(4.3)	(4.9)
Level of Illiteracy	−0.016	−0.022
	(−2.2)	(−3.0)
Differential in per capita income, as compared with developed countries' average	−0.026	−0.058
	(−6.2)	(−10.3)
Recipient country's population size	−0.104	−0.154
	(−6.1)	(−7.9)
Degree of openness of recipient country's economy in current account	0.026	—
	(3.3)	
Average of degree of openness of source country's economy in current account	0.026	—
	(0.9)	
Degree of openness of recipient country's economy in capital account	—	0.012
		(2.2)
Average of degree of openness of source country's economy in capital account	—	0.028
		(1.4)
Economic (real GDP): growth of the recipient country	0.025	—
	(2.4)	
Economic (real GDP): growth of developed country	−0.0001	—
	(−0.3)	
Phase of economic cycle that the recipient country is experiencing	—	0.088
		(8.9)
Phase of economic cycle that the developed countries are experiencing	—	−0.115
		(−4.9)
Adjusted R^2	0.863	0.884
Number of observations	991	958

Notes: (a) The dependent variable is the workers' remittances received by each developing country in relation to its GDP;
(b) The numbers in parentheses below the parameter estimates are the t-values. A parameter estimate is statistically significant at 1%, 5%, and 10% levels if its t-value is, in absolute sense, not less than 2.6, 2.0 and 1.6, respectively. The estimates were derived through fixed-effect OLS technique, based on heteroscedasticity correction technique suggested by White (1980).
(c) Level of illiteracy, per capita income (as a ratio of that of developed countries' average) and population size are in logarithm. Economic growth is given as a percentage. Phase of economic cycle is derived as the residuals generated from regressing the logarithm of index of real GDP on a time trend while other variables, being pure fractions, were employed as *log (1 + x)* as in Table 1.3.

Source: All data are from the World Bank's *World Development Indicators* and *Global Development Statistics* (2001, online).

assistance, can be said to be for PSD. However, this extremely wide conception of PSD flows has never been used in the literature.

But, another equally broad conception exists that has been used particularly by multilateral development banks. Accordingly, foreign official sources destined to the recipient government sector are classified as being earmarked for PSD if they have some identifiable (and sometimes, incidental) benefits to the private sector. According to the World Bank (2002: 27):

> PSD activities are carried out all over the Bank. [...] Today, adjustment lending supports a PSD agenda that enhances the foundations of a positive investment climate in the Bank's client countries: a wide array of procedural, regulatory and legal reforms have come to the fore that are critical to foster private-sector led growth, including removing exit and entry barriers, reducing market rigidities, simplifying tax systems, safeguarding property rights, and liberalizing trade barriers.

It should be noted that while such a wide conception of PSD financial support may be convenient for the purpose at hand, it can pose a problem in some cases. For instance, this World Bank definition also qualifies even IMF lending as a form of PSD support, since the enhancement of business macroeconomic environment and investment climate is a centrepiece of IMF lending conditionalities. Furthermore, many such sectors and activities currently financed cannot pass the exclusivity test, that is, whether the business sector is the exclusive or major beneficiary. For example, it is doubtful that the business sector could be the major beneficiary (not to mention being the substantially exclusive beneficiary) of conditionality lending to improve public sector management, social protection and others that the World Bank includes in its PSD lending. They do not seem to benefit the business sector any better than, say, military assistance against an external aggression to a country (including its private sector). Despite the all-embracing nature of this definition, it lacks a clear and functional delineation from other forms of official financial flows like IMF lending, military aid and so on.

Thus, a narrower definition of PSD support is often adopted and this refers essentially to support aimed at individual businesses (and, in some cases, business sectors or group of actors like chambers of commerce, entrepreneur groups, etc.) in the recipient countries. Because this assistance to individual businesses and business sectors generally does not require or even entail guaranteeing by the government sector (particularly when it takes the form of lending), it is often referred to as direct support. While this concept of foreign official financing for PSD may be too narrow (by not recognizing support to improve the environment necessary for PSD), it clearly defines the present discussion and is, therefore, the concept adopted here unless explicitly mentioned to the contrary.[2]

It should be realized within the context of this narrow concept that it is not just the volume of official financial flow that matters. First, the type and extent of entrepreneurial assistance packaged with it also count. In the context of multilateral sources, such entrepreneurial support (which includes the provision of a 'template' for private investors to replicate and the undertaking of pioneering experimental projects) is actually a part of their role as a development bank.

Second, the investment banking role (co-financing, loan syndication, risk and credit guarantees, etc.) is also important due to the catalytic effect it might have.[3] Such a catalytic effect (foreign source or cross-border) is expected to be high (in sectors and/or countries) where foreign private investors (including foreign banks) are likely to be interested in or where they can be 'cajoled' relatively easily into committing funds. Thus, middle-income developing countries may have an advantage over low-income ones in this respect, just as telecommunication and extractive industries – even in low-income countries. And here exists an inherent conflict between achieving a high foreign-source catalytic effect or leverage ratio and the need to reduce crowding-out of foreign private sources through foreign official financing of PSD. Countries and sectors that naturally appeal to foreign private investors are those where foreign official support for PSD can 'cajole' such investors with relative ease and, hence, achieve maximum catalytic effects. But at the same time, foreign private investors may already be present in these same countries and sectors, and these can be displaced or crowded-out through the same process of official foreign support for PSD. There is virtually no scope for such crowding-out if, as in the case of low-income countries (without mining sector), no foreign private investors are present, or even in middle-income countries, in sectors like small-scale and microenterprises. This is where a high catalytic effect is most difficult to achieve. Maximum additionality (defined here as the difference between cross-border catalytic effect and cross-border crowding-out effect) is attained conceptually by striking a balance between the two. The issues of catalytic effect, crowding-out and additionality have recently attracted the attention of policymakers and donor agencies concerned with PSD.[4]

A similar balance has to be maintained between profitability (to ensure continuity and growth in the scale of operations) and the social or developmental roles.[5] More important, Chapter 5 by Nissanke has brought to the fore the inherent conflicts between the targets of financial *sustainability* and the *outreach* of the poor that donors supporting microfinance institutions in developing countries often expect these organizations to achieve.

There are both bilateral and multilateral official foreign sources for PSD, as discussed below. The magnitudes, trends and structure of some of the bilateral and multilateral instruments of direct financial support are given in Tables 1.5 to 1.7 and Figures 1.5 and 1.6.

Table 1.5 Selected bilateral and multilateral direct financial support for PSD, 1970–2000 (US$ million, annual average)

	Gross disbursements			Net disbursements		
	1970–80	1981–90	1991–2000	1970–80	1981–90	1991–2000
PSD multilateral development banks (biggest)						
IFC	183.7	704.3	1 439.0	119.8	369.8	600.3
EBRD*	NA	NA	1 634.7	NA	NA	800.7
Selected bilateral financial instruments						
ODA equity acquisition	26.0	94.4	157.7	24.2	82.6	116.3
OOF joint venture equity acquisition	367.1	528.2	376.1	214.7	65.0	−7.2
Total ODA and OOF equity acquisition	393.1	622.6	533.8	238.9	147.6	109.1

Notes: Statistics, except for EBRD, are for developing countries other than those in transition (Part II countries); * indicates 1994–2000 average for gross and the 1992–2000 average for net disbursements for EBRD.

Source: OECD/DAC (online).

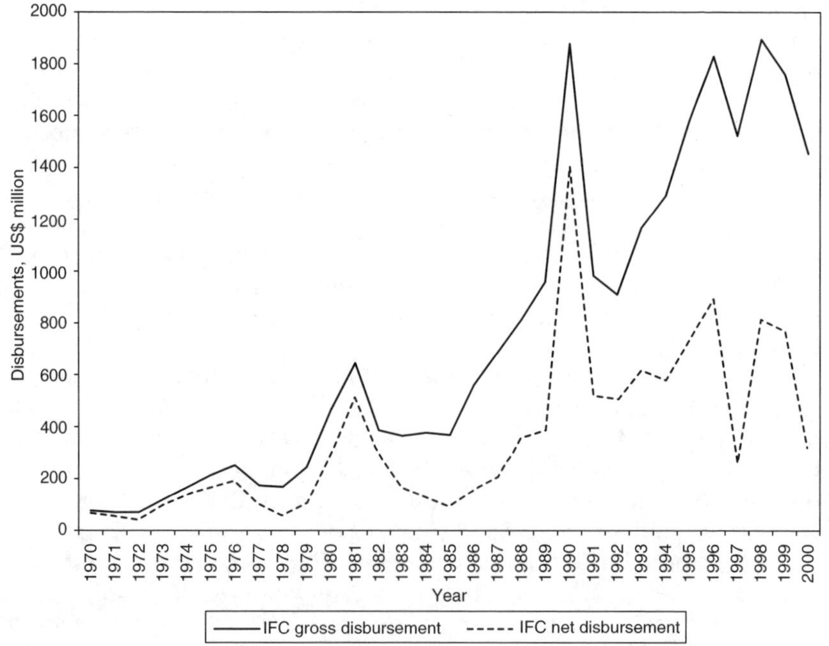

Figure 1.5   IFC's gross and net disbursements, 1970–2000 (US$ million)

Source: OECD/DAC (online).

Table 1.6 Major instruments of bilateral official support for PDS in developing countries, 1995–2000 (US$ million, annual average)

	Equity acquisition	Export-related transactions				Investment-related transactions							
		Total	Official export credits to developing countries	Loans to national private exports	Interest subsidies to national private exporters	Total	With developing countries				With residents		
							Total	of which joint ventures (JV)					
								Total	of which JV-loans	of which JV acquisition of equity	Total	Loans to national private investors	Subsidies to national private investors
Australia	—	110.6	110.6	—	—	—	—	—	—	—	—	—	—
Austria	—	93.7	93.7	—	—	—	—	—	—	—	—	—	—
Belgium	0.2	16.1	—	—	16.1	—	—	—	—	—	—	—	—
Canada	—	2011.1	2011.1	—	—	—	—	—	—	—	—	—	—
Denmark	27.5	182.0	113.4	17.4	—	10.4	9.0	8.5	8.5	—	17.4	17.4	—
Finland	2.7	467.6	467.6	—	—	7.9	7.9	—	—	—	—	—	—
France	—	320.0	320.0	—	—	396.9	427.2	—	246.9	—	—	—	—
Germany	36.0	897.3	897.3	17.9	—	228.7	252.9	—	—	—	17.9	17.9	—
Greece	—	6.2	6.2	—	—	—	—	—	—	—	—	—	—
Ireland	—	—	—	—	—	—	—	—	—	—	—	—	—
Italy	—	373.5	1 107.9	14.1	96.6	32.2	43.4	43.4	29.8	13.6	11.7	14.1	—
Japan	88.2	2 029.4	837.2	—	—	7,644.3	—	—	5 614.2	—	—	—	—
Luxembourg	—	—	—	—	—	—	—	—	—	—	—	—	—
Netherlands	—	297.5	297.5	76.6	—	73.8	17.8	—	—	—	63.1	76.6	47.8
New Zealand	—	—	—	—	—	—	—	—	—	—	—	—	—
Norway	7.8	—	—	—	—	—	—	—	—	—	—	—	—
Portugal	—	—	—	20.8	—	103.2	115.4	93.2	93.2	—	14.1	20.8	7.1
Spain	—	3.2	3.2	—	—	—	—	—	—	—	—	—	—
Sweden	2.5	—	—	—	—	5.9	5.9	5.9	2.0	3.5	—	—	—
Switzerland	7.6	—	—	7.7	—	21.3	15.3	11.7	—	13.0	14.3	7.7	5.1
United Kingdom	133.7	36.1	27.8	—	44.4	202.3	173.5	178.1	156.8	23.2	—	—	—
United States	—	1 115.7	1 115.7	—	—	659.4	659.4	668.7	—	688.6	—	—	—

Notes: (a) Figures do not necessarily add up where they should. They should therefore be regarded as being only indicative.
(b) — means either zero value, or non-availability of statistics. Also, the average value is computed over only the years between 1995 and 2000 for which statistics actually exist. We did take the lack of statistics for a particular year to mean zero value.

Source: OECD/DAC (online).

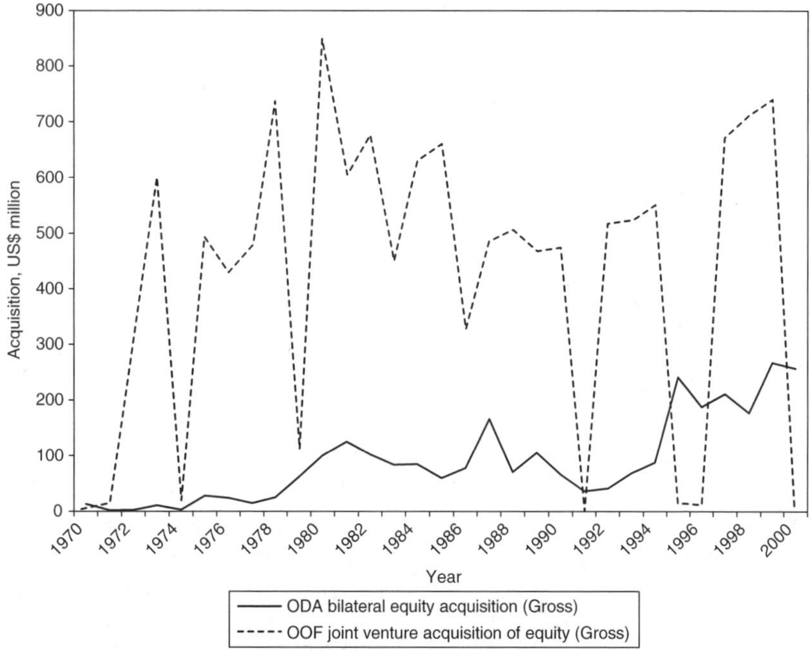

Figure 1.6   Gross ODA and OOF acquisition of equity, 1970–2000 (US$ million)
Source: OECD/DAC (online).

Bilateral official sources for PSD

Bilateral donors have various instruments through which they support PSD in developing countries (see Chapters 2, 3 and 5 by Gibbon and Schulpen, Jimoh and Nissanke, respectively, for details). The specific instruments used would, presumably, depend on the self-interests of the donors concerned (see Table 1.6).

Table 1.6 shows that equity acquisition on a concessional basis (qualifying it as ODA) is one such instrument. This, among others, can take the form of debt swaps or participation in joint ventures with the recipients. Another broad instrument is investment-related transactions (IRTs), which are non-concessional in nature (or, at least, not enough to qualify as ODA). Because of limited or nil concessionality, IRTs are simply called other official flows (OOF), as opposed to ODA. There are two broad types of IRT. The first entails direct financial flows to developing countries. These can be loans or equity investments that are a part of joint venture with the recipients. Thus, there are two forms of equity investment: concessional (qualifying as ODA) and the non-concessional. Both can, apparently, be said to be similar except for the degree of concessionality. But in reality, the difference goes beyond the

Table 1.7 Level of development-based and geographical allocation of IFC gross disbursements, 1970–2000 (%)

	% of total				Avg annual nominal growth rate[a]			
	1970–80	1981–90	1991–2000	1970–2000	1970–80	1980–90	1990–2000	1970–2000
Level of development-based:								
Countries in transition	NA	NA	7.8	4.9	NA	NA	23.7	NA
Developing countries	100.0	100.0	92.2	95.1	17.6	12.0	3.8	11.6
Least developed countries	5.8	4.3	3.8	4.1	29.9	7.1	16.7	11.5
Other low-income countries	11.0	16.5	24.4	20.9	5.8	14.2	−2.0	14.9
Lower-middle income countries	31.4	24.4	19.5	21.9	21.9	6.8	5.2	10.0
Upper-middle income countries	51.8	54.6	44.6	48.2	20.5	14.0	2.6	12.1
All	100.0	100.0	100.0	100.0	NA	NA	NA	NA
Geographical classification:								
Africa, north of Sahara	2.9	6.1	2.7	3.7	45.4	13.3	−0.8	14.0
Africa, south of Sahara	8.3	13.3	9.6	10.7	23.4	21.7	0.7	13.4
North and Central America	16.3	16.0	13.4	14.5	45.2	12.1	3.7	14.6
South America	26.1	32.1	31.6	31.3	14.8	12.8	2.1	12.0
Far East Asia and Oceania	16.0	8.1	17.2	14.2	7.4	9.6	9.0	10.5
South and Central Asia	3.7	8.3	13.7	11.1	12.9	10.9	0.7	19.0
Middle East	4.8	1.3	2.9	2.5	18.9	−23.7	29.0	8.0
Europe	21.9	14.9	9.0	12.0	15.4	13.8	3.1	6.9
All	100.0	100.0	100.0	100.0	18.3	11.8	2.9	11.3

Notes: NA means not applicable;
[a] The annual growth rates were computed through the least squares method.

Source: OECD/DAC (online).

degree of concessionality, as it can be seen in Figure 1.6, with the aggregate ODA-type flow rising steadily over the 1970–2000 period while the aggregate OOF-type flow is extremely volatile. The second type of IRT may not entail direct financial flows from donor governments to developing countries, and is directed merely at assisting donor-country businesses (with loans and/or subsidies) to finance-specified investments in aid recipient countries.

Another form of financial support is the export-related transactions (ERT). This can involve a direct financial flow to a developing country if it is in the form of official export credits. But no direct flow would be involved if the ERT is intended to support the donor country's private exporters, either via loans (to partially finance export credits extended by such private exporters to developing countries) or interest subsidies (to reduce the interest rate charged on private export credits). Broadly speaking, IRT and ERT are similar and an equal underlying degree of donor self-interest can be impugned in each, but both can potentially also provide advantages for the recipients' PSD.

Table 1.6 shows that official export credits to developing countries constituted the bulk of such finances during 1995–2000, followed by IRT with developing countries. The table also shows that donor countries differ in their preference of delivery instruments, and it appears that, even after allowing for differences in donor sizes, bigger donors use these more frequently than the smaller donors (see Chapter 3 by Jimoh for some econometric explanation of why different donors prefer different instruments). An interesting recent development is the attention now being focused by bilateral donors on microfinance and microenterprises, as they now see this channel as a way of accomplishing poverty-reduction objectives in developing countries (see Chapter 5 by Nissanke).

Multilateral official sources for PSD

There are many multilateral development banks and non-bank institutions that provide PSD assistance in one form or another. Many UN agencies (UNIDO, IFIAD, UNDP, UNESCO, etc.) provide technical support and grants, particularly for the development of small-scale businesses and microenterprises (see Chapter 5 by Nissanke for details). Also, many multilateral development banks, particularly the World Bank Group, provide indirect support that aims at improving the business environment in developing countries through their adjustment lending (see Chapter 2 by Gibbon and Schulpen). More importantly, they also provide direct financial and non-financial support. First, some banks have been established to provide financial support for PSD exclusively, as in the case of the European Bank for Reconstruction and Development (EBRD) which assists 27 former communist countries in Europe and Central Asia to build market economies. Second, some other institutions, whose original mandate was to provide direct support to the public sector, have since diversified into establishing more or less autonomous affiliates charged with the provision of direct support for PSD.

Thus, the World Bank Group (comprising originally only the International Bank for Reconstruction and Development, IBRD) established the International Finance Corporation (IFC) in 1956. IFC activities are examined later in Chapter 4 by Mavrotas. Another affiliate, the Multilateral Investment Guarantee Agency (MIGA), was created in 1988 to provide insurance cover to foreign investments in developing countries against political risks (risks of expropriation, transfer restrictions, breach of contract, wars and civil disturbances) and to provide other investment and marketing services. The Inter-American Development Bank (IADB) followed the World Bank's footsteps by establishing the Inter-American Investment Corporation (IIC) in 1986 to perform similar roles as the IFC. But IADB went further in 1994 by establishing yet another affiliate, the Multilateral Investment Fund (MIF), that is specifically focused on microfinance and microenterprise development. Third, other multilateral development banks, albeit without similar autonomous affiliates in their organizational structures, also provide direct financial support (i.e. without government guarantee) and non-financial assistance to enterprises in the countries of their domain, usually through some non-autonomous organizational units or departments. Generally, they also have specialized units for microfinance and microenterprises, as in the case of the ADF Microfinance Initiative for Africa (AMINA) unit of the African Development Bank. See Chapter 5 by Nissanke on AMINA and Chapter 2 by Gibbon and Schulpen for the list of multilateral development banks and their respective functions.

The IFC and EBRD are on the top in terms of recent financial flows (Table 1.5). But, in terms of geographical coverage, the IFC is the obvious leader – and, to a large extent, is also the prototype, pioneer and pacesetter. See Chapter 4 by Mavrotas for an evaluation of the specific activities and performance of IFC. For this leadership position of IFC, further analysis and discussion of multilateral support of PSD in this chapter is based on the IFC as a complement to Mavrotas' study.

Figure 1.5 shows the volumes of IFC financial support (both gross and net disbursements) to developing countries. These rose fairly steadily to a peak in the very early 1980s, declined for about 3 years before rising again very fast to attain an all-time pinnacle around 1990. This pinnacle was almost 'conquered' again around 1998. As is further shown in Table 1.7, gross disbursements (in nominal US dollars) recorded an average annual growth of 11.6 per cent between 1970 and 2000, although the rate fluctuates from one decade to the next, from a high of 17.6 per cent in the 1970s, to 12 per cent in the 1980s, and finally just 3.8 per cent in the 1990s. Thus, the rate of increase in the tempo of IFC financing has been declining and the level of its finances more or less constant in the 1990s, particularly in real terms.

In terms of regional destinations, the bulk of financing has gone to the lower-middle income and especially upper-middle income country groups (based on DAC's classification). Only a negligible, declining proportion

(4.1 per cent over 1970–2000) has been allocated to the least developed countries and a small proportion to other low-income countries (see Table 1.7). Geographically, North and Central America and, more specifically South America, have been major recipients, followed by the Far East and Oceania and Europe. Africa (north and south of the Sahara), the Middle East and South and Central Asia have received relatively little.

What factors account for this distribution pattern? There are no analytical assessments of IFC in the literature (except the attempt reported in Chapter 4 by Mavrotas) to provide some explanation. Here, we complement Mavrotas' effort. We observe that a number of developing IFC-member countries have never received financial support from the Corporation throughout the 1970–2000 period. Others have received support only occasionally, say, during 2 or 3 years. On the other hand, some countries (notably, Argentina, Brazil, Colombia, India, Indonesia, Kenya, Mexico, Philippines, Thailand, Turkey and Zimbabwe) have benefited almost annually. It thus appears that some member countries are favoured by IFC while others are not. This raises the question of the factors that make a country an IFC favourite.

To attempt to answer this question, we assume the IFC to be involved in a two-stage decision process. First, there is the decision as to which countries to operate in and, then, the decision on the allocation of financial support for each country that passed the first screening. To test this proposition, we adopt a special econometric test tailored to that specific type of situation.[6] Specifically, because the decision to invest in a country in a particular year is a binary factor, factors affecting the first stage of the Corporation's decision process are examined by fitting a probit equation to a panel of annual data (over 1970–2000) for IFC member countries (totalling about 90, mainly those with the 2000 population over one million). The binary dependent variable is whether or not a country receives IFC finance during each year. Testing the second stage of the decision process, on the other hand, consists of running OLS panel regression (using fixed-effect panel method) with the dependent variable now being the IFC financing received in relation to the recipient's GDP. Coverage is now limited to those data points with non-zero values for this dependent variable.

We tested for several possible explanatory variables assumed to be relevant in the first-stage decision process. One of these is the size of the country, alternatively measured by population and real GDP. We expect each of these to affect positively the chance of a country being an IFC favourite in a particular year. A high level of economic development (measured by the per capita income level), high level of industrialization (proxied by industry value added in relation to GDP), rate of economic (real GDP) growth and rising phase of a business cycle (measured as described in Table 1.6) are also assumed to have a similar positive effect. On the other hand, the opposite effect is hypothesized to be induced by a high external debt burden (total external debt/GDP ratio) and the dominance of agriculture in the overall economic activities or agricultural value added/GDP ratio (as IFC rarely finances agriculture). Also posited to have a negative effect is the adverse domestic political performance (alternatively proxied by a high index of the lack of political rights; an index of the lack of civil liberties and an index of the lack of political freedom, which is a combination of the first two).[7] We also included a trend variable. To test the second-stage decision process on the factors affecting allocation amounts to the 'winners' of the screening process, we repeated the same explanatory variables listed above, plus an econometric term called 'inverse Mills ratio', which seeks to account for some dependence of the second stage on the first (see McGillivray and Oczkowski 1991).

Based on the above specification, we estimated the equations with annual panel data over the 1970–2000 period for about 90 developing countries. The results are presented in Table 1.8. The coefficients of all explanatory

Table 1.8 Econometric results of identifying factors affecting IFC's allocation of financial support across countries, 1970–2000

	Probit equation results			Corresponding panel OLS equation results		
Trend	0.026	0.017	0.018	0.000	0.0001	0.00002
	(7.5)	(4.8)	(5.3)	(0.3)	(1.9)	(0.8)
GDP per capita (log, 1995 US$)	—	0.171	—	—	−0.001	—
		(4.9)			(−2.4)	
Total real GDP (log, 1995 US$)	—	—	0.33	—	—	−0.001
			(18.8)			(−2.3)
Total population (log)	—	0.35	—	—	−0.002	—
		(17.6)			(−1.2)	
External debt/GDP ratio	−0.106	—	—	0.0001	—	—
	(−2.8)			(1.3)		
Real GDP growth	—	1.10	1.13	—	−0.0002	−0.001
		(2.2)	(2.3)		(0.1)	(−1.0)
Rising phase of economic cycle	1.033	—	—	0.0001	—	—
	(3.4)			(0.1)		
Industry value added/ GDP ratio	—	0.108			0.003	—
		(0.3)			(2.0)	
Agriculture value added/ GDP ratio	−1.39	—	—	0.0002	—	—
	(−6.4)			(0.1)		
Index of lack of political freedom	−0.027	—	—	−0.000	—	—
	(−3.0)			(−0.1)		

Table 1.8   Continued

	Probit equation results			Corresponding panel OLS equation results		
Index of lack of political rights	—	−0.10	—	—	−0.0001	—
		(−5.8)			(−0.6)	
Index of lack of civil liberty	—		−0.06	—	—	0.00002
			(−3.1)			(0.3)
Statistical inverse Mills ratio	—	—	—	0.0004	0.001	−0.001
				(0.2)	(0.6)	(−0.6)
Adjusted R^2	—	—	—	0.255	0.254	0.250
Log likelihood	−1480.7	−1337.3	−1343.9	—	—	—
Number of cases correct	1421	1606	1582	—	—	—
Number of observations	2279	2312	2323	1057	1055	1067

Notes: (a) The dependent variable is gross disbursement of IFC financial support in relation to recipient's GDP; (b) See Table 1.4 for reporting and interpretation of t-values as well as for the econometric techniques of deriving the estimates.

variables are statistically significant and have the expected signs in our first stage decision-making (or probit) equations, except for the coefficient of the share of industrial value added in GDP which (though with the expected sign) does not pass the statistical significance test. This evidence suggests that the chance of a country being allocated IFC financial support is enhanced by factors such as large size, a high level of per capita income, a high rate of economic growth and a rising phase of the economic cycle. The prospects of the country are also enhanced if it has a low external debt burden; if its total economic activities are not dominated by agriculture, and if its score in domestic political indicators is satisfactory. On the other hand, none of the factors tested for show expected and statistically significant effect in explaining the second-stage decision-making concerning how much to allocate to those countries that pass the first-stage screening test. Thus, unlike in the first-stage process for the selection of beneficiary countries, one can infer that the allocation of IFC financial support has not been consistently based on identifiable factors (or at least on the wide range of factors tested here). This is perhaps a reflection of the fact that the 'allocation' is mainly demand-driven by potential beneficiary countries, instead of being at the discretion or initiative of the IFC.

5   Private flows to multilateral institutions

Multilateral institutions, in the past and the present, raise funds from private markets in the developed countries. These funds are used to augment other sources in financing their resource transfers to the developing countries, and the bulk of private-market funds are obtained through the issue of new securities. Available statistics do not identify the specific institutions

Table 1.9   Private flows to the multilateral development
banks, 1979–2000 (US$ billion, annual average)

Gross disbursements		Net disbursements	
1979–89	1990–2000	1979–89	1990–2000
9.12	11.88	3.42	−2.10

Source: OECD/DAC (online).

issuing debt instruments, but they are most likely to be the multilateral
development banks.

This channel is, however, declining in importance. As is shown in Table 1.9,
while the annual average of new issues increased between 1979–89 from
US$9.12 billion to US$11.88 billion for the period 1990–2000, reflows
(i.e. repayment by multilateral institutions of maturing debts) outweighed
new issues in the latter period. The result is a net flow to multilateral
institutions from private investors to the tune of US$3.42 billion per annum
during the first period and a net (reverse) flow of US$2.10 billion per annum
from the multilateral institutions during the second period.

One fact explains the observed trend is interest rate. A high domestic
interest rate is likely to reduce the relative attractiveness of these multilateral securities while foreign interest rate (say, average interest rate prevailing
in other developed countries) – which is indicative of the rate of interest on
the securities of the multilaterals – is likely to have the opposite effect.
A high level of per capita income in the investor country is also posited to
affect the volume of these securities since this indicator signifies high savings and investible resources. On the other hand, a high level of per capita
income in other developed countries combined is expected to have the
opposite effect, since these are, in effect, alternative outlets for the investor.
Odedokun reports empirical findings that support these propositions (2003:
Table 1.12).

6   Private commercial flows: foreign direct investment and portfolio capital flows

Concepts of foreign direct investments and portfolio capital flows

Unlike the multilateral private flows discussed earlier, private investments,
although also characterized by commercial or profit motives, are bilateral in
nature. A major component of these bilateral private flows is FDI, comprising (according to DAC's definition)[8] net financing by an entity in a developed country 'which has the objective of obtaining or retaining a lasting
interest in an entity resident in an aid recipient (developing) country'.

Lasting interest, in turn, is defined as:

> ...a long-term relationship where the direct investor has a significant influence on the management of the enterprise, reflected by ownership of at least ten per cent of the shares of the enterprises, or the equivalent in voting power or other means of control.

The other component is portfolio capital flows (PCF), which is a concept of cross-border capital flows that seems to have no precise meaning. According to a survey of PCF definitions by Wilkins (1999: Box 1):

> ...a range of definitions became apparent. The broadest usage included all investments going to a host country that were not classified as FDI, including short- as well as long-term capital movements.... Many authors include, as I do in this paper, only long-term investments other than FDI.... Others include only securitized investments (bonds and stock), once more excluding FDI, but now excluding long-term bank lending as well.... Some sources classify as FPI (foreign portfolio investment) only equity investments that are not FDI....

Within the context of this chapter, we adopted the specific PCF concept applied also by Wilkins, which is 'only long-term investments other than FDI'.

FDI and PCF together constitute what is conventionally referred to as total private capital flows. The trend in the volumes of total net private capital flows from the developed to the developing countries is shown in Figure 1.2 and described earlier.[9] Corresponding patterns for FDI and PCF are shown in Figure 1.7. As can be seen, FDI prior to the early 1990s showed a more or less steady upward trend, after which it made drastic jump to an all-time peak in 1998. It declined in 1999 and 2000 from that pinnacle. Net PCF, on the other hand, has been more volatile. It rose steadily from the very low pre-1975 level to an initial peak in the early 1980s. Thereafter, it declined until around 1985 when it dipped into the negative side, where it remained for most of the pre-1991 period. After 1991, the volume rose rapidly, first becoming positive and then rising to an all-time crest in 1997. It fell again after the East Asian financial crisis of 1997 and by 2000 was already below the initial peak attained in the early 1980s.

Table 1.10 shows the destinations of both total and components of net private capital flows over 1995–2000, analysed according to the level of per capita income, while Table 1.11 shows the regional classification of the target countries. Figure 1.8 gives a graphic perspective of the trend for the different PCF components. For a source-country analysis of the flows and the size relative to GDP of both the source and destination countries, see Chapter 8 by Odedokun.

In this section, capital flows are limited to those from the 22 DAC member countries to the rest of the world, collectively labelled the 'developing

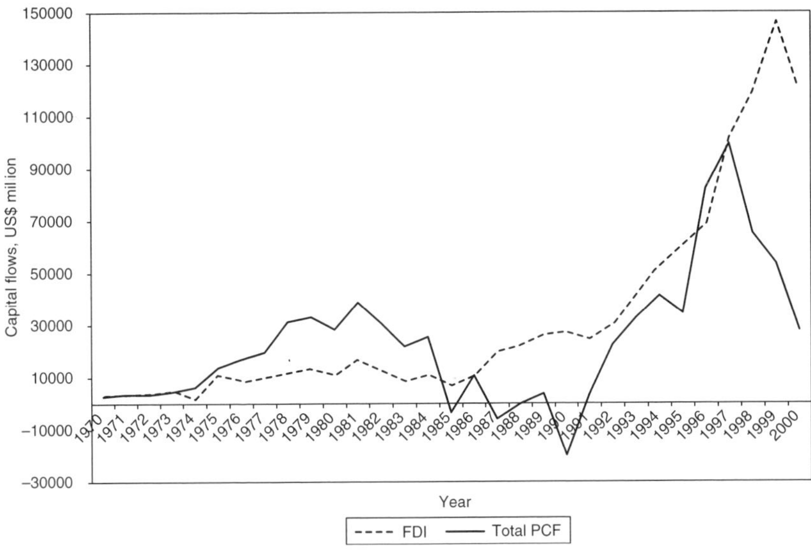

Figure 1.7   Trends in FDI and PCF from DAC member countries to other countries, 1970–2000 (US$ million)
Source: OECD/DAC (online).

countries', a term which sometimes includes countries in transition. Flows between developing countries as well as between developed countries, are excluded as they are not relevant to the present objective. Thus, statistics may not be comparable to those relating to total net outflows from each developed country or to total receipts for each developing country (or group of developing countries).

Foreign direct investments (FDI)

FDI, when compared to portfolio capital, is a relatively stable and less volatile form of private capital flows. In principle, FDI also has the attraction of embodying entrepreneurship and technology, which should make it more growth-friendly to host economies.

The trend in aggregate net FDI flows from developed to developing countries over 1970–2000 is given in Figure 1.7 (see also Chapters 6 and 8 by Akinkugbe and Odedokun, respectively). Its distribution according to a breakdown by various income levels and regional destination countries for the six-year period 1995–2000 is given in Tables 1.10 and 1.11. Geographically, North and Central America received the largest share in relation to the recipients' GDP, accounting for 4.4 per cent of the region's GDP. Following at some distance is South America, with 2 per cent. South and Central Asia received the least, 0.3 per cent, with Africa next (0.61 per cent of GDP for north of Sahara and 1.07 per cent for south of Sahara).

Table 1.10 Destination of PCF: level of income-based destination classification, 1995–2000 (annual average)

	Least developed	Other low	Lower-middle	Upper-middle	High income	All developing	Part II (transition)	Total
				Amounts in US$ billion, current values				
Total private flows	1.15	9.88	13.94	51.38	0.90	110.33	52.72	163.05
FDI	0.77	8.44	9.78	32.44	0.19	72.31	30.33	102.64
Portfolio capital:								
Total	0.44	1.57	4.52	19.01	0.72	38.66	20.57	59.22
Banks	0.31	−0.21	2.78	8.68	0.35	19.38	4.36	23.74
of which banks' net export credit	−0.01	0.02	−0.14	0.17	0.02	0.11	−0.05	0.06
Non-banks	0.13	1.78	1.74	10.34	0.37	19.28	16.20	35.48
of which non-banks' net export credits	0.11	0.78	0.50	0.99	−0.01	3.21	0.18	3.39
of which non-banks' securities and others	0.11	0.67	1.15	9.21	0.38	15.58	16.08	31.66
				% of GDP (1995–2000)				
Total private flows	0.83	0.60	1.43	2.53	4.04	2.05	4.03	2.44
FDI	0.56	0.51	1.00	1.60	0.83	1.34	2.32	1.54
Portfolio capital:								
Total	0.31	0.10	0.46	0.94	3.21	0.72	1.57	0.89
Banks	0.22	−0.01	0.28	0.43	1.55	0.36	0.33	0.36
of which banks' net export credit	0.00	0.00	−0.01	0.01	0.09	0.00	0.00	0.00
Non-banks	0.09	0.11	0.18	0.51	1.67	0.36	1.24	0.53
of which non-banks' net export credits	0.08	0.05	0.05	0.05	−0.04	0.06	0.01	0.05
of which non-banks' securities and others	0.08	0.04	0.12	0.45	1.70	0.29	1.23	0.47

Source: Computed from OECD/DAC (online).

Table 1.11 Destination of PCF, 1995–2000: regional/geographical destination classification[a] (annual average)

	Africa: north of Sahara	Africa: south of Sahara	North and Central America	South America	Far East, Asia and Oceania	South and Central Asia	Middle East	Europe
Amounts in US$ billion, current values								
Total private flows	−0.10	3.65	36.65	38.24	41.74	2.79	7.14	4.51
FDI	1.08	3.21	21.54	26.53	24.24	1.75	2.12	1.86
Portfolio capital:								
Total	−0.84	0.60	15.12	11.79	17.52	1.06	5.02	2.66
Banks	−0.52	0.88	5.70	6.65	4.24	0.43	2.30	0.60
of which banks' net export credit	−0.12	−0.03	0.07	0.09	−0.06	0.08	0.11	−0.11
Non-banks	−0.33	−0.28	9.42	5.14	13.28	0.63	2.72	2.06
of which non-banks' net export credits	−0.11	0.11	0.26	−0.05	2.00	0.13	0.56	0.36
of which non-banks' securities and others	−0.22	−0.32	9.51	5.14	10.63	0.44	2.03	1.60
% of GDP (1995–2000)								
Total private flows	−0.06	1.21	7.49	2.89	1.76	0.48	1.50	1.78
FDI	0.61	1.07	4.40	2.00	1.02	0.30	0.45	0.73
Portfolio capital:								
Total	−0.48	0.20	3.09	0.89	0.74	0.18	1.06	1.05
Banks	−0.29	0.29	1.16	0.50	0.18	0.07	0.48	0.24
of which banks' net export credit	−0.07	−0.01	0.01	0.01	0.00	0.01	0.02	−0.04
Non-banks	−0.19	−0.09	1.92	0.39	0.56	0.11	0.67	0.81
of which non-banks' net export credits	−0.06	0.04	0.05	0.00	0.08	0.02	0.14	0.14
of which non-banks' securities and others	−0.12	−0.11	1.94	0.39	0.45	0.08	0.43	0.63

Note: [a] Transition countries excluded.

Source: Computed from OECD/DAC (online).

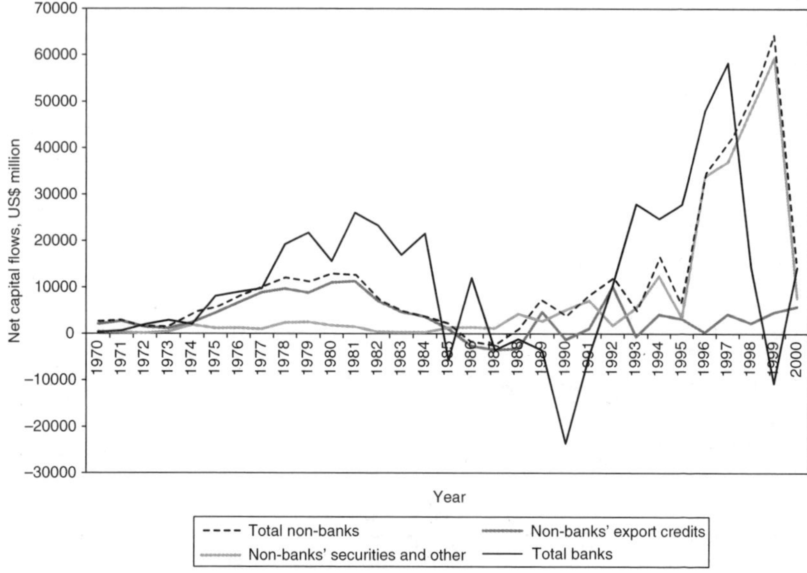

Figure 1.8   Trends in different components of net PCF from DAC members to other countries, 1970–2000 (US$ million)

Source: OECD/DAC (online).

But more interesting is the wide disparity that exists in FDI–GDP ratio between countries at different level of development. As is shown in Table 1.10, FDI in relation to GDP varies more or less directly according to the level of development (per capita income). Thus, while net FDI flows on the part of the least developed countries were equivalent to only 0.56 per cent of their GDP, and a mere 0.51 per cent for other low-income countries, corresponding figures for the lower-middle income, upper-middle income and high-income developing countries were 1 per cent, 1.6 per cent and 0.83 per cent of their respective GDPs. The transition economies (also high income) received the highest share, 2.32 per cent of GDP. Furthermore, it is generally recognized that even the minimal FDI amount received by the least developed and other low-income countries constitutes a flow mainly to their extractive industries.

The lopsided distribution of FDI has intrigued analysts and worried development policymakers and donors (see Swedish Foreign Affairs Ministry 2002, online). This has prompted many studies to attempt to explain the FDI flow. Some of these studies simply adopt the case study method while others, in turn, are micro-oriented in approach, seeking to identify factors that make a particular multinational locate in a specific country or another. Others are macroeconomic in approach, in which factors affecting the aggregate flows of FDI from a particular country (or group of countries) to another country (or group of countries) are reviewed. Several factors have been identified in these studies as the determinants of FDI flows. These include macroeconomic environmental factors in the developing countries, recipient-specific institutional and political variables, and circumstances prevailing in the rest of the world (particularly with regard to actual and potential source countries) – what are popularly known as 'push' factors in the literature (see Chapter 8 by Odedokun for a review). But the above approaches are not suitable for shedding light on the immediate problem as to why FDI does not flow to certain countries, specifically the low-income ones that have no extractive or mining industry enclaves. Literally speaking, some countries have never recorded FDI flows in the last decade or so. What is therefore needed, is finding a substitution for the micro-oriented and macroeconomic method which would identify the reasons as to why some countries are favoured with FDI flows while others receive nothing. One such approach is reported in Chapter 6 by Akinkugbe, who is able to iden-tify a few factors, including the level of per capita income and degree of eco-nomic openness, which together may produce results that deprive some developing countries of FDI receipts.

Portfolio capital flows (PCF)

In Figure 1.8, the movements of the different categories of PCF during 1970–2000 are shown. Commercial bank sources constitute the largest group between 1974 and 1984 and, again, after 1992. Non-bank sources are also sizeable during the 1974–84 period (mainly due to export credits) and became the largest source after the mid-1990s. Following the Asian financial crises, bank sources pummelled in the 1997–99 period – this time, solely because of securitized debt flows, as export credits have since become almost negligible (but rose somewhat in 2000) while non-bank sources also nosedived in 1999 and 2000.

Table 1.10 shows that the total volume of net PCF – amounting, on an annual average, to US$59.2 billion and accounting for only 0.89 per cent of the recipients' GDP – was barely more than half of FDI volume for the 1995–2000 period. The bulk of PCF (annual average of US$35.48 billion) was from non-bank sources, mainly in the form of securitized and related flows (US$31.66 billion), as opposed to export credit sources. The remaining US$23.74 billion was from commercial banking sources (again, mainly from non-export credit sources). Net export credits from bank and non-bank sources, which were relatively important in the 1974–84 decade (see Figure 1.8), now accounted for a negligible fraction of net PCF during the middle and latter part of the 1990s.

The net PCF earmarked for the poorer developing countries – and for the other low-income country group in particular – was disproportionately lower when compared to the already limited volume of net FDI these countries received. The high-income group fared better; their share of PCF was substantially more than that of FDI. Also, countries in transition performed better than average in comparison to the FDI they received. Despite the negligible volume of export credits mentioned above, it still constituted a sizeable portion of the total PCF to the least developed countries, and over 50 per cent of even that volume went to the other low-income country group. Export credits to the upper-middle income and high-income groups as well as countries in transition accounted for a negligible fraction of their total net PCF receipts. Concerning the relative volume of commercial bank PCF in total, countries in transition received much lower than the average for other group of countries while the other low-income group of countries even suffered a net outflow. On the other hand, the lower-middle income and the least developed groups of countries received net PCF from banks than from non-bank sources. Developing countries (excluding countries in transition) as a whole received similar amounts of net PCF from banks and non-banks.

Concerning the geographical distribution of the net PCF, Table 1.11 shows that North and Central America received the highest share by far in relation to the recipients' GDP, or 3.09 per cent of its GDP, followed by the Middle East and Europe, each receiving slightly below 1.1 per cent of GDP. By contrast, South and Central Asia and Africa (south of Sahara) just received about 0.2 per cent of GDP while the African region north of the Sahara suffered a net outflow of every component of PCF.

What factors have accounted for the above trends and distribution of net PCF? Some answers are found in the literature on the subject. After each financial crisis episode (Mexico in 1984–85 and East Asia in 1997–98), a plethora of studies has sprung up, trying to explain the reverse PCF that characterized the episodes (see Chapter 8 by Odedokun for a review of these). Some explanations emanating from these studies have to do with a limited and narrow range of indicators of rates of return and risk considerations. But most of the studies adopted essentially *ad hoc* approaches, invented for the particular financial crisis under consideration, with limited application to some earlier episodes. Thus, the study reported in Chapter 8 adopts a different approach in analysing past financial crises with a more general and enduring applicability as its objective.

7   Reverse net flows from developing to DAC member countries

On the whole, it should be noted that not all types of net financial flows move from developed to developing countries. Some finances on a net basis actually flow in the opposite direction to developed countries, and one important category – the cross-border bank transactions connected with international banking – is examined here. Cross-border transactions drains resources from developing countries, and can be regarded as a vehicle for capital flight (see Chapter 7 by Hermes, Lensink and Murinde).

A widely known source of published information on cross-border transactions with international banks used to be the IMF's *International Financial Statistics, IFS* (World Tables). But the most recent statistics are for year-end 1994 which were last published in the 1995 IFS issues. Table 1.12 is based on the.1995 IFS statistics.

First, non-bank residents of developing countries lodge cross-border deposits with banks located either directly in the developed countries or indirectly, as in the case of offshore banking centres, notwithstanding that most of these are legally sited in the developing countries. Table 1.12 shows that the deposit volume is enormous and has also been growing rapidly over the period for which statistics are published.[10] While it is remarkable that the stock of gross deposits (about US$1.6 trillion at end-1994) from the developed countries greatly exceeds that of developing countries (US$588 billion at end-1994), this is because of the enormous wealth of the former and, as discussed next, gross deposits are being re-cycled to the same developed countries.

Of course, non-bank residents in developing countries also obtain credits from these international banks, thereby moderating net outflows somewhat. After netting out such cross-border lending to non-bank borrowers residing in developing countries, we arrive at an item labelled 'net deposits by residence of depositors' in Table 1.12. Despite this adjustment, Table 1.12 still shows that resource outflows from developing countries remained enormous, and that subsequently these 'lost' US$125.8 billion over the 1984–94 period. Although the flow of gross deposits over the 1984–94 period from developed countries to the international banks was substantial, over the same period there was actually a huge reverse net flow amounting to US$875 billion, from the banks to the developed countries. This reflects the fact that gross deposits received from the developed countries, together with the bulk of what the banks received from the developing countries, were being lent to non-bank borrowers residing in developed countries. Only a small portion of the gross deposits from developing countries eventually found their way back to the original source, that is, developing countries.

For a more complete picture, we also took cognisance of, and made adjustment for, the fact that international banks not only received deposits from, but also lent to, the banks (as opposed to non-banks discussed so far) in developed and developing countries. The resulting net deposits[11] of the banks in these two country groups are consolidated with the non-bank net deposits discussed earlier, giving us the item 'net deposits and liabilities by residence of depositor and borrowing bank' in Table 1.12. Again, the enormity of resource flows from developed to developing countries is not reduced by this adjustment. What the adjustment highlights more clearly is the role of the offshore banking centres (e.g. Bahamas, Bahrain, Barbados, Bermuda, Cayman Islands and Singapore) as the pipeline through which resources are being mopped up from the developing to the developed countries. While the 1984–94 overall net resource flow from developing countries was US$134.4 billion, major offshore banking

Table 1.12   Cross-border banking activities as a vehicle for net private financial outflows from developing countries, 1984–94 (US$ billion)

	Developed countries	Developing countries						
		All	offshore banking	Africa	Asia	Europe	Middle East	Western hemisphere
Increase (flow) between 1984–94								
Cross-border bank deposits of non-banks by residence of depositor[a]	1 157.6	288.0	105.7	22.7	44.7	17.3	25.7	141.4
Net deposits by residence of depositor[a]	−875.1	125.8	9.7	23.5	−23.5	−5.2	15.8	101.5
Net deposits and liabilities by residence of depositor and borrowing bank	−834.7	134.4	190.7	9.8	107.3	−35.4	−7.8	44.7
End-1984 stock value								
Cross-border bank deposits of non-banks by residence of depositor[a]	487.2	300.2	59.6	13.5	31.0	3.6	65.4	130.5
Net deposits by residence of depositor[a]	53.5	−44.4	25.2	−36.6	−42.7	−13.1	37.0	−111.9
Net deposits and liabilities by residence of depositor and borrowing bank	77.4	−36.3	51.6	−31.1	−46.0	2.5	−34.0	−48.5
End-1994 stock value								
Cross-border bank deposits of non-banks by residence of depositor[a]	1 644.8	588.2	165.3	36.2	75.7	20.9	91.2	272.0

| Net deposits by residence of depositor[a] | −821.5 | 81.4 | 34.9 | −13.1 | −66.2 | −18.3 | 52.8 | −10.4 |
| Net deposits and liabilities by residence of depositor and borrowing bank | −757.2 | 98.2 | 242.3 | −21.3 | 61.4 | −32.9 | −41.8 | −3.8 |

Notes: [a] There were unallocated portions (in the data source) of global cross-border bank deposits (by residence of depositors) of non-banks and cross-border bank credits received (by residence of recipients) because the residences of the non-bank transactors could not be determined. We prorated these on the basis of the share of each region from the allocated portions. By this, the regional shares now add up to the global volumes.

Source: IMF (1995).

centres alone accounted for US$190.7 billion, more than the total, suggesting that international banks (other than offshore centres) probably even recorded some net resource flows to developing countries. Given that the total bilateral ODA net flow over the same 10-year period was US$345.8 billion, this conservatively estimated net resource flow (US$134.4 or about 40 per cent of bilateral ODA) through offshore banks is, without a doubt, substantial.

Regional distribution shows that the bulk of net resource flows to the international banks originates from Latin America. This is in line with the finding reported in Chapter 7 by Hermes, Lensink and Murinde in their study of capital flight (a rather nebulous concept) of which the cross-border banking transactions being discussed here are a specific form.

The question that naturally arises from Table 1.12 concerns the reasons for the observed resource movements and the motives of non-bank economic agents for patronizing international banks, particularly offshore banking centres. The answer depends on whether the agents are residents of a developed or a developing country. Developed country residents are likely to patronize banks on the basis of return-risk investment considerations. Money laundering for tax evasion could also be a major reason, particularly for deposits to offshore banking centres. While similar reasons can also apply to non-bank residents of developing countries, other motives are likely to loom larger, such as the urge to put their mostly illegally acquired wealth in safe havens beyond the reach of national laws. While illegality and money laundering could arise from narcotics transactions, the bulk is likely to be relation to corruption. This could also partly explain the increasing importance of offshore banking centres, given the recent clamour for anti-secrecy in banking laws in the traditional safe havens for illegal wealth (in countries like Switzerland and the UK), which would make these less secure.

These outward flows of resources from developing countries are a major component of capital flight, as it is known within the development policy circles. As discussed in detail by Hermes, Lensink and Murinde in Chapter 7, some capital-flight researchers use similar statistics to what we present above as their measure of capital flight. But, as also discussed in the same Chapter 7, capital flight can encompass more than the just outward movement of corrupt enrichment or illegally procured wealth. Legitimately acquired wealth can also give rise to capital flight (just as it can be a component of developing country residents' deposits with international banks, including offshore centres). Also, not all capital flight (regardless of whether legitimately or ill-gotten wealth) involved in cross-border movements is lodged in foreign banks, as it can be used to buy other financial assets (e.g. stocks, bonds, etc.) and non-financial assets (real estate abroad). In the absence of statistics on the uses of cross-border resource flows among various foreign assets categories, capital flight continues to be based on rough estimates, as surveyed in Chapter 7, as does the measurement of cross-border transfers of ill-gotten resources, as we have done here. Various factors affecting capital flight are reviewed comprehensively in

Chapter 7, and most would be applicable in explaining the observed distribution and trends in cross-border banking transactions in Table 1.12.

8 Short-term and net liquid resource flows from developing to developed countries

We do not have access to statistics on short-term private capital flows (i.e. those with maturity of no more than a year). The combined private and non-private sources that are published (e.g. in the World Bank sources) do not tell much, particularly as interest arrears on long-term debts are included. Thus we are unable to infer much on the trends and magnitudes for short-term capital flows, but we do not believe that these differ markedly from the PCF discussed earlier, because maturity is the only distinguishing element between short-term capital flows and PCFs.

But in addition to conventional short-term capital flows, there is also cross-border flow of liquid capital, including cross-border holding of currencies (of other nations). While we have no statistics to determine to whether there is a net outflow of conventional short-term capital from developing countries, available evidence suggests that a net flow of liquid capital exists from the developing countries to the developed. The flow of international reserve assets[12] is an example of these. According to the IFS (World Tables), total reserves (gold excluded) held by all developing countries at the end of 1970, 1980, 1990 and 2000 were 17, 135, 241 and 850 billion SDRs, respectively. This suggests that the net resource flows on the account of (non-gold) foreign reserve movements during the 1970s, the 1980s and the 1990s amounted to about 118, 106 and 609 billion SDRs, respectively, totalling 833 billion SDRs over the three decades.

Our main concern here, however, is the financial flows directly affecting the private sector in the developing countries. Foreign reserve movements directly impact on the public sector through central banks, except for the share held by the commercial banking system directly affecting the availability of cross-border funds to the private sector. But in addition to the commercial banks' share of foreign reserves, the private sector also holds portfolios of foreign currencies and other liquid assets (i.e. liabilities of developed countries) outside the banking systems. The official sector maintains foreign reserves for transactions and precautionary reasons, but so does the private sector, but there are no statistics on the volumes held by the private sector. In almost every urban centre, parallel and informal (at times, illegal) foreign exchange markets exist for trading major currencies, especially the US dollar, followed by the British pound, European Union Euro and Japanese yen. Across all developing countries, the equivalent of trillions of US dollars is likely to be involved in similar reserves of foreign liquid assets. A small annual percentage accretion to this huge stock of foreign currency translates into substantial net resource flows from the developing countries.

This situation is further compounded by the macroeconomic problems many developing countries are faced with; domestic residents lose confidence in their national currencies, thus preferring to effect most of their exchanges through, and holding much of their wealth in, the so-called 'hard currencies'. Studies on currency substitutions and the so-called dollarization have identified a number of factors responsible for this phenomenon (e.g. see Mulligan and Nijsse 2001 for studies on transition economies; Dontsi 2001 for African economies; and Mourmouras and Russell 2000 for some theoretical exposition).[13] We do not have statistics with respect to all of these, but casual empiricism leads us to believe that the amounts involved are enormous.

9   Summary and conclusion

The chapter has presented a comprehensive survey of the 'shopping list' of sources of external finance that are directly channelled to the business sector of the developing countries. Generally, our survey and statistical analysis cover the 1970–2000 period. The distribution of foreign sources according to different income-based and geographical classifications of the developing countries were reviewed. We examined the aggregate net resource flows in the form of saving–investment gap and current account surplus in the developed country BOP. We also examined the institutionalized component of this aggregate, which encompasses both official and private flows. In addition, we discussed the different components of private flows, including unrequited private transfers (grants by NGOs and worker remittances) and commercial capital flows (private flows to multilateral institutions and bilateral private capital flows in the form of foreign direct investments and portfolio capital flows) to developing countries. Official foreign flows for business sector development were also examined and the recent pre-occupation with assistance to microfinance and microenterprises in the developing countries to promote poverty reduction and gender balance in the recipient countries was highlighted. These official sources are bilateral flows and multilateral flows, including those from the IFC. Items that by their nature are inherently net outflows from the developing countries were included: the cross-border international banking transactions by residents of developing countries that often give rise to capital flight. Also included are the foreign currency and other liquid liabilities of the developed countries, whose holding by the residents of developing countries seems to be ever-increasing over the years.

While most of these components have been discussed and analysed in various contributions within current research project, questions and issues still remain. Also, some have hardly been examined at all in any previous study. Within the limited space available, we attempted to address each issue. Where feasible, we also reported our own studies that seek to explain the trends over the years and distribution across countries. As mentioned earlier, not all the types of movement of funds involve net resource flows to developing countries. A number of these actually are inherently a form of resource outflows from the third world to developed countries. Whether there has been a net resource flow on balance to or from developing countries over the years is difficult to ascertain. Only the increased availability of requisite statistics in the future will permit a more categorical assessment in this regard.

Notes

1. For example, El-Sakka and McNabb (1999) who reported exchange rate and interest rate differentials as remittance determinants.
2. This, however, does not infer that the aforementioned wider concept is not useful within some contexts (as are used by Jimoh, Chapter 3 and Gibbon and Schulpen Chapter 2).
3. This cross-border catalytic effect, together with additionality effect of their role, seem to lack precise usage in the literature. Within the context of this paper, we are interested in the cross-border catalytic, crowding-out and additional effects of PSD support and we adhere to their concepts as explained below: If US$1 direct foreign official PSD support is able to fund, say, a project costing US$13 through co-financing, loan syndication and others then the leverage ratio or multiplier would be said to be 13. But, let us assume that US$2 out of the US$13 project cost comes from domestic sources (government and private sector), then the cross-border leverage ratio or multiplier would be just 11. For a number of reasons, this is only a pragmatic definition, at best. First, the increased domestic investment opportunity brought about by the existence of the project could have prevented some domestic sources from finding their way outside the country (like through capital flight). This, if known, should be added to the cross-border leverage ratio. Second, some of the foreign sources that are now mobilized through co-financing, loan syndication, and so on would still have likely found their way into the country in other forms, so that, at best, the foreign official PSD support merely affect the timing of their availability. To the extent that the amounts involved are known or can be estimated, they should be used in adjusting (by being deducted from) the cross-border leverage ratio above. But, in real life, the above two adjusting factors cannot often be known or reasonably estimated. Hence, we stick to the pragmatic cross-border leverage ratio of 11 mentioned above, which then constitutes the cross-border catalytic effect (albeit, pragmatic or practical) of foreign official financing of PSD. But undertaking of the project can displace existing foreign investors already undertaking the same or similar activities and discourage potential investors contemplating doing so. The foreign investments so displaced and discouraged would then be the cross-border crowding-out effect. The difference between the catalytic and crowding-out effects constitutes the (net) additionality of the official support for the PSD.
4. Attempts at making conceptual distinctions between the concepts and efforts aimed at maximizing additionality are discussed in IIC (2002, online).
5. Chapter 4 by Mavrotas discusses how the IFC, has been performing on this score.
6. See McGillivray and Oczkowski (1991) for the exposition and application and Akinkugbe (Chapter 6) for a similar application to foreign direct investors' allocation decision.

7. The statistics are from the Freedom House (online).
8. DAC Statistical Reporting Directives (online).
9. Although NGO grants are included in the private capital flows discussed in Section 2, the inclusion hardly makes a difference.
10. See Table 1.12, the row titled: Cross-border Bank Deposits of Non-banks by Residence of Depositors, from page 7xr d of the IFS World Tables.
11. This is arrived at by subtracting cross-border inter-bank liabilities by residence of borrowing bank or page 8ya d of IFS World Tables from cross-border inter-bank claims by residence of lending bank or page 8ya d of IFS World Tables.
12. Here we imply items other than gold and relatively small items like the IMF's special drawing rights (SDRs), whose value is a little above one US dollar.
13. Some use currency substitution and dollarization interchangeably while others (e.g. Alami 2002) defines currency substitution as holding foreign money as a medium of exchange and dollarization as holding foreign money as a store of value.

References

Ahlburg, D. A. and R. P. C. Brown (1998). 'Migrants' Intention to Return Home and Capital Transfers: A Study of Tongans and Samoans in Australia'. *Journal of Development Studies*, 35 (2): 125–51.

Alami, T. H. (2002). 'Currency Substitution versus Dollarization: A Portfolio Balance Model'. *Journal of Policy Modeling*, 23 (4): 473–79.

Brooks, R. (2000). 'Aging and Global Capital Flows in a Parallel Universe'. IMF Working Paper WP/00/151. Washington, DC: IMF.

Brown, R. P. C. (1997). 'Estimating Remittance Functions for Pacific Island Migrants'. *World Development*, 25 (4): 613–26.

Browning, M. and A. Lusardi (1996). 'Micro Theories and Micro Facts'. *Journal of Economic Literature*, 34 (4): 1797–855.

DAC/OECD (online). International Development Statistics, IDS. Paris: OECD.

Dontsi, D. (2001). 'Substitution Monetaire dans les Pays Africains'. *African Development Review*, 1382: 250–75.

El-Sakka, M. I. T. and R. McNabb (1999). 'The Macroeconomic Determinants of Emigrant Remittances'. *World Development*, 27 (8): 1493–502.

Freedom House (online). Available at: www.freedomhouse.org/ratings/index.htm.

Funkhouser, E. (1995). 'Remittances from International Migration: A Comparison of El Salvador and Nicaragua'. *Review of Economics and Statistics*, 77 (1): 137–46.

Gibbon, P. and L. Schulpen (2002) 'Comparative Appraisal of Multilateral and Bilateral Approaches to Financing Private Sector Development in Developing Countries'. WIDER Discussion Paper WDP2002/112. Helsinki: UNU/WIDER.

IIC (Inter-American Investment Corporation) (2002). 'Additionality Roundtable: Presentations of First, Second, and Third Thematic Workshops'. Washington, DC: IIC. Available at: www.iadb.org/iic/english/additionality/.

Loayza, N., K. Schmidt-Hebbel and L. Serven (2000). 'What Drives Private Saving Across the World'. *Review of Economic and Statistics*, 82 (2): 165–81.

Lopez, J. R. and M. A. Seligson (1991). 'Small Business Development in El Salvador: The Impact of Remittances', in *Series on Development and International Migration in Mexico, Central America, and the Caribbean Basin*, vol. 4 of *Migration, Remittances and Small Business Development: Mexico and Caribbean Basin Countries*. Boulder and Oxford: Westview Press, 175–206.

McGillivray, M. and E. Oczkowski (1991). 'Modelling the Allocation of Australian Bilateral Aid: A Two-Part Sample Selection Approach'. *The Economic Record*, 67 (197): 147–52.

Mourmouras, A. and S. H. Russell (2000). 'Smuggling, Currency Substitution and Unofficial Dollarization: A Crime-theoretic Approach'. IMF Working Paper WP/00/176. Washington, DC: IMF.

Mulligan, R. F. and E. Nijsse (2001). 'Shortage and Currency Substitution in Transition Economies: Bulgaria, Hungary, Poland and Romania'. *International Advances in Economic Research*, 7 (3): 275–95.

Multilateral Investment Fund (2002). Conference Document 'Remittances to Latin America and the Caribbean'. Presented at the regional conference, Remittances as a Development Tool, 17–18 May.

Nishat, M. and N. Bilgrami (1993). 'Determinants of Worker's Remittances in Pakistan'. *Pakistan Development Review*, Part 2, 32 (4): 1235–43.

Odedokun, M. (2003). 'A Holistic Perception of Foreign Financing of Developing Countries' Private Sectors: Analysis and Description of Structure and Trends'. WIDER Discussion Paper No. 2003/01. Helsinki: UNU/WIDER. Available at: www.wider.unu.edu/publications/publications.htm.

OECD/DAC (n.d.) *International Development Statistics* (online). Available at: OECD.org/DAC/stats.

Swedish Foreign Affairs Ministry (2002). 'Interim Report: Increasing Foreign Direct Investments in Least Developed Countries: The Role of Public Private Interaction in Mitigating Risks'. Final Part of the Series of Reports comprising the Research Project: Development Financing 2000. Stockholm: Swedish Foreign Affairs Ministry. Available at: www.utrikes.regeringen.se/inenglish/policy/devcoop/ financing.htm.

White, H. (1980). 'A Heteroscedasticity-consistent Covariance Matrix Estimator and Direct Test for Heteroscedasticity'. *Econometrica*, 48: 817–38.

Wilkins, M. (1999). 'Two Literatures, Two Storylines: Is a General Paradigm of Foreign Portfolio and Foreign Direct Investment Feasible?'. *Transnational Corporations*, 8 (1): 53–116.

World Bank (online). *Global Financial Statistics*. Washington, DC: World Bank.

World Bank (2002). 'Private Sector Development Strategy – Directions for the World Bank Group'. April. Washington, DC: Private Section Advisory Services of the World Bank.

2

Comparative Appraisal of Multilateral and Bilateral Approaches to Financing Private Sector Development

*Peter Gibbon and Lau Schulpen**

1 Introduction

In the minds of a large majority of development thinkers and agencies, there is no longer any doubt that the private sector is the real 'engine of growth', the motor that will lead to economic progress and thereby to poverty reduction. On the other hand, the lack of conceptualization and, certainly, operationalization of the poverty reduction objective is a major problem for the development cooperation policies of the donors. This is of particular importance when looking at those interventions and programmes which seem at best to be tackling only one dimension of poverty reduction, such as those falling under the rubric of private sector development (PSD).

According to the OECD's Development Assistance Committee (DAC 1994: 4), this is less of a problem than it might seem. For the DAC, private sector development is itself related to poverty reduction in a multifaceted way. First, it contributes to growth, and creates employment and income leading 'to a more equitable diffusion of the benefits of growth to more people'. Furthermore, in the case of microenterprises 'these factors are [...] enhanced by virtue of their particularly direct impact on poverty reduction and on the integration of women and other marginalized segments of society into economic life'. Second, PSD contributes to the political aspects of poverty reduction because it promotes participatory development and good governance, by engaging 'people more actively in the productive and decision-making processes that affect their lives'. The development of the private sector is even seen as contributing to a more pluralistic civil society 'that can lead to more accountable political systems and rising labour standards'. Finally, certain aspects of PSD, in particular privatization, address the social dimension of poverty reduction. They do so because they imply more efficient use of resources and thus create possibilities to divert funds from loss-making public enterprises to such laudable causes as education and health. These consequences do not follow automatically though. Rather, whether they follow or not is dependent on good governance and good policies.

Similar claims for multifaceted links between PSD and poverty reduction are made by the World Bank (2002). It is debatable whether these arguments for multiple but largely indirect links compensate for the absences of clear definitions of poverty reduction, and of stronger demonstrations of a direct link between PSD and the latter.[1] Even so, it is clear from the strength of efforts to make such links that donors now consider it not only worthwhile but also necessary to assist the growth and performance of developing countries' private sectors. While most development agencies (from bilateral donors to regional development banks) have always had some focus on the private sector, it has been only since 1990 and in the context of a broader new development consensus that something termed 'private sector development' has achieved the status of a catchword.

This chapter identifies the rationale behind this trend, describes the main elements and instruments of the PSD policies, and provides an overview of the differences and similarities between the PSD activities of bilateral and multilateral development agencies. Beginning with the underlying arguments for PSD promotion, the chapter goes on to investigate the nature of the instruments used by both sets of donors. It examines these in relation to their practical effectiveness and their consistency with donors' broader development objectives and development assistance norms. This discussion raises broader issues concerning aid coherence, coordination and inter-donor competition. The chapter concludes with a general comparison between bilateral and multilateral donors, and a discussion of the implications of this comparison for future donor interventions.

2 The content of PSD

The increasing focus of bilateral and multilateral organizations on the private sector was a logical outcome of the reorientation in development thinking that began in the 1980s. The first stage of this reorientation was a shift from the belief of the state being the prime mover of economic development to the neoliberal resurgence of the early 1980s when the state was regarded with 'major disillusionment' (Killick 1989: 9) and privatization and structural adjustment were seen as the solution to a broad range of problems. A more nuanced view emerged during the 1990s, when a synthesis of public and private initiative became recognized as the way forward. Together with the end of the cold war, therefore, came an end of the 'ideological cleavage' in development thinking and the emergence of the present-day consensus on the role of the private sector in development and on PSD as a policy objective.

This consensus acknowledges complementary roles for the state and the private sector, in which the latter generates economic growth and the former ensures that the private sector is able to fulfil its role while at the same time making sure that growth contributes to poverty reduction, does not lead to environmental degradation and pays attention to gender equality. The paradigmatic status of this view dates from the 1991 World Bank *World Development Report* which argued that while the role of private firms and markets was to produce and distribute goods and services in an efficient manner, government was needed in order to provide a legal and regulatory framework (including strengthened property rights), macroeconomic stability, investments in infrastructure and essential services for the poor. A decade later, *World Development Report 2003* (World Bank 2002: i, 183) still takes this point of departure, albeit with an increased emphasis on the importance of non-market institutions. These institutions, which may be government or non-government, are now also considered necessary for supplying environmental and social assets.

What is perhaps most striking about the consensus is that it still pays much more attention to (re-)defining the role of the government than it does to the nature of the private sector and the effects of its development. Agencies depart from the notion that, in the long run, the private sector will deliver equitable growth spontaneously – provided that an enabling environment is present. In practice, therefore, policy discussion of suitable interventions has been confined to how the government can be directed to create this enabling environment. At the same time, many practical PSD interventions by donors are aimed directly at the private sector, but in ways that lack detailed policy justification.

Intellectually, the consensus can be interpreted as distinguishing two basic levels of PSD, the second of which is sub-divided into three sub-levels. Each comprises a different group of parameters in which specific private sectors operate, whose regulation may act as a stimulus to or constraint on PSD. To this extent, designing and coordinating policies addressed to all four levels can be considered a prerequisite for the coherence of donor activity in this field.[2] At the first, *international* level, these parameters include effective participation in international trade. This entails participation in the WTO. However, in regard to the WTO, incoherence is still the order of the day, since donor countries' enthusiasm for the recipients to conform to WTO agreements is not usually matched by an equal willingness for opening up from their own side. At the second, *national* level, a distinction can be made between *macro*-level parameters such as macroeconomic policy, physical infrastructure, human capital formation and good governance; a *meso*-level includes the presence of institutions such as employers' organizations, labour unions and training institutions; and a *micro*- or firm-level includes access to capital/credit, technology, labour, and market information.

Specific types of intervention may be identified within each of these levels of PSD, ranging from advocacy on behalf of developing countries in international fora to direct support to private firms. Table 2.1 provides a summary of the content of these levels, and of some related actual and proposed instruments. Corresponding to the distinctions between these levels,

Table 2.1   Levels, elements and proposed interventions for PSD

	Elements	Proposed intervention
International	• Free and rule-governed international trade • Access to international markets • Debt reduction • Donor policies and practices (including coordination)	• Lobby and advocacy on behalf of poor countries in multilateral fora such as World Bank, WTO, IMF; with the EU and member states to open up the European market; with the MAI; with donor countries to promote coherence in foreign policies (particularly in relation to aid policies); • Increase trade with the southern countries (e.g. through tariff reductions, exemption schemes, or providing (technical) assistance and knowledge on northern markets to southern exporters); • Set up bilateral investment treaties with poor countries regulating foreign direct investments; • Set up a coherent PSD policy within the overall development policy by donors; • Increasing coordination between donors and reducing tied aid.
Macro	*Macroeconomic policies* • Trade policy • Privatization • Exchange rate, monetary, labour market and fiscal policies • Inflation reduction • Financial institutions (capital market) • Balance of payments regulation *Physical infrastructure and human capital* • Education and skill training • Health • Roads, railways, telecommunication, etc. • Social security and pension schemes *Good governance* • Fight against corruption • Transparency • Legal system • Competition policy • Corporate governance	• Strengthen economic and industrial policy of developing countries through technical assistance, training and exposure; • Support economic reform programmes while paying attention to sequencing and timing; • Support debt relief measures and provide bilateral debt relief assistance; • Improve (physical) infrastructure (roads, railways, telephones, harbours); • Provide technical and financial assistance to improve the human capital situation in poor countries (including such issues as skill training, education, health); • Provide technical assistance in the fields of labour laws and pension funds; • Provide assistance in the field of policymaking, transparency of governments, the fight against corruption; • Increased coordination between donors.

Table 2.1   Continued

	Elements	Proposed intervention
Meso	*Institutional infrastructure* • Chamber of commerce • Employers' organization • Labour unions • Intermediary financial Institutions • R&D institutions • Training institutions	• Strengthen the institutional framework through increased cooperation between northern labour unions, employers; organizations and chambers of commerce and their southern counterparts through funding, training, exposure; • Provide training to sensitize social partners (labour and employers' organizations, civil society and the government) to work together; • Institutional development through training, exposure; • Increased coordination between donors
Micro	• Access to technology, expertise and capital • Manpower • Management and entrepreneurship • Market access and information	• Support to enterprises through, for instance, transfer of technology, training and competence building (e.g. in the fields of marketing or export), financing, supervision; • Support for improving access to financing by micro credit schemes of governments and NGOs, providing risk capital, loan schemes, guarantee schemes and local investment funds to the private sector; • Support for local market improvements, storage systems and marketing knowledge; • Provide assistance to increase agricultural production as a base for economic growth; • Increase local or regional procurement and the use of local or regional consultants within aid (including emergency aid) interventions; • Increased coordination between donors.

Source: Adapted from Schulpen and Gibbon (2001: Table 1.1 and Table 1).

some of the latter are directed at the international community, some to assisting governments in developing countries, some to assisting governments together with other 'partners' in society, and some at individual enterprises in developing countries. Those directed at the international community include action to reduce tied aid and increase donor coordination. Generally, interventions tend to become more specific, and more in the form of targeted technical and financial support,[3] the further one moves down from the international to the micro-level.

Probably because the parameters recognized in the consensus are so many, and the resources of individual donors are few, most concentrate interventions at only one or two levels. The choices this involves tend to reflect the different degrees of attention paid in broader policy discourses to the behaviours of developing country governments and the international community, respectively. While it is arguably more rational for donors to assume that these are of equal importance, selection of instruments is in practice influenced by the belief that 'external factors [are] invariably less significant than internal policies and practices' (DAC 1999: 3). Therefore the instruments chosen are those addressing national macro-, meso- and micro-levels.

There may also be a problem with some of the assumptions governing how specific instruments are devised to address issues at these levels. Many of these reflect a highly normative conception of what a 'national enabling environment' should look like, reflecting an idealized model of such environments in the north. The result is a form of 'one size fits all' thinking that fails to take its point of departure in the realities of the south. Only within this somewhat narrow framework is it possible to identify meaningful differences between donors on issues addressed and instruments chosen. Nonetheless, some important differences are present, which are examined in the following section.

3   Bilateral and multilateral agencies: policies, programmes, instruments and funding

Having described PSD thinking in general terms, this section sets out to provide a presentation of the policies and instruments of both bilateral and multilateral donors. Not all donors can or will be covered here. Thus, whereas for the discussion on bilateral donors reference is made particularly to those donors that have formulated explicit PSD policies, discussion on multilateral donors is restricted to what are probably the major players (in the PSD field) as far as developing countries are concerned. These include the World Bank Group (e.g. IFC, MIGA, IBRD/IDA) and the main 'south'-oriented regional development banks (IADB, AfDB, AsDB and IsDB). Many (smaller) or less 'south'-oriented players are omitted, or referred to only in passing. It is expected, however, that including more (multilateral) organizations would only lead to 'variations on the same theme'.

Bilateral donors

At the end of the 1990s and the beginning of the new century, several bilateral donors brought out policy papers dealing directly with PSD. In 1999, for instance, Norway presented its strategy for the support of the private sector in developing countries (NORAD 1999), and during the next year Australia (AusAID 2000) and the Netherlands (DGIS 2000) produced PSD policies. Although Belgium still has no explicit PSD strategy, recent policy statements clearly emphasize the development of the private sector as part of development cooperation. In the meantime, Finland is preparing a

PSD policy. The group of bilateral donors with an active policy and specific programmes in the field of PSD is growing and now comprises Australia, Canada, Denmark, Germany, New Zealand, Norway, the Netherlands, the United States and the United Kingdom. Other DAC donors have not yet begun formulating an explicit PSD policy but all have to a greater (e.g. Sweden, France, Belgium) or lesser (e.g. Spain, Portugal, Italy, Ireland) extent programmes aimed at the private sector.

As already suggested, most of the issues addressed by these policies are government-related in the sense that they refer to tasks and responsibilities that governments have to perform and implement to prepare for a private sector-led development path (i.e. they address the role of the government in creating an enabling environment). Furthermore, in a majority of the cases, they refer to the national rather than the international enabling environment. This national enabling environment in practically all cases covers elements described earlier under macro-level, but also quite often meso-level, elements. Finally, all donors clearly distinguish the enabling environment level from more direct interventions at the micro-level. Of course, not all donors distinguish explicitly all four PSD levels or even implicitly acknowledge all levels within their PSD policies. Table 2.2 shows the levels and central elements distinguished by a selection of bilateral donors.

Table 2.2   Donor policies and PSD: some examples on central issues

| | **PSD levels** | |
International	**Macro/meso**	**Micro**
Australia	• Macroeconomic policy • Trade, investment and finance sector policies • Legal and regulatory system • Effective public administration • Development of civil society • Physical and social infrastructure	• Access to financial market • Access to business services
Canada	• Labour market policies • Public sector reform • Financial sector reform • Trade, investment, and exchange rate reform • Legal and regulatory framework • Physical and social infrastructure • Competitive internal market linked to global economy	• Access to financial and non-financial services (particularly for micro-enterprises and SMEs) • Linkages with Canadian business

Table 2.2   Continued

PSD levels		
International	**Macro/meso**	**Micro**
Norway • Access to international markets • Regulations of international trade • Debt relief • ODA levels	• Macroeconomic policy • Good governance • Physical and institutional infrastructure (including the legalframework)	Covers factors at enterprise level, e.g. • Access to technology • Access to expertise • Access to capital Workforce • Skills
The Netherlands • Trade • Investment • Debt relief • Primary products • Coherence of policy	• Macroeconomic policy • Political stability, good governance and legal system • Market development • Physical and social infrastructure • Protection of men and environment	A large number of (bilateral and multilateral) programmes are captured here. These are divided in three fields: • Knowledge (e.g. training in management, investments) • Profitability (e.g. financial support for investments, exports) • Risks (e.g. guarantee schemes)

Notes:
– The table only covers the major elements mentioned by the concerned DAC donors in their PSD policies and is thus not all-inclusive. Moreover, the table does not cover all elements regarded as important for the development of the private sector in developing countries. Norway represents a special case here. The table only shows a selection of those policies it states as central. A more thorough discussion and analysis of these elements is presented in a background paper for Norway's PSD policy.
– The macro- and meso-level, together forming the national enabling environment, are taken together here, as most donors do not make a distinction between these two levels.
– Macroeconomic policy in general includes such issues as balanced public budgets, satisfactory external balances and acceptable rates of inflation and interest.
– Social infrastructure generally covers health and education, whereas physical infrastructure relates to roads, railways, energy and so on. Institutional infrastructure (as in the case of Norway) refers to 'functioning organizations able to strengthen the dialogue between the business community and the authorities as well as between the social partners' (e.g. labour unions, employer organizations and chambers of commerce).

Sources: AusAID (2000); CIDA (1999); DGIS (2000); EC (1998); NORAD (1999).

As far as specific programmes and instruments are concerned, one way of providing a clearer picture of donor interventions in the field of PSD is to distinguish between financial and non-financial (or technical) aid[4] (Pietilä 2000: 2; also see the next chapter by Jimoh). Donors provide technical assistance at the macro-, meso- and micro-levels, in the form of export training, investment advice, provision of experts in managerial roles and so on. Most bilateral donors are involved in such types of assistance. The same holds for financial aid instruments such as grants and loans for macro-level activities (e.g. infrastructure), equity financing, risk capital, guarantees, mixed credits, lines of credit and micro-loan programmes. Annex 1 provides some examples of such instruments for bilateral donors while more comprehensive examples are in Gibbon and Schulpen (2002). A glance at these indicates (potentially) high levels of duplication, indicating that coordination might pose a major challenge (see below).

Multilateral donors

The major multilateral players providing PSD assistance in developing countries comprise international organizations (primarily the World Bank Group) and regional and quasi-regional organizations with developing countries members (primarily the various development banks). Members of the UN family of organizations such as UNCTAD, UNIDO and UNDP also acknowledge the importance of the role of the private sector in their sector-specific strategies, and provide technical assistance and 'matchmaking' services around PSD issues. While they act as intermediaries in providing financial assistance, they do not normally provide this directly from their own resources.

These multilateral organizations began directing assistance to or opening windows for PSD at rather different times. The World Bank Group has operated one exclusively private sector window since the 1950s, namely the International Finance Corporation (IFC), and another since the 1980s (the Multilateral Investment Guarantee Agency [MIGA]), while at least one of the regional development banks (the Inter-American, IADB) opened a private sector division (the Inter-American Investment Corporation [IIC]) in the 1980s. Other development banks opened windows or divisions much later – the Islamic Development Bank (IsDB) with its Business Development Department in 1995 and the African Development Bank (AfDB) in 1996.[5] Some other development banks still have no dedicated private sector windows, although all lend a part of their funds to private enterprises. This group includes the Caribbean Development Bank (CDB), the European Bank for Reconstruction and Development (EBRD) and the European Investment Bank (EIB). A similar picture exists with regard to explicit policy discourses around PSD. The World Bank's first PSD policy was unveiled in 1987,[6] while the AsDB, AfDB and IsDB all have published formal statements only between 1997 and 2000. The IADB, CBD, EBRD and EIB still have no such formal policy statements at all.

Here, the policies, programmes and instruments of five multilateral donors are considered in detail, while the others mentioned above are considered in passing. The five comprise the World Bank and four regional or quasi-regional development banks (African, Asian, Inter-American and Islamic). At the time of writing, only three of these organizations (the World Bank, the Asian and the African Development Banks) had what might be called fully articulated PSD policies or strategies (that of the IsDB consists of only a few sentences).

The PSD policies of the three organizations with explicit policies resemble each others' programmes, and those of the bilateral agencies, to a very great extent (see Table 2.3). All fall within the broad boundaries of the 'PSD consensus' described earlier. At the same time, there are some minor differences in emphasis with respect to the way the common policies are articulated in detail, and the World Bank and the AsDB can be said to have developed their policies further than the AfDB, in that their policies address areas not covered by earlier generations of PSD strategy.

Assisting the development of an *enabling (business) environment* is seen in each case in terms of a combination of legal and judicial reforms (particularly the elaboration and enforcement of property rights), continuing internal (competition-related) and external (trade policy-related) market reform and taxation system reform. The emphasis of the AsDB in relation to this issue is somewhat distinct. On the one hand, it highlights labour market as well as other reforms, while on the other it registers an exception to more comprehensive proposals for market opening. In its view, governments should retain the freedom to close the capital account in order to favour longer- over shorter-term investment flows. In the World Bank's latest (2002) PSD strategy, the centrality of the 'enabling environment' is strongly underlined by the prioritization of 'investment environment assessments'

Table 2.3   Components of multilateral donors' PSD policies

	World Bank	Asian Development Bank	African Development Bank
1 Enabling business environment	×	×	×
2 Enterprise reform/privatization	×	×	×
3 Assistance to private sector firms	×	×	×
4 Assisting the financial sector	×	×	×
5 Private participation in infrastructure	×	×	×
6 Corporate governance	×	×	
7 Compliance of actions with development and/or poverty reduction goals	×	×	

Sources: World Bank (2002); AsDB (2000); AfDB (1997).

for each recipient country. These assessments are intended to be instruments for 'mainstreaming' PSD into country assistance strategies, and a precondition for decisions on the allocation of direct support to private enterprises between countries.

Reform or privatization of state-owned enterprises (SOEs) is again a common component. In relation to this issue, the policy of the AsDB and the latest policy of the World Bank are somewhat more nuanced than earlier generations of donor privatization policies. The AsDB mentions support for types of enterprise reform falling short of privatization, while the World Bank's latest statement refers critically to earlier generations of 'shock treatment' privatization and places more emphasis on securing a supportive market environment than on the volume or pace or privatization.

Direct assistance to private sector firms is another policy shared by this group of donors. The development banks and the IFC and MIGA wings of the World Bank emphasize loans, syndications and guarantees for, and equity partnerships in, private enterprises of all sizes. Similar sets of limitations and conditions for loans and other forms of financial assistance are mentioned in each case: direct lending is said to be on strictly non-concessionary terms[7] (but see below) and maximum levels of equity holding range between 25 per cent and 40 per cent. Direct lending (and technical support) by the World Bank proper to private firms is said to be aimed primarily at small- and medium-enterprises (SMEs).

Assistance to the financial sector is generally formulated in terms of a combination of technical assistance and direct lending to financial institutions. Technical assistance is discussed mainly in relation to issues of regulation, supervision and financial market development. On-lending by development banks to financial institutions is described as being targeted both at national banks and at institutions specifically serving SMEs and microenterprises.

Promoting *private participation in infrastructure* provision also features in all the policies considered, with support to 'build-operate-transfer' projects being the most frequently mentioned instrument. The AsDB's policy strongly emphasizes the importance of private participation being accompanied by the development of an adequate regulatory framework.

More recent policy development is reflected in two new emphases, found so far only in the prescriptions of the AsDB and the World Bank. First, these embody proposals to assist reform of *corporate governance*. This can be read as an incorporation of some of the arguments developed by IMF and World Bank economists in relation to the Asian crisis of 1997–98. According to these arguments (e.g. Claessens 1998; World Bank 1998; Iskander *et al.* 1999), important causes of the crisis included weak minority shareholder rights, lack of transparency in corporate financial reporting, interlocking ownership between the corporate and financial sectors and dependence of the corporate sector on bank debt rather than equity financing.[8] Policy proposals concern mainly the first two of these issues.

Second, the PSD policies of the AsDB and World Bank are also relatively distinct in their reference to the necessity of explicit *compliance-based links between PSD programme design and broader aid objectives*. The AsDB states that direct lending to the private sector will be henceforth conditional on projects having demonstrable 'development' implications, and proposes 'scorecards' for monitoring these implications. The World Bank proposes somewhat more detailed conditions for support to private participation in infrastructure projects, namely that they should include mechanisms to ensure poor people's access to services (as well as environmental sustainability). Whereas these two organizations' emphasis on corporate governance issues can be considered an extension of more familiar themes within the PSD policy discourse, proposing 'compliance' mechanisms represents a qualitatively new departure. Prior to this point, the link between PSD programmes, development and poverty reduction had been made by donors only in theoretical, rather than direct, terms.

While most multilateral donors that have PSD policies cover a wide range of issues in them, in practice all those examined here other than the World Bank, concentrate essentially on direct financial support to the private sector rather than more general lending for PSD (including to governments). In the development bank realm, the substantive presence of specific programmes aimed at improving the business environment, enterprise reform/ privatization and modifying corporate governance is low. Where they are present, they generally take the form of technical assistance programmes concerned with training/capacity building, commissioning transaction designs and undertaking feasibility studies.

Programmes or (much more commonly) programme components around business environment, enterprise reform and corporate governance issues are very common in World Bank lending, however. According to the latest World Bank (2002: 26) strategy document, around 100 PSD conditionalities of these kinds were included in new adjustment loans *each year* between 1996 and 1999 (see Table 2.4). The main trend in their internal distribution

Table 2.4 Distribution of PSD conditionalities in World Bank adjustment operations, 1996–99

	1996	1997	1998	1999	Total
Business environment	26	15	13	23	77
Corporate restructuring	2	2	32	15	51
Legal and judicial reform	9	13	5	11	38
Privatization	32	36	29	18	115
Public enterprise reform	17	9	2	3	31
Private participation in infrastructure	13	25	19	30	87
Total	99	100	100	100	

Source: World Bank (2001a: 26).

was away from public enterprise reform/privatization (presumably reflecting a reduction in possible targets for this) and towards private participation in infrastructure and 'corporate governance', particularly in the wake of the Asian crisis.

Independently of its adjustment lending, the World Bank has also run a substantial number of technical assistance programmes related to business environment reform, privatization, private participation in infrastructure and so on. On the last of these, the most important such programme is the 'public–private infrastructure advisory facility', which funded 75 activities between 1998 and 2000 at a cost of US$15 million, US$8 million of which went to IDA countries (World Bank 2001c: 21).

Although the World Bank's reporting terminology is somewhat confusing, it nonetheless appears that – even in the World Bank Group – lending to the private sector (mainly through IFC) overtook adjustment loan-based and technical assistance-related PSD lending combined during the 1990s. By 2000, IFC alone accounted for 56 per cent of total PSD-related lending (ibid.).[9] The central element of any survey of multilaterals' PSD programmes should, therefore, be that of their direct lending to the private sector. The principal multilateral programmes falling under this heading are listed in Table 2.5.

In addition, Table 2.6 provides an overview of bilateral (ODA and other official flows (OOF)) equity investments and total IFC funding, and compares these with total foreign direct investments and total private capital flows. This table shows that total bilateral equity investment (taken here as a form of direct financial support for PSD) is only a fraction of total IFC financing and that IFC funding and bilateral equity investment taken together is even a smaller fraction of total FDI. Perhaps more importantly, the table shows that LDCs score badly when compared to higher income countries. This holds for bilateral equity investment as well as the already mentioned IFC funding and FDI. It also holds for total private flows. Over the period 1995–2000, the least developed countries only receive 1 per cent of total (bilateral) private flows to developing countries and FDI, moving up to 9 per cent of all IFC funding and 15 per cent of all bilateral (ODA plus OOF) equity investments.[10]

These tables suggest a number of provisional observations. The first is that, in terms of volume of financial commitments to destinations normally counted as developing countries, the World Bank Group accounts for the overwhelming bulk of all private sector-directed lending. What is probably the largest single multilateral or quasi-multilateral lender to the private sector, the European Development Bank (EDB), lends over 85 per cent within the EU itself. Second, funding goes largely to only two sectors: infrastructure and financial services. Third, levels of lending to LDCs are extremely low. Because some development banks have no or only one or two LDCs amongst their members, it is better to try to estimate an overall proportion of

Table 2.5 Multilateral donors' programmes for lending to the private sector

Donor	Programme/window	Type of assistance	Cumulative value		Main sectors	% to LDCs
			US$ bn	Years		
WB						
	IFC	Loans, equity, quasi-equity, risk management, syndications, securitizations	51.6	1956–2000	Financial services 2.6% Utilities 8.5%	4.1
	MIGA	Guarantees	9.0	1988–2002	NA	NA
	IBRD/IDA	On-lending to private credit providers	7.7	1990–2002	NA	NA
	Contribution to CGAP	Grants to micro-finance institutions	0.008		NA	NA
AsDB						
		Loans, equity, guarantees, export credit finance	18.0	1983–2000	Financial services 63.0% Infrastructure 32.6%	NA[a]
		Credit lines for on-lending to SMEs (but overwhelmingly via public sector)	4.4	1983–2003		
AfDB						
		Loans, equity, guarantees, syndications, on-lending to SMEs	0.58[b]	of which 0.24 in 2001	Financial services 77.3% Infrastructure 22.6% (2001)	22.6 (2001)

Table 2.5 Continued

Donor	Programme/ window	Type of assistance	Cumulative value		Main sectors	% to LDCs
			US$ bn	Years		
IADB						
		Loans, equity, guarantees, syndications, re-insurance	3.6	1995–2000[c]	Infrastructure 100%	0
	IIC	Loans, equity	0.76	1993–2002	Financial sector 51.9% Manufacturing 12.9%	0
	MIF	Equity, small enterprise development, micro-finance	0.8	1994–2001		0
IsDB						
	ICDPS	Term finance, equity	<0.1	2000–	Manufacturing 40% Private healthcare 30%	10
CDB						
		Loans, equity	<0.1	2000 only	Tourism 100%	0
	Rural enterprise development	Micro-enterprise and marketing support	<0.1	1995–2000		0
EIB						
	Includes private sector finance in general lending	Term finance, equity guarantees	Unstated portion of total of portfolio 159.4	1996–2001	Infrastructure 56% Manufacturing 8%	1.2% in APC countries (includes some LDCs)

European Investment Fund	Venture capital and guarantees for 'SMEs'	5.3	2001	NA	NA
EBRD					
'Mainly private sector investment', but no specific window	Term finance, equity guarantees	20.2	1991–2001	NA	0 (dedicated to Central and Eastern Europe and CIS)

Notes

a During 1983–90, 60 per cent of AsDB's lending to private sector support operations went to only six countries (Bangladesh, PR China, India, Indonesia, Pakistan and Philippines), of which only Bangladesh is a LDC. Twenty of its 43 regional member countries received no private sector lending (AsDB 2001a).

b At the same time, public sector operations still dominate AfDB operations with 81 per cent of total approvals in 2001. Many of these have a clear link with PSD elements, making total PSD-related funding of the AfDB substantially higher than US$241 million for 2001, certainly when also activities of the African Development Bank Fund and the Nigeria Trust Fund are also taken into account.

c Including to projects under public sector ownership.

Sources: World Bank (2001a, c); IFC (2000); MIGA (2001); AsDB (2000, 2001a, b); AfDB (2001); IADB (2001); IIC (2001); MIF (2001); CDB (2001); EBRD (2002); EIB (2002).

Table 2.6 Bilateral and IFC 'direct financial support' in comparison with FDI, 1995–2000 (in million US$)

Country groups	ODA equity investment (bilateral)	OOF equity investment (bilateral)	Total (ODA + OOF) equity investment (bilateral)	IFC financing (multilateral)	Foreign direct investments (bilateral)	Total private capital flows (bilateral)
Developing countries total	657.7	−14.9	642.8	3 375.2	433 874.7	661 995.5
Least developed countries	81.8	15.1	96.9	305.0	4 642.2	6 904.0
Other low-income countries	265.7	35.0	300.7	627.0	50 669.4	59 290.4
Low-middle-income countries	124.3	70.3	194.6	718.9	58 705.6	83 651.5
Upper middle-income countries	16.2	−142.2	−126.0	1 565.4	194 621.3	308 268.3
High income countries	0.4	2.6	3.0	−18.0	1 115.1	5 429.5
Part II countries	71.3	55.8	127.1	397.5	181 933.4	316 308.4
Grand total	729.0	40.9	769.8	3 772.7	615 868.2	978 303.9

Notes: Figures are totals for the period 1995–2000; Part II countries are countries in transition.

Source: DAC International Development Statistics (online).

multilateral and quasi-multilateral lending going to private sectors in LDCs than to discuss the performance of particular banks (with the exception of those whose remit is global) in this respect. The authors' estimate is that LDCs probably account for between 1.5 per cent and 2.0 per cent of this total lending. As for multilaterals with global remits, IFC allocates 4.1 per cent of lending to LDCs. These figures seem very low, although it should be noted that LDC's share of total world inward private FDI stock in 1999 was much lower still – only 0.6 per cent (UNCTAD 2000: Annex Table B3). Fourth, on-lending to private credit institutions for SME, and microenterprise finance is usually hived off to separate units whereas (except in the case of the World Bank Group) term loans, equity investments and guarantees are covered by generic, presumably 'core' administrations. Fifth, microfinance and lending to SMEs, however broadly defined, comprise only a tiny part of direct lending for PSD. At the same time, regional development banks appear to dedicate far higher proportions of their resources to this than does the World Bank Group, where the contribution is negligible.

Bilateral funding for PSD

Levels of bilateral PSD funding are difficult to determine, if only because some donors have a tendency to hide PSD-related programmes under different headings and 'sectors'. Some of these programmes are, at first sight, neither recognizable, nor described, as PSD programmes. A possible way for determining the magnitude of PSD funding in relationship to total development aid is to look at the latter's distribution according to purposes of aid, as reported to the DAC. Annex 1 matches the purposes as distinguished by the DAC with the different levels of PSD described earlier. In theory, of course, basically all purposes could be linked to one or more PSD levels. This could even be said of purposes such as emergency aid, whereas the private sector provides goods and services. This would mean that basically all aid is directed at PSD, which naturally is not the case.[11]

One could also count in those purposes that are either directly linked to the economy (i.e. economic infrastructure and services, and production sectors) and add commodity aid and general-purpose aid (mainly because it includes structural adjustment assistance via the World Bank/IMF plus other general programme and commodity assistance). On this basis, Table 2.7 shows that Japan (as can be expected because of its emphasis on infrastructure projects) is the biggest bilateral donor with more than 60 per cent of bilateral aid commitments in 1998 going to PSD. Using the same criteria, most donors can be said to be spending 20 to 30 per cent of their bilateral aid on activities related to PSD. Even a donor like Ireland, which hardly claims to be active in the field of PSD, still spends more than 16 per cent.[12]

An overview of funding

The uncertainty with regard to determining levels of funding for PSD is further strengthened by the fact that not all interventions categorized under

Table 2.7   Funding to 'PSD' following DAC classification of purposes (in % of bilateral ODA commitments for 1998)

Donor	Bilateral PSD (in %)	Donor	Bilateral PSD (in %)	Donor	Bilateral PSD (in %)
Australia	25.0	Germany	26.4	Norway	15.3
Austria	7.0	Ireland	16.6	Portugal	16.9
Belgium	21.5	Italy	15.6	Spain	20.8
Canada	22.9	Japan	62.1	Sweden	17.6
Denmark	15.7	Luxembourg	17.6	Switzerland	27.2
Finland	21.6	Netherlands	16.4	United Kingdom	28.8
France	20.9	New Zealand	11.7	United States	29.7
				TOTAL	35.6

Source: Own calculations on the basis of DAC (2000).

PSD necessarily fall under budgets for development cooperation (and thus ODA). Table 2.7, for instance, does not cover official aid (OA) figures for PSD-related activities, nor ODA contributions to multilateral organizations which in turn use such funds (also) for PSD programmes. Moreover, PSD programmes are also supported through non-ODA funds, particularly by multilateral organizations such as the IFC and the regional development banks (but also by bilateral donors). For calculating total funding for PSD, therefore, the so-called OOF should also be taken into account. Data on the distribution of such funds for PSD by multilateral organizations are not readily available, however.

The only thing left to do, then, is to turn to each agency individually. Although this is not accurate, financial data from each separate multilateral donor can provide additional insight in the funding pattern. Table 2.5 already provided some aggregate figures for the multilateral donors considered here. The table clearly showed IFC to be the major funding agency for PSD-related activities. In fiscal year 2001 alone, for instance, the IFC signed and processed a total of 194 projects in 70 countries, 18 regional projects and five worldwide projects with a total commitment of US$3.9 billion.[13] In the same year, another 245 country, regional and worldwide projects were approved for financing to the tune of US$5.4 billion. MIGA, another World Bank Group member whose main objective is to promote 'the flow of investment to and among developing countries', implemented in fiscal year (FY) 2001 a total of 59 technical assistance or advisory service projects in 38 countries under the banner of investment marketing services.[14] The same year, MIGA also provided investment guarantees for an amount of nearly US$2 billion for 45 projects in 27 countries for such diverse activities as equity investment by the Habib Bank AG Zurich in its Pakistan branches and a shareholder loan from Dole Food Company, Inc. to the Ecuadorian company Bananapuerto Puerto Bananero S.A. (MIGA 2002).

Although the above perhaps does not provide a definitive answer to the question of funding of PSD by bilateral and multilateral organizations (whether falling under ODA, OA and/or OOF), the broad picture is clear. The increased attention to private sector development that can be seen in the policy discourse, can also be detected in substantial funding. As such, PSD is increasingly important in 'word and deed'.

4   Issues arising from bilateral and multilateral donors' programmes

While bilateral and multilateral donors share very similar analyses of the significance and preferred focus of PSD, they do not necessarily emphasize the same issues and interventions. In this section we take a closer look at the similarities and differences between the two channels of development cooperation. Four issues considered to be central to the discussion of PSD are raised here (also see Schulpen and Gibbon 2002): (i) justifications for public intervention in supporting developing country private enterprise as such; (ii) justifications for programme and country selection; (iii) inter-donor competition and coordination; and (iv) internal and external coherence.[15] These issues relate not only to bilateral donors but also to multilateral ones, in some cases in more acute forms.

Justifications for public intervention

A central issue for public support to private firms and markets in developing countries is whether such support 'crowds out' private provision. Related arguments concern the opportunity cost of using public assistance in this way, and possible linkages between such support and political patronage on the one hand and the imposition of political conditions on private investment on the other.[16]

In relation to the middle-income countries that provide many of the leading destinations for the interventions described here, the 'crowding out' argument probably has some merit. On the other hand, even in these countries the leading sector subject to support (infrastructure) is one where private capital is universally reluctant to invest without public support, due to long project gestation times, high risk and typically low rates of return. Furthermore, many infrastructure projects concern public goods, in the sense that the majority of benefits accrue to users, rather than owners. With regard to LDCs, the core argument here simply appears to be wrong. FDI into these countries tends to be very low and directed mainly at 'enclave' projects with low multiplier effects, while local private investors and investment institutions are typically thin on the ground, highly risk adverse and expensive to use (e.g. spreads between deposit and lending rates tend to be very high, possibly justifying an element of subsidy). Moreover, there is a series of direct obstacles to local borrowing. For example, weak property rights and commercial dispute settlement procedures militate against collateralization of assets. In these circumstances, it can be more convincingly argued that selective public support is a pre-condition of larger-scale private sector activity outside of extractive sectors.

Counter-arguments of the latter kind provide the basis for claims which suggest that, rather than 'crowding out' private investment, public support reins in additional investment. This argument is advanced by some of the regional development banks themselves (e.g. AsDB 2000: 15–16; AfDB n.d.). The AsDB (op. cit.) claims, for example, that every dollar it lends catalyses US$8 finance from other sources. More recently, efforts have been made to distinguish and provide definitions of different forms of such 'additionality' (catalytic effect, value-added effect and 'template'-cum-demonstration effect).[17] However, a common problem of such claims is their counter-factual: it is virtually impossible to know whether 'catalysed' finance would have been activated in one form or another without co-financing and loan syndication arrangements.

Programme and country selection

Despite the plethora of interventions mentioned in Annex 2, in practice there are only a few instruments that make up most bilateral PSD programmes (see for some examples Schulpen and Gibbon 2002). In general, bilateral donors focus on macro- and micro-levels. At the former level, programmes cover almost everything from bilateral policy dialogue to technical aid for specific interventions such as privatization, all with the aim of creating a conducive environment for the private sector. A few donors (e.g. Germany) include in these macro programmes elements such as support to chambers of commerce, labour unions and employers' organizations (or, in general, instruments aimed at strengthening aspects of the institutional infrastructure). Second, they concern elements at the micro-level, with instruments ranging from direct financial support to MSEs to management training, from sending out (senior) experts to individual enterprises, to assisting self-help groups, and from export promotion programmes (to and from developing countries) to the promotion of joint ventures and the provision of investment guarantees. The Dutch FMO, the Danish IFU, the Canadian PSDI fund, the Belgian technology and know-how transfer programmes, the Finnish Export Credit Ltd, and the Norwegian NORFUND and GIEK are all examples of this emphasis on direct micro-level support. Moreover, these programmes incorporate bilateral donors' own private sectors (see below).

While the multilaterals share with bilaterals very similar analyses of the significance and preferred direction of PSD, the overall shape of their programmes is much simpler. As noted above, these tend to comprise only two broad groups of components, namely conditionality-based adjustment lending and direct lending to the private sector (including, in the regional development bank case, on-lending for SME and micro-finance development).

Conditionality-based adjustment lending for PSD is typically not undertaken at all by bilateral donors, although the latter do fund it through World Bank operations. Arguably, since the conditions set by the World Bank are supposed to be based on a close analysis of the recipient countries' economic environments, in its lending to the private sector the World Bank Group should be in a particularly good position to base its choices between countries on the relative favourability of their business environments. Bilateral donors, who at least until recently have tended not to conduct independent evaluations of the recipient's economic and business environments, do not have the advantage of this kind of direct knowledge when allocating private sector support. Yet, there seems to be no association between the World Bank's assessments of recipient countries' economic and business environments and the destination of the World Bank Group's direct lending to the private sector. Nine countries account for well over half of IFC's cumulative commitments, for example. These are, in rank order, Brazil, Argentina, Mexico, Turkey, Thailand, India, Indonesia, Pakistan and the Philippines. Brazil, Argentina and Mexico (in the same rank order) also happen to be the leading recipients of IADB support to the private sector, while India, Indonesia, Pakistan and the Philippines make up four of the six largest Asian Development Bank PSD recipient countries.

Most of these countries have been subject to international criticism with respect to macroeconomic policy and IMF stabilization programmes especially during the 1980s and early 1990s (see e.g. Berry 1998). Nonetheless, multilateral donors have directed the bulk of their PSD lending to them, presumably on commercial grounds, regardless of how 'enabling' their environments were considered. It is clear that these destinations were considered attractive both by private investors and by multilateral agencies on the grounds of potential short-term profitability deriving from the size of their markets alone. Since all the multilaterals (with the exception of the IsDB) have recently affirmed the strictly commercial nature of their lending, this discrepancy seems likely to increase rather than to decrease. Similar arguments can be advanced in relation to bilateral donors' country selections for PSD support, which usually seem to be based on traditional aid partners or commercial interests or both.

Internal and external coherence

The fact that multilaterals' motives in selecting partner countries and projects for direct lending to the private sector are mainly commercial, directly raises the question of 'internal' coherence between these interventions and objectives such as long-term economic growth, poverty reduction and environmental sustainability. Not all private investment leads to long-term growth. And while economic growth – where it is attained – is a precondition of long-term poverty alleviation, not all growth leads to poverty reduction and, historically, much of it has been environmentally harmful. Even where growth is pro-poor, the links may be highly indirect rather than direct.[18]

As noted earlier, two of the five multilateral donors considered here have adopted (albeit very recently) 'compliance' mechanisms requiring at least some private sector operations to have tangible development and even 'pro-poor' consequences. In regard to the latter, privatization operations can now be required to have safety-net elements,[19] while utility schemes can be required to demonstrate an extension of services to poor customers and so on. But the setting of such requirements appears to be confined to financing for former SOEs and/or enterprises supplying 'public goods' and a majority of multilaterals do not apply them at all. Some even utilize guidelines for lending that directly appear to encourage low-wage employment. For example, the IADB's (2002) operational policy on industrial development gives explicit preference to 'projects based on [...] efficient [plants] that can compete at least with the lowest cost level in the region'.

It is, therefore, not surprising that, where multilaterals' policies discuss explicitly the relation between PSD and poverty reduction, *direct links* are typically referred to only in relation to SMEs and microenterprises. As shown in Table 2.5, many multilateral donors have run or supported programmes of this kind, usually on concessionary terms. In most cases, however, the amounts committed as part of explicit PSD initiatives (i.e. through private intermediaries) have been small.[20] Moreover the current tendency, at least in the World Bank, appears to be to lend only on non-concessionary terms or to replace on-lending for SMEs and micro-finance by technical assistance to capacity building of institutions specializing' in these purposes (World Bank 2001a: 13, 2002: 40).[21]

Identical issues of internal coherence exist in the case of the bilateral donors. As already noted, most of the bilateral donors who have developed a clear PSD policy have also tried, formally at least, to align their PSD activities with the objective of poverty reduction. The Canadian International Development Agency (CIDA), for instance, distinguishes (besides interventions regarding the informal sector) three levels of PSD intervention with links to poverty reduction. The first is the macro-policy level, with interventions here aimed at affecting the policy environment to 'address the root causes of poverty of the country as a whole'. The specific policy areas mentioned include trade policy, financial and public sector reform, the removal of systematic constraints that prohibit the ownership of assets by women and reallocation of public expenditures towards basic infrastructure services. The second level is the focused programmes that benefit the poor disproportionately but do not have specified groups of the poor as direct beneficiaries. This description is given to interventions such as capacity building with micro-finance organizations or agricultural research and training. Finally, there are programmes directly targeted at poor groups but which are not part of interventions aimed at the informal sector. These include, for instance, training of microentrepreneurs (CIDA 1995a,b).

Germany uses a similar distinction between the levels of PSD policy interventions and poverty reduction (DAC 1998), while the US depicts poverty reduction as a consequence of interventions to create an open and democratic environment in which the private sector is given the space to develop. Other donors, who have not (yet) developed an integrated PSD policy, nevertheless also consider their activities in this field, in accordance with the views expressed within the DAC, as part of the fight against poverty. An overall impression is that the PSD interaction – poverty reduction connection – is asserted more often than demonstrated, however. Even where a connection is reasonably clear intellectually, mechanisms for assuring compliance in practice are generally absent. While the importance of support for general macroeconomic policies which promote poverty reduction is clear, it is still worthwhile asking whether donor policy coherence does not demand a stronger and more direct link between other aspects of PSD policy and poverty reduction.

A second type of (in)coherence (*external*) refers to the question of whether PSD-related activities are consistent with broader donor country policy concerns with a bearing on developing countries and not simply those seen as the objects of development cooperation. Tables 2.2 and 2.3 showed that only some bilateral and no multilateral donors explicitly acknowledge the international level in their PSD policies. At the same time, the overview of programmes and interventions presented in Annex 2 shows that most donors are aware that it is insufficient to look only at internal obstacles to and preconditions for PSD. This still leaves open the issue of whether donor insistence that recipient countries open up their markets, integrate with the world market and increase exports goes hand in hand with efforts to eliminate donors' own domestic subsidies and non-tariff barriers to trade. As the DAC (1994) puts it:

> OECD Member countries' [own] policies, particularly in the sphere of trade, investment and financial flows, must be coherent with policies espoused by donor agencies vis-à-vis private sector development in the developing world, such as the need for recipient countries to facilitate foreign direct investment, liberalize capital movements and financial markets and promote export-led development.[22]

Where issues of coherence have been acknowledged at all by donors, these have been somewhat perversely in terms of recognizing a lack of 'PSD consciousness' in their own organizations. In most instances, this recognition translates into a call for 'mainstreaming' PSD and more staff training in the field of PSD. Norway (NORAD 1999), for instance, acknowledges that 'the [PSD] approach [...] will require increased competence and capacity within this area in the aid administration both at home and at the embassies'. Although perhaps misidentifying the central problem, it is clear that a lack of understanding of PSD issues and perspectives amongst core agency staff also has negative effects. It is no better to only state that 'private sector considerations must be taken into account in designing and appraising all ODA activities' (NZODA 1998: 21) than it is only to say that poverty considerations should be mainstreamed into PSD activity. Both require systematic thought and planning. A possible way forward in both cases is to expand the development of criteria and guidelines in the direction started by AsDB and the World Bank, so that a selection of instruments occurs which is based on what is needed and not simply on what is available. More important still, both require institutional change (e.g. staff motivation and incentives, institutional culture, organizational change) and capacity strengthening (e.g. human resource development and skills, resources and knowledge, instruments, planning and management). Up to now, little evidence can be found of donors taking the need for mainstreaming very seriously, whether of poverty reduction into PSD, or PSD into broader development work.

Competition and coordination

Except at the level of major overlaps in formal policy pronouncements, it seems clear that there is little in the way of coordination between multilateral or bilateral donors in general, within multilaterals or bilaterals as distinct groups of donors, or even amongst different divisions or windows of the same multilateral agency, with respect to PSD. At least, there is little evidence of any clear division of labour, which might reflect such coordination. Amongst multilaterals, while regional development banks have some micro- and SME finance focus (reflected in specialized units like IADB's MIF and AfDB's AMINA) that is lacking in the World Bank, the bulk of private sector lending in both cases is made up of equity loans, guarantees and technical assistance to specific enterprises. As noted, there is also a strong overlap in terms of destinations by sector and country. Lack of coordination between multilaterals has almost certainly increased in recent years, for up to the mid-1990s an implicit division of labour was detectable between the regional development banks, which then lent overwhelmingly to the public sector, and the World Bank Group's IFC and MIGA wings, who were lending to private business. With the new increased emphasis on PSD by the regional development banks, this division of labour has evaporated.

The same is true with respect to traditional divisions of labour within single multilateral donors themselves. Two or three generations of internal reorganization within the World Bank Group still leaves a confusing picture concerning the provision of private sector advisory services, for example. In the late 1990s, a joint IFC-World Bank foreign investment advisory service (FIAS) was created, although both wings continued to provide advisory services separately (the IFC through its Corporate Financial Services Division [CFSD]). This was followed by a further reorganization in 2000, when a private sector advisory service was created by a merger of FIAS, CFSD and part of the World Bank PSD Department. Within the World Bank Group, such services are still being provided separately by MIGA's Investment Marketing Services Division, however. The recent World Bank (2002: 70) strategy document acknowledges another dimension of this problem: 'IDA, IFC and MIGA have sometimes all been independently engaged on the same projects (using similar or different) forms of financing...'.[23]

Such problems of 'internal coordination' are not restricted to the World Bank Group, however. One of the main criticisms of the micro-level PSD interventions of the Netherlands expressed by Dutch enterprises over the years has been that there was no single window these companies could turn to. They were correct: although all micro-level PSD programmes with a connection to Dutch enterprises and supported by ODA fall under the responsibility of one department within the Ministry for Development Cooperation, the implementation of these programmes is in the hands of different agencies, often working independently of each other and of the Ministry. Particularly because donors regard PSD as an increasingly important element for development (cooperation) and new types of interventions are appearing, there is a need for streamlining interventions.

While steps have been taken to improve the inter-donor coordination around lending for SME finance, none have been reported with regard to lending to larger enterprises. As long as there has been a discussion on the merits of tied aid (i.e. since the 1970s), injunctions to avoid competition between bilateral donors in the field of export credits have been made repeatedly. Not only have these fallen on deaf ears, but inter-bilateral competition appears now to extend also to other elements of PSD, from trade and investment instruments at micro-level (whether or not connected to the donor country's own private sector), through the increasing range of technical, financial and/or training facilities made available, to policy advice. Furthermore, there still appears to be no mechanisms at all within the World Bank Group for coordinating the activities of MIGA with its other wings. Similar problems are recognized by the AsDB (2000) in its PSD work. A discussion of the 'lessons learned' states that AsDB's 'public and private sector windows should have worked more closely together to increase benefits to its member countries and optimize development benefits...'.

As a result, developing countries can feel constrained to enter into relationships with export (or import) promotion commissions from different donor countries, while their government ministries and agencies draw on similar programmes from a variety of sources, and it becomes easy for them to lose sight of all the private sector-strengthening donor interventions and of all the PSD assistance coming their way. This shows that, even if the similarity between PSD interventions does not lead to greater competition between donors, there is a growing need for coordination, mutual learning and (perhaps) cooperation between donors.

Where some donor coordination on PSD does exist, it appears to be mainly found at three levels. At the policy level, there have been some important developments mainly, through the coordination role of the DAC, that have lead to mutually agreed (but very broad) policy guidelines (DAC 1994, 1995, 1997). Second, there is a degree of coordination around a handful of highly specialized PSD-related projects, such as the 'Eco Trade Manual', covering environmental regulations and standards in OECD . This is funded by CBI (Netherlands), NORAD (Norway), Danida (Denmark) and Sida (Sweden) (DAC 1997: 18). Third, there is localized cooperation in a few recipient countries around specific programmes, such as the 'Business Environment Strengthening of Tanzania' programme supported by DFID, Sida, DGIS and Danida. Within some agencies at least, resistance exists even to such incremental changes.[24]

The poverty reduction strategy process, engaged in by a number of recipient countries that have applied for debt relief under the Highly Indebted Poor Country (HIPC) Initiative, may lead to greater coordination in practice. This process is supposed to involve the recipient country's private sector as 'stakeholders' and to formulate a centralized list of poverty reduction-relevant private sector projects that donors can choose to support. Since this is a relatively new development, it is too early to see if it is making much of a difference.

5   PSD in practice

Norway's PSD policy ends with a short reference to evaluation where it is stated that 'an important basis for future evaluation of Norwegian support for private sector development has been laid through the preparation of this strategy' (NORAD 1999). Formally, the statement is correct. Before being able to evaluate interventions in the light of their contribution to PSD, one needs, as the statement continues, 'precise specification of objectives and expected results'. Unfortunately, in relation to PSD, such 'precise specifications' are either missing or are of a such recent nature that few policy-based evaluations are yet available. Simultaneously, the large diversity of what goes under the name of donor PSD interventions presents a further difficulty. First, it is not always clear whether all these interventions have been actually and directly implemented with a view to strengthening the private sector in developing countries. The fact, for instance, that many parts of PSD programmes are aimed at economic development in general or at individual enterprises, rather than the development of the private sector as such, is a case in point here. In such cases, the relation between intervention and the intended consequences with regard to the private sector is at best indirect and, thus, by definition difficult to assess. Finally, although it is true that development aid is in general an activity that is subject to frequent evaluation, many such studies that touch upon PSD-related issues are of a project type and not easy to generalize conclusions from.

Nevertheless, an attempt by Schulpen and Gibbon (2001) to draw generalized conclusions from a number of such PSD-related evaluation studies of bilateral donors identified some provisional findings. On the basis of 15 evaluation studies from six bilateral donors, the assessment concluded, among other things, that bilateral donors' PSD-related interventions frequently lacked a clear set of objectives, reflected in a general lack of guidelines and selection criteria. Moreover, the selection of intermediaries chosen to implement programmes often suffered from problems concerning their ability to conform to donor 'best practice' and 'ownership' of broader aid objectives, while the selection of target firms, and even of countries of operation, sometimes suffered from a lack of transparency. In general, the evaluation studies showed an excessive focus on simple hardware or training package-related transfers, and a lack of focus on institution building (a point strengthened by the tendency for PSD interventions to have a strong tied-aid component). Finally, most PSD-related interventions seemed to lack a point of departure in the real capacities, modes of operation and internal relations found in private sectors in recipient countries, both in their firms and institutions. Instead, interventions were usually based on models of business development derived from developed countries. Finally, given the highly specialized nature of the mind-frame and perspective necessary for successful work with the private sector, and their fundamental difference from those necessary for other types of development agency activity, these evaluation studies posed the question whether bilateral donor agencies were a suitable home for PSD activities as such.

Unfortunately, evaluations of multilaterals' PSD operations are also rather thin on the ground. Overview evaluations or assessments are available only for the World Bank and the AsDB. Furthermore, that of the AsDB mostly comprises a discussion of its lending's financial performance. Unpublished evaluations by the AfDB and IADB, referred to in these organizations' annual reports for 2001, also appear to be largely financial in focus. It should be noted that *all* the multilateral evaluations referred to were conducted internally, rather than by external consultants.

As in the case of bilateral donors' PSD interventions, the main issues concerning aid (in-)effectiveness raised by recent evaluations of World Bank programmes (World Bank 2001a, 2002) include the consistency of interventions with broader aid objectives (as well as some of the specific objectives of PSD support itself); consistency with donors' 'best practice' in specific areas; and relevance to the particular circumstances of recipient countries. Certain observations in the AsDB's published evaluation can also be considered under these headings.

Inadequate consideration of institutional issues, and on this basis of the distributional consequences of PSD interventions, is mentioned several times in the World Bank's evaluation from 2001. Privatization-related PSD programmes are acknowledged to have had benefits of improved efficiency, particularly through reductions in fiscal burdens following sale or liquidation of loss-making SOEs. But, as a result of 'underestimation [of] both the importance and complexity of the institutional underpinnings of PSD ...' (World Bank 2001a: 2) and of 'the time required to develop effective regulative capacity' (op. cit.: 23), these benefits proved either one-off and/or 'not widely shared by society' (op. cit.: 2). This had been exacerbated by the continuing absence of a conceptual framework for understanding 'pro-poor' enterprise reform (op. cit.: 22).

An identified related issue concerns a lack of internalization of more specific PSD-centred aims in certain PSD programmes or operations. Whereas PSD programmes aim to promote greater competition and more transparent regulation, certain privatization and 'public participation in infrastructure' operations have not reflected these principles (op. cit.: 21) The same observation is made in the AsDB (2000: 46) report. The relation between specific PSD interventions and promotion of competition is raised on a more general plane by the apparent admission by the World Bank (2002: 54) that IFC credit *in general* embodies an element of subsidy, despite the supposed prevalence of market-based lending principles.

Proposals to overcome these problems revolve around the introduction of 'performance-based investment' and/or 'output-based aid' (op. cit.: 65), whereby donor lending to certain private sector activities is back- rather than front-loaded. That is, finance is released when 'development outcomes' have become visible. In this context, subsidies would be made explicit, reserved for interventions with explicit pro-poor content, and released only when agreed targets have been met. By implication, the subsidy element would be withdrawn from all other PSD lending. Little detail has so far been provided of what performance standards might look like, how private partners might finance installation or start-up costs alone, or the methodology for determining and removing subsidies on other PSD lending.

Since multilateral donors do not operate tied aid programmes administered through intermediaries, problems arising from the latter's failure to absorb donor 'best practice' do not emerge as an issue in their evaluations, as they do in those of bilaterals. On the other hand, diluted forms of the same problem of 'ownership' are identified, arising from the dispersal of private sector operations *within* multilateral agencies. According to the World Bank's 2001 evaluation (World Bank 2001a: 2) only 91 of its (up to this point) 250 credits with PSD components were actually managed by the Bank's PSD Department. A large proportion of the balance seems to have represented components relating to the financial sector, which although a major subject of PSD policy was not officially part of PSD 'work'. As a result, 'the record of assistance for financial sector reform [has] not been strong ...' (op. cit.: 8, 10).

As in the case of bilateral donors, a considerable volume of criticism in evaluation reports is devoted to a lack of relevance of interventions to the particular circumstances of recipient countries. Most commentary under this heading is again directed at a lack of focus on (national) institutional issues. However whereas for bilaterals, recipient country institutional issues were held to be neglected in favour of 'supply-driven' hardware and training packages, in the case of the World Bank they were neglected in favour of pursuing more visible and tangible structural reforms such as the privatization of specific enterprises and enactment of specific laws (ibid.). The prioritization of such structural reforms is questioned on the basis of its derivation from 'a tendency to apply the same solution to all countries', thereby ignoring differences in institutional underpinnings (op. cit.: 14). In low-income countries as a group, patient development of institutions should have preceded 'promotion [of reforms of] corporate governance, insolvency/bankruptcy reform [or even] property rights...' (op. cit.: 8).

In the World Bank's new PSD strategy, the lesson derived from these criticisms appears to be that – where they are detected – 'flawed investment climates' require rectification before established forms of PSD support, including direct lending to private enterprise, can be effective. It is not very clear whether this position represents an acknowledgement of the 'one size fits all' criticism or a restatement of a 'one size fit all' view in a different form. For it is apparently still planned to identify 'flaws' in investment climates on the basis of local departures from an (Anglo-Saxon) ideal type.

Over and above these concerns, both the World Bank and the AsDB evaluations share the concern of some bilateral evaluations with inadequate monitoring. Lack of effective financial reporting is identified as an issue in both cases. In that of the AsDB (2001a: 5), it appears that the only financial reporting undertaken prior to 2000 was of too aggregate a nature to distinguish the performance of private from public sector lending. In the case of the World Bank (2002) there are also calls to initiate monitoring both of non-financial but still economic measures of performance (e.g. productivity changes following investments) as well as non-economic dimensions. For private participation in infrastructure projects, the latter include changes in access to services for low-income groups and levels of charges/subsidies levied on/provided to low-income groups.

6   Conclusions

On the basis of comparing bilaterals' PSD policies, programmes, instruments and funding, Schulpen and Gibbon (2002: 12–13) identified five main challenges that needed to be taken into account in re-designing existing PSD interventions or initiating new generations of policies and interventions. First of all, there is need for clarification of PSD objectives and for mainstreaming core objectives of the donor agencies' (i.e. poverty reduction) into them. Second, in order to underwrite this process, donors should consider integrating specialized sub-agencies responsible for PSD into the organizational, cultural and procedural routines of agency head offices. Third, the challenge of phasing-out tied aid is stressed. Fourth, it is necessary to examine how to reorient programmes away from transfers of hardware and finance, in order to bring PSD interventions more in line with agencies' comparative advantage. Finally, there is the challenge of moving PSD programmes away from a standardized format and to root them instead on a clear analysis of the strengths, weaknesses and dynamics of local private sectors in developing countries.

To what extent do these challenges also apply to multilateral agencies? With the exception of tied aid (which is far less an issue for multilateral donors), the answer is a straightforward yes. This is because of the high level of convergence in outlook and practice between the two groups of donors. Although there are some differences in policy emphasis between multilaterals and bilaterals, and although multilaterals have posed more 'new' policy issues in recent years – ranging from the obligations of western countries to open up their own markets to demands for better 'corporate governance' in developing ones – the policy similarities still outweigh the differences. This goes particularly for their 'one size fits all' models of what 'enabling environments' should look like.

Both groups of donors also show a strong preference for instruments and programmes at national macro- and micro-level, although the instruments of the multilateral donors are much simpler and basically comprise adjustment lending, direct lending to the private sector and support to micro/SME finance.

There is also is a strong overlap in the two groups' beneficiary countries, and in the facts that their selection is not generally based on any assessment of their national environments for doing business and can be often questioned from a poverty or development perspective.

Meanwhile, although for obvious reasons it is only bilaterals that (can) insist on involving their 'own' private sectors in PSD, the fact that the content of multilaterals' and bilaterals' programmes is similar tends to place them in competition with each other and highlights their lack of coordination. There is little current evidence of information-sharing or even of knowledge of each other's portfolios. Although this lack of coordination (and the fact that donors tend to formulate similar programmes) could be regarded as positive as it provides developing countries with a large reservoir of funding, it also militates against their ability to chose between programmes on a strategic basis and generates a lack of coherence. This, in turn, makes ownership of PSD by developing countries more difficult. Hopefully, the poverty reduction strategy route may offer a path out of this maze, by encouraging recipient countries to formulate their own PSD policies, but probably this route will be taken only by countries applying for HIPC relief, and even in their case the extent to which this generates self-designed policies and programmes remains to be seen.

To sum up, the differences between multilateral and bilateral donors follow from differences in their organizational objectives (bank lending as such versus broader forms of assistance) and their 'ownership' (international rather than national). It does not follow from major differences in analytical sophistication or in the degree to which experience is reflected on critically.

Annex 1: Examples of bilateral donor's PSD programmes
(See Gibbon and Schulpen (2002: Annex 2) for more comprehensive examples)

Country and programmes

AUSTRALIA
General
- Supporting effective governance (technical assistance, policy analysis, training and scholarships for institutional strengthening, privatization, tax and trade reforms, and effective legal systems);
- Strengthening social services and infrastructure (financial and technical aid for education, health and infrastructure);
- Facilitating enterprise development (aimed at SMEs, micro-finance, business development services).
Policy dialogue and studies
Technical assistance and seminars
- WB SPF: WB South Pacific Facility;
- PIPS: Pacific Island Private Sector programme.
Vocational and technical training
- TGS: Training Grants Scheme (short-term training);
- PIPS: Pacific Island Private Sector programme;
- TIPS: Trade and Investment Promotion Section of the Department of Foreign Affairs and Trade (business skills courses);
- SPTC: South Pacific Trade Commission (technical training).
Technical assistance, training, access to finance
- AESOP: Australian Executive Service Overseas Programme (volunteer programme);
- SPPF: IFC South Pacific Project Facility (advisory services project preparation).

CANADA
Regional and country strategies
Africa
- MDF: Mahgreb Development Fund (transfer of technology);
- RSF CEA: Regional Support Fund Central and Eastern Africa;
- CAPSSA: Canadian Association for the Private Sector in Southern Africa (joint ventures/licensing arrangements);
- DCS: Development Programme of Canadian-Senegalese joint ventures (research investment opportunities, advice + information, studies and project support through CIDA INC funds);
- Egypt PSD (capacity building public sector, promotion of enabling environment, direct incentives to private sector, privatization, transfer of technology, collaboration Canadian and Egyptian private sector);
- CABBSA: Canadian Association for Black Business in South Africa;
- Cameroon entrepreneurial support (to 'enterprise incubators and SMEs, institutional reinforcement of consultancy firms and financial institutions')
Asia
- Technology transfer, joint ventures, industrial cooperation at policy and project levels + aid at institution/organization level and educational institutions level, mostly through partnerships between Canadian and Asian organizations and institutions);
- Direct support to microenterprise development (examples: Grameen Bank and regional industrial development programmes);
- PSDI Fund: Private Sector Development Initiatives Fund (formation of joint ventures and other forms of collaborative arrangements);

Annex 1   Continued

Country and programmes

- ETC: Enterprise Thailand Canada (transfer of technology and expertise through joint ventures);
- EMC: Enterprise Malaysia Canada (see ETC);
- CAC: Canada-ASEAN Centre (human resource development and institutional cooperation, business cooperation in support of investment and trade, regional public affairs to raise awareness of Canada in ASEAN countries)

Latin America and the Caribbean

- Jamaica: export promotion to Canada, training and credit to SMEs, agricultural credits to cooperative banks, practical technical and entrepreneurial training;
- South America: lines of credits (particularly to public sector institutions), counterpart funds (to inance community-based, productive sector initiatives), private sector development fund (to encourage linkages between Colombian and Canadian firms);
- CRPSM: Costa Rica Productive Sector Modernization programme (including linkages with Canadian firms);
- RISPCA: Regional Initiatives Support Programme in Central America (aimed at improving effectiveness of governmental and private sector institutions to manage process of economic modernization).

Canadian Partnership Branch (CPB)

- Supports efforts of Canadian firms, (international) NGOs, universities, professional associations and municipalities. Broad range of programmes across whole range from direct support of PSD through business-to-business joint ventures, investment and technology transfer, support to microenterprises, creation of enabling environment;
- Direct business-to-business support through INC (Industrial Cooperation) (assistance to Canadian firms in investment (joint ventures), professional services, and/or specialized activities;
- Microenterprises support through Canadian and international NGOs (e.g. Women's World Banking);
- Enabling environment support through strengthening pluralistic civil society favouring a vigorous private sector (e.g. regulatory framework for capital markets, judicial information systems to improve business dispute resolution system).

Multilateral branch

- Support to international finance institutions in strengthening capacity of governments to adopt and sustain sound economic policies through policy dialogue, training, education and research programmes, lending for infrastructure and sector loans for SMEs;
- Encouraging regional development banks (RDBs) to use technical aid for sector studies for formulating and implementing policy reforms, institutional development and public sector restructuring, including privatization;
- Support to direct lending facilities of the RDBs (particularly the Asian Development Bank).

DENMARK

- IFU: Industrial Fund for Developing Countries (provides share capital in joint ventures with Danish companies and companies in developing countries, pre-investment studies, loans);

Annex 1   Continued

Country and programmes

- Investment guarantee system (in connection with Danish companies investments in developing countries covers against loss associated with political risks);
- PSD programme (assistance to institutional development of private sector environment, commercialization and privatization of government-owned enterprises, and business-to-business cooperation between companies in Denmark and in the recipient country. Aid granted within these components varies according to situation in country. Includes also various types of preparatory action, training and education). The main thrust of the PSD programme is the business-to-business programme, which includes grants for initial investigations, initial visits, external consultants in drafting project proposal. The PSD programme is restricted to six developing countries: Egypt, Ghana, India, Uganda, Vietnam and Zimbabwe;
- TechChange (linked to the PSD programme, offers paid travel and accommodation to representatives from selected enterprises in the six PSD countries and allows for small exhibition areas at Danish trade fairs);
- South African business-to-business programme aims to reinforce and develop the business opportunities and employment of the target group by supporting the establishment of collaborations between Danish and South African 'black-owned' enterprises; covers expenses for preliminary studies, training and technology transfers from the Danish partner, and provides guarantees for investment loans to a limited extent;
- Mixed credits (in support of the supply of Danish goods and services for development projects);
- DIPO: Danish Import Promotion Office for Products from Developing Countries promotes contacts between exporters from developing countries and Danish importers; arranges, among other things, visits and seminars;
- Danced's Partnership Programme support, comparable to the PSD programme, to enterprises in Thailand and Malaysia for the development of business ideas in the environmental field, where Danish environmental know-how or technology can be transferred to Southeast Asia.

FRANCE
Policy measures aimed at strengthening institutional partners;
Developing networks of private enterprises through forging links with and between chambers of commerce, employers' associations. Can include technical assistance through personnel of volunteer workers VSNE), cooperation at local level and mechanisms, which allow French regional authorities to provide support to firms operating in Africa (guarantee funds, venture capital companies, etc.);
Action aimed at small and microenterprises
- AIPB credits (Aid for Basic Productive Initiatives) through CFD: Caisse Française de Développement (loans to support creation and development of such enterprises);
- Local loan schemes (operated by CFD and Ministry of Cooperation).
Instruments used by CFD to provide funding to the private sector
- PROPARCO (subsidiary of CFD, finance company, loans to assist in the creation of new firms, restructuring of existing firms and asset purchases in the event of privatization);
- CFD: providing loans where PROPARCO cannot provide;

Annex 1   Continued

Country and programmes

– ARIA: Assurance du Risque des Investissements en Afrique (venture capital insurance);
– FGAO: Fonds de Garantie d'Afrique de l'Ouest (credit guarantees for banks that finance medium and long-term investment in private sector firms);
– Joint venture funds (feasibility studies, audits, joint ventures, training programmes.

GERMANY
Private–public partnership
Basically this is the name under which most of Germany's bilateral PSD programme related to German companies is known. It covers a range of different interventions which all depart from the fact that the costs are shared by the German government and the (German) private sector together. Financially supported activities falling under the PPP are:
– Technical, sector and project studies (institutions involved KfW, GTZ and DEG);
– Pilot projects (DEG and GTZ);
– Investment projects (DEG);
– Technical training in developing countries or Germany (GTZ, DEG and CDG);
– Experts (SES and CIM);
– Joint ventures (SEQUA).
Below is an overview of PSD programmes from the 1995 DAC survey. At that time, the concept of PPP was not operational.
– Technical cooperation/advisory services and training;
– Policy dialogue (state level);
– Policy advice agreement (state level);
– Advisory services to governments and administrations (state level);
– Advisory services for institutions working in trades and crafts, SMEs, export, technology, investment in joint ventures, chambers of commerce and business credit guarantee fund associations, twinning;
– Arrangements, financial institutions, savings banks and cooperatives, development of vocational commercial training, management centres (intermediary/APEX institutions level);
– Institution building (intermediary/APEX institutions level);
– Federal Ministry for Research and Technology: technology transfer (intermediary/APEX institutions level);
– Twinning arrangements with the federal states (chambers of commerce) (intermediary/APEX institution level);
– Promotion of companies (company level);
– SES: Senior expert service (company level).
Financial cooperation/funding
– Financial cooperation funds for physical and social infrastructure, mixed financing, commodity aid and/or structural adjustment programmes (state level);
– Financial cooperation for banks (credit lines for the private sector) (intermediary/APEX institutions level);
– DEG: German finance company for investment in developing countries (funds-in-trust) (intermediary/APEX institutions level).
Foreign trade promotion
– Investment guarantee agreement (state level);
– Double taxation agreement (state level);

Annex 1 Continued

Country and programmes

– General customs preferences for developing countries GATT (state level);
– Joint economic missions (state level);
– German Chambers of Commerce abroad, BfAI (Federal Agency for Foreign Trade
  Information), Associations or specific regions (company level);
– Export guarantees, business services at the embassies (company level);
– 'The promotion of German exports to developing countries' (company level).
Multilateral development cooperation
– World Bank, IMF, MIGA, IDA, IFC (state level);
– Regional development banks (state level);
– ILO, UNDP, UNIDO (intermediary/APEX institutions level);
– European Commission (intermediary/APEX institutions level);
– Centre for Industrial Development (company level);
– UNIDO-IPS (companies level);
– IFC (companies level).

JAPAN
Direct approach to private sector promotion
– Technical cooperation between governments through JICA ([Japan International
  Cooperation Agency] facilities and equipment for vocational training, experts and
  receiving trainees);
– Private sector technical cooperation (training of workers, dispatching of experts
  to private enterprises in developing countries. AOTS [Association of Overseas
  Technical Scholarship provides training and JODC [Japan Overseas Development
  Corporation] takes care of experts);
– Two-step loans (loans to the private sector via financial institutions in developing
  countries);
– Promotion of exports from developing countries (via JETRO [Japan External Trade
  Organization] through trade missions, advice on product quality, technology trans-
  fer and research and information provision);
Indirect approach to private sector promotion
– Establishment of appropriate economic and social infrastructure (mainly through
  loans for infrastructure, but also annual dialogue).
– Government technical cooperation (transfer of know-how on capacity building and
  institution building, i.e. taxation, finance, industrial standardization, intellectual
  property through dialogue and experts);
– Promotion of imports from developing countries (in Japan) (through import mis-
  sions, exhibitions, trade seminars, information via JETRO);
– Promotion of investment in developing countries (trade insurance and soft loans by
  Export-Import Bank of Japan, and promotion of investment in joint ventures by
  JAIDO [Japan International Development Organization], and information via JETRO).

THE NETHERLANDS
Bilateral channel
General
– Support to micro- and small-scale enterprises;
– Support to structural adjustment programmes which are aimed at the creation of the
  macroeconomic and monetary conditions, and the legal and regulatory framework
  for PSD;

Annex 1   Continued

Country and programmes

– Support to the creation and safeguarding of the conditions for the effective operation of free markets (including privatization as a means to further the efficiency of the national economy).
Provision of rural infrastructure
– Reinforcement of the educational system;
– Institutional development activities;
– Matchmaking and information services for Dutch companies.
More specific
– FMO: Netherlands Development Finance Company (loans and equity for small- and medium-scale private enterprises either directly or through local banks and other financial institutions);
– KB: Small-scale enterprise funding programme under FMO (financial assistance in local currency to small enterprises);
– SC: Seed capital programme under FMO (financial participation in starting enterprises, particularly in Africa);
– IFOM: Investeringsfaciliteit Opkomende Markten (loans to joint ventures by Dutch companies);
– IBTA: Investment promotion and technical assistance (via FMO, grants or concessional loans for management advice and technical assistance to promote investment and business performance);
– NMCP/PUM: Netherlands Management Consultancy Programme/Programma Uitzending Managers (sending out experienced advisors in the technical and management fields to small- and medium-sized companies);
– RHI: Regeling Herverzekering Investeringen (insurance for specific political risks for investments by Dutch companies);
– POPM: Garantieregeling Particuliere Ontwikkelings Participatie Maatschappijen (guarantees for commercial risks with investments by Dutch development participation companies);
– CBI: Centre for the promotion of Imports from Developing Countries (through market information, trade fairs, support to exporters);
– PESP: Programma Economische Samenwerkingsprojecten (financing of feasibility studies for trade and investment relations);
– PSO: Programma Samenwerking Oost-Europa and PSOM–Programma Samenwerking Opkomende Markten (supporting trade and/or investments by Dutch companies by setting up local firms through financial assistance);
– NIMF: Netherlands's Investerings Matching Funds (comparable to IFOM);
– ORET/Miliev: Ontwikkelingsrelevante Export Transacties/Milieu en Economische Verzelfstandiging (financial support for non-commercially viable local investments requiring Dutch goods and services with the aim of strengthening the local infrastructure);
– NCM: Nederlandse Credietverzekerings Maatschappij (insurance against commercial and political risks in the case of exports or investments);
– GOM: Garantiefaciliteit Opkomende Markten (insurance scheme for transactions following from the ORET/Miliev programme).

Annex 1 Continued

Country and programmes

Multilateral channels
- World Bank and regional banks;
- IFC, MIGA, FIAS;
- UNIDO, ILO;
- AMSCO, APDF, RPED;
- EIB;
- Micro credit (WWB and CGAP).

SWEDEN
SwedeCorp (aid authority formed to promote a favourable business environment and sustainable profitable enterprises in developing countries and Eastern Europe) provides aid within three main areas:
Competence development in trade and industry
- Training, institutional support, industrial environment protection with emphasis on involvement of Swedish private companies and institutions.
Business development
- Information, advice, market research, business contracts, import guarantee schemes, promotion of joint ventures and alliances for exporters and Swedish importers.
Provision of risk capital
- Loans and equity investments through investment banks, venture capital funds, leasing companies and other specialized local financial institutions in order to promote investments and improve financial strength of small- and medium-scale companies in developing countries, equity participation mostly in cooperation with Swedfund International AB, technical assistance for development of financial markets, support to privatization projects, investment seminars.
Interventions at macro-level
- (Co)financing of structural and sectoral adjustment programmes;
- (Co)financing of debt reduction programmes;
- Support of international networks, coordination and policy dialogue mechanisms;
- Commercial policy measures for PSD, e.g. double taxation treaties, investment protection treaties, investment insurance or guarantees;
- Policy dialogue at international and local levels.
Interventions at meso-level
- Promotion of institutions actively involved in private sector promotion, e.g. in fields such as finance, banking, professional training, advisory and consultancy services in technical and managerial aspects;
- Promotion of international, regional and national sector specific networks.

UNITED KINGDOM
Correcting policy fundamentals
- Programme aid in support of structural adjustment supported by technical cooperation (aimed at macroeconomic stabilization, adopting realistic exchange rates, sound public finance, price liberalization and liberalizing' investment).
Helping markets work more efficiently
- Technical cooperation and consultancy mainly in context of structural adjustment programmes (aimed at financial sector reform, company law reform, new rules for capital markets, removing legal and regulatory barriers to entry and labour mobility).

Annex 1   Continued

Country and programmes

Helping design promotional and confidence-building measures
– Technical cooperation and policy dialogue (in/for investment promotion, establishing investment assistance and promotion services).
Support for CDC (Commonwealth Development Corporation) investment and lending activities
– Investments in profit-making enterprises.
Help for small and microenterprises
– Financial, technical and training services (often via NGOs).
Direct help, outside normal government-to-government channels, for selected enterprises
– Technical cooperation grants (often with a cost-sharing or cost-recovery element) for the formal private sector or (preferably) organizations representing them, in the form of training in technical, administrative, financial and management skills and of product development and marketing.

UNITED STATES
Priority
– Financial and technical support for policy reform and structural adjustment policies in close cooperation with the World Bank and the IMF.

Individual and sectoral topics
Financial markets development
– Trade and investment promotion (with focus on long-term private enterprise ties).
Privatization, and private provision of social services: (through contacts with)
– CFP: Centre for Privatization;
– IPG: International Privatization Group providing technical and advisory services with focus on design, preparation and implementation of privatization transactions);
– Microenterprise development (also through NGOs);
– CEG: Center for Economic Growth (technical support to USAID missions, management of USAID's loan and guarantee programme, developing programmes in areas of economics, agriculture, business development, microenterprise development, and financial markets development).
– OPIC: Overseas Private Investment Corporation (political risks insurance, loans, guarantees, equity, etc. to US business to invest and compete in emerging markets and developing countries).

Sources: DAC (1995: 31–110; 1997); Bosch (1998); DGIS (2000); BMZ (Folder over PPP); CIDA (1999); Sida (1997); AusAID (2000); Danida (1999).

Annex 2: Examples of multilateral donor's PSD support
(See Gibbon and Schulpen (2002: Annex 3) for more comprehensive examples)

Types of support

<table>
<tr><td rowspan="1" style="writing-mode: vertical-rl">World Bank Group</td><td>

IBRD/IDA project lending
– 260 active Bank projects (in March 2001) with substantial PSD components. 60 projects classified as PSD projects. The rest are categorized under other sectoral or thematic heads.

Interventions fall into four categories

(i) Improvements in the investment climate aim to enhance deregulation and competition by ensuring a legal and regulatory framework that encourages competitive provision of goods and services, property rights and corporate governance, and development of institutions related to PSD;

(ii) Privatization and concession-type arrangements include management contracts, leases, concessions, build-operate-and-transfer (BOTs) operations and outright divestiture;

(iii) Direct assistance to enterprises includes lines of credit to financial institutions which then on-lend to private companies, provision of technical assistance such as business advisory services, matching grants facilities, project financing facilities for infrastructure projects and guarantees;

(iv) Social funds typically support small projects in infrastructure, social services, training and micro-credit. They support the PSD agenda by developing alternative, non-governmental delivery mechanisms.

IBRD/IDA adjustment lending
– Adjustment lending programmes support the implementation of a number of key measures to strengthen the investment climate. These measures focus on competition policies and strengthening competitiveness through (i) regulatory reform; (ii) improving logistics and reducing transaction costs; (iii) strengthening inter-firm linkages and government-business consultations, and (iv) supporting global integration through institutional and policy reforms for greater export orientation, corporate governance and foreign direct investment.

International Finance Corporation (IFC)
– IFC's traditional and largest activity is to finance private sector projects in developing countries. IFC provides loans, equity finance and quasi-equity. It also offers financial risk management products and intermediary finance;

– IFC investments go to a variety of sectors. About two-thirds were concentrated in three sectors: financial sector, which includes financial services and collective investment vehicles, infrastructure and manufacturing. IFC's latest strategy signalled a change in its strategic focus. It calls for a move towards areas with high multiplier effects, i.e. whose impact goes well beyond the capital investment. It calls for increased intervention in frontier countries (high risk/low-income countries with very limited access to foreign capital and/or undeveloped domestic financial markets) and in frontier regions or sectors within other countries. Five sectors of emphasis were identified: domestic financial institutions, infrastructure, information technology and communications, SMEs and the social sectors (health and education).

</td></tr>
</table>

Annex 2   Continued

Types of support

<table>
<tr><td rowspan="1">World Bank Group</td><td>

Multilateral Investment Guarantee Agency (MIGA)
– MIGA provides investment guarantees against certain non-commercial risks (i.e. political risk insurance) to eligible foreign investors for qualified investments in developing member countries. MIGA's coverage is against the following risks: Transfer restriction; expropriation; breach of contract; and war and civil disturbance.

Non-financial activities
– The World Bank Group is involved in a wide range of non-lending activities related to PSD issues. The most important of such activities being advisory services (to governments, private sector institutions and firms), economic and sector work, research and training. Arbitration, standard setting and ratings have emerged as an important area in recent years.

The Consultative Group to Assist the Poorest (CGAP)
– World Bank in association with a number of bilateral donors is a founding member of CGAP. CGAP is a consortium of 29 bilateral and multilateral donor agencies who support micro- finance. Its mission is to improve the capacity of micro-finance institutions to deliver flexible, high-quality financial services to the very poor on a sustainable basis;
– CGAP serves micro-finance institutions, donors and the micro-finance industry through the development of technical tools and services, the delivery of training, strategic advice and technical assistance, and action research on innovations.

</td></tr>
<tr><td rowspan="1">Inter-American Development Bank (IDB)</td><td>

Structured and corporate finance lending
– Project finance basis: Loans can be made on a project finance basis. This structure is particularly useful for new or 'greenfield' operations, where a special purpose company is generally established to build, own, operate and act as borrower for the project with limited recourse to sponsors during the project completion and/or operation stage;
– Corporate finance basis: Loans are also structured on a corporate finance basis, most typically required for expansions and modernization of the existing productive capacity of a corporation, and often for privatized public utility companies.

Political risk and credit guarantees
– In addition to loans, the IDB also provides credit and political risk guarantees to private sector lenders seeking coverage for their loans to projects.

Capital markets initiatives
– Debt financing and/or guarantees to regional or national investment funds to mobilize venture capital equity resources and/or debt capital that are otherwise not commonly available to private sector projects or other long-term capital investments. These funds may be invested in projects that develop infrastructure or expand the long-term capacity of other productive sectors;
– Debt financing and/or guarantees for funds, leasing companies or other financial intermediaries. This support is designed to enhance the efficiency of financial intermediaries, to generate additional sources of long-term local currency funding;

</td></tr>
</table>

Annex 2   Continued

Types of support

<table>
<tr><td rowspan="1" style="writing-mode:vertical-rl">Inter-American Development Bank (IDB)</td><td>

– Start-up debt financing and/or guarantees for local companies that guarantee locally-issued private sector debt. The IDB seeks to enhance the local company's ability to mobilize funds for private sector projects and capital-intensive productive sectors, to further develop the secondary markets of those debt obligations;
– Guarantees for local institutions, such as investment banks, commercial banks and leasing companies, to allow them to securitize assets and to develop a medium-term corporate debenture market that will facilitate the channelling of long-term, local currency financing;
– Co-lending arrangements with local financial institutions and institutional investors that have a developmental impact on the domestic capital market's long-term financing capabilities. Since the IDB does not provide risk capital, it does not participate in the equity of investment funds or individual companies.

Inter-American Investment Corporation (IIC)
– The IIC's developmental financing programme targets small- and medium-sized private companies in Latin America and the Caribbean that have limited access to long-term financing, through loans and equity investments.

The Multilateral Investment Fund (MIF)
– Market functioning;
– Regulatory framework; facilitation of trade and investment; labour market modernization;
– Financial and capital markets;
– Market transparency measures; regulatory reform and supervision; capital market development;
– Small business development;
– Streamlining regulations; innovative business relationship; eco-efficiency; quality management; financing options; information technologies; skills standards and credentialing;
– Microenterprise;
– Innovation partnerships; regulatory and supervisory framework; strengthening micro-finance institutions.

IDB is a donor agency member of CGAP.
</td></tr>
<tr><td rowspan="1" style="writing-mode:vertical-rl">EU/EC</td><td>

Dialogue and reform
Permanent discussion between donors and governments on content and timing of measures for further liberalizing' and deregulating the economy, reducing the size of the public sector, and creating enabling environment (e.g. macro-economic factors [taxation, prices], price controls, dismantling of entry and exit barriers, tax reforms, property rights, etc.).

Financial instruments
– ECIP: European Community Investment Partners (financial backing for joint ventures (particularly SMEs) at various points in project's development through subsidies, participatory loans, equity participations, interest-free advances);
– EIB: European Investment Bank (venture capital);
</td></tr>
</table>

Annex 2   Continued

Types of support

EU/EC	– EDF: European Development Fund (opening credit lines to local SME financing institutions); – Import programmes (used to fund imports of intermediate products by ACP export industries); – Counterpart funds (used to finance farm loans, job creation programmes, etc.). Technical assistance – CID: Centre for Industrial Development (technical or economic feasibility studies for industrial projects, seeking out EC partners for ACP-EC joint ventures) (technical assistance, joint ventures, subcontracting, licensing). General – Studies, experts, training, dissemination of information, investor forums, technology transfer. Instruments for creating contacts between enterprises – Europartenariat, Med Partenariat or enterprise meetings; – BCC: Business Cooperation Centre (Mediterranean); – BC-NET: Business Cooperation Network (Latin America and Asia); – COOPECO network (Latin America) (networks for tracing possible partners); – Information; – MED-INVEST (Mediterranean) and ALL-INVEST (Latin America) (information clearing-houses) Also one in Philippines.
The European Bank for Reconstruction and Development (EBRD)	The EBRD finances projects in the private sector. The Bank also finances infrastructure projects that support the private sector. In addition, it supports privatization, restructures state-owned firms and improves municipal services. Many projects are too small to be funded directly by the EBRD. To give entrepreneurs and small firms greater access to finance, the EBRD supports financial intermediaries, such as local commercial banks, micro-business banks, equity funds and leasing facilities. The Bank supports trade facilitation through guarantees for import and export-related transactions, as well as financing to banks for on-lending to traders. The EBRD also supports several business development programmes. Programmes include the TurnAround Management Programme, business advisory services, Joint Vienna Institute seminars and the MBA loan programme. EBRD is a donor agency member of CGAP.

Annex 3: Abbreviations specific to the chapter

AfD   Agence Française de Développement
ARIA   Assurance de Risque des Investissements en Afrique (France)
AusAID   Australian Agency for International Development
CABBSA   Canadian Association for Black Business in South Africa.
CAC   Canada-ASEAN Centre
CAPSSA   Canadian Association for the Private Sector in Southern Africa
CBI   Centre for the promotion of Imports from Developing Countries
           (the Netherlands)
CDB   Caribbean Development Bank
CDC   Commonwealth Development Corporation
CDG   Carl-Duisburg-Gesellschaft e.V. (Germany)
CEG   Center for Economic Growth (United States)
CFP   Center for Privatization (United States)
CID   Centre for Industrial Development (EU)
CIDA   Canadian International Development Agency
CIM   Centrum für Internationale Migration und Entwicklung
           (Germany)
CRPSM   Costa Rica Productive Sector Modernization programme (Canada)
DAFs   Development Assistance Facilities (New Zealand)
DCS   Development programme of Canadian-Senegalese joint ventures
DEG   Deutsche Investions und Entwicklungsgesellschaft (Germany)
DGIS   Directoraat-Generaal Internationale Samenwerking (the
           Netherlands)
DIPO   Danish Import Promotion Office for Products from Developing
           Countries
ECIP   European Community Investment Partners
ETC   Enterprise Thailand Canada
FISA   Foreign Investment Advisory Service
FMO   Financiering Maatschappij voor Ontwikkelingslanden (the
           Netherlands)
FY   Fiscal year
GIEK   Guarantee Institute for Export Credits (Norway)
GOM   Garantiefaciliteit Opkomende Markten (the Netherlands)
GTZ   Deutsche Gesellschaft für Technische Zusammenarbeit (Germany)
IBTA   Investment promotion and technical assistance (the Netherlands)
ICDPS   Islamic Corporation for the Development of the Private Sector
IFOM   Investeringsfaciliteit Opkomende Markten (the Netherlands)
IFU   Industrial Fund for Developing Countries (Denmark)
ILO   International Labour Office
IPG   International Privatization Group (United States)
KfW   Kredietanstalt für Wiederaufbau (Germany)
MDF   Mahgreb Development Fund (Canada)
MIGA   Multilateral Investment Guarantee Agency
NCM   Nederlandse Credietverzekerings Maatschappij (the Netherlands)
NIMF   Nederlands Investerings Matching Fonds
NMCP   Netherlands Management Consultancy Programme (the
           Netherlands)
NORAD   Norwegian International Development Agency

NORFUND   Norwegian Risk Capital Fund for Developing Countries
NZODA   New Zealand Official Development Assistance
ORET/Miliev   Ontwikkelingsrelevante Export Transacties/Milieu en Economische
              Verzelfstandiging (the Netherlands)
PESP   Programma Economische Samenwerkingsprojecten (the
              Netherlands)
PIIDS   Pacific Islands Industrial Development Scheme (New Zealand)
POPM   Garantieregeling Particuliere Ontwikkelings Participatie
              Maatschappijen (the Netherlands)
PROPARCO   Société de Promotion et de Participation pour la Coopération
              Economique (France)
PSDI Fund   Private Sector Development Initiative Fund (Canada)
PSO   Programma Samenwerking Oost-Europa (the Netherlands)
PSOM   Programma Samenwerking Opkomende Markten (the Netherlands)
PUM   Programma Uitzending Managers (the Netherlands)
RHI   Regeling Herverzekering Investeringen (the Netherlands)
R&D   Research & Development
RISPCA   Regional Initiatives Support Programme in Central America
              (Canada)
RSF CEA   Regional Support Fund Central and Eastern Africa (Canada)
SES   Senior Experten Service (Germany)
SEQUA   Stiftung für wirtschaftliche Entwicklung und berufliche
              Qualifizierung (Germany)
VASS   Voluntary Agencies Support Scheme (New Zealand)

Notes

* The authors wish to thank Matthew Odedokun for his comments on earlier drafts.
   Responsibility for the content remains, of course, with the authors.
1. Many (particularly bilateral) donor formulate the link between PSD and poverty
   reduction in terms of the notion of 'pro-poor growth'. This formulation tends to
   simply beg the question in a slightly different form.
2. Coherence refers to 'the consistency of policy objectives and instruments applied
   by OECD governments, individually and collectively, in the light of their combined effects on developing countries' (DAC Informal Network on Poverty
   Reduction 2000).
3. Instruments in the field of international negotiation can also be in the form of targeted technical support, as in the case of programmes to enhance developing
   countries' trade negotiation capacity.
4. Non-financial aid includes micro-interventions grouped under business development services.
5. Although the IsDB's Business Development Department was created in 1995, lending to the private sector only started to be recorded as a distinct activity in
   2000–01, with the setting up of the Islamic Corporation for the Development
   of the Private Sector (ICDPS).
6. The World Bank's PSD policy has been revised at least twice, in 1995 and 2002.

7. The policy of the ICDPS states that its lending principles are based upon Sharia (Islamic) Law, with the implication that its loans are interest free.

8. Basically these 'causes' can be read as a summary of the unique features of the Asian corporate governance model in relation to an idealized account of the Anglo-Saxon one. For a critical discussion, see Dore (2000).

9. The World Bank's 2002 strategy document reports only shares of total assistance and sizes of changes in magnitudes rather than actual magnitudes themselves. The Bank's (2001c) OED report is only slightly less cryptic. A central problem in quantifying adjustment operation-based PSD lending is that such operations were almost always embodied in broader programmes. The 2001 Review states that around 250 credits made by the World Bank between 1994–99 had one or more PSD component. The total value of these credits was US$11.4 billion.

10. There is no discrepancy between the data presented here and that in Table 2.5, and the latter's subsequent discussion. The earlier discussion refers to FDI stock rather than recent FDI flows and to IFC funding over a much longer period. A comparison between the two sets of data suggests some recent marginal improvements in LDC's shares of both sources of funds.

11. Interesting in this regard is, for instance, the remark by New Zealand (DAC 1995) with regard to social policy and infrastructure development as elements of PSD: 'There is some doubt whether this category is appropriate to classify under 'private sector development' given that the primary purpose of social policy and infrastructural development is for the 'public good'.

12. One of the few bilateral donors for whom data on PSD related expenditure are readily available is New Zealand. Over 1995, NZODA calculated that 18 per cent of its total bilateral budget was to be considered as PSD assistance and this would even increase to 32 per cent if one would assume 'that 100 per cent of the private education and training awards result in increased skills for private sector activity' (DAC 1995: 81). It would, of course, be possible to add all expenditures for specific PSD programmes together but this would still leave out expenditures for other elements that are not grouped under a specific programme. In its 1999 annual report, AfD (France), for instance, notes total commitments of slightly more than €217 million under the heading for PSD (including PROPARCO, ARIA and Equity guarantees funds). However, this excludes commitments for microfinance and for specific banking and financial subsidiaries under AfD, to name just a few PSD related elements (AfD 2000).

13. The majority of funds were committed as loans (40.4 per cent), followed by syndications (30.6 per cent), guarantees (11.7 per cent), equity (9.9 per cent), quasi-equity (6.7 per cent) and risk mitigation products (0.6 per cent).

14. These projects were often implemented in collaboration with the World Bank – IFC Foreign Investment Advisory Service (FISA) (see below).

15. A fifth issue worth mentioning is that of tied aid. For a more general discussion on aid tying, see elsewhere in this publication and for a discussion on aid tying in relation to bilateral PSD support, see Schulpen and Gibbon (2001). All bilateral donors stress the necessity of involving their own private sector justifying this not only in altruistic terms (providing investment, technology, know-how and employment) but also sometimes explicitly instrumental ways – providing the opportunity to support their own (foreign and domestic) economic interests vis-à-vis those of other countries (and other donor countries in particular). For multilateral organizations, not having a private sector of their 'own', these issues

are not relevant, although some also emphasize the close interaction between improving flows of developed country private finance and opening (capital) accounts in recipient countries.

16. See, for example, the criticisms of the US's Overseas Private Investment Corporation by the Institute for Business Research and the Competitive Enterprise Institute, two Washington-based right-of-centre think tanks, available at: www.progress.org/banneker/cwopic.htm.

17. Cf. papers presented at a recent IFC/IIC Workshop on Additionality, available at: www.iadb.org/iic/ english/additionality/index.htm.

18. Cf. Eurodad's (2002) reaction to the World Bank PSD strategy. Eurodad states that 'there is no clarification in the document on what the WBG means by the "market", nor is there any specification of how the "poor" would benefit from the strategy'. More specifically, the PSD strategy is criticized for focusing 'exclusively on the needs of private firms' thereby 'neglecting to address the main concerns of the poor'. As such, Eurodad questions the automatic link between PSD and poverty reduction which forms the point of departure in the World Bank strategy (and in the strategies of practically all other donors).

19. An important question here, however, is whether safety-nets should precede or accompany privatization. This seems to have been one of the issues giving rise to tensions within the World Bank around the writing of *World Development Report 2000*. Those arguing for 'precede' did so on the grounds that evidence suggests that safety-nets are effective only when they are constructed in advance; those arguing the other position took the view that construction before could lead to prevarication with privatization itself (Wade 2002).

20. Of course, if definitions of SMEs are loosened, the amounts become much bigger. The IIC (2001) claims that 87.1 per cent of all its disbursements have been to SMEs, but an analysis of these indicates an average commitment of US$6.7 million. Another IADB affiliate, the MIF, actually defines 'small enterprises' as ones with 'sales of US$3–5 million and fewer than 100 employees' (www.iadb/mif.org).

21. The World Bank (2002: 41, 51) also proposes to end direct financial support for business advisory support services to SMEs, in favour of technical assistance for the development of 'market-based SME support systems…'. The IADB already ended such support in the 1990s. But an evaluation from 2000 (IADB 2000) noted 'a potential conflict between fee-based sustainability and the mission to serve smaller and less-established firms'.

22. See Schulpen and Gibbon (2002) for a short description of the rather mixed performance of bilateral donors in the field of external coherence.

23. This is not only important from a coordination point of view but certainly also to ensure greater internal coherence.

24. While being involved in PSD missions, one of the present authors has been informed by donor agency staff that they consider inter-donor coordination problematic. This is because it involves them in agreeing to common management practices, accounting methods, and so on, and because it is more difficult to show quick results when a lot of time has to be invested in 'learning about each others' expectations'.

References

AfD (2000). *Annual Report 1999*. Paris: Agence Française de Développement.

AsDB (2000). 'Private Sector Development Strategy'. March. Manila: AsDB.

AsDB (2001a). 'Private Sector Operations: Strategic Directions and Review'. September. Manila: AsDB.

AsDB (2001b). 'Annual Report'. Manila: AsDB.

AfDB (1997). 'Private Sector Development'. Abidjan: AfDB.

AfDB (2001). 'Annual Report'. Abidjan: AfDB.

AfDB (n.d.). 'Co-financing Operations – Summary of ADB Group Co-Financing Operations 1967–98'. Available at: www.afdb.org/financial/cofinancing operations. htm?n1=2=9&n3=0.

AusAID (2000). 'Private Sector Development through Australia's Aid Program'. January. Canberra: AusAID.

Berry, A. (ed.) (1998). *Poverty, Economic Reform and Income Distribution in Latin America*. Boulder CO: Lynne Reiner.

Bosch, F. van den (1998). 'De ontwikkeling van de particuliere sector – beleid, organisatie en programma's in de DAC donorlanden'. The Hague: DGIS.

CDB (2001). 'Annual Report 2000'. Barbados: CDB.

CIDA (1995a). 'Canada in the World: New Challenges for CIDA'. *Express Outlook on Development Issues*, 8: November.

CIDA (1995b). 'Microenterprise Financing: Global Agent for Poverty Reduction'. *Express Outlook on Development Issues*, 9: December.

CIDA (1999). 'CIDA's Draft Policy for Private Sector Development in Developing Countries'. March. Quebec: CIDA.

Claessens, S. (1998). *Systemic Bank and Corporate Restructuring*. Washington, DC: World Bank.

DAC (1994). 'DAC Orientations for Development Cooperation in Support of Private Sector Development'. Paris: OECD/DAC.

DAC (1995). 'Private Sector Development – A Guide to Donor Support'. Paris: OECD/DAC.

DAC (1997). 'Survey of DAC Members' Cooperation for Capacity Development in Trade. Paris: OECD/DAC.

DAC (1998). 'Development Cooperation'. Review Series – Germany no. 29. Paris: OECD/DAC.

DAC (1999). 'Development Cooperation: Efforts and Policies of the Members of the Development Assistance Committee'. Paris: OECD/DAC.

DAC (Development Assistance Committee) (2000). 'Development Cooperation: Efforts and Policies of the Members of the Development Assistance Committee'. Paris: OECD/DAC.

Danida (1999). 'Review Report – Danida's Private Sector Development Program'. September. Copenhagen: Danida.

DGIS (2000). 'Ondernemen tegen armoede – notitie over economie en ontwikkeling'. October. The Hague: DGIS.

Dore, R. (2000). *Stockmarket Capitalism, Welfare Capitalism: Japan and Germany vs. the Anglo-Saxons*. Oxford: Oxford University Press.

EBRD (2002). 'EBRD Investment 1991–2001 – Moving towards a Better Future'. London: EBRD. Available at: www.ebrd.com/pubs/index.htm.

EC (1998). 'A European Community Strategy for Private Sector Development in ACP Countries'. Brussels: Commission of the European Communities.

EIB (2002). 'Annual Report 2001'. Luxembourg: EIB. Available at: www.eib.org.

Eurodad (2002). 'Private Sector Development – Pro-poor, or Merely Poor Service Delivery? A Reaction to the World Bank Group's Strategy for Private Sector Development and the Link to PRSPs'. April. Brussels: Eurodad.

Gibbon, P. and L. Schulpen (2002). 'Comparative Appraisal of Multilateral and Bilateral Approaches to Financing Private Sector Development in Developing Countries'. WIDER Discussion Paper No. 2002/112. Helsinki: UNU/WIDER.

IADB (2000). 'Evaluation Office Report RE 249'. Washington, DC: IADB.

IADB (2001). 'Annual Report'. Washington, DC: IADB.

IADB (2002). 'Operational Policy for Lending for Industrial Development'. Washington, DC: IADB. Available at: www.iadb.org/cont/poli/OP-722E.htm.

IsDB (2002). 'The Islamic Corporation for the Development of the Private Sector'. Available at: www.idb.org.

IFC (2000). 'Paths Out of Poverty – The Role of Private Enterprise in Developing Countries'. Washington, DC: IFC.

IIC (2001). 'Annual Report'. Washington, DC: IIC.

Iskander, M., G. Meyerman, D. Gray and S. Hagan (1999). 'Corporate Restructuring and Governance in East Asia'. *Finance & Development*, 36 (1).

Killick, T. (1989). 'A Reaction Too Far – Economic Theory and the Role of the State in Developing Countries'. London: ODI.

MIF (2001). 'Annual Report'. Washington, DC: MIF.

MIGA (2001). 'Annual Report'. Washington, DC: MIGA.

MIGA (2002). 'List of Projects Insured by MIGA in Fiscal Year 2001'. Washington, DC: MIGA. Available at: www.miga.org/screens/projects/projects.htm.

NORAD (1999). 'Strategy for Norwegian Support of Private Sector Development in Developing Countries'. Oslo: NORAD.

NZODA (1991). 'A Strategy for Implementing NZODA to the Private Sector in Developing Countries in the South Pacific'. March. Wellington: NZODA.

NZODA (1998). 'Investing in a Common Future – Policy Framework for New Zealand Official Development Assistance (NZODA)'. Wellington: NZODA.

Pietilä, T. (ed.) (2000). 'Promoting Private Sector Development – Issues and Guidelines for Aid Agencies'. Policy Papers I/2000. Helsinki: Institute of Development Studies.

Schulpen, L. (2000). 'Private Sector Development and Poverty Reduction: An Inbuilt Incoherence?', in T. Pietilä (ed.), 'Promoting Private Sector Development – Issues and Guidelines for Aid Agencies'. Policy Papers I/2000. Helsinki: Institute of Development Studies.

Schulpen, L. and P. Gibbon (2001). 'Private Sector Development – Policies, Practices and Problems'. CDR Policy Paper. Copenhagen: CDR.

Schulpen, L. and P. Gibbon (2002). 'Private Sector Development – Policies, Practices and Problems'. *World Development*, 30 (1): 1–15.

UNCTAD (2000). *World Investment Report*. Geneva: UNCTAD.

Wade, R. (2002). 'US Hegemony and the World Bank: the Fight over People and Ideas'. *Review of International Political Economy*, 9 (2): 201–29.

World Bank (1991). *World Development Report 1991 – The Challenge of Development*. Oxford: Oxford University Press.

World Bank (1998). *East Asia: the Road to Recovery*. Washington, DC: World Bank.

World Bank (2001a). 'Private Sector Development Strategy – Directions for the World Bank Group'. Washington, DC: World Bank.

World Bank (2001b). *World Development Report 2002*. Washington, DC: World Bank.

World Bank (2001c). 'OEC Evaluation Review', in *Review of Private Sector Development in IDA 10–12*. May. Washington, DC: World Bank.

World Bank (2002). *World Development Report 2003 – Sustainable Development in a Dynamic World*. New York: Oxford University Press for the World Bank.

3

Bilateral Official and Non-Governmental Organizations' Support for Private Sector Development

Ayodele Jimoh

1   Introduction

In the 1980s, development thinking shifted from seeing the state as the conducive force behind economic activities to viewing it as the facilitator of an enabling environment for the private sector which, in turn, is increasingly recognized as the prime mover of economic activities. By the mid-1980s and the early 1990s, the socialist systems were under strain and, indeed, crumbling. In 1991, the Soviet Union collapsed and market reforms progressed (Exeter and Fries 1998: 26). As if awakened by these events, the donor community, academics, policymakers and professionals in the aid business, increasingly focused attention on the effectiveness of previous aid efforts. It is worth noting that until very recently, virtually all recipients of official aid were governments and such aid was for public sector development (Van de Walle 1999: 345).

Today, the conventional wisdom is that the private sector should be the engine of growth in developing countries. This being the case, it is only logical that development aid efforts be directed, increasingly, at private sector development (PSD) which provides the best hope for ending poverty in the less developed countries (LDCs) and for ending the need for development aid that could be replaced by private capital flows (Riddell 1999: 310).

Indeed, as reviewed in Jimoh (2002), there is growing evidence that the current target of major development aid programmes is PSD and a good share of this is being channelled through the NGOs rather than through the governments of LDCs. Thus, the PSD aid phenomenon is a reality and the role of civil societies (NGOs, in particular), is becoming significant by all accounts (see Charlton and May 1995: 1; Stewart 1997: 1).

Despite the significant role being ascribed to PSD by major donors and the prime place given to NGOs in this regard, a good number of issues surrounding this new strategic direction are yet to be thoroughly examined or evaluated. For example, it needs to be determined whether the new focus and the corresponding practices are indeed superior to earlier approaches. Specifically, there is the need to review the channels and instruments used by donors to determine their effectiveness a priori. While existing studies have examined some of these issues, most are focused on either donor instruments or channels. But rarely have the two aspects been examined comprehensively together, especially through the use of relevant aggregate time-series. For instance, employing case studies and relevant theories, Edwards and Hulme (1992) and Meyer (1992) examine only the role of NGOs in aid delivery, as donors shift their attention from public to the private sector. Similarly, Pedersen (2000), Gibbon (2000), and Schulpen and Gibbon (2002) focus on PSD aid instruments, while Phelan (1995) conducts a comparative analysis of Japanese PSD aid programmes in Philippines and Thailand. Even though Kragh *et al.* (2000) outline PSD aid instruments and channels, their main focus is on the relevant delivery instruments. Thus, issues like the relative merits of alternative channels of PSD aid delivery are not examined. Further, a conceivable channel of PSD aid delivery is not mentioned in Kragh *et al.*'s (2000) study. Second, none of the existing studies address in a satisfactory manner the issue of whether PSD aid efforts have catalytic effects on foreign direct investment flows (FDI) to poor countries. The aim of this chapter is to examine these issues with a view to enhancing our understanding. This we do by examining the theoretical literature as well as data relevant to channels and instruments of PSD aid delivery to provide answers to some of the questions raised above. To ensure a manageable scope, this study focuses on bilateral official flows in support of PSD.

Towards this end, the rest of the chapter consists of the following: Section 2 on alternative channels of official finance for private sector development, Section 3 on private sector development aid instruments, activities commonly financed and the catalytic effects of official PSD aid flows. Section 4 closes with a summary and concluding remarks.

2   Alternative channels of official finance for private sector development

In identifying the alternative channels through which official finance can be made available to the private sector, we are greatly assisted by Kragh *et al.* (2000: 319). In particular, from their diagram of aid channels (Figure 3.1), five channels of PSD finance are identifiable. In addition to these five channels, two more may be added:

(1) From a donor government to a multilateral institution which, in the recipient country, channels aid either directly to a firm or through institutions, associations, NGOs, and other such organizations, or even through the receiving government,

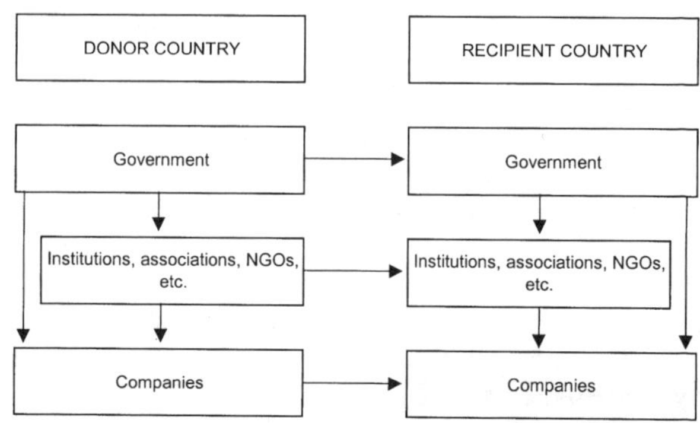

Figure 3.1   Channels of PSD aid

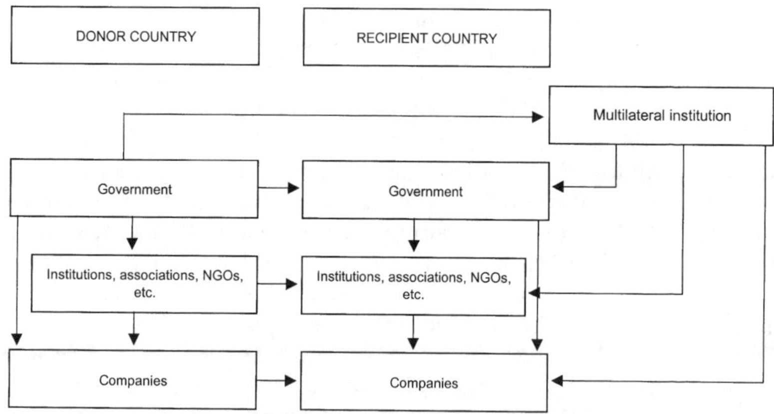

Figure 3.2   Conceivable channels of PSD aid, a modified version

Source: A modified version of Kragh *et al.*'s (2000) diagram.

(2) From a donor government to individuals as, for example, scholarships for studies in marketing, or courses that are specific to the private sector.

Figure 3.2 modifies Figure 3.1 on the part of the first additional channel, thereby presenting six identifiable channels; the second channel is not shown because it is not significant for the delivery of PSD aid, nor is it likely to be one in the future. It must be noted, as fully discussed by Gibbon and Schulpen in Chapter 2, that in all these six cases, the aid or finance is either directed at the international-, macro-, sector- (meso-) or enterprise-level activities.

Merits and demerits of the alternative aid delivery channels[1]

Each of these six channels has its merits and shortcomings, which we examine next.

Channel (i): Donor government–government–recipient businesses
This channel is similar to the traditional vehicle for aid delivery. Its major advantage is that it allows for better coordination of donor efforts, and as a government is in a good position to fit the disbursed aid into its own sector plans. This is particularly important for PSD aid because of the decentralized nature of the private sector, and this can, for instance, be done through the adoption of a sectoral investment programme approach (Riddell 1999: 333). Further, the government's administrative machinery can easily be deployed for PSD aid delivery to achieve substantial savings in overhead costs. Also, because government has the power to enact laws, regulate the production of social goods and social 'bads', it can often resolve the free-rider problem that hinders its optimal production (Meyer 1992: 1116). Consequently, aid that is channelled through *good* government and designed to promote the production of social goods which were under-produced in the first instance because of free-rider problems, has a greater chance of reaching the beneficiaries targeted by the donor. Finally, government would have a sense of project ownership, a fact which usually facilitates effective and efficient delivery of aid services or execution of the associated projects.

But if the government is corrupt, inefficient or ineffective, some of these merits are lost. In such instances, governmental *red tape* impairs aid delivery, especially in terms of delivery time and quality of work. Similarly, corruption makes aid delivery more costly and results in poor quality. Through the same political process that often allocates resources disproportionally so that some are over-satisfied and others (mainly the less privileged) remain under-satisfied (Meyer 1992: 1116), corruption furthermore works to bypass the targeted beneficiaries, because such aid commonly goes to those who would normally be excluded by donors. This often results in a very perverse outcome, giving the impression that such aid is ineffective. Further, because corruption worsens the problems generally associated with the lack of incentives for efficient operations by bureaucrats as they do not share in these efficiency gains (Meyer 1992: 1116), the expected savings in overhead costs cannot be realized. Finally, as with all aid targeted at the enterprise level, it can create an unequal environment for the non-assisted firms of the industry and at its worst, can induce rent-seeking behaviour instead of encouraging competition.

Channel (ii): Donor government–government–local institutions–businesses
By local associations and institutions, we mean NGOs,[2] which include chambers of commerce, trade unions, labour unions, village associations (usually age-grade groups), trader associations, farmers' associations, voluntary (and often unregistered) craftsmen/artisan associations (e.g. bricklayers, plumbers, mechanics, radio and electronics technicians, air conditioner technicians, etc.), cooperative societies and self-help groups. While most chambers of commerce represent only a tiny minority of the well-to-do entrepreneurs, trade and labour unions are often more broad based. In

particular, most voluntary trade/craftsman/artisans organizations in poor countries that have been in existence for over five years, are attracting large memberships. These are credible, and enjoy the trust and respect of their members partly because they meet regularly (sometimes weekly) and make regular contributions with which they help their members. Discipline is high and obligation defaults very rare (Ibe 1990). Similarly, most village (age-based) associations are mandatory. Set up to execute communal development projects, these organizations are usually governed by customs and traditions, and are highly disciplined (Ibe 1990 and 1992).

One of the principal advantages of this channel lies in the general belief that southern NGOs have a comparative advantage in reaching the poorest of the poor, and those in the remote areas that are often difficult for the authorities to reach. Local NGOs can handle aid delivery faster and cheaper, especially when local institutions consist of grassroots-based and popular organizations.

Furthermore, believed to be innovative, bureaucracy-free, flexible, small, and smart, these local NGOs have a comparative advantage in capacity building and participatory development (Smillie 1997). Voluntarism is a major feature of NGOs and probity one of their guiding principles, therefore the trust of the public and donors in their operations is somewhat higher (Charlton and May 1995; Davis and McGregor 2000). Finally, as illustrated by a number of donors' self-evaluation reports, NGO programmes are effective, and it is likely that donors will favour engaging NGOs in aid delivery (see Smillie 1997: 571). Thus, their involvement in PSD is expected to promote a higher level of donors' funding, and aid programme effectiveness.

Another advantage of this channel is the involvement of both the domestic government and local NGOs. This may combine the best of the two worlds because the government has the legislative means to resolve the free-rider problem, and regulate the production of social goods and bads, as necessary. The participating NGOs would provide the flexibility, responsiveness, expertise in reaching the poor to ensure efficiency and effectiveness of aid delivery (Meyer 1992). Each partner can also be a check on the other.

The major disadvantage of this channel is the lack of incentives for the government and the NGOs to operate efficiently, as they do not share in the efficiency gains (Meyer 1992). However, voluntarism and the missionary spirit of the NGOs are expected to be the guiding principle. Another demerit is that NGO/government involvement creates the possibility of conflict between the two, with disappointing outcomes, particularly if the government is corrupt.

Some scholars (e.g. Stewart 1997) have expressed doubts about the benefits usually credited to NGOs. But it is worth noting that while these critical observations can be rather helpful in avoiding past mistakes, they do not negate the generally acknowledged virtues of NGOs.

Available evidence, furthermore, suggests that the donor/NGO 'partnerships' may have proven to be satisfactory. The role of NGOs in aid delivery has, over time, become significant and their activities increasingly diversified.[3] As NGOs rely on official donors for their financing (see Table 3.1), and as official donors have shifted their focus to PSD, this would be correspondingly reflected in the diversified NGO involvement in PSD activities.[4]

Today, donors support NGOs by channelling through them some of the ODA and engaging them as contractors in the delivery of aid. As can be seen from Table 3.1, and Figure 3.3, the percentage of ODA channelled by donor governments through the NGOs was 4.4 during the 1970–2000 period. Even though a noticeable decline has been recorded after the peak (of 6.9 per cent) during the 1980–89 period, a deeper analysis suggests that the honeymoon between the NGOs and donor governments may not be over yet.

A legitimate question that arises from Table 3.1 and Figure 3.3 relates to the factors that have accounted for the observed size and trend movement in the size of NGO grants to developing countries as well as the amounts of ODA support received from donor governments. This is an intriguing issue and all we do here is to attempt to provide some tentative empirical explanation by analysing relevant statistics. To conduct such an analysis, we formulate and estimate a panel regression model on the basis of annual (1970–2000) statistics for the donor countries (Development Assistance Committee (DAC) member). The estimates of the model are reported in Table 3.2.

The model postulates a number of determinants of ODA financial support given by the donor governments to the NGOs (in relation to overall ODA as well as in relation to the GDP of the donor country). These determinants expected to enhance the financial support include high level of economic prosperity in the donor country (rising per capita income level and upturn in economic cycle), high level of donor government expenditures, and the

Table 3.1 Bilateral development assistance and NGOs' levels of activities, 1970–2000

Period average	1970–79	1980–89	1990–99	2000	Average[a]
			($ billion)		
Bilateral ODA net disbursements	9.3	22.9	39.1	36.0	24.1
Grants by NGOs to developing countries	1.3	3.0	5.7	6.9	3.5
Support received by NGOs from the official sector	0.3	1.6	1.3	1.2	1.1
			(in %)		
Support received by NGOs from official sector as % of ODA	3.7	6.9	3.4	3.3	4.4
Grants by NGOs to Developing Countries as % of ODA	14.3	13.2	14.7	19.2	14.4

Note: [a] Average for the years 1970–2000.

Source: DAC's International Development Statistics (online).

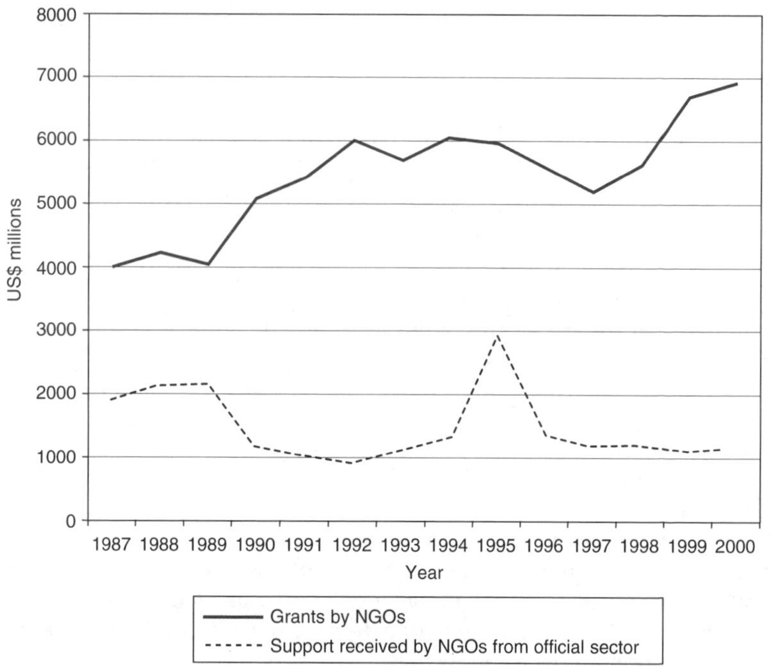

Figure 3.3   Official support and NGOs' activities, 1987–2000

extent to which the donor government is not of the right wing type.[5] Similarly, it postulates that the level of NGO grants to developing countries relative to GDP (of the NGO's country of origin) is determined by the same set of factors. In all cases, we also include a trend variable to capture the effects of other (miscellaneous) time-variant determinants not explicitly considered here.

A priori, it is expected that prosperity in the donor country (rising per capita income level and an upturn in the economic cycle) and the large size of donor government (i.e. high donor government expenditure–GDP ratio) would increase ODA support to the NGOs so that positive coefficients of these determinants are expected. Following a similar logic, we also expect their positive coefficients in the equation for the grants by NGOs to developing countries in relation to the GDP of the NGO's country of origin. On the other hand, as right wing government can be said to be parsimonious with respect to ODA in general and charity-like foreign activities of NGOs in particular, the extent of the donor government being right wing is expected to have a negative coefficient in an equation for donor government support to the NGO.

Judging by the statistical properties of the estimated equations in Table 3.2 and noting the fact that panel data (like cross sectional data) are often

Table 3.2 Determinants of selected variables, model of NGOs

Dependent variables	Trend variable	Per capita income (log) (t−1)	Upturn in economic cycle (t−1)	Govt. expenditure GDP ratio (t−1)	Extent of govt. being right wing (t−1)	No. of observations	Adj. R^2
ODA-type support received by national NGOs from official sector in relation to:							
(1) GDP	−0.000002	0.00007	0.00068	0.000008	0.00001	348	0.750
	(−0.6)	(0.5)	(2.9)	(4.3)	(1.5)		
(2) Total ODA	0.00166	−0.1040	0.2235	0.00092	0.00023	348	0.515
	(2.3)	(−2.9)	(3.7)	(1.9)	(0.2)		
Net grants by total NGOs in relation to							
(3) GDP	−0.00001	0.00047	−0.00037	0.000004	NA	476	0.758
	(−3.9)	(4.0)	(−1.7)	(2.2)			

Notes

(a) The dependent variables are indicated in the first column and they are all sourced from the OECD's IDS (online), except the GDP which is from the World Bank's Global Development Indicators, GDI, (online). The regressors (except the political variable) are also from the World Bank's GDI indicators. Political variable is from Beck *et al.* (2000).

(b) The estimates are panel data-based and the fixed-effect OLS method was employed in deriving the estimates.

(c) The figures in parentheses below the parameter estimates are the t-values. At 10%; 5%; and 1% levels of significance, a parameter estimate is statistically significant if its t-value, in absolute sense, is not less than 1.6; 2.0; and 2.6, respectively.

(d) The dependent variable in equation 1 is the portion of ODA given by the national government to the NGOs, expressed as a fraction of the GDP. In equation 2, it is expressed as a fraction of the total ODA. In equation 3, the dependent variable is the total grant given by the NGOs to developing countries, expressed as a fraction of GDP of the countries where the NGOs are resident.

associated with low R^2, we believe that the estimated models have good statistical properties and that the sign expectations are, in most cases, met. Therefore, they are reliable estimates on the whole, from which some valid inferences can be made.

These empirical results in Table 3.2 imply that the share of official support to national NGOs in relation to GDP increases with an upturn in the economic cycle, with increased government expenditures and with increased per capita incomes in the donor countries, but the per capita income variable is not statistically significant. Official support to national NGOs relative to total ODA increases as the economic cycle upswings and as government expenditures increase, but decreases with increased per capita incomes in the donor country (suggesting that a high per capita income enhances overall ODA more than it enhances the portion given to the national NGO). Similarly, grants by NGOs in relation to the host-country GDP increase with rising per capita income and increase in the size of host-country government, but decrease with an upturn in the economic cycle (though this is not statistically significant at 5 per cent level of significance) and have a negative significant trend.

Channel (iii): Donor government–donor businesses–recipient businesses
In this option, as in channels (iv)–(vi) discussed below, the government in the recipient country is not involved in the delivery of official support. Thus, the government does not provide any form of guarantee, unlike delivery options (i) and (ii) above where it does. This channel is most suitable for partnership and investment support programmes. Its effectiveness is less influenced by the quality of government in the recipient country. It has the advantage of being able to demonstrate the values of private sector organizing principles because, as they say, charity begins at home. However, because it lacks a built-in arrangement for the coordination of donor programmes, it has a greater likelihood of creating a situation in which one donor's activities undermine the activities of others. This is true of all channels in which the recipient government is not involved in the delivery of aid. Further, doubts could easily be raised about donor sincerity, as it may be difficult to ascertain which objectives are paramount to the donor: promotion of their business interests or the provision of genuine assistance to poor countries (Schulpen and Gibbon 2002: 10).

Channel (iv): Donor government–donor institutions/associations–
donor businesses–recipient businesses
This, like channel (iii) above, is significantly different from the traditional form of aid delivery, and both have similar merits and demerits, especially with respect to bypassing the government. The involvement of northern NGOs encompasses all the advantages of NGOs discussed in channel (ii) above, so there is no need to repeat them here. However, because local NGOs are not involved, the ability to reach the poorest of the poor may be

compromised without their in-depth knowledge of local conditions. Also, this option may be prone to transparency problems, inadequate consultation with intended beneficiaries and over-reliance on private consultants from the donor country, as observed by Smillie (1997). The free-rider problem is observed and accountability to the local public questionable. This channel may be very suitable for advocacy, investment support and partnership programmes as well as for sector-level donor interventions.

Channel (v): Donor government–donor institutions or association–
local institutions/associations–recipient businesses
Channel (v) is similar to the foregoing (iv), with the only difference being the involvement of institutions and associations in the recipient country. All the virtues of NGOs discussed under channel (ii) apply. The involvement of institutions and associations in both the donor and recipient countries allows for greater monitoring, and control by donors as NGOs are easier to control than governments. However, because the chain of aid delivery is lengthened, the probability of a breakdown in communication is increased. Similarly, the chances of bottlenecks are increased. Further, as with all channels by-passing the government and concerned with the provision of social services, the free-rider problem is present, and NGOs' accountability to the local public is doubtful. Similarly, there is no built-in arrangement for the coordination of donor programmes. This channel could be very suitable for advocacy, training and education.

Channel (vi): Donor government–multilateral institutions
At present, donors do contribute to multilateral institutions in support of their programmes. The common vehicles for these flows are mainly grants, loans and purchase of securities. Table 3.3 shows these donor government flows to multilateral institutions between 1970 and 1999. Together, they constitute an average of about 22 per cent of total official flows.

In addition to this common practice, it is conceivable to have a specialized multilateral institution to which donors contribute funds in support of PSD. Such an institution would then channel the resulting resources for PSD in the LDCs. This multilateral agency could be modelled along the lines of the International Financial Corporation (IFC) for coexistence with it. Thus, while IFC would strive to source the funds for PSD from the international capital market, the specialized institution would obtain its funds from official donors, for a common pool from which disbursements are made to beneficiaries.

The major attraction of this channel is that it creates room for effective coordination of donor efforts (see Riddell 1999: 33). Furthermore, as with multilateral institutions in general, this channel is most likely to ensure that aid allocations are based more on needs and swayed less by the strategic and political factors that commonly influence donor governments. The overall effectiveness of aid delivered through this alternative would depend on the

Table 3.3 Disbursements and commitments of official flows to multilateral institutions, 1970–2000

Period average	1970–79	1980–89	1990–99	2000	Average
	(in US$ billion)				
1. Total official flows, gross	20.9	49.4	88.0	70.5	53.3
2. Disbursements to multilaterals, gross (MGD)	4.4	11.1	19.5	18.1	11.9
(a) ODA to multilaterals	3.8	10.2	17.3	17.8	10.7
(b) OOF to multilaterals (MOOF)	0.6	0.9	2.2	0.2	1.2
3. Total OOF disbursements, gross	6.1	13.5	24.0	10.5	14.4
	(in %)				
MOOF as % total gross OOF	11.4	6.8	9.0	2.2	8.9
MGD as % of total official flows	20.4	22.4	22.1	25.6	21.8

Notes: The average column records the average for 1970–2000.

Source: DAC's International Development Statistics (online).

channel being used in the delivery of aid from the multilateral institution to the recipient.

The proposal for a new multilateral approach to PSD aid delivery being put forward here envisages an arrangement whereby a good proportion of ODA-eligible flows is channelled through a specialized multilateral institution whose main focus is PSD. This is capable of increasing the magnitudes of flows passing through this channel manifold. It is worth noting that both the EU and Organization for Economic Co-operation and Development (OECD) have bodies with similar features and roles to what is being proposed here, albeit on a much smaller scale.

3 PSD instruments, activities commonly financed and the catalytic effects of official PSD aid flows

Kragh *et al.* (2000) identified four PSD aid instruments, namely, programmes to support (i) an enabling environment, (ii) privatization and commercialization, (iii) investment, and (iv) business partnership programmes. Alternatively, PSD aid instruments may be classified into just two categories, namely, financial or non-financial instruments (Schulpen and Gibbon 2002: 5–6; Pietilä 2000: 2; Schulpen 2000: 88–94; etc.). Donors use either financial or non-financial instruments or a combination of both in their various support programmes. Financial instruments include, for example, grants, loans, credit lines, subsidies, equity acquisitions, risk capital and guarantees, and other such instruments. Non-financial instruments include technical aid, vocational aid, training assistance (e.g. export training), provision of information and advice, management and consultancy services, and so on (see Appendix Table A3.1). For details of these, and other instruments and channels, see Appendix Table A3.2.

The major features of these programmes as well as the extent to which they are used by official donors in PSD are reviewed next.

PSD instruments that benefit the private sector indirectly

By their very nature, programmes for supporting an enabling environment and those supporting commercialization and privatization benefit, for most part, the private sector indirectly. We outline their major features first before reviewing the instruments that benefit the private sector directly.

Enabling environment support programmes

This type of support is usually provided at the international-, macro- and sector-levels. An environment favourable to a business concerns forces and resources created outside the business and therefore beyond its control, but which affect operations within the business. These forces include rules and regulations, business services, physical and financial infrastructure, research and development, education, training, societal attitudes (including trust or social capital in general), information preparation and dissemination framework, access to world market, and so on. Creating an enabling environment means paying attention to numerous aspects of the environment, such as the usual factor and demand conditions, the nature, scope and structure of linkages among firms and sectors, and the nature and degree of competition that exists (Porter 1990). A further elaboration of these environmental obstacles and the need for removing them is provided in Jimoh (2002).

Major donors include the World Bank, German aid agencies, European Union (especially via the Lome convention), regional development banks (e.g. Asian Development Bank, African Development Bank, etc.), among others. Typical beneficiaries are the national export promotion agencies (capacity building with respect to trade regulations, export credits, export promotion, seminars, collection and dissemination of market intelligence, etc.), and governments in transition (training and education in marketing and modern management, support for environmental protection, occupational health and safety through education programmes, networking and subcontracting among firms, etc. and for chambers of commerce and industry).

Generally, the effects of donor aid instruments for promoting an enabling environment are difficult to isolate. For instance, they are often implemented in conjunction with privatization and commercialization measures within a much larger structural adjustment policy (SAP) package and also often form an integral part of adjustment lending by multilateral development banks. It is, therefore, difficult to evaluate their impact. However, some major problem areas which need donor attention have been identified by many existing studies (Grierson 2000: 42; Kragh *et al.* 2000: 325; Schulpen and Gibbon 2002, among others). First, it is generally agreed that recipient countries are not sufficiently involved in the design of many of the enabling environment support programmes (Putzel 1998). Consequently, these are supply-driven rather than demand-driven (Kragh *et al.* 2000: 325), which calls for increased donor–recipient dialogue. Second, there is not sufficient coordination among donors, which means that there is duplication of effort (Riddell 1999: 315–6; Hyden 1997: 64). Third, donors are commonly reported to have excessive concern for the export of the hardware at the expense of institutional building (Schulpen 2000; Schulpen and Gibbon 2002). For instance, insufficient attention is commonly given to the development of inter-business and inter-industry linkages. Yet, if greater attention were to be given by donors to promoting and enhancing these linkages among businesses in the recipient countries, a significant dividend could be realized (Grierson 2000: 42). But all this notwithstanding, there is no evidence to suggest that the traditional approach to aid delivery could have been more effective, as it also suffers from similar problems.

Commercialization and privatization programmes
One of the major activities financed by donors that aims to improve the effectiveness and efficiency of resource utilization in poor countries is the facilitation of privatization and commercialization measures, usually within a larger SAP programme. The most direct theoretical justification for privatization/commercialization measures can be found in private sector-led development literature that has become dominant since the 1980s. Thus, to facilitate the transition from a hitherto public sector-dominated economy to a private sector-led economy, ownership must be transferred from the public to the private sector, that is, privatization must be implemented.

Similarly, efficiency arguments favouring private over public ownership – the first indication of the shift in development thinking – provide further justification. These, together with market-discipline arguments, justify the commercialization of natural monopolies. Even though these measures are needed, the huge adjustment costs involved are often beyond the means of the LDCs. Furthermore, the successful design and implementation of reforms require skill, experience and knowledge – which the donor countries have in relative abundance. Consequently, donor assistance in this regard could significantly reduce the associated adjustment costs, making the change smoother.

The major donor in this area is the World Bank Group; its efforts are also supported by some bilateral donors like the United States (through the USAID) and Japan. The modes of support include provision of technical assistance and advice, equity investments, and loans and grants in support of the following activities: (i) establishment of mechanisms for controlling natural monopolies, for example, anti-trust laws, commercial courts, and so on, (ii) preparation of privatization and commercialization programmes, (iii) providing support in the formulation and facilitation of the implementation of appropriate regulatory environment for the privatized sector and to enable firms to adjust to the new dispensation, (iv) assisting the financial sector to better understand the needs of the privatized enterprises, and (v) conducting necessary training, and other such activities. In addition, outright grants may come in the form of debt cancellation, while equity investments may, among others, come in the form of debt-for-equity swaps.

Efforts of the donors are difficult to evaluate here for the same reason as outlined in the previous section on the enabling environment support programmes. In general, the implementation of privatization has been sluggish and gains slow in coming. Privatization may even be associated with deteriorating social conditions in recipient countries, resulting in massive and hostile opposition. These have often beclouded the positive impacts. In a number of cases, difficulties in finding potential buyers have delayed implementation (Van de Walle 1989) either because many enterprises are operating at a loss (Larsson 1994) or because of the general atmosphere of policy uncertainty in LDCs. Potential buyers are often put off by the unattractive conditions attached to the sale of state-owned enterprises (SOEs), mainly in terms of buyer obligations regarding the old company's debts or workforce, or in terms of conditions crafted deliberately to make the sale difficult and preserve the privileges of some groups. On the whole, however, efficiency gains have been reported at company-level in a number of countries implementing privatization and commercialization programmes. These appear to be more successful in Asia than in Africa because the former has an environment more conducive for success (Kragh *et al.* 2000).

PSD instruments inducing direct benefits to the private sector

The instruments are mainly investment support programmes, partnership support programmes and mixed credits that benefit the private sector directly. These and issues related to the catalytic effects of official investment flows are discussed in this section.

Investment support programmes

Investment programmes are of two broad varieties. One is the type in which donor governments or their agencies invest directly. Another variety is that in which donor governments or their agencies facilitate private direct investment in the recipient countries. Under the first type, a government using financial instruments, undertakes an equity or portfolio investment in a project in a recipient country. Commonly, finance flows directly from the donor government to the recipient business through the donor government's venture capital funds and such investments are later disposed off at prevailing market terms.[6] Under the second variety, donors encourage their private companies to set up subsidiaries in the target countries. This is slightly different from partnership programmes that involve 'twinning'. Under this variety, incentives provided by donors may be financial or/and non-financial.

Notable donor governments that have used venture capital funds to provide investment support include some European countries (e.g. Denmark through Danish Industrialization Fund for Developing Countries, etc. [see Appendix Table A3.1]). But, as also apparent from the discussion in the previous chapter by Gibbon and Schulpen, this instrument seems to be more commonly used by multilateral development institutions.

The most direct support for investment support programmes can be found in the two-gap growth models where savings and/or foreign exchange shortage constrains economic growth. Thus, through this instrument, donors, by injecting or facilitating capital inflows to the LDCs, loosen the constraint on growth in the recipient countries imposed by low savings and poor foreign exchange earnings. When donors promote, under this programme, direct investment by foreign private firms in the LDCs, subsidiary firms thus established could facilitate technology transfer through the training of engaged local staff and the introduction of new methods of production/machinery (Kragh *et al.* 2000: 319).

The extent to which official donors use investment support instruments of the first variety is reflected in their equity acquisitions, joint venture investments and other investment-related transactions in the LDCs. As can be seen from Table 3.4, Development Assistance Committee (DAC) members' bilateral ODA-eligible equity acquisitions between 1970 and 2000 are a small proportion of bilateral ODA and of total bilateral official flows, being on average of about 0.3 per cent and 0.2 per cent, respectively. Similarly, it shows that donors' other investment-related transactions per annum in the OOF (other official flows) category between 1995–2000 are about 6 per cent of average annual ODA, 4 per cent of average annual total official flows and 88 per cent of average annual total official investments in support of LDCs. In a similar manner, Table 3.5 shows that between 1995–2000, official flows in support of joint ventures constituted about 17.7 per cent of total official investment flows and about 0.5 per cent of total official flows.

In terms of the channels discussed in the previous section, Table 3.5 presents the breakdown of the official investment flows of donors between 1995 and 2000 according to the identifiable channels. Table 3.5 indicates that official bilateral donors channelled directly to the LDCs about 77 per cent of their investment-related support in the OOF category or 66 per cent of their total investment support, mainly through governments of LDCs and their national agencies.

The overall picture emerging from Table 3.5 is that financial flows through investment support programmes have recorded a significant downward trend. And this leads to the issue of what factors could have accounted for the observed movements in the financial flows over the years. We carry out

Table 3.4   ODA eligible equity acquisitions and other investment-related transactions, 1970–2000

Period average	1970–79	1980–89	1990–99	2000	Average
	(in US$ billions)				
Bilateral ODA gross disbursements	11.07	25.66	46.71	42.18	28.28
Bilateral OOF gross disbursements	5.46	12.55	21.83	10.29	13.19
Total bilateral official disbursements (TOD), gross	16.54	38.21	68.55	52.48	41.47
ODA bilateral equity acquisition (ODAEA), gross	0.02	0.10	0.14	0.26	0.09
Investment-related transactions (IRT), gross			3.14	0.73	2.73
Total official investment (TOI)			3.35	0.98	2.96
	(in %)				
ODAEA as % gross bilateral ODA	0.1	0.4	0.3	0.6	0.3
ODAEA as % TOD	0.1	0.3	0.2	0.5	0.2
TOI as % of TOD			4.8	1.9	4.3
IRT as % ODA			6.9	1.7	6.0
IRT as % TOI			90.7	73.9	87.9
IRT as % TOD			4.5	1.4	4.0

Notes: The average column records the average for 1970–2000; IRT is the support with respect to investment transactions that do not qualify as ODA.

Source: DAC's International Development Statistics (online).

a tentative and preliminary analysis, by estimating some panel regression equations for the ODA-type and OOF-type of equity investments by the 'donor' countries. Each is alternatively expressed in relation to GDP and total ODA, and annual data for available years and the DAC-member countries are employed. The explanatory variables of the model set out in Table 3.6 are the same as those in the NGO model in Table 3.2. A priori, it is expected that prosperity in the donor country (rising per capita income and an economic cycle upturn) and increased donor government expenditures increase the portion of donor GDP to be allocated to the ODA-type equity acquisitions, and will tilt resources away from the OOF-type. While a right-wing government often discourages ODA in general, the government, if it has to give aid at all, would favour OOF-type transactions that are undertaken more at market terms. A trend variable is also included for the same reason as in equation estimates of Table 3.2.

Judging by the statistical properties of the estimated equations in Table 3.6 and noting the fact that panel data (like cross sectional data) are often associated with low R^2, we are encouraged that the estimated models have

Table 3.5   ODA, joint ventures and some investment channels, 1970–2000

Period average	1995	1996	1997	1998	1999	2000	Average
	(in US$ billions)						
1. ODA-bilateral joint ventures equity acquisitions, net	0.02	NA	NA	0.004	0.01	−0.01	0.01
2. Gross IRT with developing countries (IRTDCs)	0.67	1.28	2.01	1.24	1.68	0.67	1.26
of which gross joint ventures (gross JV)	0.08	0.26	0.68	0.81	0.13	0.09	0.34
of which gross JV loans	5.67	0.25	0.15	0.11	0.41	0.44	1.17
of which gross JV acquisition of equity (JVAE)	0.02	0.01	0.67	0.71	0.74	0.00	0.36
3. Gross IRT with residents (IRTR)	0.12	0.13	0.11	0.12	0.02	0.06	0.09
IRTR, gross loans to national private investors (IRTR loans)	0.05	0.07	0.10	0.04	0.02	0.01	0.05
IRTR, subsidies to national private investors (IRTR sub)	0.07	0.06	0.01	0.09	0.00	0.04	0.05
	(in %)						
4. Gross IRT	8.79	1.41	2.11	1.67	1.70	0.73	2.73
RTDCs as % of total bilateral official investments (TOI)	7.4	80.2	86.3	67.2	85.4	68.3	65.8
IRTDCs as % of IRT	7.6	90.9	94.9	74.3	98.8	92.4	76.5
Gross JV as % of TOI	0.9	16.3	29.3	43.9	6.3	9.4	17.7
Gross JV as % of TOD	0.1	0.4	1.1	1.2	0.2	0.2	0.5

Notes: IRT stands for support for investment-related transactions; The average column records the average for 1995–2000; TOD stands for total bilateral official disbursements.

good statistical properties and the sign expectations are met in most cases, as no significant coefficient had the wrong sign. Therefore, these are reliable estimates on the whole, and valid inferences can be made.

The empirical results in Table 3.6 suggest that economic prosperity and government expenditures in donor countries, on the whole, have positive impacts on the ODA-type of PSD aid instruments and that they steer allocations away from the OOF-type to the ODA-type. Also, they suggest that right-wing governments favour OOF-type equity acquisitions, though the negative impact of their preference on ODA-type acquisitions is not statistically significant.

Business partnership programmes
Under business partnership programmes, companies in the donor country are encouraged to be involved in partnership with firms in the recipient

Table 3.6 Determinants of selected variables – investment support variables

Dependent variables	Trend variable	Per capita income (log) (t−1)	Upturn in economic cycle (t−1)	Govt. expenditure/ GDP ratio (t−1)	Extent of govt. being right wing (t−1)	No of obs	Adjustments R²
ODA-type acquisition of equity in relation to:							
(1) GDP	0.00001 (2.1)	−0.0004 (−1.8)	0.0008 (2.7)	0.000003 (2.4)	−0.000002 (−1.0)	88	0.583
(2) Total ODA	0.0023 (2.1)	−0.1041 (−1.8)	0.1743 (2.4)	0.00068 (1.8)	−0.000093 (−0.1)	88	400
OOF-type joint venture acquisition of equity in relation to:							
(3) GDP	0.00003 (1.6)	−0.0015 (−1.7)	0.0005 (0.5)	−0.000018 (−4.0)	0.000008 (1.8)	70	0.670
(4) Total ODA	0.0078 (1.7)	−0.4386 (−1.8)	0.1559 (0.6)	−0.0050 (−4.4)	0.0027 (2.3)	70	0.636

Note: The dependent variables are as indicated in the first column. See also Table 2 notes (a), (b) and (c).

country, thus sharing their experience. In addition to capital provision for firms in the recipient country, these partnerships enhance the transfer of technology, know-how and management skills and open access to foreign markets. The encouragement given by donors may be in the form of financial incentives (flows) including investment-risk guarantees or non-financial incentives like the exchange of information, advice, facilitation of pre-investment studies or visits, and so on.

Theoretical support for the donor partnership programmes can be found in the evolutionary and network theories of firms. A major conclusion in the evolutionary theory is that for a firm to upgrade its technology and innovate, it needs to have the in-house capabilities that come with education and training (Evenson and Westphal 1995). Another major observation, especially of network theories, is that cooperation among firms often facilitates the upgrading and renewal of their capabilities (Grabher 1993).[7] Thus, cooperation between a firm in the donor country and a firm in a developing country is expected to facilitate technology transfer as it provides the most conducive atmosphere for the development of internal capabilities of the firm needing assistance. In addition, it provides the recipient firm with access to foreign markets.

Donors that have funded partnership programmes include Norway through the Norwegian Enterprises Facility (NEF); Canada through the Canadian

Industrial Cooperation; the EU through its Centre for Development Industry as well as through the European Community Investment (Appendix Table A3.1 of this Chapter and Appendix 1 of Chapter 2 by Gibbon and Schulpen).

Though some progress is reported with respect to this instrument in general (Schulpen and Gibbon 2002), there are a number of problem areas. First, the design of the technology and business models being transferred are commonly reported not to match the needs of local circumstances (Sverrisson 2000: 24–9; Gibbon 2000: 61). Second, because there are no clearly defined objectives for many of the programmes, monitoring and evaluation are problematic (Schulpen and Gibbon 2002). Third, some donors have multiple aid agencies; therefore activities are not coordinated and there is no transparency in the selection of target firms and benefiting partners (Putzel 1998). Fourth, problems related to the lack of capacity on the part of the private companies implementing aid are reported in a number of cases (Schulpen and Gibbon 2002).[8] This is a major weakness in view of the fact that the capacity of the private intermediaries is generally identified as a key success factor (Schulpen and Gibbon 2002; Schulpen 2000).

Thus, it is necessary for the donors to adopt more innovative approaches to technology transfer to ensure that partnership programmes fit local conditions because, first of all, significant technological and knowledge gaps exist between the donor and recipient countries. The improvement and diffusion of existing engineering and technical capabilities in poor countries is bound to be a more effective approach than a wholesome importation of donor technology. Alternatively, donors, by redesigning their programmes to enhance south–south business partnerships rather than north–south partnerships (Sverrisson 2000: 24–9), could propagate the technology of the relatively more advanced developing countries to the poorer or less advanced ones, the advantage being that the corresponding technology and knowledge gaps would be minimal.

Second, local universities and technology institutes could be used to adapt donor technology and knowledge to local conditions and diffusing these in the recipient countries to bridge the gaps between the donor and recipient countries for better results (Sverrisson 2000: 27). Third, donors could, through the use of appropriate incentives, promote industry-based vocational training using the large foreign-technology-based companies in the recipient country (Sverrisson 2000: 28).[9]

It is worth noting that the effectiveness of PSD aid within this category is enhanced when efforts are made, as is done by some donors, to provide potential investors with some investment risk insurance coverage. Other than this, a specialized guarantee arrangement, modelled after the Multilateral Investment Guarantee Agency (MIGA) could better serve the purpose. Under this arrangement, donor governments contribute to a specialized multilateral institution whose only agenda is to insure investment risks with respect to suitable foreign private-sector investments in eligible poor countries.

Overall, existing studies suggest that partnership programmes are popular with donors and participating firms alike; drawing from Denmark's experience, official flows through this channel could be as much as three to four times of those associated with investment support programmes (Danida 1995) and about 12 per cent of total official flows pass through this instrument. There is every reason to believe that this instrument has recorded significant gains in poverty alleviation in places where it has been directed at small-scale enterprises; again the Danish experience clearly illustrates this fact (Danida 1995). However, in the final analysis, the most conclusive evidence of the effectiveness of this instrument is determining whether it eventually has a catalytic effect on direct foreign capital flows to the LDCs, the issue investigated in the subsequent section. But notwithstanding the outcome of such an investigation, available evidence suggests that traditional approaches, with the same objectives, may not have been as effective as this instrument.

Mixed credit programmes
Some other donor instruments, which are primarily designed to promote donors' interests, also promote PSD in the LDCs. These are the mixed credit programmes. Examples of these are the credits and subsidies directed at promoting donors' own exports, although they can be considered as aid to importers in the recipient countries and classified under the enabling international environment support programmes[10] (promoting international linkage). But as these instruments raise unique issues on their own, they are treated as a distinct category.

As reported in Jimoh (2002, Table 7), between 1970–2000, official export-related credits (i.e. a component of the OOF category) constituted about 15.8 per cent of total bilateral official flows for the same period, with a noticeable downward trend. Also, Jimoh postulated and empirically tested for certain explanatory factors for the observed temporal and cross-country variations in the volumes of official export-related credit flows to developing countries. Specifically, it is posited that during periods of prosperity in the donor country (rising per capita income level and an economic upturn), the incentive for donors to stimulate their own exports through government policy is reduced. Thus, a negative relationship is expected between export-related PSD aid and donor per capita incomes or/and an upturn in economic cycle. Also, in periods when (and in countries where) the ratio of government expenditures to GDP is high, a decrease in export-related PSD aid is expected, because an expansionary fiscal stance is expected to tilt aid allocations away from OOF to ODA. Also, when right-wing governments, which generally are known to oppose subsidies (or government interventions in general), are in power, export-related aid, especially in the form of subsidies to domestic exporters, is expected to decrease. These postulated effects are found to be supported by the estimates of panel regression equations reported there.

The catalytic effects of official PSD financial flows
A central objective of official direct financial support for PSD is to leverage foreign private flows so that the total (i.e. combined official and private) foreign flows for PSD could be a multiple of the initial official support. We investigate in this section whether official financial flows supporting PSD encourage private capital flows or they are led by private flows. In factual terms, there are four possible outcomes. First, official financing stimulates private capital flows so that these together produce greater effect, the so-called 'additionality' phenomenon. Second, official financing crowds-out or displaces private capital flows, causing private financing to flee as official financing flows in. Third, the two types of financing are independent, so that one does not affect the other. Fourth, private capital flows lead official flows so that they add up, but in this case (as with the first case) the 'additionality' phenomenon is present, but with a reversed lead-lag structure. Of these possible outcomes, the first is the most conducive to PSD. This being the case, it needs to be known which of these phenomena is applicable so that appropriate development financing programmes can be reformulated.

With this objective in mind, we undertook some empirical tests by estimating some panel regression equations based on annual data for the 'donor' countries over the 1970–2000 period. What we seek to identify is whether donors' direct financial support for PSD leads foreign private flows for the PSD; it is official support that passively follows the private flows; both follow each other to some extent; or both are independent of each other. We therefore resort to a variant of Granger's (1969) causality test that is suited to identifying this form of lead-lag relationship (as also discussed in Chapter 4 by Mavrotas). Details of the specified models, including the explanatory and the dependent variables as well as the estimates, are given in Tables 3.7 and 3.8.[11]

The explanatory variables include all those reported earlier in Tables 3.2 and 3.6 as well as the economy's degree of openness index, direct foreign investment (FDI) relative to GDP (present and lagged values); as well as current and lagged values of the dependent variables (other than FDI–GDP ratio). As in Table 3.6, a priori, it is expected that the coefficients of prosperity variables (rising per capita income level and an upturn in the economic cycle) and size of donor government (share of government expenditure in GDP) would be positive. On the other hand, the coefficient of donor government's ideological inclination (extent of being right-wing) will be negative. Further, as the economy becomes more open, FDI as well as donors' direct support for PSD should be facilitated. The statistical significance of the coefficients of FDI, ODA-equity acquisitions and their lagged values as well as OOF-equity acquisitions and their lagged values, in these catalytic effect models would determine which one (if any) leads the other.

Based on the statistical properties of the estimated equations and taking note of the fact that panel data (like cross-sectional data) are often associated with low R^2, we believe the estimated models have good statistical properties and that the sign expectations are virtually met. Thus, these are reliable estimates and valid inferences can be made. Estimates in Tables 3.7 and 3.8 suggest that foreign official flows do not lead and, hence, have no catalytic effects on private capital flows. Neither do the private capital flows lead and, hence, have any effect on foreign official support for PSD because none of the relevant coefficients are statistically significant. The two types of flows are independent of each other.

Because the long-run objective of the donors is to ensure that private finance flows are leveraged by official support for the PSD, the absence of any significant catalytic effects that are associated with official PSD finance flows is worrisome. This suggests that it is necessary for donors to introduce measures that would further enhance catalysis and additionality in their financial supports. A measure that readily comes to mind is the redirection of donor efforts to sectors with low patronage by foreign private investors such as microenterprises so as to reduce the potential crowding-out effects of official flows. This, combined with deliberate measures that would give greater returns or/and ensure some improved scheme for guarantee against risk within donors' current co-financing and loan syndication arrangements, could enhance catalysis and additionality in their financial supports.

Official and private investment flows – regional and income-based spread
Though official investment flows, based on our empirical analysis above, do not appear to lead private investments, it is possible that official and private flows may have some common features in terms of their distribution across world regions or/and income grouping of recipient countries. This may suggest the existence of some sort of modest catalytic or additionality effects that might mitigate the evidence of lack of additionality reported above. This would be the situation, for instance, if the focus of official donors is the poorest of the poor and private investors also follow by directing their funds to these target countries. The same arguments apply to regional distribution of PSD financial flows.

In this section, we examine the relevant data to see if there is any similarity in the regional spread of official (bilateral/multilateral) and private investment flows, as well as in their distribution across income-based groups of the LDCs. Table 3.9, presenting the volume and percentage distribution of development finance according to the income categories of the recipient countries, shows that the focus of bilateral official investors is on the low- to middle-income countries. About 39 per cent and 25 per cent of total bilateral official investments go to 'other low-income' and 'low-income' categories of poor countries, respectively. However, the IFC (representing multilateral official investors) and private investors behave alike, focusing on the 'upper middle-income' group with about 42 per cent of IFC financing and about 32 per cent of private investments going to this income group.

Table 3.7 Testing for the catalytic effect of ODA-type acquisition of equity on direct foreign investment

Dependent variables	Trend	Per capita income (log) (t−1)	Upturn in economic cycle (t−1)	Government expenditure/ GDP ratio (t−1)	Openness of economy	FDI/GDP ratio in: period t	ODA AQU period t−1	period t−1	No. of obs.	Adj. R^2
ODA-type acquisition of equity in relation to:										
(1) GDP (ODA AQU)	0.00001 (1.6)	−0.00027 (−1.4)	0.00050 (2.0)	0.000001 (1.2)	NA	0.00274 (1.5)	NA	NA	99	0.569
(2) GDP (ODA AQU)	0.00001 (1.6)	−0.00027 (−1.3)	0.00049 (1.9)	0.000001 (1.0)	NA	NA	0.0008 (0.6)	NA	99	0.560
FDI in relation to:										
(3) GDP	−0.0000 (−0.0)	0.0017 (0.2)	0.0003 (0.02)	NA	0.00003 (0.5)	NA	NA	8.109 (1.1)	97	0.453

Notes: The dependent variables are as indicated in the first column. See also Table 3.2 notes (a), (b) and (c);

Catalytic role of PSD type of aid means it should also bring into the recipient countries additional private capital as the involvement of the donor should signal to their investors that they are encouraged to invest in the host country. If it is effective in accomplishing this, we expect either current or especially past value of ODA AQU to have a positive causal effect on the current value of FDI (in the 3rd equation above). But if, instead, it is the current or especially the past value of FDI that has a positive effect on ODA AQU in the first or especially second equation above, it means the ODA AQU simply follows the initiative of private investors rather than lead or signal to them.

Table 3.8 Testing for the catalytic effect of OOF-type acquisition of equity on direct foreign investment

Dependent variables	Trend	Per capita income (log) (t−1)	Upturn in economic cycle (t−1)	Government expenditure/ GDP ratio (t−1)	Openness of economy	FDI/GDP ratio in: ODA AQU			No. of obs.	Adj. R^2
						period t	period t−1	period t−1		
OOF-type joint venture acquisition of equity in relation to:										
(1) GDP (ODA AQU)	0.00002 (2.1)	−0.0013 (−2.2)	0.00029 (0.4)	−0.00002 (−3.2)	NA	0.00427 (0.4)	NA	NA	88	0.763
(2) GDP (ODA AQU)	0.00003 (2.5)	−0.00015 (−2.5)	0.00035 (0.5)	−0.00002 (−3.4)	NA	NA	−0.00105 (−0.2)	NA	86	0.765
FDI in relation to:										
(3) GDP	0.0001 (0.5)	−0.0051 (−0.5)	0.0121 (1.1)	NA	0.00012 (1.5)	NA	NA	−0.2564 (−0.2)	85	0.362

Notes: As given in Table 3.7.

Table 3.9   Distribution of official and private finance according to recipient income categories, totals for the 1995–2000 period

	Equity investment (bilateral)			IFC financing (multi-lateral)	FDI (bila-teral)	Total private (bila-teral)
	ODA	OOF	Total			
Value (in US$ billions)						
Developing countries, total	0.66	−0.01	0.64	3.38	433.87	662.00
Upper-middle income countries, total	0.02	−0.14	−0.13	1.57	194.62	308.27
High-income countries, total	0.00	0.00	0.00	−0.02	1.12	5.43
Least developed countries, total	0.08	0.02	0.10	0.31	4.64	6.90
Other low-income countries, total	0.27	0.03	0.30	0.63	50.67	59.29
Low middle-income countries, total	0.12	0.07	0.19	0.72	58.71	83.65
Part II-countries, total	0.07	0.06	0.13	0.40	181.99	316.31
Developing and Part II-countries combined	0.73	0.04	0.77	3.77	615.87	978.30
Share (in %)						
Developing countries, total	90.2	−36.6	83.5	89.5	70.4	67.7
Upper-middle income countries, total	2.2	−348.2	−16.4	41.5	31.6	31.5
High-income countries, total	0.1	6.3	0.4	−0.5	0.2	0.6
Least developed countries, total	11.2	36.9	12.6	8.1	0.8	0.7
Other low-income countries, total	36.4	85.6	39.1	16.6	8.2	6.1
Low middle-income countries, total	17.0	172.1	25.3	19.1	9.5	8.6
Part II countries, total	9.8	136.6	16.5	10.5	29.6	32.3
Developing and Part II-countries combined	100.0	100.0	100.0	100.0	100.0	100.0

Source: DAC's International Development Statistics (online).

Similarly, Table 3.10 which provides the same data as Table 3.9, but broken down by regions of the recipient countries, shows that the focus of bilateral official financial flows is different from that of the IFC and private investors. While the majority of bilateral official investments (46 per cent) goes to Asia and is allocated almost evenly between the Far East and South/Central Asia, the focus of IFC and private investors is on Latin America. About 38 per cent of IFC financing, about 51 per cent of FDI and about 49 per cent of total private investments go to this region. These figures suggest that private investors, in terms of their regional and income grouping of poor countries, do not follow the directions set by bilateral official donors in channelling their PSD investments.

Table 3.10 The regional/geographical distribution of destinations of official and private finance, totals over the 1995–2000 period

	Equity investment (bilateral)			IFC financing (multi lateral)	FDI (bila-teral)	Total private (bila-teral)
	ODA	OOF	Total			
Value (in US$ billions)						
Developing and Part II-countries, total	0.73	0.04	0.77	3.77	615.87	978.30
Far East Asia, total	0.12	0.05	0.17	0.86	145.40	251.03
South and Central Asia, total	0.14	0.04	0.18	0.48	10.50	16.77
Europe, total	0.02	0.02	0.04	0.26	12.71	42.85
Africa, north of Sahara, total	0.01	−0.02	−0.01	−0.05	6.50	−0.62
Africa, south of Sahara, total	0.11	0.03	0.13	0.17	19.27	21.91
North America, total	0.12	−0.15	−0.03	1.45	314.00	474.65
Middle East, total	0.01	0.01	0.02	0.20	11.15	27.07
Oceania, total	−4.44	−0.62	−5.06	7.09	42.06	−591.42
Share (in %)						
Developing and Part II-countries, total	100.0	100.0	100.0	100.0	100.0	100.0
Far East Asia, total	15.9	131.4	22.0	22.7	23.6	25.7
South and Central Asia, total	19.4	106.8	24.0	12.6	1.7	1.7
Europe, total	2.7	38.3	4.6	6.9	2.1	4.4
Africa, north of Sahara, total	1.5	−40.3	−0.7	−1.2	1.1	−0.1
Africa, south of Sahara, total	14.9	63.4	17.4	4.6	3.1	2.2
North America, total	16.6	−373.6	−4.1	38.4	51.0	48.5
Middle East, total	1.5	14.3	2.1	5.3	1.8	2.8
Oceania, total	−3.8	−1.2	−3.0	0.8	0.03	−0.2

Notes: Part II countries are those in transition.

Source: DAC's International Development Statistics (online).

Private sector development, poverty alleviation and gender-based programmes

It is also worth noting that the current donor objectives with respect to poverty alleviation, minority-focused and gender-related programmes can be achieved simultaneously with PSD aid instruments. For instance, PSD aid directed at small-scale businesses, rural economic activities (including agriculture), and women-owned businesses, would at the same time achieve the multiple goals of poverty eradication, PSD, promotion of gender equality and empowerment of minority groups (Schulpen 2000: 96–8). A critical appraisal of this, in the context of donors' support of PSD relating to microfinance and microenterprises, is provided in Chapter 5 by Nissanke.

4   Summary and concluding remarks

The study has examined aid practices currently utilized by official bilateral donors, with a particular focus on their major instruments and channels for private sector development aid delivery. It was observed that the major donor instruments for PSD are investment support, enabling environment support, privatization and commercialization, and business partnership programmes. Major participants in the alternative channels are NGOs, governments of poor countries, firms in recipient countries and donors' own firms. After a review of the merits, demerits and effectiveness of these channels and instruments, the study concludes that there is still a pertinent role for poor country governments in the delivery of PSD aid, especially when the provision of public services (or social goods) is involved and free-rider problems major. Also, as a result of the decentralized nature of the private sector, the chapter acknowledges the need for the coordination of donor efforts. In PSD aid delivery, this would require either the involvement of recipient governments or/and the creation of a multilateral institution specializing in the task. With respect to instruments, the chapter identifies a number of factors that have limited the effectiveness of PSD aid. These include the gap between donor design and local conditions, and insufficient dialogue between donors and intended beneficiaries of aid. However, these limitations notwithstanding, the study finds evidence that suggests that these channels and instruments are effective and preferred by donors over the traditional approaches to aid delivery. Furthermore, the chapter finds that official investment-related aid flows are yet to have a perceptible catalytic effect on private direct foreign capital flows.

Based on these findings, the study recommends that donors consider new approaches to their investment and partnership programmes so as to encourage technology and knowledge transfer. These alternative approaches include (1) the upgrading and diffusion of existing engineering and technical capabilities in poor countries rather than a wholesome importation of donor technology; (2) propagating the technology of relatively more advanced poor countries to the more severely disadvantaged countries, which would require donors to favour south–south business partnerships rather than north–south partnerships (Sverrisson 2000: 24–9).

Similarly, the analysis suggests that, if donors were to give greater emphasis to promoting and enhancing inter-business linkages among businesses in the recipient countries, a significant dividend could be reaped from their enabling environment programmes.

Table A3.1 Instruments for investment and partnership support programmes of selected donors

Instruments	Instruments (specific)	Donors (programmes popular names)	Description
Part A – Instruments for investment support programmes			
Financial	Venture or risk capital	Canada (CPB), Germany (DEG), Norway (NORFUND), Denmark (IFU)	Providing equity capital directly to commercial projects
Financial	Loans	France, the USA, Belgium, the Netherlands (IBTA), Denmark (IFU), Canada (CPB), Sweden (Swedfund)	For recipient 'countries' enterprises often via support to local financial institutions
Financial	Grants	Australia, Belgium, Denmark, Germany, Japan, New Zealand, Portugal, Sweden and the Netherlands	Feasibility studies train, advice and visits
Financial	Guarantees	Germany, Finland, Fancy (ARIA), Sweden, Switzerland, United States and the Netherlands (RHI, Popm and IBO)	Insurance against mistral or trade risk which focuses on political risks
Non-financial	Information provision advice	Denmark, Canada and the Netherlands	Provision of information on market conditions, regulations, contact addresses, etc.
Part B – Instruments for partnership support programmes			
Financial	Loans	Canada (CRPSM and Egypt PSD), Denmark (PSD Program and IFU); the Netherlands (IBTA)	For a donor country's own private enterprises and for joint ownership with local firms
Financial	Grants	Canada (PSOP), Denmark (PSD Program, IFU), the Netherlands (PSOM), New Zealand (PIIDs and DAF), Sweden (Swedfund)	Feasibility studies training advice and visits
Financial	Guarantees	Canada (PSOP), Denmark (investment guarantee), the Netherlands (RHI, POPM and IBO)	Insurance against investment or trade risk, with focus on political risks
Non-financial	Provision of information, training and human development	Denmark, Canada, the Netherlands and Germany	Provision of information on market conditions, regulations, contact addresses and through training of staff of participating firms especially those of local partners

Table A3.2   PSD aid delivery channel-instrument mix

Channels from donor government to:	Invest-ment support	Partnership support	Mixed credit support	Enabling environment support	Commer-cialization and privatization
Government–recipient business, flow (i)		Y	Y	Y	Y
Government–local institutions–recipient business, flow (ii)				Y	Y
Donor business–recipient business, flow (iii)	X	X	X	Y	
Donor institutions–donor business–recipient business, flow (iv)	Z	X		Y	
Donor institutions–local institutions–recipient business, flow (v)	Z			Y	
Multilateral institutions, flow (vi)	Z	Z	Z	Z	Z

Notes:

X = most suitable for the indicated instruments;

Y = suitable for only some sub-sets of the indicated instruments for example, advocacy and training are subsets of enabling environment; assistance in form of provision of business intelligence, advisory services and business visits in partnership support; writing-off old but bad debts of banks being privatized;

Z = suitable for the indicated instruments;

If PSD assistance is defined to include indirect benefits to the recipient firms, then all 'Y' ratings for enabling environment support and for commercialization and privatization in channel (i) turn to 'X' rating.

Notes

1. The literature citations in this section and most of the other sections of this chapter have been abridged due to space consideration. More extensive citations relating to the same discussion are in Jimoh (2002).
2. The term non-governmental organization (NGO) includes, in a very broad sense, religious associations and even some educational institutions (provided that they are not government-owned), but in this chapter, the term does not apply to these groups. It is used here to include all non-religious private voluntary organizations (PVOs) supported by either voluntary private contributions or/and official contributions (external or local), membership-based PVOs, often called grassroots organizations, and non-profit-seeking non-governmental associations including non-profit business and trade associations.
3. In addition to their initial preoccupation with the delivery of emergency and relief aid, NGOs are also increasingly involved in policy advocacy and education, citizenship projects, poverty-reduction programmes, promotion of entrepreneurial

activities, and private sector development (Charlton and May 1995: 237; Grugel 2000: 89–90).

4. They are engaged in activities that support private sector development such as training to facilitate the establishment of an enabling private sector environment, promoting health and safety in the sector's workplaces, providing credits for small-scale enterprises, promoting foreign–local firm partnership in business, and so on.

5. If the executive arm of government is right wing, centre or left wing, a value of 1, 0 and −1 is awarded, respectively. The same is repeated if the legislature is dominated by the right wing, centre, and left wing party. This means that the value of this variable ranges between −2 (both executive and legislature are of left wing type) and 2 (both executive and legislature are of right wing type).

6. When the investments are at market terms, the only aid element is the forgone risk premium. However, when loans are given at below market rates, the aid element is more feasible.

7. Even though the focus of most network theories is on cooperation among firms in same country, the same rationale is applicable to cooperation among firms across national frontiers, especially in today's world of globalization.

8. Donors should, therefore, make greater efforts at ensuring that the donor companies selected as agents of technology transfer have adequate capacity for their envisaged role as agents of change. Available evidence suggests that the chances of success in technology transfers increase with the size of the donor country company serving as partner because size determines the capability to transfer technology (Danida 1995), and donors are thus advised to give some weight to this in the selection of change agents.

9. Such incentives could include a scheme to compensate trainer-firms for the competition that graduates are likely to pose in setting up similar businesses or being employed by competitors.

10. Because firms in the LDCs require considerable output from the industrialized countries as inputs, the shortage of these outputs usually impacts adversely on the business environment in developing countries. Production becomes disrupted as a result of shortage of inputs or the lack of foreign exchange. Thus, it can be argued that this type of aid promotes the recipient country's international linkages, promoting, as a consequence, an enabling environment. Therefore, it can be said that export-related aid that is primarily designed to promote donors' own exports impacts on the business environment of firms in the LDCs.

11. Though more appropriate statistics for estimating catalytic models are those for the destination countries as opposed to the source-country data utilized here, such data are difficult to come by. However, because source-country data are expected to be destination-country data order-preserving, it is expected that our estimates are still reliable.

References

Beck, T., G. Clarke, A. Groff, P. Keefer and P. Walsh (2000). 'New Tools and New Tests in Comparative Political Economy: The Database of Political Institutions'. Washington, DC: World Bank Economic Growth Research, Online. Available at: <u>www.worldbank. org/research/growth /political datal.htm.</u>

Charlton, R. and Roy May (1995). 'NGOs Politics, Projects and Probity: A Policy Implementation Perspective'. *Third World Quarterly*, 6 (2): 237–55.

Danida (1995). 'Review of the Danish PSD Programme'. Copenhagen: Ministry of Foreign Affairs.

Davis, P. R. and J. A. McGregor (2000). 'Civil Society, International Donors and Poverty in Bangladesh'. *Common Wealth and Comparative Politics*, 38 (1): 47–64.

Edwards, M. and M. Hulme (eds) (1992). *Making a Difference: NGOs and Development in a Changing World*. London: Earthscan.

Evenson, R. E. and L. E. Westphal (1995). 'Technological Change and Technology Strategy', in I. Behrman and T. N. Srinivasan (eds) *Handbook of Development Economics*, Vol 3a. Amsterdam: Elsevier.

Exeter, J. and S. Fries (1998). 'The Post-Communist Transition: Patterns and Prospects'. *Finance & Development*, 35 (3): 26–9.

Gibbon, P. (2000). 'Global Commodity Chains and Private Sector Development in Less Developed Countries', in T. Pietilä (ed.) *Promoting Private Sector Development*. Helsinki: Institute of Development Studies, University of Helsinki. Policy Papers I/2000.

Grabher, G. (ed.) (1993). *The Embedded Firm: on the Socioeconomics of Industrial Networks*. New York: Routledge.

Granger, C. W. J. (1969). 'Investigating Causal Relationships by Econometric Models and Cross-Spectral Methods'. *Econometrica*, 37: 424–38.

Grierson, J. (2000). 'Business Linkages in Zimbabwe: Interdependency, Growth and Benefit Dispersion', in T. Pietilä (ed.) *Promoting Private Sector Development*. Helsinki: Institute of Development Studies, University of Helsinki.

Grugel, J. (2000). 'Romancing Civil Society: European NGOs in Latin America'. *Journal of Interamerican Studies and World Affairs*, 42 (2): 87–107.

Hyden, G. (1997). 'Foreign Aid in Longer-term Perspective', in *Development Cooperation in the 21st Century*. Stockholm: Sida.

Ibe, A. C. (1990). 'The Structure of the Informal Credit Market in Nigeria: Lessons from Awka Town of Anambra State'. *African Review of Money Finance and Banking*, 1.

Ibe, A. C. (1992). 'Provision of Life Insurance Services in the Informal Sector: The Case of Igbo Clubs in Ilorin, Nigeria'. *African Review of Money Finance and Banking*, 2: 185–93.

Jimoh, A. (2002). 'Bilateral Official Finance for Private Sector Development and the Role of Non-government Organizations'. WIDER Discussion Paper No. 2002/117. Helsinki: UNU/WIDER.

Kragh, M. V., J. B. Mortensen, H. Schaumburg-Müller and H. P. Slente (2000). 'Foreign Aid and Private Sector Development', in Finn Tarp (ed.) *Foreign Aid and Development: Lessons Learnt and Directions for the Future*. London and New York: Routledge.

Larsson, K. A. (1994). *Structural Adjustment, Aid and Development*. Stockholm: Sida.

Meyer, C. A. (1992). 'A Step Back as Donors Shift Institution Building from the Public to the "Private" Sector'. *World Development*, 20 (8): 1115–26.

OECD (1995). *Private Sector Development: A Guide to Donor Support*. Paris: OECD.

Pedersen, P. O. (2000). 'Business Services in the Globalizing African Economies', in T. Pietilä (ed.) *Promoting Private Sector Development*. Helsinki: Institute of Development Studies, University of Helsinki.

Phelan, B. E. (1995). 'Japanese ODA and Private Sector Development in the Philippines and Thailand, A Comparative Analysis'. *Philippine Review of Economics and Business*, 32 (1): 18–49.

Pietilä, T. (2000). 'Introduction', in T. Pietilä (ed.) *Promoting Private Sector Development*. Helsinki: Institute of Development Studies, University of Helsinki.

Porter, M. E. (1990). *The Competitive Advantages of Nations*. New York: Macmillan.

Putzel, J. (1998). 'The Business of Aid; Transparency and Accountability in European Union's Development Assistance'. *Journal of Development Studies*, 34 (3): 71–96.

Riddell, R. C. (1999). 'The End of Foreign Aid to Africa? Concerns about Donor Policies'. *African Affairs*, 98: 309–35.

Schulpen, L. (2000). 'Private Sector Development and Poverty Reduction: An In-built Incoherence', in T. Pietilä (ed.) *Promoting Private Sector Development*. Helsinki: Institute of Development Studies, University of Helsinki.

Schulpen, L. and P. Gibbon (2002). 'The Private Sector Development: Policies, Practices And Problems'. *World Development*, 30 (1): 1–15.

Smillie, I. (1997). 'NGOs and Development Assistance: A Change in Mind-Set?'. *Third World Quarterly*, 18 (3): 563–77.

Stewart, S. (1997). 'Happy Ever After in the Market Place: Non-government Organizations and Uncivil Society'. *Review of African Political Economy*, 71: 11–34.

Sverrisson, A. (2000). 'Technological Development in Networked SME Clusters', in T. Pietilä (ed.) *Promoting Private Sector Development*. Helsinki: Institute of Development Studies, University of Helsinki.

Van de Walle, N. (1989). 'Privatization in Developing Countries: A Review of the Issues'. *World Development*, 17 (5): 601–15.

Van de Walle, N. (1999). 'Aid Crisis of Legitimacy: Current Proposals and Future Prospects'. *African Affairs*, 98: 377–52.

4

Multilateral Development Banks and Private Sector Financing: The Case of IFC

*George Mavrotas**

1 Introduction

Recent years have witnessed important changes in the area of development finance, both internal and external. Regarding external development finance in particular, the volume of net official flows has been decreasing and the net private flows have been not only very volatile but also geographically concentrated in favour of just a few countries. External official support for private sector development (PSD) in these countries is a way of rectifying this situation and, arguably, this is better implemented within a multilateral framework than if donor countries do so individually. This realization has thus prompted a resurgence of specialized affiliates, units or windows of the existing global and regional multilateral development banks that provide direct support for PSD in these countries. Some multilateral development banks, particularly the European Bank for Reconstruction and Development (which exists solely for providing support for PSD in the transition economies), have also been established. There is a clear need to shed light on how these multilateral institutions have been performing, how they allocate their portfolio, how they accomplish their missions, and so on. This can be done by looking at a prototype or representative one, as a case study, although a substantial degree of variation may be expected among different multinational development banks (MDBs).

Against this background the present chapter examines the role of the MDBs in private sector financing with a particular focus on the International Finance Corporation (IFC), the private sector arm of the World Bank Group, which was established in 1956 to provide equity and loan finance to the private sector. The IFC is examined as a case study because it is not only the oldest but also the largest and most evolved of the specialized affiliates of multilateral development banks that provide direct support for the PSD. This

"

has positioned it as a sort of role model for others, especially its equivalent affiliates in the various regional multilateral development banks.

It is notable that hitherto a discussion of the activities and portfolios of these multilateral development banks in private sector financing has been mainly confined to their respective annual reports. Few or no concerted efforts (outside the banks' annual reports) have been reported in the literature on this issue, despite the growing need for it to be critically analysed. The aim of the present chapter is to bring to focus, in an analytical manner, the past activities and operations as well as problems and prospects of the IFC. In addition, IFC's portfolio, sectoral and regional allocation of its lending and equity finance, and other activities will be highlighted (see Section 2). Simple econometric analysis will also be undertaken to test a number of hypotheses regarding IFC finance such as whether IFC's financing is additional or substitute to private capital flows as well as the relationship between IFC finance and growth in IFC finance–recipient countries and regions (see Section 3). Finally, areas which need reforms will also be discussed.

2   IFC finance: trends, features and key issues

Origins, objectives and IFC's role in private sector financing

IFC was founded in 1956 to act as the private arm of the World Bank with a main aim of promoting development through catalysing private sector investment in developing countries. It is owned by 175 member-countries and shares commercial risks with sponsors and other financial partners when they are not yet prepared to invest independently. IFC invests in private enterprises that benefit the economy, promote a sound environment and social well-being, and are examples of good business for other entrepreneurs. IFC is also trying to mitigate country risk and advises governments independently as well as private sector companies in the context of a transaction (IFC 2002a).

According to IFC

> the IFC, a part of the World Bank Group, fosters sustainable economic growth in the developing world by financing privates sector investment, mobilizing capital in the international financial markets, and providing technical assistance and advice to governments and businesses. (IFC 2002a)

Furthermore, '...IFC's mission is to promote sustainable private sector investment in developing countries, helping to reduce poverty and improve people's lives' (IFC 2001a).

IFC acts as both a commercial and a public entity. IFC argues that it invests principally on a commercial basis, but as a public entity does so where market failures exist, in order to complement and catalyse funding from private financial markets. IFC also acts in part on a non-commercial basis, where its shareholders believe its experience and expertise make it the most appropriate institution for supporting the delivery of certain public goods.

According to IFC, the Corporation's recent role as the private sector arm of the World Bank Group is characterized by (IFC 2002b):

– A *primary focus on frontier markets*. This means a focus on countries where there is little or no foreign capital flow, especially debt capital, or areas and sectors within a country where there is very limited capital availability. IFC argues that it tries to act as a catalyst to help companies implement investment plans and to provide the risk mitigation that enables investors to proceed with plans they otherwise would not implement, given perceived risks. At the same time, the relative scarcity of good investment opportunities in many frontier markets requires IFC to complement its investment work with extensive technical assistance, and to transfer know-how and best practices from more developed areas. IFC also supports governments' efforts to develop small and medium enterprises (SMEs), improve the investment climate, and undertake privatization.

– A *counter-cyclical role in non-frontier markets*, when their access to alternative sources of financing dries up. Capital flows to emerging markets are expected to remain depressed and volatile for the foreseeable future. Private sector companies in many countries, even those with good access to financing in the mid-1990s, may have only very limited or sporadic access to private financing over the medium term. In view of the above, IFC can play an important counter-cyclical role in those countries. Such a role will be particularly important in countries – many of them middle-income – which depend on cross-border flows to finance their investment needs.

– *Provision of support to international companies increasingly reluctant to invest in developing countries* (e.g. infrastructure).

– *Increasing emphasis on high-impact sectors*. IFC currently seeks to emphasize sectors that contribute disproportionately to development, where 'spill-over' effects in addition to the economically productive use of capital are significant. These have included domestic financial markets, infrastructure, information and communications technology (ICT), and social sectors.

– *An increasingly important role in providing know-how to domestic companies in developing countries*. This is done for a full range of technical knowledge (e.g. on financial issues, accountancy, marketing and technology), and to both domestic and international companies in areas related to sustainable development (corporate governance, environmental management and local community development). International companies also seek IFC's know-how and experience in frontier markets. IFC's know-how services are often 'bundled' with its investments, where they can be an important part of strengthening a project's long-term viability.

IFC's portfolio

Recent years have witnessed an expansion of IFC's portfolio and activities (see Table 4.1). Three hundred and four projects in total were approved in

Table 4.1   IFC operations and resources, 1997–2001 (millions of US$)

Operations	FY 1997	FY 1998	FY 1999	FY 2000	FY 2001
Investment commitments					
Number of projects[a]	—	—	228	210	205
Total commitments signed[b]	5558	5138	3688	3909	3931
For IFC's own account[b]	2402	2699	2890	2379	2732
Held for others	3156	2439	798	1530	1199
Investment approvals					
Number of projects	276	304	255	259	240
Total financing approved[c]	6722	5905	5280	5846	5357
For IFC's own account[c]	3317	3412	3505	3505	3742
Held for others	3405	2493	1775	2341	1615
Total project costs	17945	15726	15578	21136	16427
Investment disbursements					
Total financing disbursed	5110	4291	3296	3307	2370
For IFC's own account	2003	2054	2102	2210	1535
Held for others	3107	2237	1194	1097	835
Committed portfolio[d]					
Number of firms	1046	1138	1280	1333	1378
Total committed portfolio[b]	18992	20608	21685	22168	21851
For IFC's own account[b]	10512	11448	13364	13962	14321
Held for others	8471	9160	8321	8206	7530
RESOURCES AND INCOME (millions of US$)					
Capitalization					
Borrowings	10123	11162	12429	14919	15457
Paid-in capital	2229	2337	2350	2358	2360
Retained earnings	2503	2749	2998	3378	3723
Operating income	432	212	249	380	241
Net income	432	246	249	380	345

Notes: Certain prior period amounts have been reclassified to conform to current period presentation;

[a] Includes first commitment to projects in the fiscal year. Projects involving financing to more than one company are counted as one commitment. Figures maintained for commitments prior to FY99 do not compare;

[b] Includes loan guarantees and risk management products for FY 1999–2001;

[c] Includes loan guarantees and risk management products for FY 1997–2001;

[d] Total committed portfolio and held for others include securitized loans.

Source: IFC (2001a).

the 1998 fiscal year. Since then, mainly due to the impact of the Asian financial crisis, the number of approved projects declined to 240 projects in the fiscal year 2001. Compared to previous years, total financing over the period 1997–2001 increased substantially to reach almost US$7 billion in 1997, and then to follow a declining trend during the period 1998–2001. Total committed portfolio reached almost US$22 billion in 2001 and the number of firms involved in IFC's financing activities was 1378 the same year.

Sectoral allocation of IFC projects and activities

IFC's projects range across many sectors: financial services, infrastructure (including communications technologies, power, water and sewerage, and transportation), oil, gas and mining, food and agribusiness, social services (including private health care and education), chemicals and petrochemicals, and hotels and tourism.[1]

The financial sector attracted about 40 per cent of IFC commitments on average during the period 1999–2001 followed by infrastructure (13 per cent on average), transport and other infrastructure (7.5 per cent), power sector (6 per cent), information communication technologies (5.5 per cent) and social sectors (2 per cent). The above priority sectors attracted almost 70 per cent of IFC's commitments in the fiscal year 2001 (see Table 4.2).

Recent years have also witnessed a growing emphasis on behalf of IFC on SMEs and SME-related projects. Indeed, as Table 4.2 seems to suggest, IFC investment commitments associated with SME-related projects increased significantly during the period 1999–2001 from US$1.5 billion in 1999 to

Table 4.2   IFC investment commitments by sector

	Fiscal year 1999		Fiscal year 2000		Fiscal year 2001	
	US$ million	%	US$ million	%	US$ million	%
Financial sector	1 170	40.5	747	31.5	1 154	42.6
Infrastructure (excluding ICT)	244	8.5	471	19.8	334	12.3
Power sector	82	2.9	237	9.9	141	5.2
Transport and other infrastructure	162	5.6	234	9.9	193	7.1
Information communication technologies	51	1.8	88	3.7	294	10.8
Social sectors	37	1.3	24	1.0	106	3.9
Total priority sectors	1 502	52.0	1 330	56.0	1 888	69.6
SME-related projects	370	12.8	349	14.7	521	19.2

Source: IFC (2002b).

almost US$2 billion in 2001 with the share of the relevant sector increasing to almost 20 per cent in 2001 compared to 13 per cent in 1999.[2]

Regional allocation of IFC lending

Turning to the regional allocation of IFC investment commitments, both the Latin America and the Caribbean and the Middle East and North Africa regions attracted half of IFC's commitments in 2001 (26 per cent and 25 per cent, respectively) followed by the Asia and the Pacific region (20 per cent), Sub-Saharan Africa (16 per cent) and Europe and Central Asia (13 per cent) (see Table 4.3).[3]

In the case of the Sub-Saharan Africa region, IFC's focus in 2000–01 was mostly on the financial sector, infrastructure projects, SMEs and tourism businesses with a total committed portfolio above US$1.8 billion in 2001 as compared to US$1.5 billion in the previous year.

Asia and the Pacific attracted more than US$6.5 billion in 2000–01, with most of the IFC commitments directed to the financial sector and SMEs (sectors particularly affected by the recent financial crisis in the region). A number of projects were approved in the above sectors for China, Indonesia, the Philippines, Thailand and South Korea among others. At the same time, IFC's commitments in South Asia increased substantially in 2001 with a particular emphasis on new products to new clients in new sectors.

In Europe and Central Asia, IFC's committed portfolio exceeded US$3.6 billion in 2000 to decline slightly to US$3.3 billion in 2001. Growing emphasis was given to sectors and countries in the region with the most acute need to advance the pace of private sector development.

Turning to the Latin America region – the main recipient of IFC's investment commitments in recent years – IFC's portfolio ranged between US$8.5 billion and US$9 billion in the 2000–01 period. Priority was given to those businesses where private sector participation can provide a visible impact on living standards such as housing finance, health, education and infrastructure.

Table 4.3   IFC commitments by region ($ millions)

Regions	$ millions	%
Sub-Saharan Africa	642	16
Asia and the Pacific	784	20
Europe and Central Asia	510	13
Latin America and the Caribbean	1017	26
Middle East and North Africa	956	25
Global	22	
Total	3931	

Source: IFC (2001a).

Finally, in the case of the Middle East and North Africa region (the other major recipient of IFC's financing in recent years), IFC invested mainly in infrastructure (Egypt, Morocco), small information technology companies (Egypt), large capital market investments (Syria) as well as institution-building investments in the financial sector (Algeria). IFC committed almost US$1 billion in 18 investments in the 2001 fiscal year. It is notable that, for IFC, this was a record level of loan syndications for the region, partly due to the commitment of a number of sizeable infrastructure investments. The total committed portfolio reached US$1.6 billion in 2001.

Discussion of IFC's products and services

IFC has a variety of products and services. They include the following:

- *Equity and quasi-equity*: IFC buys shares in project companies, other project entities, financial institutions, and portfolio or private equity funds. It generally subscribes to between 5 and 20 per cent of a project's equity. It will not normally hold more than a 35 per cent stake and is never the single largest shareholder in a project. Through quasi-equity instruments, IFC invests in products that have both debt and equity characteristics.
- *Loan and intermediary services*: IFC finances projects and companies through A-loans, which are for IFC's own account. IFC does not accept government guarantees. Maturities of A-loans generally range between 7 and 12 years at origination, but some loans have been extended to as long as 20 years. Finally, IFC makes loans to intermediary banks, leasing companies, and other financial institutions through credit lines that result in further on-lending. These credit lines are often targeted at small businesses.
- *Syndicated loans, or B-loans*: IFC broadens its impact by mobilizing loans from other financial institutions that are willing to lend to projects only with IFC's participation. Along these lines, syndicated loans, or B-*loans*, are an important part of IFC's finance products. Through this mechanism, financial institutions share fully in the commercial credit risk of projects while IFC remains the lender on record.
- *Guarantees and risk management*: Loan and bond guarantees and standby financing allow IFC's clients to use IFC's credit to help them secure financing from international capital markets. IFC offers credit enhancement structures for debt instruments. IFC's risk management services enable clients to access derivatives markets through IFC as an intermediary.
- *Advisory services*: IFC's advisory services are designed to improve the investment climate in member countries and the business practices of companies in which IFC invests. They play an increasingly important role in the way IFC approaches its investment activities. IFC undertakes a wide array of financial market advisory assignments, specializing in securities markets and banking and credit institutions. Another newly

created and jointly managed unit, the Small and Medium Enterprise Department, focuses on business environment issues, capacity building, and the development of innovative financing techniques.

- *Technical assistance*: Technical assistance further complements IFC's investment activities by providing advice and training to governments and private companies. Cumulative contributions to IFC-managed technical assistance programmes reached US$582 million in 2001, compared with a cumulative total of US$525 million at the end of 2000 (fiscal years). Seventy-one per cent of the above technical assistance programmes were supported by donor countries, about 20 per cent by the World Bank Group and 10 per cent by donor institutions (IFC 2001a).

Evaluating IFC's effectiveness

Recently IFC published the cumulative findings from four years of evaluating IFC's investments. It draws from evaluations of 176 randomly-selected IFC operations that were approved in 1991–94 and evaluated in 1996–99. The results of the evaluation process became available from the Annual Review of IFC's Evaluation Findings (2001). The main findings seem to suggest that

- IFC's operations have generated substantially greater benefits for others – customers, employees, suppliers and taxpayers – than they have for the owners and financiers of the projects;
- IFC's effectiveness – how well IFC does its job throughout the project cycle – is strongly associated with positive outcomes. When IFC's effectiveness was consistently good, it achieved good development results in 91 per cent of cases, and good development *and* investment results in over two-thirds of cases.
- Among IFC's strategically important sectors, infrastructure projects yielded significantly better than average development results. Similarly, investments in targeted high-risk countries performed better developmentally. This finding, according to IFC, may not hold for the future, as fewer countries currently are designated high-risk, and they may be more challenging environments in which to work.

Obviously, the above relatively satisfactory findings need to be assessed on the basis of the evaluation criteria that IFC is employing to evaluate its activities. In what follows we discuss the IFC's evaluation approach in detail as well as further findings related to specific performance indicators.

Each year IFC evaluates a random sample of investments that have reached early operating maturity (typically five years following approval by which time the projects have been established and built up a track record of operating performance). Within statistical limits the sample is representative of each year's entire approvals. First, self-evaluations of the investments in the sample are undertaken by IFC's investment department staff. They complete the research and analysis necessary to rate each investment on 11 indicators. Using corporate guidelines, they rate each indicator on a four-point scale: unsatisfactory, partly unsatisfactory, satisfactory, and excellent. Next, the Operations Evaluation Group (OEG) conducts independent research, verifies each rating to ensure that evaluation standards are applied consistently throughout IFC, then synthesizes its findings in each year's annual review. The *Annual Review 2000* is based on evaluations conducted during 1996–99 of investments approved during 1991–94. It also draws on findings from previous annual reviews as well as four years of OEG evaluation research.

Each of the 11 performance indicators used in IFC's evaluation process relates to one of three outcome ratings:

– *Development outcome*: a project's contribution to a country's economic development and improved living standards;
– *Investment outcome*: an investment's contribution to IFC's profitability; and
– *IFC's effectiveness*: how well IFC does its job throughout the project cycle. IFC's effectiveness is evaluated on the basis of achieving good development *and* investment outcomes that is, 'win–win' outcomes. 'Win–win' operations are the ones that simultaneously foster development and are sufficiently profitable relative to their risk to contribute to IFC's own sustainability for supporting development. Two-thirds of the evaluated operations had successful development outcomes. Development outcome ratings are a judgemental synthesis of six indicators.

The following findings are reported from IFC's Operations Evaluation Group, from highest- to lowest-rated indicator:

– *Living standards*: IFC's operations have generated substantially greater benefits for others – customers, employees, suppliers, and taxpayers – than they have for the projects' owners and financiers. This outcome is measured by the difference in projects' economic (social) and financial (private) rates of return. For 102 investments in which analysis was possible, OEG estimated that they generated net present values of approximately US$1.4–1.6 billion in direct net benefits in developing countries, US$0.9 billion more than that received by the owners and financiers.[4]
– *Private sector development*: Three-quarters of IFC's projects have contributed to the development of local private sectors through linkages supporting other private enterprises, demonstration effects, privatization, or regulatory changes.
– *Environmental impact*: Two-thirds of operations, including many whose profitability for their owners fell short, met IFC's high standards for environmental sustainability.[5]

- *Growth of the economy*: About two-thirds of evaluated projects yielded tangible benefits to the economy. For example, a project to modernize the production facilities of a beverage company allowed it to respond efficiently to an unforeseen increase in consumer demand and at the same time realize economies of scale, as labour productivity increased.
- *Project business success*: This indicator, reflecting whether a company earned an attractive profit on its investment, was the lowest-rated. When a project's financial returns are less than the cost of capital, the business success is rated less than *satisfactory*. This was the rating for about half of the projects.[6]
- *Company business success*: Notwithstanding the success or otherwise of their projects, a higher proportion of companies, particularly those that were established enterprises with proven expertise, remained clearly viable despite concerns.

Results versus IFC's strategic objectives and priorities

As already mentioned, IFC's strategy in recent years focuses on (i) high-risk or low-income countries and 'frontier' regions or sectors within countries; and (ii) targeted sectors (mainly financial markets and infrastructure). More precisely

- In targeted sectors, the evaluation results were mixed. Infrastructure projects performed better, but some credit lines to financial institutions lacked a clear IFC role or contribution to needed capacity-building.
- In low-income countries, there was no discernible difference in performance of IFC's operations other than on average poorer environmental impacts.
- Operations in countries that were regarded by institutional investors as high-risk at the time of approval (i.e. 1991–94) had a significantly higher proportion of 'win–win' outcomes than projects in other countries.[7]

Needless to say, the above evaluation results are not based on an independent external evaluation and, hence, the findings should be accepted with caution and the reservation that any other internal assessment deserves.

The profitability issue

A key issue for IFC seems to be related to the improvement of its profitability. It has been correctly argued that the impact of the global slowdown and the crisis in Argentina have put pressure on IFC's profitability and have highlighted the need to focus on improving the IFC's profitability as a top priority. In view of the above, IFC goes further by arguing that it is rather important to ensure that IFC's partners experience their investments as profitable opportunities, and that IFC continues to provide a positive signal to other investors that good business can be done in developing countries, in particular when their apprehension about investing in emerging markets has increased.

Two further arguments have been put forward by IFC recently on the profitability issue: first, *replicability*, that is, if the projects do not earn a return corresponding to what private investors can earn on other investments, IFC projects will not be replicated and nothing sustainable will have been created, and second, *crowding out*, that is, if IFC accepts, for otherwise viable projects, a lower return for itself, the IFC would be crowding out the private financial market and hinder its development (Lysy 2001).[8]

The OEG also stresses the importance of profitability for IFC on the basis that there is a close correlation between the business success of projects and their development outcomes, and better quality investments should translate into a stronger development impact for IFC. The OEG argues that improving profitability will require, in particular, continued efforts to work out problem investments, as well as to ensure that good quality new investments are booked by IFC, and that improvements in efficiency continue to be sought. In the same vein, it has been argued that if IFC is not profitable, its financial capacity could be eroded, and a negative signal would be sent about good business to be done in developing countries (IFC 2002b).[9] In view of the above arguments, the OEG's annual review has recently recommended that the current top priority for IFC is strengthening profitability.

3   Evaluating IFC finance: what the data really tell us

In this section we evaluate IFC's private finance by using data from a number of sources regarding its financial flows, GDP growth rates and per capita income in recipient countries. We use two types of empirical analysis. First, we use simple correlation analysis among a number of crucial variables, namely IFC finance and other private capital flows, as well as IFC finance and GDP per capita in recipient countries. The purpose of this simple, albeit important, statistical analysis is to test IFC's own conclusions and statements regarding the features as well as impact of IFC finance on its recipients (see Section 2). Second, since correlation analysis is indicative only of the degree of correlation among the variables in question, we also conduct Granger-causality type tests within a panel of 59 recipients of IFC financial flows for which data are available over the period 1980–2000 (and also replicate the same for corresponding regional aggregate of statistics), to explore the direction of causation between the economic relationships under investigation.

A focus on frontier markets?

The first claim of IFC we tried to test relates to whether it actually focuses on frontier markets (see Section 2). More precisely, according to IFC, a primary focus on frontier markets means a focus on countries where there is little or no foreign capital flow. We tried to investigate the above assertion by testing whether there exists a negative correlation between the access of a country or a region to capital flows (measured as total net FDI financial flow in relation to GDP) and IFC's own net investment in that country or region (IFC finance–GDP ratio). The data employed cover the period 1980 to 2000.[10] Initially we started with 126 countries, but almost half of them were dropped from the statistical analysis due to lack of data. At the end, 59 countries representing all geographical regions (although with a different degree of representation) remained in the final sample.

Correlation statistics regarding the relationship between total net FDI share in GDP and the share of IFC finance in GDP are reported in the first column of Table 4.4. The results concerning this relationship are rather mixed. In 30 out of 59 countries in the sample, a negative correlation was found between the two variables, thus confirming a 'focus on frontier markets'. For the remaining 29 countries in the sample, however, a positive correlation seems to exist, thus not supporting the theory of a focus on markets with little or no capital. It is also notable that, with a few exceptions (Uganda, Turkey, Uruguay, Tunisia, Togo and Malaysia), in the majority of cases the degree of correlation is also very low.

Does the picture change if we focus on regions instead of countries? The bottom part of Table 4.4 reports correlation analysis results between the same variables but this time for each region. A focus on countries with little or no capital is confirmed only in the case of the East Asia and Pacific

Table 4.4 Correlation analysis results

Country	Correlation coefficients between	
	FDI capital flows & IFC finance	**GDP per capita & IFC finance**
1. China	−0.271	−0.081
2. Fiji	0.255	−0.079
3. Indonesia	−0.305	0.589
4. Malaysia	−0.468	−0.223
5. Philippines	−0.005	0.168
6. Thailand	−0.131	0.076
7. Cyprus	0.072	0.320
8. Hungary	−0.201	−0.418
9. Turkey	−0.579	0.733
10. Argentina	0.284	0.194
11. Barbados	0.113	0.074
12. Bolivia	0.302	−0.178
13. Brazil	−0.283	0.178
14. Chile	0.088	−0.363
15. Colombia	−0.032	−0.005
16. Costa Rica	−0.368	0.124
17. Dominican Republic	−0.154	0.120

Table 4.4   Continued

Country	Correlation coefficients between	
	FDI capital flows & IFC finance	GDP per capita & IFC finance
18. Ecuador	−0.040	−0.004
19. El Salvador	0.124	0.277
20. Guatemala	−0.008	−0.261
21. Honduras	−0.081	−0.068
22. Jamaica	−0.058	0.289
23. Mexico	0.063	0.323
24. Panama	0.139	0.398
25. Paraguay	−0.237	0.683
26. Peru	0.201	0.140
27. Uruguay	0.438	−0.216
28. Jordan	−0.261	−0.028
29. Morocco	0.368	−0.063
30. Tunisia	0.504	−0.202
31. Bangladesh	0.209	0.381
32. India	−0.291	0.039
33. Nepal	0.244	0.751
34. Pakistan	−0.113	0.185
35. Sri Lanka	−0.117	−0.168
36. Benin	0.359	0.798
37. Cameroon	−0.055	−0.256
38. Congo, Republic	−0.147	0.043
39. Côte d'Ivoire	−0.054	−0.230
40. Gabon	0.082	0.397
41. Ghana	0.451	−0.443
42. Kenya	−0.105	0.361
43. Madagascar	−0.400	0.052
44. Malawi	0.366	−0.037
45. Mali	−0.316	0.438
46. Mauritania	0.145	−0.465
47. Mauritius	0.089	−0.608
48. Mozambique	0.117	−0.005
49. Nigeria	−0.211	−0.026
50. Rwanda	0.374	−0.233
51. Senegal	0.231	0.410
52. Seychelles	0.157	0.305
53. Sierra Leone	−0.091	0.456
54. South Africa	−0.508	−0.837
55. Swaziland	−0.150	−0.030
56. Togo	0.529	−0.414
57. Uganda	−0.873	−0.086
58. Zambia	−0.016	0.226
59. Zimbabwe	−0.007	−0.180
Regions		
East Asia and Pacific	−0.242	0.444
Europe and Central Asia	0.162	0.395
Latin American and Caribbean	−0.165	0.354
Middle East and North Africa	0.314	−0.125
Sub-Saharan Africa	0.234	0.414
South Asia	0.181	0.496

region (though with only six countries being included in the final sample due to data problems) and Latin America (18 countries in the sample). For the remaining four regions (Sub-Saharan Africa, South Asia, Middle East and North Africa, and Europe and Central Asia) the emerging sign is positive, thus rejecting the hypothesis concerning a focus on frontier markets.[11]

IFC capital flows and other foreign private finance: complements or substitutes?

A very central question in the present chapter is whether IFC finance leads (and hence encourages or catalyses) other forms of foreign private finance or merely passively follows them.[12] To test the above relationship we again use data on IFC capital flows to countries/regions (the share of IFC finance in GDP) as well as data on other private capital flows (the share of FDI from other sources in GDP) over the 1980–2000 period for the same group of 59 countries for which data are available. We conduct Granger-causality tests within a panel (see Attanasio *et al.* 2000 as well as notes to Table 4.5, for further details), over the same period for our panel of 59 countries. Results are reported in Table 4.5, and the emerging conclusion is that other private finances in the form of FDI do Granger-cause IFC finance, but IFC finance does not cause other FDI flows. Thus, it is doubtful, on the basis of this empirical evidence, whether IFC finance catalyses private capital flows.

Table 4.5   Causality analysis results

	Current and lagged (first-differenced) FDI values in IFC finance equation	Current and lagged IFC finance in (first-differenced) FDI equation	Current and lagged values of economic growth in IFC finance equation	Current and lagged IFC finance in economic growth equation
Panel of 59 countries	−0.2958* (0.1326)	0.0022 (0.0032)	0.4088** (0.2124)	−0.0009 (0.0077)
Panel of 5 regions	0.1819* (0.5287)	−0.0014 (0.0081)	1.3948* (0.4134)	0.0065 (0.0052)
Latin American region	−0.3198 (0.2715)	0.0139 (0.0086)	0.8706 (0.5934)	−0.0098 (0.0132)
Sub-Saharan African region	−0.2521 (0.1594)	0.0037 (0.0069)	−0.0152 (0.0966)	0.0302* (0.0145)

Notes: Standard errors are the figures reported in parentheses: * = significant at 5% significance level; ** = significant at 10% level. Within this framework, IFC finance is deemed to have causal effect on the first-difference of FDI if (in column 1) the reported estimate is jointly significant. Also, FDI would be deemed to have causal effect on IFC if (in column 2), the estimate is significant statistically. IFC is said to cause economic growth if (in column 3) the coefficient is significant. Finally, economic growth would be driving IFC flows if (in column 4), the coefficient of economic growth is significant.

We also try to explore the direction of causation between the two variables within a panel of regions instead of countries. The results reported in Table 4.5 seem to suggest no causality between the two variables, namely IFC finance and FDI flows. In view of the disproportionate representation of countries in the five regions due to data problems, however, we conducted the same exercise for two regions, Latin America and Sub-Saharan Africa, for which a substantial number of countries are included in each region (18 and 24, respectively). Granger-causality test for Latin America (Table 4.5) seems to suggest that IFC finance leads other forms of foreign private finance, thereby indicating the presence of a catalytic effect of IFC finance. However, the above conclusion is region specific. Indeed, our Granger-causality test for the Sub-Saharan Africa region suggests that FDI flows do Granger-cause IFC finance and not vice versa, implying that IFC finance does not leverage (but merely passively follows) foreign private capital flows.[13]

IFC finance and growth: what causes what?

It would be of equal importance for us to know whether IFC finance leads economic growth or passively responds to economic growth. Initially, we conducted simple correlation analysis to shed some light on the correlation between IFC flows (the share of IFC finance in GDP) and GDP per capita for our panel of 59 countries.[14] The correlation statistics reported in column 2 of Table 4.4, suggest a positive and varying degree of correlation in 30 countries in the sample. For the other half of the countries in our sample (29), the emerging relationship, as expected, is negative with a varying degree of correlation. Correlation analysis by region was also undertaken and the results are reported in the bottom part of column 2 in Table 4.4. With the exception of the Middle East and North Africa region, there exists a clear positive correlation between the two variables in all regions with the degree of correlation ranging between 35 per cent (Latin America) and 49 per cent (South Asia). Thus, on the whole, there is no consistent positive or negative association between per capita income level and IFC finance–GDP ratio.

In view of the descriptive nature of the above type of analysis, however, Granger-causality tests were also carried out to explore further the IFC finance–growth relationship. In columns 3 and 4, first row of Table 4.5, we report the Granger-causality test results for our panel of 59 countries. The emerging conclusion is one-way causality, with the direction of causation running from GDP growth to IFC finance (IFC's finance share in GDP) and not vice versa. The above finding is also confirmed within the context of our panel of regions (see columns 3 and 4, second row of Table 4.5). Thus, the evidence suggests that IFC finance is influenced by the growth performance of the recipient countries while it has no perceptible effect on growth of the recipient economies.

Finally, in line with our previous methodology, we tested the above relationship for the Latin America and Sub-Saharan Africa regions which are better represented (18 and 24 countries, respectively) compared to the other geographical regions. Results related to the Latin American region (columns 3 and 4, third row of Table 4.5) seem to suggest lack of any causality between the two variables, however. In the case of Sub-Saharan Africa (columns 3 and 4, fourth row, Table 4.5), IFC finance does cause growth and not vice versa, thus suggesting that causality between the two variables might be region-specific. The finding for the Sub-Saharan Africa region is quite interesting though since it indicates a positive role for IFC finance in the region and a clear potential for a much more significant role in the future. However, the evidence based on regional statistics is not only mixed (with that for Africa differing from that of Latin America), it also negates the fairly robust evidence based on individual country statistics that is discussed in the previous paragraph. Thus, on the whole, there is no consistent evidence either way regarding the effect of IFC finance on the growth performance of recipient economies or the effect of economic growth on IFC finance. Further research is needed in reaching some definite conclusions on these.

4   Criticism, recommendations and the way ahead

Of particular relevance to the present chapter is the Meltzer Commission's recommendation regarding private sector financing from the MDBs, and in particular about the future of IFC. The Meltzer Report recommends that private sector involvement by the development institutions should be limited to the provision of technical assistance and the dissemination of best practice standards. Investment, guarantees and lending to the private sector should be halted. The Commission's view for IFC, in particular, is that the Corporation should be merged into the World Bank (the 'world development agency'), to more closely integrate its function into the Bank's activities. Its capital base would be returned to shareholders as existing portfolios are redeemed. The US share of the IFC's US$5.3 billion capital is US$1.3 billion (Meltzer Report 2000). Equivalent changes should be made at the regional agencies. The IFC should also become an integral part of the redefined 'world development agency'.[15]

Another critic, Alex Wilks of the Bretton Woods Project argues that

> … despite various strategy and policy restatements over the years the IFC still appears to operate without any clear methodology for estimating or evaluating development impacts. Moreover, the IFC has no mechanism in its project cycle to articulate the intended development impact of a given project. Without such a mechanism, the IFC is unable to factor development effectiveness into either project design or implementation. Thus, on the evidence available outside the institution it is hard to conclude that it has a clear approach to selecting projects that will maximize benefits for poor people and the environment. (Wilks 2000)

Some observers think that closer cooperation between IFC and the World Bank in drawing up country assistance strategies, designing sector strategies, and crafting the private sector development strategy may help the IFC to support sectors and initiatives that are most appropriate for the poorest. This is basically the argument behind the recommendation of the Meltzer Commission for IFC. Others fear that the Bank and IFC together will persuade governments to privatize strategic sectors, regardless of whether this is the best option for the poorest. There is also concern about conflicts of interest. Where the IFC has merged departments with those in the World Bank, the same group of people will be advising governments on privatization and regulation strategies as well as discussing private sector investment plans in the same sector (Wilks 2000).

On the basis of the detailed discussion of IFC's activities, portfolio, evaluation procedures and strategic priorities, as well as our econometric analysis in Section 3, our view is that the above criticism of IFC's investment activities is devoid of sound arguments for IFC's work. Furthermore, Meltzer Report conclusions about IFC are not based on an in-depth discussion of IFC activities.

The IFC has taken a number of efforts since 1998 to address many of the issues of particular importance for the institution. For example, sustainability has recently emerged as a key priority for IFC, and an increasingly important way in which IFC can support member countries' sustainable development efforts and add value to clients. Examples include concentrated efforts to ensure that large projects are no longer carried out on an 'enclave' model, but are closely 'linked' to the local economy: this, according to IFC, broadens the benefits of these investments, and at the same time reduces risks for investors. IFC further argues that its ability to help firms in the management of environmental, social and governance risks as well as responding to demands for IFC's expertise in local capacity building and extending benefits to local communities, increasingly differentiate the IFC from other lenders. Its expertise in these areas enables it to take on large, risky projects which others avoid (IFC 2002b).

Furthermore, on the basis of the evaluation findings regarding IFC investment activities (see Section 2), the OEG of IFC recommends that it should

- Enhance measurement of its performance against its mission by introducing a system that tracks the development of its portfolio and investment outcomes and IFC's operational effectiveness. As it relates to development outcome measures, this system's measures and IFC's evaluation methodology should be closely aligned;
- Pursue a corporate objective that focuses on achieving successful investment outcomes *and* development outcomes. To this end, strategies and strategy-linked budget allocations should consider investment and development result patterns by sector and country risk/income group;

- Expand training programmes for core investment and development skills in project screening, appraisal and structuring, and project supervision. Such training programmes should strengthen the rigour of economic analysis and the appraisal of sponsors, markets and competition. They also should increase the profitability of equity investments, for example through greater use of quasi-equity in financial structuring; and
- Extend credit lines to financial intermediaries in projects in which IFC's role is strong and it can contribute to needed capacity building that is identified at appraisal (IFC 2001b).

The World Bank (2002), in a recently published Private Sector Development Strategy document refers also to IFC. The report argues that IFC should operate under three basic principles: it should continue to avoid crowding out the private sector and to seek additionality in its projects. Furthermore, it is argued that IFC should need to earn at least the full risk-adjusted cost of capital on its portfolio of commercial operations; this would prevent the pursuit, according to the above report, of substandard projects.

On the basis of the discussion of IFC's activities as well as recent efforts undertaken by IFC (see Section 2), one might argue that the Meltzer Report is not entirely right in its recommendation for the merger of IFC with the World Bank: IFC's semi-independent status gives it flexibility, comparative advantage, and a distinct role regarding private sector financing which will be lost in the case of a merger with the World Bank.

Our empirical analysis in Section 3 suggests, however, that IFC's claim regarding 'a focus on frontier markets' is not fully supported by available data. Our correlation analysis suggests that this is the case in only half of the countries included in the sample. A focus on countries with little or no capital is confirmed, however, in the case of the East Asia and Pacific region and Latin America. Furthermore, in view of the Granger-causality tests employed in the previous section, there seems to be no clear evidence regarding IFC's role as a catalyst in the area of private sector financing. The results are again mixed and region-specific, thus leaving little room for generalization. Finally, a positive growth effect of IFC finance was found in the case of the Sub-Saharan region, which has not been confirmed, however, in the rest of the regions.

Nevertheless, even in view of the rather mixed results above, it would be fair to say that IFC has played an important role in the area of private sector financing in many developing countries and this should be continued in view of depressed capital flows, volatility of private finance, macroeconomic instability, and so on, in international capital markets.

It is also true that until very recently, IFC's primary focus has been on emerging markets. Therefore, critics of IFC may be partly right in the sense that by doing so, IFC seems to have neglected low-income countries. Furthermore, and in relation to the previous point, IFC's claim regarding an emphasis on high-impact sectors is debatable, at least for the poorest of developing countries. More precisely, it could be well argued that financial markets, infrastructure and ICT are not necessarily the most important impact sectors in economies bedevilled with famine, conflict, epidemics, and other misfortunes, as compared, say, to substantial improvements in agriculture (an area IFC rather seems to neglect). Having said this, however, it would be rather inappropriate to argue that currently IFC is moving towards the right direction (and balance) in view of its growing attention and focus on high impact sectors in both middle- and low-income countries. At the same time, it has been trying to assess performance by also looking at the development impact of its projects in developing countries.

In our view, a key problem of IFC seems to be the conflict of interest between two rather different objectives, that is, improving its profitability (absolutely reasonable objective for a semi-private bank like IFC) and at the same time strengthening its developmental impact (of crucial importance if IFC wants to be identified as a development bank with a mission 'to promote private sector investment in developing countries, which will reduce poverty and improve peoples' lives' [IFC 2001a]). Our own view is that IFC should give more focus to its developmental role, trying at the same time to operate with reasonable profits. There are a number of arguments, however, against the above recommendation, some of them already mentioned in Section 2. It has been argued, for example, that IFC invests on a parallel basis with other financiers, always taking a minority position, and generally only providing 20–30 per cent of the financing needed. The returns IFC earns are tied to the returns on the project with adjustment only for the nature of the risks for IFC's share in the investment package (i.e. equity vs. loan, senior loan vs. junior loan etc.). Furthermore, the returns that IFC's B-loan partners earn are quite explicitly tied to the returns IFC earns on its A-loans.[16]

Lysy (2001) has recently argued that IFC should concentrate on areas of demonstrated competitive advantage. It has been particularly argued that IFC's competitive advantage derives from its unique status as a global multilateral institution and the value of IFC's involvement in an investment stems from this. Therefore, IFC needs to build the skills that are important to the exploitation of the above competitive advantage and to seek projects where this competitive advantage is most important.

The discussion of IFC activities and investment projects in the present chapter as well as the empirical analysis of the previous section seem also to suggest that at present, the main recipients of IFC's investment are mostly middle-income countries and emerging markets. In view of that, IFC should try to re-direct its emphasis on low-income countries with weak prospects for private sector financing rather than to emerging and middle-income countries with better prospects and chances to attract private capital.

An important issue, though partly relevant to IFC's activities, is related to 'output-based aid', that is, a strategy for improving the delivery of services that depend at least in part on public financing (e.g. infrastructure projects). Output-based aid, in contrast to traditional approaches of channelling support to inputs consumed by public sector providers, delegates service delivery to third parties under contracts that tie payment to the outputs or results actually delivered (Brook and Smith 2001; see also World Bank 2002). IFC can play a significant role in this case in view of its good links with the private sector in developing countries.

Overall, our view is that IFC plays a rather significant role in development financing in many developing countries, although its role as a catalyst in private sector development needs to be re-examined in view of the mixed findings reported in the previous section. Moreover, there is growing evidence that the IFC is now moving to new directions and sectors and this change of orientation will soon reveal some positive effects on the poverty reduction front. In view of the above, we do not personally think that IFC should be merged with the World Bank as the Meltzer Commission suggests. IFC is different in many ways from other multilateral development banks, and we do not agree with the Meltzer Report that IFC should not retain its independence and flexibility. Having said this, there are, however, important challenges for IFC to meet. These include, inter alia

- Africa's share in IFC's investment commitments should be increased in view of the severe economic difficulties, weak financial systems and the rather poor prospects on the poverty reduction front. It is notable that in the fiscal year 2000, 80 per cent of IFC's approvals were in targeted sectors, and 40 per cent were in high-risk or low-income countries. However, our view is that IFC approvals in Africa and in low-income countries should be increased in line with the mission of IFC for poverty reduction.
- Until very recently, the share of IFC projects related to the social sector (education, health etc.) has been unacceptably low (about 2 per cent of the total). Although there is a clear indication from IFC's recent budget that the above share will increase in the near future, it is absolutely vital that future increases are sustainable and have the highest possible development impact.
- Related to the previous point, IFC also needs to define its strategic approach more clearly to promote poverty reduction and sustainable development. For a rather large group of low-income countries, emphasis on the financial sector and infrastructure (IFC's so-called 'high-impact sectors') is not necessarily what is needed at the moment. As pointed out earlier, financial markets, infrastructure and ICT are not necessarily the most important impact sectors in an economy bedevilled with famine, epidemics, and so on which, in the first instance, may have favoured measures to improve agriculture (an area IFC seems rather not to focus on at the moment).

– It also needs to reduce substantially its involvement in projects with rather ambiguous (or even minimum) development impact, such as hotel projects in middle-income countries and instead to re-direct its financing, expertise, efforts and products to projects with high development impact in low-income countries (particularly in the education and health sectors, microfinance, institutions, housing, etc.).
– As the discussion of the profitability issue seems to suggest, there is a clear need to improve IFC's performance evaluation criteria by placing more emphasis on the developmental impact of projects rather than on their profitability outcomes.
– Last, but not least, organizational changes – like absorbing the private sector development department and activities of the World Bank – may be necessary if the IFC is to perform its important role more efficiently. Needless to say, IFC's possible expansion also raises budget issues and adjustment of donors' policy towards that option.

In conclusion, a number of fruitful avenues of research could be opened regarding future work in this important, though neglected, area. Obviously, the empirical analysis that was carried out in the present study, though important, is at this stage indicative only of the trend and the nature of IFC's capital flows to countries/regions. At the same time, our tentative conclusions, based on rather mixed empirical findings regarding the relationship between IFC finance and other private capital flows, should be treated with some degree of caution. A much more appropriate analysis for future work in this interesting area should be, inter alia, the development and estimation of an allocation model for IFC finance. Similar work on private sector arms of other multinational development banks could also be undertaken so that useful conclusions concerning the role of the above institutions in the area of development financing can be drawn.

Notes

* The author is grateful to Matthew Odedokun and Ayodele Jimoh for helpful discussions and suggestions during the preparation of the chapter as well as the participants of the UNU/WIDER Project Meeting for comments. He wishes also to thank two anonymous referees for comments and suggestions which improved the chapter significantly. The usual disclaimer applies.
1. IFC specifies certain criteria for a project to be financed by it. The project must be (i) technically and financially viable, (ii) economically competitive, (iii) beneficial to the local population and (iv) environmentally and socially sound.
2. IFC's support for the SME sector is increasingly focused on: (i) working through and with local financial intermediaries to provide access to financing for smaller companies; (ii) creating new local financial intermediaries such as microfinance institutions, venture capital funds, leasing companies and others; (iii) providing funding from the SME capacity building facility to scale up global best practice institutions; and (iv) providing technical assistance and advisory support through

project development facilities, which assist SMEs by developing local SME service providers, preparing project feasibility studies, accessing financing, and obtaining a broad range of management and technical assistance including post-financing. This approach has replaced that of direct financing, which in IFC's experience has proven an expensive and ineffective way to reach smaller companies.

3. More comprehensive statistics and discussion of regional allocation, together with some econometric analysis of geographical allocation of IFC portfolio, are in Section 4 and Tables 1.7 and 1.8 of Chapter 1 by Odedokun.

4. For example, a mine in an isolated area has considerably improved the standard of living for 3000 local inhabitants by providing well-paid jobs, housing, health care, schooling, better communications and amenities.

5. For example, an IFC investment in an expansion project helped reduce effluent and air emissions from a wood pulp and paper company's existing operations. Moreover, bio-mass from the plant was used as a coal replacement at an adjacent power station.

6. This finding is fully consistent with the results of a recent survey, conducted by an independent consulting firm, of multinational companies operating in the same regions as IFC. Based on ratings standards that mirror those IFC uses, the firm judged the companies' projects as financially successful in 44 per cent to 74 per cent of cases, depending on the region. IFC achieved project business success rates of between 35 per cent and 63 per cent across these same regions, but in a higher-risk mix of countries.

7. Furthermore, the OEG looked at all of IFC's equity investments approved between 1985 and 1995 and found that IFC had significantly better returns in countries that were high-risk at the time of investment approval.

8. It is notable that issues of profitability are currently in the heart of the agenda for IFC in view of the fact that the average overall return on equity (ROE) that IFC has earned over the period 1997–2001 (fiscal years) was 6.4 per cent, well below the ROE of US investment banks/security houses (11.2 per cent) and of most European banks (8.2 per cent) (Lysy 2001).

9. There is also a need for some clarification with regard to IFC's profitability. IFC's consolidated income includes expenditures on activities undertaken in line with IFC's developmental mandate, but without commercial compensation. Examples include IFC's work in capacity-building for SMEs, participation in World Bank Group advisory efforts to improve the investment climate, management and delivery of technical assistance (including overseeing technical assistance activities funded by donor trust funds), and for economic and environmental work above and beyond what would be required purely for risk management (IFC 2002b).

10. The data on IFC capital flows comes from the OECD–DAC (2002, online database). The data on FDI and GDP, GDP per capita and GDP growth are obtained from World Bank (2001).

11. Again, it is notable that in the case of South Asia, Europe and Central Asia and Middle East and North Africa regions, five, three and three countries are included, respectively. The exception is Sub-Saharan Africa with 24 countries being included in the region.

12. See Chapter 3 by Jimoh for a similar approach, using bilateral official financial flows instead of multilateral ones used here.

13. However, the results should be treated with caution in view of the low significance of coefficients for both regions.

14. The data on FDI and GDP, GDP per capita and GDP growth are obtained from World Bank (2001). GDP per capita is based on purchasing power parity (PPP). Annual percentage growth rate of GDP at market prices is based on constant local currency. Aggregates are based on constant 1995 US dollars.
15. For a detailed discussion of recent proposals to reform the MDGs (including the G7 proposals of 2001) see also Kapur (2002).
16. See the discussion of IFC products and services above for a definition of A-loans and B-loans. Furthermore, to argue that IFC supported projects should earn a return less than what private financiers could earn on 100 per cent private projects would be to argue that either IFC (along with its B-loan partners) accepts a sub-par portion of the project returns (which has not been IFC policy), or the IFC funded-projects are sub-par projects (i.e. they do not earn a return commensurate with the risk). Neither should be the case, however, according to IFC (Lysy 2001).

References

Attanasio, O., L. Picci and A. Scorcu (2000). 'Saving, Growth and Investment: A Macroeconomic Analysis using a Panel of Countries'. *Review of Economics and Statistics*, 80 (2).

Brook, P. and W. Smith (2001). *Contracting for Public Services: Output-Based Aid and Its Applications*. Washington, DC: Private Sector Advisory Services, World Bank.

IFC (2001a). *Annual Report 2001*. Washington, DC: International Finance Corporation.

IFC (2001b). 'Operations Evaluation Group, Annual Review of IFC's Evaluation Findings'. September. Washington, DC: International Finance Corporation.

IFC (2002a). *IFC: Building Business, Creating Opportunity 2002*. Washington, DC: International Finance Corporation.

IFC (2002b). *IFC's Strategic Priorities*. March. Washington, DC: International Finance Corporation.

IFC (various years). *Annual Reports*. Washington, DC: International Finance Corporation.

IFC (various years). IFC: Lessons of Experience Series (1–7). Washington, DC: International Finance Corporation.

Kapur, D. (2002). 'Do As I Say Not As I Do: A Critique of G-7 Proposals on Reforming the MDBs', Working Paper No. 16, Centre for Global Development, Washington, DC.

Lysy, F. (2001), 'Utilizing Commercial Discipline to Improve the Effectiveness of the IFC'. November. Washington, DC: International Finance Corporation. Mimeo.

Meltzer, A. (2000). 'Report of the International Financial Institutions Advisory Commission'. Washington, DC: US Congress.

OECD–DAC (2002). *International Development Statistics* (online database). Available at: www.oecd.org.

Wilks, A. (2000). 'Analysis of IFC's Role and Impact'. Bretton Woods Project. September. Available at: www.brettonwoodsproject.org.

World Bank (2001). *World Development Indicators*. Washington, DC: World Bank.

World Bank (2002). *Private Sector Development Strategy – Directions for the World Bank Group* (April). Washington, DC: World Bank.

5
Donors' Support for Microcredit as Social Enterprise: A Critical Reappraisal

*Machiko Nissanke**

1 Introduction

Over the last decade or so, we have observed a proliferation of microfinance institutions (MFIs) in developing and transitional economies as well as in some developed countries such as USA and Canada. Modelled on infamously 'successful' institutions such as the Grameen Bank of Bangladesh, the Badan Kredit Kecamatan (BKK) of Indonesia or BancoSol of Bolivia, new strands of 'innovative' microfinance institutions have been established specifically for reaching 'the poor', in the field of 'micro-enterprise finance' and 'poverty lending'. Drawing lessons from the widely acknowledged failure of the earlier experiments with credit interventions such as the targeted rural credit programmes based on subsidized interest rates, new microcredit programmes lean heavily towards 'market-based solutions', with use of concepts such as group lending and joint liability contracts.

At the Microcredit Summit in November 2002 organized by Consultative Group to Assist the Poorest (CGAP), it is reported that the number of 'microfinance' clients has risen to 54.9 million at the end of 2001, from 30.7 million a year earlier, and 13.5 million in December 1997. They included 26.8 million of the world's poorest, defined as those people living in the bottom half below their country's poverty line. The number of the poorest served has showed a more than triple increase in four years from 7.6 million in 1998. *Microcredit Summit Report* proclaimed that this annual increase of 37 per cent achieved is just one point below the rate required to meet the Summit Campaign's goal of providing microcredit to 100 million of the poor households by 2005 (Microcredit Summit 2002).

Indeed, the international donor community as well as northern and southern NGOs have enthusiastically embraced the concept of microcredit and microfinance as one of the most promising mechanisms to poverty alleviation and eventual eradication. Reflecting their preference of providing financial and technical assistance on a 'wholesale' rather than a direct 'retail' basis by working through intermediaries, many donor agencies view MFIs and microcredit programmes as the key component of their lending towards microenterprise development (DAC/OECD 1994). Microenterprise development is, in turn, recognized as a central part of the private sector development agenda, microenterprises being referred to as a unique channel for achieving the donors' targets of 'poverty reduction through private sector development', while attending the growth and equity objectives of economic development. For example, the Development Assistance Committee (DAC) of OECD identifies the role of microenterprises not only in creating jobs and incomes with a more equitable diffusion of the benefits of growth, but also in having 'direct impact on poverty reduction and on the integration of women and other marginalized segments of society into economic life' (DAC/OECD 1994: 4).

As found in many of the documents that have spelled out donors' strategy towards poverty reduction, a very high hope is placed on the success of MFIs to serve hitherto credit constrained poor households. Indeed, amid the high expectation raised towards MFIs' ability to carry out the ascribed mission, a myth has been generated that MFIs could have a significant impact on the livelihoods of millions of poor people around the world. High-profile speeches have been delivered and documents issued with many impressive 'performance' indicators and achievements, producing inadvertently an unfounded claim that MFIs could be the *ultimate* solution to poverty reduction.

This rhetoric has sometimes prevented the donor community from tackling real challenges and issues confronting MFIs on the ground. It has obscured the need for understanding the scope and reality of microfinance in different local conditions, and hence, the required care for the diversity of approaches towards incentive and delivery mechanisms. While acknowledging the potential for economic development and poverty alleviation embedded in the microfinance concept, we feel it is important to evaluate underlying economic theories and empirical evidences concerning the premise of MFIs and microcredit programmes, so that we could have a more realistic picture of the likely impact of microcredit programmes on the poverty profile and enterprise development as well as of their limitations.

The objective of this chapter is to examine critically the nature of support rendered by the donor community to MFIs and microcredit programmes and the effectiveness of this particular outlet of official aid for microenterprise development and poverty alleviation.[1] The chapter is structured as follows. The next section (Section 2) provides a brief review of economic theories of microfinance. It examines main analytical rationales for the role of MFIs in microenterprise development and poverty reduction as well as the delivery mechanisms adopted by microcredit programmes. Section 3 discusses features and trends in bilateral and multilateral donor support for microfinance and microenterprises. Section 4 critically assesses empirical evidence on the performance of microfinance institutions and the impact of microcredit programmes on poverty alleviation. The final section (Section 5) discusses policy implications of our analysis for donors' support towards microfinance and microcredit programmes.

2   Economics of microfinance institutions

The poor and financial services

The central premise of the microfinance credit approach is that the lack of access by the poor to credit constitutes one of the most critical impediments to poverty reduction and broad-based economic development. The poor are conventionally viewed as 'unbankable'. To start with, *borrower net worth* of the poor is too low to get access to financial services provided by formal financial institutions such as banks.[2] Second, the poor cannot easily overcome the informational and enforcement problems that normally exist as frictions in the borrower–lender relationships.[3] Third, the poor usually cannot offer collateral to overcome the agency problems characteristic to a principal–agent relationship.[4]

Indeed, in information-constrained economies such as low-income countries or transitional economies, where endowments of information capital is very low, banks are burdened with the problems caused by costly and imperfect information – adverse selection, moral hazard and contract enforcement – in dealing with idiosyncratic risks of private borrowers (Stiglitz and Weiss 1981). In particular, banks are constrained to serve the poor, as transaction costs for obtaining information on them for screening and monitoring are too high. Banks usually resort to collateral requirements as a credit-rationing device, though the foreclosure of collateral property is known to be difficult in view of inefficient judiciary systems and the ambiguities surrounding property rights. Banks do not also posses a comparative advantage in offering financial products and services required by the poor, that is, small-scale and short-term liquidity and saving facilities.

In these low-income country environments, informal financial market segments[5] have developed devices and mechanisms in coping with the agency problems resulting from imperfect information.[6] These mechanisms operate within geographically and socially confined community settings, and are firmly rooted in indigenous social codes and norms. In this set of circumstances, as found in many rural credit markets and most group arrangements, the relationship between borrower and lender is often exclusive and repeat transaction is critical. Then the promise of repeat borrowing and social sanctions serve as effective incentives for borrowers not to default. Clearly, borrowers repay loans for fear of losing access to future loans upon default (particularly in schemes involving groups). In addition, defaulters are subject to effective and severe sanctions by the whole community.

Social sanctions could include exclusion from other financial transactions (such as informal insurance) or other economic or social penalties. Social sanctions are available only in reasonably cohesive social groups, providing yet another reason for the propensity to transact credit within the confined community settings.

Similarly, informal commercial lenders could also rely less on collateral assets than on social pressure, reputation and personal knowledge of borrowers or interlinked credit contracts for screening, monitoring and contract enforcement. In short, all informal agents and groups effectively use a relatively accurate communalized information-base in order to reduce the risk of dealing with small borrowers, who remain high-risk for formal lending institutions. However, in many parts of the world, informal financial services are used mainly for cash flow and liquidity management for consumption smoothing at a low-income equilibrium. The effective lending rates charged by commercial informal lenders are often too high for these funds to be used by micro- and small-scale enterprises or rural small farmers as a regular source of working capital, let alone for financing fixed capital investment. Most informal insurance mechanisms are weak with regard to frequent external shocks that can be highly covariant across households. They hardly provide adequate protection (Morduch 1999b).

Now, in the face of shrinking formal employment opportunities, micro- and small-scale enterprises/firms are increasingly viewed as an important vehicle in reducing poverty and meeting simultaneously the growth and equity objectives of developing and transitional economies. Yet, it is not uncommon for these enterprises to have insufficient working capital even for day-to-day operations. Indeed, most surveys conducted in these economies report that *financial constraints*, that is, the lack of access to and cost of finance, remain the binding constraint on operation and expansion for small-scale establishments. Of course, these shortages and constraints may be symptomatic of supply and marketing problems or of managerial inefficiencies, which could be the real cause of their liquidity problems and lack of creditworthiness. Nevertheless, for many enterprises the potential for growth takes the demand for capital beyond the limits of self-finance, and such needs are not easily met from either banks or informal lenders. Thus, there is a sizeable shortfall in the provision of financial services for microenterprises.[7]

At the same time, while poverty is increasingly recognized as a multi-dimensional condition (Sen 1984 and 1993; Chambers 1997) rather than merely a shortfall in income and consumption, the microfinance concept has become regarded as one of powerful mechanisms for poverty reduction, by providing the poor with the means for risk management. In the face of frequent income shocks with meagre asset endowments, the poor have to engage in different risk coping as well as risk reduction and mitigation strategies.

Risk reduction and mitigation are methods of *ex ante* risk management, which could involve various decisions ranging from migration to crop and income diversification (Holzmann and Jorgensen 1999). Risk coping refers to *ex post* risk management, in which the poor seek to cushion against the imminent consumption risk and choose to smooth consumption across time and space. While inter-temporal consumption smoothing is effected by saving–borrowing and self-insurance at individual/household levels, spatial consumption smoothing amounts to pooling idiosyncratic risks of individuals/households and co-insuring against risks (Alderman and Paxson 1992; Besley 1995; Nissanke and Aryeetey 2000). It is claimed that MFIs could provide the poor with these vital financial services for risk management, known as *poverty lending*.

Thus, microenterprise finance and poverty lending have become twin-pillars of MFIs' activities. While microenterprise finance centres on poor people with enterprises of their own, poverty lending aims at concentrating on lending toward income-generating activities of the very poor with a view of mitigating poverty rather than enterprise development.[8] However, this distinction has been increasingly blurred in recent years, since microenterprises are viewed by the donor community as 'a key ingredient for helping families and communities out of poverty' (Eversole 2000: 45).

Credit delivery mechanisms of microfinance institutions

With considerable perceived gaps in credit service delivery to the poor and microenterprise, the mission of MFIs is set to address this market failure by serving the 'unbankable' segments of the population in the name of poverty reduction. For this purpose, MFIs have adopted a set of delivery mechanisms with 'innovative' contracts and incentives with the view of minimizing the risks in dealing with the poor. MFI's risk-minimization approaches are adopted from those practised by 'informal' finance in solving the information and enforcement problems.

One of most prominent features of new innovation is the use of the mechanism of group lending in creating *joint liability*, so that social pressure, collateral substitutes and other group dynamics do motivate repayment.[9] In particular, peer pressure or group dynamics is used as a way of reducing the transaction costs of microfinance in lending to the poor by solving information problems such as adverse selection, moral hazards, auditing and enforcement (Hulme and Mosley 1996). Like 'informal' lenders, the joint liability lending institutions are supposed to utilize the local information and 'social capital' that exist among borrowers in close-knit social environments for peer selection, peer auditing and peer monitoring (Stiglitz 1990; Ghatak 1999 and 2000; Ghatak and Guinnane 1999).[10] Hence, a creation of joint liability is viewed to act as a mutual guarantee mechanism with a particular structure of incentives to ensure high repayment without demanding physical collateral assets to back up loans. It is seen effective in mitigating the problem of strategic default in particular.

MFIs also adopt mechanisms such as progressive lending, frequent repayment schedules and compulsory savings to generate dynamic incentives for repayment. Progressive lending refers to the system by which borrowers obtain increasingly larger loans if repayment is made promptly. As long as the system is credible and alternative sources of finance are less attractive, this type of incentive can enhance repayments (Morduch 1999a). Frequent repayment schedules are also seen to act as an added mechanism to secure repayment. As most microfinance organizations collect repayments before investments bear fruit, they are, in fact, lending against the borrower's steady income stream (not just the investment) and, hence, securing part of the loan repayment even if projects fail. Compulsory savings, along with emergency funds and other group funds, play the role of collateral substitutes, used as insurance against loan defaults.

MFIs are also recommended to levy relatively high 'market-based' interest rates to cover operational costs. As discussed below, this certainly reflects a clear apathy to subsidized cheap interest rates, which are blamed to be the chief culprit in the failure of many donor support programmes for SMEs as well as the targeted rural credit schemes in the 1960s and 1970s (Adams *et al.* 1984).

It has been claimed that by effectively overcoming key constraints for credit delivery to the poor through this innovative financial engineering, the MFIs enjoy high repayment rates so as to ensure their financial viability and sustainability in the long run. At the same time, it is contended that the MFIs could make significant contribution towards poverty reduction through a reduction in the vulnerability of the poor to shocks as well as to enhanced gender and community empowerment.

3   Donors' support for microfinancial institutions

Based on these up-beating premises of microfinance, most bilateral and multilateral donor agencies have established a specialized microenterprise and microcredit unit within their lending programme for private sector development, though the budget for these units typically accounts for a rather insignificant share in their overall PSD programme.[11] The donor community's involvement has been particularly strong in the movement to advance the microfinance concept worldwide as a viable, self-sustaining vehicle for poverty reduction.[12] Towards this objective, the donor community formed a consortium – Consultative Group to Assist the Poorest (CGAP) – in 1995 with a team of microfinance specialists housed in the World Bank. CGAP's main mission is identified as promoting 'best practice' in microcredit especially in the way donors would like MFIs to evolve. CGAP is also to act as the central funding channel for microfinance initiatives with the provision of small grants, often 'performance based' linked to the attainment of 'financial sustainability' as discussed below.[13]

At its inception in 1995, CGAP had nine donor members. At the Microcredit Summit of 1997,[14] a global campaign was launched to promote micro-finance with the explicit aim of raising US$22 billion to reach 100 million poor people by the year 2005. In 1997, 618 NGOs and related organizations became associated with the global microfinance campaign; by December 2000, the number grew to 1567 organizations which operate worldwide in many corners of developing and transitional economies, while 20 more bilateral and multilateral donors became CGAP members. In the first three years since its establishment, CGAP provided around US$32 million in grants to MFIs and its networks, while CGAP participating donors committed over US$400 million to microfinance activities (*Microcredit Summit Report* 1998).

On the eve of the Microcredit Summit (Summit Plus Five) in November 2002, 29 bilateral and multilateral donors were registered as members of CGAP. At least 1580 NGOs and other related self-help organizations, which are members of the Microcredit Summit Campaign, are delivering micro-finance services as a central strategy for attacking poverty worldwide, and a large number of national governments currently endorse their political commitment to microfinance through this campaign (CGAP 2002). With this unified donor support, MFIs worldwide, as at the end of 2001, serve 54.8 million of the poor, of whom 26.8 million identified as the poorest.[15] The poorest clients include 21.2 million women, an increase of 7 million on the previous year.[16]

While providing about US$5 million per annum in grants, CGAP's main function is to offer services to microfinance industry, donors and MFIs mainly in the form of policy development, institution- and capacity-building such as technical tools and services; training and capacity-building; and technical advice and exchange. This may or may not require the provision of credit to firms or intermediaries (World Bank 2002).

On the whole, donors' support for this movement is firmly based on the strategic positions drawn from the evaluation of the past experiences with their support for SMEs development. For example, citing in-house research papers such as Batra and Mahmood (2001) and Caprio and Demirgüç-Kunt (1998), World Bank (2002: 39) concludes:

…the financial support to larger private firms, SMEs, microfinance schemes and rural borrowers has typically resulted in mediocre outcomes, when based on credit with subsidized interest rates. Incentives to divert such subsidized credit to powerful parties or to support substandard projects have reduced effectiveness. [...] Subsidized credit does not lead to superior firm-level performance and the provision of finance in weak investment climates is ineffective.

Hence, their policy conclusions resulting from these evaluations are: First, 'Credit operations for private firms should be *un-subsidized*. This requires sufficient flexibility in interest rate policy, in particular the revision of usury laws that hamper the development of microfinance operations.' Second, it is best to shift to 'wholesale' SME support through financial intermediaries, since 'direct financing of SMEs is costly and ineffective in meeting the needs of the clients, as evidenced in the case of IFC' (World Bank 2002: 40).[17]

A distinct feature of CGAP's use of its grant fund is an investment-style approach that ties tranched funding to MFIs' performance in two critical performance indicators: financial *sustainability* and poverty *outreach*. Outreach measures performance by the number of poor people who gained access to superior financial services as a result of the programme, while financial sustainability refers to the programme's independence from concessional funding.

It is contended that performance-based grants provide MFIs with strong financial incentives to reach the twin targets of sustainability of financial intermediaries and the outreach of the poor for the poverty reduction objective. Hence, CGAP takes a 'hand-off' position towards the use of this equity-like funding, leaving it to the discretion of the MFI's own management. It is argued that the performance contract accompanying its funding ensures that 'reporting, monitoring, and continuation of disbursements are tied to the MFI's fulfilment of performance thresholds at the institutional level'. MFIs are expected to achieve 'full financial sustainability' to cover the commercial cost of funds as well. This implies that MFIs are expected to be 'subsidy-independent' in a relatively short time frame and able to generate substantial surpluses over time to fulfil their social mission on an ever-expanding scale.[18]

While there has been an intensive debate within the Campaign group whether financial sustainability and social mission of poverty reduction could be reconcilable without causing organizational tension in MFIs, CGAP has been pushing hard on the twin goals of achieving sustainability and deepening poverty outreach in recent years.[19] It cites, as examples, several MFIs such as Comparatamos in Mexico, who serves the very poor with an average outstanding loan balance of US$66, but stayed on track to financial sustainability with the very high repayment rate and attracting commercial funds.

Within this broad framework set out by CGAP, multilateral financial institutions, numerous UN agencies, and many donor agencies have microcredit support programmes. It is very interesting to note that a remarkably high degree of donor coordination has been achieved, under the leadership of CGAP, in donors' approach to microfinance and microcredit programmes, which is not quite prevalent in other aid programmes. They all provide both financial and non-financial technical support with specifically agreed objectives within the CGAP forum. Non-financial components are emphasized in all programmes on the recognition that MFIs require considerable technical assistance for capacity building in reaching out to the poorest of the poor.

Among multinational financial institutions, the World Bank is a key player in the donor community under CGAP in advancing the Microcredit Summit's pledge in building a robust microfinance industry. It provided over US$900 million in grants and concessional loans to MFIs worldwide in the 1990s. At the end of 2001, the World Bank managed over 100 and about 150 active projects with a microfinance component and with a rural finance component, respectively. Both Asian Development Bank and Inter-American Development Bank have accumulated very rich experiences in supporting microfinance institutions over many years and plan to expand their technical and financial support with a specially drafted microfinance development strategy, as well as through different operational windows. In contrast, European Bank for Reconstructions and Development (EBRD) and the African Development Bank are relatively new to the field, but both have rapidly built up active microfinance portfolios.

In addition, many UN agencies have been actively supporting microcredit and microfinance programmes. These include UNDP, which established a special initiative called Microstart in 1997, as well as specialized agencies such as the FAO, IFAD and ILO. Among bilateral donor agencies, USAID has been historically very active in supporting MFIs. It has long committed to enterprise development and building market-based financial institutions. On the other hand, both CIDA and DFID place their microfinance and microdevelopment programmes as a central component of the overall poverty reduction strategy. The two agencies run a substantial number of microfinance and microcredit programmes worldwide. Other donors such as European Union, GTZ of Germany as well as Nordic and Scandinavian aid agencies are all known to provide technical and financial support to microenterprise and microfinance programmes. The scope and other features of these main donor programmes are presented in the appendix.

4   Performance of microfinance institutions and impact of microcredit

Performance

Several 'high-profile', well-established microfinance institutions such as the Grameen Bank of Bangladesh, the BKK of Indonesia or BancoSol of Bolivia have captured the imagination of the donor community who have been searching for an effective conduit of channelling official aid for poverty lending. While the public has often been dazzled by the claim that MFIs are an unqualified success in achieving the twin targets of financial sustainability and poverty outreach, this is far removed from reality. First of all, these 'successful' institutions themselves have followed quite a different path of institutional evolution. Dunford (2000) classifies them, for example, in a continuum from *traditional business* (a purely financial bottom line) at one end to *traditional social service* (a purely social bottom line) at the other end. Second, newer MFIs that have replicated innovative practices in different parts of the world have produced highly varied results in their financial performance as well as in the poverty impact (Hulme and Mosley 1996; Morduch 1999a; Marr 1999).

The Grameen Bank, the most celebrated microfinance institution in the world, has expanded fast its 'poverty lending' operations, with 2.4 million members, 95 per cent of whom are women, with an average loan size of US$134 as in 2002. It rigidly follows the original 'innovative' delivery mechanisms (and hence known as the Grammen formula) with group lending methodology, joint liability incentives, weekly repayment schedules and meetings, 10 per cent compulsory savings and progressive loans.

However, despite consistently producing a very high loan repayment rate as well as charging an interest rate of 20 per cent, it has remained subsidy-dependent on the donor funds. Morduch (1999a) estimates that the effective subsidies to the Grameen Bank amounted to about US$176 million between 1985 and 1996. In order to wean away from this dependence, the Grameen Bank has tried to shift the major source of funding over time from donor agencies to the central bank and money markets and most recently, it has sought financing through bond sales.

Bolivia's BancoSol is one of the exceptional cases in not being subsidy-dependent. However, it specializes in lending to the relatively well off and charges a high interest rate, 45–48 per cent at an annualized base rate plus 2–3 per cent of commission fees in 1998. It was converted into a full-fledged bank in 1992 from Prodem, an NGO, affiliated to the US-funded Accion International, which has been firmly in support of striving for financial sustainability. While promoting the group-lending methodology in 20 developing countries and 30 US cities with half a million members worldwide as of 2002, Accion places less emphasis on social issues than on business viability. BancoSol itself has moved away from group lending to individual lending.

At the other end of spectrum, village or communal banking programmes, which have been operating under the Foundation for International Community Assistance (FINCA), continue to target the poor and make an explicit commitment to building community-based networks that could serve as financial and social self-help organizations (Marr 1999). FINCA serves, as in 2002, nearly 165000 members in 20 countries, 95 per cent of whom are women with an average loan size of US$191. The concept of village Banking has been replicated in over 5000 places in 32 countries by NGOs including CARE, Catholic Relief Services, Freedom from Hunger, Project Hope, Save the Children and World Relief. However, many of these programmes have found it difficult to attain financial self-sufficiency.

Generally, unlike the credit cooperatives in Germany and other European countries in the nineteenth century, which relied on local funds, the contemporary microfinance schemes obtain most of their lending funds from donors (Ghatak and Guinnane 1999). It is not surprising to find that although subsidization is supposed to cover start-up costs only, many programmes remain heavily subsidy-dependent, requiring constant injections of donor funds, against aims and aspirations of MFIs and donors alike. Morduch (1999a) offers several estimates of programme sustainability. One estimate suggests that no more than 1 per cent of NGO programmes worldwide were financially sustainable at the close of the 1990s, and perhaps only a further 5 per cent of NGO programmes will ever cross the hurdle. Even using a less strict measure of sustainability, namely, *operational* sustainability that measures the ability of institutions to cover operational costs only but not the full cost of capital, the emerging picture is not encouraging: the microfinance programmes that target the poorest borrowers generate revenues sufficient to cover just 70 per cent of their full operation cost. Eversole (2000) provides another estimate, suggesting that typically MFIs require seven years of subsidies before they can become sustainable, and then success is not guaranteed.

This is not surprising, since the innovative microcredit mechanisms tend to incur high administrative costs if they are adopted and initiated by NGOs and banks. As outsiders to the community, rather than insiders, as in the case of informal associations and lenders, they have to engage in intensive monitoring of groups and are obliged to rely heavily on the promise of repeat and progressive loans in successive periods as incentives for high repayment. Yet, the agency problem characterizing the principal–agent relationship in borrower–lender interactions often remains unsolved between programme officers and groups. Such problems are compounded, when groups are large or put together by programme officers, since group cohesion cannot be guaranteed.

The start-up and administration costs of microfinance programmes tend to be higher in areas of low population density such as are found in Sub-Saharan Africa.[20] It is not surprising that microfinance is most successful in densely populated regions of Asia, which accounts for 87 per cent of microfinance clients. If administrative costs were to increase significantly, many NGOs and banks, in the short run, would find it difficult to make the necessary adjustments to accommodate new approaches, without cross-subsidizing internally or externally funded subsidies. The high loan repayment rates of 95 per cent or above, often reported by MFIs in the initial loan cycles to assure donors of low default risk, can easily mask overall high transaction costs on account of high operation costs. This can prevent them from graduating from subsidy-dependence for a considerable period.

Impact

A large number of studies have been conducted to evaluate the impact of microcredit programmes on poverty reduction, driven partly by the donor community's needs to establish whether these programmes have been successful in meeting the poverty reduction targets. Hulme and Mosley (1996) examine the impacts of microfinance programmes on income poverty through the effects on productivity, technology and employment. Khandker (1998) expands the analysis to include effects of seasonality on consumption and labour, children's nutrition and schooling, and fertility and contraception. Zeller *et al.* (1997) analyse the impacts that microfinance programmes might have on food security. Cohen and Sebstad (2000) examine the effects of the programmes on the risk management strategies of poor households, which affect the degree of their deprivation and vulnerability.

Many other studies have extended the scope of analysis to include intra-household dynamics and their impacts on individual well-being (in particular, that of women and children), the relationship between household and enterprise development, and the potential impacts on the wider community. In view of the multi-dimensional aspects of poverty, effects have been studied not only in terms of changes in income and consumption levels, but also in terms of variations in vulnerability to risk, skill development, gender empowerment and participation in community networks.[21]

These studies by and large support the claim, with some cautious notes, that 'microfinance can have the potential to help many poor people improve their lives' (Hulme 2000: 26). Khandker (1998) provides an estimate that: (1) about 21 per cent of the Grameen Bank borrowers managed to lift their families out of poverty within about four years of participation; and (2) extreme poverty declined from 33 per cent to 10 per cent among its participants. In the case of the Bank Rakyat Indonesia (BRI), there was a report in 1990, claiming that net household incomes of borrowers increased by about 76 per cent and employment increased by 84 per cent within three years of programme participation (ADB 2000).[22]

However, the potential of microfinance and the success of established MFIs appear to be somewhat exaggerated by practitioners and donors. As Hulme (2000) argues, there is a need for a much careful monitoring of these programmes by MFIs and the donors, with an acute awareness that microcredit could have both positive and negative impacts on loan recipients.

First, as Hulme aptly reminds us, the other side of the 'microcredit' is 'microdebt'. This means, while microdebt can lead to improved incomes and reduced vulnerability for the poor, it could lead to such a scale of indebtedness that the poor find it hard to get out. There is a greater need for better understanding of real economic environments in which the poor conduct their income-generating activities and microbusinesses. The targeted borrowers 'work in low-return activities in saturated markets' and they are subject to various shocks beyond their control. It has been reported that many indebted borrowers, who fail to generate returns sufficient to make a prompt repayment regularly, turn to moneylenders for buying time. As Rahman (1999) and Goez and Gupta (1996) report, borrowers from the Grameen Bank have had to sell household assets or their own food supplies, or have had to leave their homes in search of wage labour in an urban area to repay their loan. There are plenty of stories around, as found in Montgomery (1996), that delinquent borrowers of MFIs are ostracized by joint-liability groups and communities, and they become destitute in their community. Or worse, they commit suicides out of desperation, burdened with cumulative 'unbearable' indebtedness far beyond their repayment capacity.

Second, as Hulme (2000) observes, it is hard even for 'poverty-focused' MFIs to provide credit facilities to the 'hard core' of the poor. The poorer segments of the poor are usually excluded from group lending, because not many want to share joint liability with them. Even when they join MFIs at the inception as targeted clients, they are often the first to drop out through loan cycles. Marr (2002) documents the case of communal banking programmes in Peru, where group dynamics engendered by the joint-liability microcredit programme have had significant negative impacts on the well-being of participants. In her case study, tension between financial and organizational sustainability has been built up to such a scale that it has produced a fundamental instability of the system, leading to the fracturing of groups and greater exclusion of the poor.

Very high pressures to attain simultaneously the target of financial sustainability and outreach in terms of loan repayment and disbursement in a very short period, and the accompanying internal incentive structures could easily work against organizational sustainability and stability. Typically, as Marr observes, programme 'officers' performance is measured by their achievements in relation to loan repayments and lending portfolios, rather than to stable and sustainable organizations'. They tend to immediately classify delinquent borrowers as strategic defaulters. Furthermore, those with delinquent loans are under pressure to engage in similar trading activities as all other participants for loan repayment purposes, leading to over-indebtedness as well as local market saturation. Thus, Marr suggests, 'high repayment rates of loans to programme officers are often being achieved at the cost of an erosion of organizational sustainability, which in the longer term leads to instability of finances and the eventual meltdown of the system'.

The consequences of these 'wrong' incentive structures for the communities in her case study are:

1. A tendency to abandon the joint-liability system, with individually-based collateral increasingly gaining importance in relation to that of collective sanctions and social collateral;

2. The poorest and most vulnerable members of any given group leave microfinance schemes prematurely or are actively excluded, resulting in serious negative impact effects on their well-being;
3. Benefits are unequally distributed within the group and often favour the better-established households, and tend to empower people already powerful to begin with;
4. An inclination on the part of the programme officers to move away from targeting the poor segments of the population in favour of the less poor sectors, and consequently poorer people are rationed out from microfinance markets;
5. A fundamental instability and a tendency to lose cohesiveness dominate the group, which implies that not only organizational sustainability is compromised but also financial sustainability is affected in the medium and longer term, leading to negative impacts for all parties concerned.

These are sombre warnings to enthusiasts of microfinance, who tend to perceive MFIs as 'a cure for poverty'. Many structural, sociopolitical and historical factors specific to the local environments in Peru as well as institutional factors characterizing the communal banking programmes concerned, such as inappropriate programme design and implementation, did play some part in producing these results. However, similar circumstances, if not more difficult, are often present in other locations worldwide, where the microfinance concept is uncritically embraced. The proper lesson to be drawn from this experience is that the MFIs should adjust the design and implementation of microcredit programmes to the local conditions in which they operate, so that these programmes nurture the trust existing already in the communities. Unfortunately, as Marr (2002) notes, microcredit programmes established and organized in haste, tend to exploit, instead, existing social, often hierarchical, structures in order to achieve their own financial sustainability. This often results in an erosion of social fabric of the communities they serve.

Furthermore, financial products offered by MFIs are not necessarily those demanded by borrowers in the communities they are supposed to serve. The fungibility becomes an issue. In order to get access to finance their immediate consumption requirements such as school fees or medical expenses, women 'have to pretend they need "microenterprise" loans' (Holmes 2000: 27). In this regard, a weakness of many MFIs is that they focus on credit delivery, forgetting the fact that their targeted clients may also require appropriate savings mechanisms to smooth consumption. Most MFIs' compulsory savings facilities are established as collateral substitutes and insurance funds for loan defaults to sustain MFIs' credit programme operation. These facilities do not offer members flexible savings services at the time of their needs. The empirical evidence worldwide suggests poor households and microenterprises have a large demand for safe and convenient savings services as well as for insurance services (Nissanke and Aryeetey 1998).[23]

The mismatch of financial products between what is demanded and what is supplied by MFIs is an issue in relation not only to poverty lending, but also to microenterprise finance. To address the high administrative cost and to increase financial viability, many new microfinance programmes have adopted a *minimalist* credit approach, as opposed to a more *integrated* approach, including technical assistance and other forms of training. The minimalist approach, however, could claim adequacy if programmes are to deal with a specific phase of enterprise development, when enterprises' needs are concentrated in repetitive financing of working capital. Many existing 'successful programmes are, in fact, effective mainly in providing working capital in small doses' (Levitsky 1993).

Yet, the diversity of microenterprise activities is overwhelming in terms of size, market, sector, assets, experience and many other characteristics (Eversole 2000). Further, in terms of enterprise dynamics, microenterprises in both the formation and transformation phases often require more integrated assistance to overcome other obstacles and constraints. Furthermore, for development, enterprises require assistance to overcome financial obstacles other than lack of working capital (Boomgard 1989; Nissanke 2001). As production technology and marketing strategy change and enterprises expand, the need for financial services also undergoes substantial changes. To meet the need of different phases of enterprise development, as well as the wide variety of microenterprise activities, there is a need for a diversification of the loan portfolio of the microfinance programmes.

Seen from this perspective, the donor community tends to place too much emphasis on the standardization of products and services, that is, the standardization of 'successful' operating procedures or the replication of 'best practices', all in the form of simple 'financial engineering'. However, in providing microfinance services, it has to be recognized that 'enterprise finance' differs qualitatively from 'poverty lending' for income-generating activities at the lower end. The former requires a deeper understanding of evolving dynamics of credit demand on the part of entrepreneurs in terms of enterprise development (Nissanke 2001). Indeed, as Eversole (2000) notes, microloans replicated on the Grameen or BancoSol model are designed to serve well only one sub-set of a very diverse microenterprise market. For example, regular provisions for working capital in small quantities may be appropriate for meeting the financial needs of stable, high-turnover businesses, such as trading activities, but not for other diverse categories of microenterprises.

Policy implications for donors

Our discussion above suggests the urgent needs to address and re-examine the fundamental question facing the donor community: is there tension in the two goals set out to be achieved by microfinance and microcredit schemes; attaining the financial sustainability while carrying out the social mission of poverty reduction?

Some established MFIs have resolved this tension, opting consciously to be institutions operating as traditional businesses rather than *social enterprises* (Dunford 2000). BancoSol of Bolivia (mentioned above) is an example of such an institution. For these institutions, social objectives, that is, serving the poor, are only a by-product. In this sense, they disregarded measuring their progress primarily against social objectives. While they still address significant market failure to the borrowing needs of small and even microenterprises in the location they serve, they do so only incidentally. At the other end of the microfinance spectrum are traditional social service organizations, which serve the very poorest such as refugees and disaster victims as emergency operations. They should not and cannot make financial sustainability the prime objective. As Dunford suggests, their functions may lie in developing a strategy to graduate their clients into more sustainable entities.

However, donors' involvement in the microfinance movement in the past decade or so is explained mostly by their desire for creating and sustaining MFIs as social enterprises through their financial and technical support. These MFIs are supposed to have 'a double bottom line' with both financial/ institutional and social objectives. As Dunford (2000) aptly describes, this is the 'Holy Grail of Microfinance': that is, they are supposed to aim at reaching very poor people but, at the same time, aim at financial sustainability, as discussed in Section 3 above. The donor community has been rigorously and constantly redefining and advocating the frontier of 'best practices' of combined impact and sustainability.

We argue here, however, that donors should be much more aware of the trade-off between the two goals in their microcredit campaign, when microfinance mechanisms are instituted in different local conditions. The tension between the two objectives at the conceptual level is in fact directly translated into incredible pressures and stresses on both the microfinance institutions and their clients in the fields in many parts of the world, as we discussed in Section 4. There are microfinance institutions which are reported to be successful in attaining the two objectives, such as Compartamous in Mexico or Credito con Educacion Rural (CRECER) in Bolivia operating as village banking programme under an international NGO, Freedom from Hunger. They are, however, the exceptions rather than the rule, when global experiences are fully taken into account. The Grameen Bank in Bangladesh is also rather an exception, by reaching over 2.4 million people and accumulating experiences over a considerably longer period. What is required is a very careful analysis of the conditions that have engendered these successful operations, not only in relation to their service delivery mechanisms, but also in relation to specific local factors and conditions that have led to their success. Mere replication of their 'best practice' would not produce the same results in other locations in the absence of these 'facilitating' factors and conditions.

These successful cases should not be used as excuse for turning away from the reality that many other institutions have been facing so far. Even for CRECER, Dunford (2000) could not give an unqualified answer to the question as to whether they have achieved both objectives. He concludes that as social enterprises that can last long enough to bring about a major improvement in the lives of many poor people, it is not necessary for CRECER to be totally subsidy-free. He asks the critical question why should not social enterprises tap financial sources available for 'social subsidy' and 'social investment', since there is a developing market for subsidy to social enterprises – for start-up capital, for technical assistance and for loans at concessional rates.

It appears that donors' apathy to subsidy has gone too far. There are solid economic theories to provide an analytical rationale why social investment with use of tax-cum-subsidy should be made in the presence of externalities, public goods and the prevalence of market failure. The issue here is not that temporary or practical subsidies cannot be justified socially or analytically. Rather, the real challenge facing economists and the donor community is to design a microfinance programme so that the subsidy element would not be used as a mere justification for permanent inefficiency so as to perpetuate aid dependency culture, as sadly observed in many other official aid programmes.

Donors should not try to preach for the attainment of the full financial sustainability for all microcredit programmes in an unrealistically short period, standardized across the board. Instead, they should pay much more attention to projecting a realistic time frame for attaining different categories of financial sustainability for each of their sponsored MFIs in the light of local conditions, and to helping each draw a strategic plan of measures and policies to attain intermediate targets in *sequence*.

In this regard, Gibbons and Meehan (2002: 12) argue that donors should understand that MFIs have different funding requirements at different stages of development. According to information gathered from MFIs worldwide, 'quasi-equity (concessional loans) is critical in the years prior to break-even to cover (operational) deficits not financed by grants and to provide early on-lending funds that cannot yet be borrowed from banks'. They estimate that quasi-equity may be required throughout MFIs operational cycles. They also warn that the cost implications of rapid scaling up and outreach on sustainability, as scaling-up may increase substantially operational costs so that MFIs, which had once reached a breakeven point, could start experiencing substantial deficits. They urge the donor community to accept that there is a major funding problem affecting the microfinance industry, as microfinance institutions have been experiencing a dearth of equity and quasi-equity financing at any stage of maturity. In order to address this particular funding gap which is expected to remain so for the foreseeable future, Gibbons and Meehan (2002) recommend CGAP to lead the way in building the institutional capacity of national and regional-level micro credit funds by encouraging its members to finance them with grants, and by monitoring and evaluating the performance of the funds.

Donors should also take a much more *system-wide* approach to the development of financial markets in developing and transition economies. Currently, many NGO- and donor-driven programmes are operating largely in isolation from the rest of the financial system, often even with-out adequate coordination with similar microcredit programmes operating nearby.[24] This has generated *premature* market saturation in certain segments of credit demand, while leaving other segments largely under serviced. On one hand, it is not uncommon to observe a rapid increase in very similar vending and trading activities in a small locality where many microcredit programmes compete by offering standardized microloans. This sort of situation is unsustainable, often resulting in a collapse of demand for products marketed by microcredit recipients, and hence, making it difficult for microfinancial institutions to sustain high loan repayment levels beyond short loan cycles. On the other hand, a wide variety of financial services demanded by microentrepreneurs other than small working capital remains grossly under-supplied.

Consequently, the impact of microfinance programmes on financial landscapes and real sector developments has been rather disappointing. In order to make a greater contribution to the enhancement of financial market landscapes, potential roles of microfinance programmes have to be evaluated in an integrated approach to market development, wherein the types of financial products demanded locally have to be carefully analysed and the real gaps in financial services to be filled by new programmes should be identified. Options for future microfinance programmes would include linking them into local institutions (both formal and informal), or transforming these programmes into sustainable institutions anchored in local set-ups, and capable of providing a comprehensive set of financial services to different categories of the poor and microenterprises.

In this context, some valuable experiences with *microequity* programmes should be carefully evaluated. As Pretes (2002) and Eversole (2000) discuss, microequity schemes are conceived on the recognition that microcredit seldom reaches the poorest, and the very poor are too vulnerable to business risk to be indebted (see Section 4 above). The transaction costs of participating in microcredit programmes may also be too high in relation to expected returns on their income-generating activities. In contrast, microequity provided as start-up capital to the very poor can lead to reduced risk of start-up businesses and lower transaction costs, compared to microcredit provision. It can also create credit worthiness for the entrepreneur who has benefited from equity financing and has accumulated some business experiences prior to receiving microcredit. As Pretes (2002: 1345) argues, 'equity-based grants are not handouts and a welfare mentality in the recipient can be avoided by making grants to small groups, where peer pressure acts to insure that the grants are used appropriately, and where misuse may impinge upon the ability to receive future grants'.

At the same time, grants as opposed to loans to microenterprises can be justifiable on the same grounds, as for grants or concessional loans given to microfinance institutions at the start-up stage. Thus, Eversole (2000: 50) raises a legitimate question: 'if it is worthwhile to provide grants to institutions, as a kind of seed capital to get good ideas off the ground, then could it also be acceptable to provide seed capital to businesses?' Indeed, from a perspective of microequity providers, as equity financier, microequity can lead to an increase in social equity of the local community and its sustainability and independence from continued overseas aid, as equity finance could lead to the sustainability of the businesses, in which equity investment is made (Pretes 2002).

It can be suggested that equity grants could complement microcredit programmes in meeting the financial needs of those, for whom microcredit is not necessarily the most appropriate instrument. For example, as Eversole (2000) and Pretes (2002) describe, the 'trickle up' conditional grant programme experimented in Africa, Asia and Latin America has adopted the concept of microequity for start-up businesses, which is run alongside, not in competition with, microcredit programmes which cater for the needs of more experienced business people. By capitalizing businesses, the Trickle-Up Programmes target those 'who are too poor to be good credit clients, but who have the desire to invest their time and abilities in creating a business' (Eversole 2000: 51). With this objective, the Programme provides equity-grants to the fragile poor as part of a larger integrated development package. This example points to the donor community the possibility of exploring a system, wherein grant- and loan-based microfinance programme will work in tandem to offer a more complete spectrum of financial services.

All in all, it should be more explicitly recognized by donors who render support to microfinance, that microcredit schemes are not necessarily the best instrument to tackle the poverty problem of those who are at the bottom of the poverty pyramid. The poorest are as a rule risk-averse to take a loan with little fallback position. Furthermore, as Hulme argues, 'providing effective microfinance services to poor people is a part of poverty reduction strategy – but only a part' (Hulme 2000: 28). It is understandable that donors are increasingly impatient, as they realize that they could miss the 'Millennium Goals' of reducing the number of the poor by half by the year 2015. They are often dismayed by the statistics such as 'only one per cent of the world's poor households have access to financial services from MFIs' (*Microcredit Summit Report* 2000).

However, donors' policies should not be driven exclusively by political or moral imperatives or emotions. Instead, their poverty reduction strategy should be formulated on a firm basis of the deeper understanding of the *symbiotic* relationships that have been evolving between financial and real sector development. While the potential contribution of microfinance and microcredit programmes to poverty reduction is promising indeed, it is not possible to change the world easily by just applying instruments of financial engineering. The performance of microfinance and microcredit programmes always reflects, as well as impacts upon, the development of real economies.

Appendix: main features of selective donor microfinance and microcredit programmes

Main features of financial and non-financial support provided by major multilateral and bilateral donor institutions and agencies for microfinance and microcredit programmes are summarized as well as presented in Appendix Table A5.1. Unless otherwise specified, these summary descriptions and data draw on information provided at the websites of CGAP, Microcredit Summit Campaign, multilateral financial institutions, UN agencies as well as bilateral donor agencies.

Multilateral institutions

World Bank[25]

The World Bank is a key player in the donor community under CGAP in advancing the Microcredit Summit's pledge in building a robust microfinance industry, in particular with a view of its own two overriding objectives: poverty reduction and financial sector development. During period FY1991–96, the World Bank supported 55 microfinance projects with a total investment of US$713 million. Its support has accelerated over time. In 1996 alone, it provided loans of about US$88 million worldwide. It is reported that the World Bank Group provided US$200 million in concessional loans and grants for two years since the launch of the Microcredit Summit Campaign in 1997.

The World Bank provides both lending and non-lending supports to microfinance operations. The latter includes: (1) technical assistance; (2) policy dialogue; (3) grant for pilot operations; and (4) economic and sector work. In 1997, the World Bank created the Small Enterprise Development Unit in the Private Sector Development as a centre of expertise in small- and medium-enterprise development, microenterprise development, and microfinance. The World Bank also provides, through the International Finance Corporation's (IFC), loans and equity to mature microfinance institutions.

On the whole, the World Bank uses several institutional channels for microfinance support: (1) training services by the Economic Development Institute (EDI) and country departments; (2) grants through CGAP; (3) concessionally priced IDA credits; (4) market-based IBRD loans; (5) IFC equity investments.

Asian Development Bank (ADB)

ADB's microfinance projects are generally more advanced, providing more integrated services, including savings facilities. Drawing lessons from its past experience of the fragmented nature of its support for microfinance, ADB formulated in 2000 a special 'microfinance development strategy' as a central component of its overall poverty reduction strategy in the region. Microfinance policy issues are also incorporated into broader financial sector reform programmes supported by ADB. It aims, among other objectives, at: (1) promoting a common approach to microfinance operation and encouraging pro-poor products; (2) contributing to better coordination with other funding agencies. Backed with rich experiences in the microfinance concept in the region, it adopts the financial system development approach for improved financial infrastructure and apex microfinance organizations, and recognizes the need to provide a variety of financial services, including savings services, to the poor. The ADB has provided a support to two national-level apex microcredit funds in the Philippines and Nepal.

African Development Bank

African Development Bank established a special programme on microfinance, 'Micro Finance Initiative for Africa (AMINA)' in September 1997 as an initiative specifically for poverty reduction with the aim of promoting capacity-building, information dissemination, policy dialogue and donor coordination. It made US$20 million available for 10 countries for the pilot phase, including funds for on-lending by MFIs. These funds are offered on subsidized terms for loan financing schemes. The ten countries included in the pilot phase are Burkina Faso, Cameroon, Cape Verde, Chad, Ethiopia, Ghana, Malawi, Mauritania, Mozambique and Tanzania.

Inter-American Development Bank

Inter-American Development Bank (IADB) started providing support for microfinance with the 'small projects programme' in the late 1970s. So it is regarded as a pioneer with rich experiences and a growing microfinance portfolio. Between 1990 and 1996, it approved 471 microfinance operations totalling US$452 million with its estimated over 600000 microentrepreneurs as beneficiaries.

Based on this experience, it drew a new microenterprise development strategy in 1997, and launched a five-year programme, MICRO2001, in 2001 with focus on promoting policy and regulatory reform. During this phase, IADB plans to increase its investment in microenterprise development to about US$500 million, including equity investment, loans and TA from the Multilateral Investment Fund. The Microenterprise Unit at Department of Social Programmes and Sustainable Development is responsible for coordinating and monitoring the MICRO 2001. IADB disburses soft loans and grants of up to US$1 million plus technical cooperation grants through its social entrepreneurship programme (SEP). It also provides equity investments, loans and technical assistance grants of up to US$2 million to well-established, mature programmes through the Multilateral Investment Fund (MIF) for financial and nonfinancial service programmes. MIF was established in 1993 to encourage private sector development in the region with funding of US$1.3 billion. It provides technical assistance grants and investment programmes to over 400 projects in operation.

The Global Microenterprise Development Programme is fledging microcredit programmes by providing technical assistance and a line of credit.

Table A5.1 Main features of donors support for microcredit and microfinance programmes

Years considered	Programmes	Objectives	Projects	Scale of support	Scope	Features of support	Financial characteristics
World Bank Group							
1991–96	Through EDI, IDA, IBRD, IFC	Poverty reduction, financial and private sector development	55 microfinance projects	$713 million cumulative $200 million	Worldwide	Financial and technical support	Concessional loans and grants
1997–99 currently			100 microfinance projects and 150 rural finance projects				
Asian Development Bank							
1988–98		Poverty reduction, financial sector development	15 microfinance projects	$350 million	Bangladesh and Indonesia (62% of the total loan amount), Philippines and Nepal (33%), Kyrgyz (4%) Mongolia (1%)	Financial and technical support	Concessional loans and grants
			6 projects with microfinance components	$53 million			
			34 technical assistance projects	$18 million			
2000 to date	Microfinance development strategy	Poverty reduction					
African Development Bank							
Pilot phase started in 1997	Microfinance Initiative for Africa (AMINA)	Poverty reduction with capacity building, information dissemination and policy dialogue		$20 million	Burkina Faso, Cameroon, Cape Verde, Chad, Ethiopia, Ghana, Malawi, Mauritania, Mozambique, Tanzania	Financial and technical support	Concessional loans and grants

Period	Programme	Description	Projects	Amount	Countries	Support	Type
Inter-American Development Bank							
1990–96	Small project programmes		471 microfinance operations	$452 million cumulative			
1993 to date	Social entrepreneurship programme (SEP)			$10 million in 1998		Financial and technical support	Concessional loans and grants
	Multilateral Investment Fund (MIF)	Encouraging private sector development, directed to well-established, mature programmes	400 projects in operation	$1.3 billion cumulative ($31 million in 1998)		Financial and technical support	Equity investments, loans and grants for technical assistance
	Global microenterprise development programmes			$65 million in 1998		Financial and technical support	
2001–05	MICRO2001	Promoting policy and regulatory reforms		$500 million planned			Concessional loans and grants
European Bank for Reconstruction and Development							
2001	Micro and small business programmes		19 projects	EUR 403 million			Concessional loans
United Nations Development Programme							
1997 to date	Microstart	Pilot initiative for capacity building in microfinance, directed to very small institutions and investments	36 projects		25 countries	Technical support	Grants
	Special Unit for Microfinance (SUM)				42 countries, especially African rural regions	Financial and technical support	Grants

Table A5.1 Continued

Years considered	Programmes	Objectives	Projects	Scale of support	Scope	Features of support	Financial characteristics
Food and Agriculture Organization of the United Nations							
	Agri-Bank Stat	Provision of key information					
	FAO microbanking system	Software for automating banking operations			25 countries in Asia, Africa and East Europe		
	Regional agricultural credit associations	Training programmes on rural finance					
International Fund for Agricultural Development							
1979–99	IFAD funded programme and NGO/ECP grant facility	Focus on rural poor, bringing income generating activities to poor farmers and landless		$20 million cumulative			
1999 to date				$130 million annually			
International Labour Organization							
1999		Poverty reduction		$42.5 million			Grants
1999	Social finance programmes	Training, capacity building and research		$48 million			Grants

Selected bilateral donors

Years considered	Programmes	Objectives	Projects	Scale of support	Scope	Features of support	Financial characteristics
USAID							
1994 to date	Microenterprise project (MIP), of which micro-enterprise best practice project	Enterprise development		$138 million in 1996	17 countries in Africa, 11 countries in Asia and near East, 10 European	Financial and technical support, research and training	

	(MBP) and assessing the impact of microenterprise services (AIMs) Village banking		68 village banking programmes		(former socialist) countries, 10 Latin and Central American countries		
Canadian International Development Agency 1997–2000	Microfinance and microcredit development institutional action plan (MFD/MED)	Poverty reduction		$70 million in 1997–98	50 countries	Financial and technical support	
1990–99			540 projects	$1.8 billion cumulative	92 countries		
Department for International Development 1998	DFID funded programmes and joint funding scheme (JFS) with UK-based NGOs	Poverty reduction		$80 million in 1999	36 countries, with focus on 20 countries in Sub-Saharan Africa and South Asia	Financial and technical support	Grants

Source: Websites of respective donor agencies.

In 1998, IADB approved US$107 million in microenterprise development programmes, divided among the SEP (US$10 million), MIF for (US$31 million), technical cooperation programmes (US$41million) and global microenterprise loans (US$65 million). In 1998, IADB also received grant assistance from the government of Norway and established the Norway Fund for Microenterprise Development for strengthening the implementation of the microenterprise development strategy of IADB.

European Bank for Reconstruction and Development (EBRD)

The EBRD's main focus is on the private sector development, with 70 per cent of all Bank operations (by volume) devoted to private sector activities. Its central component is to build a financial sector that serves the needs of the business community, in particular, small- and medium-sized enterprises (SMEs) and microenterprises. Its financial sector operations represent almost a third of the total value of EBRD operations, the largest sector operation. It renders support to financial institutions by investing in them, developing skills and by promoting sound business practices.

As of 30 December 2001, the EBRD invested over €3.03 million in bank lending (112 projects), €1.02 million in bank equity (80 projects); €1.22 million into equity funds (63 projects); €403 million through micro- and small-business programmes (19 projects) and €236 million in non-bank financial institutions.

It posted, at its website, net cumulative business volume in micro- and small-business programmes in June 2002, amounting to €332 million in total.

UN agencies

Several UN agencies are actively supporting microcredit and microfinance programmes. These include UNDP, UNCTAD, UNICEFF, UNHCR, UNWFP, UNESCO, FAO, IFAD and UNCDF.

UNDP (United Nations Development Programme)

UNDP's programme, Microstart, established in 1997, is the best-known pilot initiative, initially with 36 projects in 25 countries for capacity-building in microfinance. It is designed to build the capacity of five to ten new or small local microfinance organizations such as NGOs and banks. In short, in terms of specialization among donors, Microstart opted for the lower end by supporting very small institutions and investments. It provides a grant of up to US$150000 to local NGOs or community organizations to receive technical support from established MFIs such as Grameen, Accion, SEWA and BRAC. UNDP also established, with UNCDF (United Nations Capital Development Fund), the Special Unit for Microfinance (SUM) in 1997. SUM supports UNDP's microfinance portfolio by providing advisory support services. At the beginning of 2002, SUM supported the UNDP and UNCDF portfolio of microfinance operation in 42 countries through technical advisory services and financial support. Many of SUM's microfinance interventions are in the rural regions of Africa.

FAO (Food and Agriculture Organization of the United Nations)

FAO provides, through its Rural Finance Group, several technical assistance programmes such as provision of key information (Agri-Bank Stat) or software for automating banking operations (the FAO Microbanking System). The latter is a collaborative venture with the German Agency for Technical Cooperation (GTZ), and is used in over 25 countries throughout Asia, Africa and East Europe. FAO also supports regional agricultural credit associations (RACAs), which organize and coordinate training programmes on rural finance.

IFAD (International Fund for Agricultural Development)

As an agency specializing in rural development with focus on rural poor, IFAD regards microcredit as an empowerment tool and as a means of bringing income-generating activities to poor farmers as well as the landless. It tries to combine credit with access to extension and better technologies and ready access to markets. Over 20 years to the close of the 1990s, it provided about US$2 billion for microfinance activities. At the end of the 1990s, it planned to commit about US$130 annually, specifically for microfinance through IFAD financed projects or NGO/ECP (extended cooperation) grant facility.

ILO (International Labour Organization)

ILO contributes to microfinance through capacity building programme and research. In 1999, it provided grants of about US$42.5 million to poverty-oriented MFIs and US$48 million for training, capacity-building and research through the social finance programmes (the trust funds).

Bilateral donor agencies

USAID

USAID has long held a perspective that enterprise development is one of the most critical conduits for economic development and growth, and has engaged in building market-based financial institutions and best-practice for serving the financial need of small and microenterprises over the last two decades in developing countries. With that strong tradition, USAID instituted in 1994 the Micro Enterprise Project (MIP), an initiative to support technical and financial assistance, research and training on microenterprise development and finance. It is an agency-wide initiative designed to integrate microenterprise more fully into its programming. It was developed in consultation with the US Congress and a policy group of microenterprise practitioners under microenterprise coalition. Indeed, the Clinton Administration advocated microcredit lending programmes internationally as well as through domestic agencies. USAID has acted to strengthen the link between the domestic and international microenterprise movements. MIP has several sub-projects, including the Microenterprise Best Practice Project (MBP) and Assessing the Impact of Microenterprise Services (AIMs) to assess the outreach and sustainability.

In FY 1996, USAID worked in about 40 countries worldwide with US$138 million devoted to microenterprise programmes. It is a major funder of village banking and supported 68 village banking programmes run by US NGOs in 1996.

USAID was active in 17 countries in Africa, in 11 countries of Asia and the Near East, in 10 European (former socialist) countries, 10 Latin and Central American countries.

CIDA (Canadian International Development Agency)

CIDA places its microfinance and microdevelopment programmes as a central component of the overall poverty reduction strategy with its own credit union movement tradition. On the basis of its history and experiences, it produced 'microfinance and microcredit development institutional action plan' (MFD/MED) for 1998–2000. It has been very active in providing both financial and technical support in MFD/MED through Canadian NGOs such as Calmeadow, MREDA (Mennonite Economic Development Association) and NGOs.

Over the 10 years (1990–99) cumulatively, CIDA spent about US$1.8 billion on 540 projects in 92 countries, while in the late 1980s and early 1990s it had a larger budget. In 1998, CIDA supported microfinance and microcredit programmes in 42 countries and planned to expand to 8 additional countries in 1998–99. In FY 1997–98, CIDA spent US$70 million on MFD/ MED related programmes. It also supported Canadian NGOs working in the field through the partnership programme on a multi-year basis.

DFID (Department for International Development)

DFID also placed its microfinance programme as a central component of the poverty reduction strategy embedded in its White Paper on International Development.

DFID supports strongly MFIs which provide voluntary savings facilities as well as credit. DFID gives grants to MFIs towards institutional capacity-building, operational costs, loan funds, as well as technical assistance for training and systems development.

In 1998 it funded microfinance programmes in 36 countries worldwide with a focus on some 20 countries in Sub-Saharan Africa and South Asia. It is reported that the commitments to microfinance programmes total approximately US$80 million annually as in 1999. DFID provides these funds to established MFIs through its bilateral country programmes, while it sets up a 'joint funding scheme' (JFS) to assist fledging institutions which are required to link up with an experienced UK-based NGOs.

Other donors

European Union provides technical assistance and credit lines to microenterprises and microfinance institutions through Rural Development Programme and European Development Funds. Local, medium, small and microenterprises are singled out as the focus of European Commission (EC), European Investment Bank (EIB) and Centre for the Development of Industry/Enterprise as well as other decentralized cooperation programmes in EU's strategy paper for private sector development in ACP countries issued in 1998. GTZ (German Agency for Technical Cooperation) is also very active in offering technical support to microfinance development and network programmes for self-help groups as part of its financial system development programme. SIDA (Sweden), Norway and the Netherlands are also known to provide technical and financial support to microenterprise and microfinance programmes.

Notes

*   The author is grateful for constructive and thoughtful comments received from the project coordinator, Matthew Odedokun, which were very helpful in revising the earlier draft. The author alone is however responsible for any remaining errors and omissions.
1. This chapter's focus is more on microcredit, though microfinance is a broader concept which includes also micro-insurance or micro-leasing that could be used as potential financial instruments for microenterprise development.
2. The borrower net worth is defined by Gertler and Rose (1994) as the sum of a borrower's net liquid assets and the collateral value of his illiquid assets, including not

only tangible physical assets, but any prospective future earnings that the borrower could offer as collateral.

3. In a principal–agent relationship that characterizes lender–borrower interactions for dealing with idiosyncratic risks, lenders are preoccupied with the question of whether they will be repaid, and the cost of acquiring information and contract enforcement becomes a critical element in realization of a proposed credit transaction.

4. When credit relationships are extended beyond the 'exclusive' borrower–lender relationship and repeated personalized transactions within the close-knit community, collateral is typically used to sustain transactions. In general, collateral pledged in exchange for loans serves the three important functions: (1) of directly reducing cost to the lender of a loan default; (2) of adding an incentive for the borrower to repay, thereby reducing the moral hazard; and (3) of mitigating the problem of adverse selection by enabling the lender to screen out borrowers most likely to default (Udry 1990). See Nissanke and Aryeetey (2000) for more detailed discussion on institutional arrangements for credit risk management in low-income countries.

5. As Sindzingre and Stein (2002) note, distinctions of institutions based on the degree of formality are conceptually *ad hoc*. While recognizing the ambiguous nature of the dichotomy of formal/informal institutions, we have adopted here this conventional term purely for the sake of an easy reference to existing literature in this field of financial economics.

6. 'Informal' segments comprise of heterogeneous agents/associations. In general, 'informal' financial transactions can be grouped into those that are non-commercial, such as transactions between relatives and friends or small-scale group arrangements, and those that are commercially-based, conducted by single collectors, estate-owners, landlords, traders or money-lenders.

7. For more detailed discussion on financing enterprise development in low-income countries, see Nissanke (2001).

8. There is a large literature on microfinancial institutions established (Levitsky 1993; Otero and Rhyne 1994; Yaron 1994, and Hulme and Mosley 1996). Morduch (1999a) contains a useful and updated literature survey on microfinance.

9. Not all MFIs adopt a group lending methodology. See Morduch (1999a) for discussion of individual-based microfinance contract.

10. As Marr (2002) notes, Stiglitz's model of peer monitoring is based on four assumptions: (1) that group members have perfect and costless information about one another; (2) that all individuals are identical in their risk types; (3) that peer monitoring is costless; and (4) that borrowers do not have alternative sources of credit. Assumptions are one by one relaxed in the subsequently developed theoretical models of joint liability. For a critical literature review of these models, see Marr (2002).

11. As Gibbon and Schulpen note in Chapter 2, it is hard to establish precise levels of donors' financial support to microcredit and enterprise programmes, since most of donors do not publish systematically the size of their microcredit programmes. The on-line Global Donor Portfolio Database, on which CGAP has been working in the past two years, may allow us to examine global donor flows in the near future.

12. Currently, the microfinance gateway posts nearly 100 websites of multilateral and bilateral donor agencies or private foundations, which cover microcredit and microfinance programmes as one of their important development-related activities (www.Microfinancegateway.org).

13. One of CGAP's first grants was its co-investment of US$2 million with another US$1 million provided from a private banker in Comparatamos, which works with very poor women in Mexico's most destitute regions (World Bank 2002, Box 8: 40–1).
14. The 1997 Microcredit summit was organized by civil society in response to the UN summits of the 1990s.
15. 'Poorest' means that the family was in the bottom 50 per cent of the population living below their country's poverty line (Microcredit Summit Report).
16. The World Bank estimates that 1.2 billion people are living in absolute poverty globally, on less than one dollar a day.
17. Webster *et al.* (1996) on IFC's experience is cited as findings supporting this position.
18. In 2000, CGAP launched the Pro-Poor Innovation Challenge, which was established to encourage MFIs to undertake innovative work in reaching the poorest with each programme entitled awards up to US$50000.
19. The Microcredit Summit Campaign states four core themes of: (1) reaching the poorest families; (2) reaching and empowering women; (3) building financial self-sufficient institutions; and (4) ensuring impact on the lives of clients and their families (Microcredit Summit Report).
20. Programmes operating in Sub-Saharan Africa are known to have incurred very high costs, in particular. Bagachwa (1995) discusses the difficulties of one such programme initiated in Tanzania, the Presidential Trust Fund for Self Reliance (PTFSR), which has adopted the Grameen Bank model. In 1991, the PTFSR extended TSh 4.3 million in loans against a cost of TSh 5.6 million. As of June 1992, it had made TSh 9.6 million in loans, yielding interest income of TSh 0.99 million against an operating cost of TSh 7.7 million. Savings are reported to have been only TSh 1.01 million.
21. For the detailed critical survey of the recent impact studies, see Marr (2002).
22. This statistic comes originally from Bank of Indonesia (1990).
23. The high demand for flexible savings services by the poor has been recognized by the donor communities for some time (e.g. DAC–OECD 1994; World Bank 1999; and Asian Development Bank 2000). The microfinance programmes supported by the Asian Development Bank now have savings facilities as a central feature of their activities, as discussed in Appendix. However, many new MFIs still tend to focus more on credit delivery. Recognizing this drawback prevalent in Africa, MicroSave-Africa was established in 2000 to conduct pilot projects in 11 countries in East and southern Africa.
24. In this respect, there is again a huge regional variation in the degree of financial market integration, involving MFIs. While coordination and linkages among institutions have gathered a pace over the last two decades and quite advanced in Asia, financial services are typically very fragmented in Sub-Saharan Africa (Nissanke and Aryeetey 1998, ADB 2000).
25. World Bank (1999, 2002).

References

Adams, D. W., D. Graham and J. von Pischke (1984). *Undermining Rural Development with Cheap Credit.* Boulder, CO: Westview Press.

Alderman, Harold and Christina Paxson (1992). 'Do the Poor Insure?: A Synthesis of the Literature on Risk Sharing Institutions in Developing Countries', in E. Bacha (ed.),

Economics in a Changing World: Development Trade and Environment. London: Macmillan.

ADB (Asian Development Bank) (2000). 'Finance for the Poor: Microfinance Development Strategy'. Manila: ADB.

Bagachwa, M. S. D. (1995). 'Financial Integration and Development in Sub-Saharan Africa: A Study of *Informal Finance* in Tanzania'. Working Paper 79. London: Overseas Development Institute.

Bank Rakyat Indonesia (1990). 'Kupedes Development Impact Survey'. Jakarta: BRI.

Batra, Geeta and Syed Mahmood (2001). 'Direct Support to Private Firms: Evidence on Effectiveness'. Private Sector Advisory Services. Washington, DC: World Bank.

Besley, T. (1995). 'Savings, Credit and Insurance', in J. Behrman and T. N. Srinivason (eds), *Handbook of Development Economics*, Vol. 3. New York: North Holland.

Boomgard, J. (1989). 'AID Microenterprise Stocktaking: Synthesis Report'. Bethesda, MD: Development Alternatives Inc.

Caprio, Gerald Jr and Asli Demirgüç-Kunt (1998). 'The Role of Long-Term Finance: Theory and Evidence'. *The World Bank Research Observer*, 13 (2): 171–89.

Cohen, Monique and Jennefer Sebstad (2000). 'Microfinance, Risk Management and Poverty'. AIMS Paper. Washington, DC: USAID.

Consultative Group to Assist the Poorest (CGAP) (2002). Available at: www.cgap.org.

Chambers, Robert (1997). *Whose Reality Counts? Putting the First Last*. London: Intermediate Technology Publication.

DAC/OECD (1994). 'DAC Orientations for Development Co-operation in Support of Private Sector Development'. Paris: OECD/DAC.

Dunford, Christopher (2000). 'The Holy Grail of Microfinance: Helping the Poor and Sustainable?' *Small Enterprise Development*, 11: 40–4.

Eversole, Robyn (2000). 'Beyond Microcredit – the Trickle up Program'. *Small Enterprise Development*, 11 (1): 45–58.

Gertler, Mark and Andrew Rose (1994). 'Finance, Growth and Public Policy', in G. Caprio, Jr, I. Atiyas and J. Hanson (eds), *Financial Reforms: Theory and Experience*. Cambridge: Cambridge University Press.

Ghatak, Maitreesh (1999). 'Group Lending, Local Information and Peer Selection'. *Journal of Development Economics*, 60 (1): 27–50.

Ghatak, Maitreesh (2000). 'Screening by the Company you Keep: Joint-liability Lending and the Peer Selection Effect'. *The Economic Journal*, 110 (July): 601–31.

Ghatak, Maitreesh and Timothy Guinnane (1999). 'The Economics of Lending with Joint Liability: Theory and Practice'. *Journal of Development Economics*, 60 (1): 195–228.

Gibbons, David and Jennifer Meehan (2002). 'Financing Microfinance for Poverty Reduction'. Paper presented at the plenary session at the Microcredit Summit, November. New York.

Goez, A. M. and R. S. Gupta (1996). 'Who Takes the Credit? Gender, Power and Control over Loan Use in Rural Credit Programmes in Bangladesh'. *World Development*, 24: 45–63.

Holzmann, Robert and Steen Lau Jorgensen (1999). 'Social Protection as Social Risk Management'. Social Protection Discussion Paper. Washington, DC: World Bank.

Hulme, David (2000). 'Is Microdebt Good for Poor People? A Note on the Dark Side of Microfinance'. *Small Enterprise Development*, 11 (1): 26–8.

Hulme, David and Paul Mosley (1996). *Finance against Poverty*. London: Routledge.

Khandker, Shahidur (1998). *Fighting Poverty with Microcredit: Experience in Bangladesh*. Oxford: Oxford University Press.

Levitsky, Jacob (1993). 'Innovations in the Financing of Small and Microenterprises in Developing Countries'. Small Enterprise Development Programme. Geneva: ILO.

Marr, Ana (1999). 'The Poor and their Money: What have we Learned?'. Poverty Briefing Paper No. 4. London: Overseas Development Institute.

Marr, Ana (2002). 'Studying Group Dynamics: An Analysis of Microfinance Impacts on Poverty Reduction and its Application in Peru'. London: University of London. Ph. D Thesis.

Microcredit Summit (various issues) (1998). 'Microcredit Summit Campaign'. Available at: www.microcreditsummit.org.

Montgomery, R. (1996). 'Disciplining or Protecting the Poor: Avoiding the Social Costs of Peer Pressure in Microcredit Schemes'. *Journal of International Development*, 8 (2): 289–305.

Morduch, John (1999a). 'The Microfinance Promises'. *Journal of Economic Literature*, 37: 1569–614.

Morduch, John (1999b). 'Between the State and the Market: Can Informal Insurance Patch the Safety Net?'. *The World Bank Research Observer*, 14 (2).

Nissanke, Machiko (2001). 'Financing Enterprise Development in Sub-Saharan Africa'. *Cambridge Journal of Economics*, 25: 343–67.

Nissanke, Machiko and Ernest Aryeetey (1998). *Financial Integration and Development in Sub-Saharan Africa*. London and New York: Routledge.

Nissanke, Machiko and Ernest Aryeetey (2000). 'Institutional Analysis of Financial Market Fragmentation in Sub-Saharan Africa: Risk–Cost Configuration Approach'. SOAS Working Paper. London: School of Oriental and African Studies, University of London.

Otero, M. and E. Rhyne (eds) (1994). *The New World of Microenterprise Finance*. London: Intermediate Technology Publication.

Pretes, Michael (2002). 'Microequity and Microfinance'. *World Development*, 30 (8): 1341–53.

Rahman, A. (1999). 'Microcredit Initiatives for Equitable and Sustainable Development: Who Pays?'. *World Development*, 27: 67–82.

Sen, Amartya (1984). *Resources, Values and Development*. New York: Basil Blackwell.

Sen, Amartya (1993). 'Capacity and Well-being', in Martha Nussbaum and Amartya Sen (eds), *The Quality of Life*. Oxford: Clarendon Press.

Sindzingre, Alice and Howard Stein (2002). 'Institutions, Development, and Global Integration: A Theoretical Contribution'. Paris: CNRS. Mimeo.

Stiglitz, Joseph (1990). 'Peer Monitoring and Credit Markets'. *The World Bank Economic Review*, 4 (3): 351–66.

Stiglitz, Joseph E. and Andrew Weiss (1981). 'Credit Rationing in Markets with Imperfect Information'. *American Economic Review*, 71: 393–410.

Udry, C. (1990). 'Credit Markets in Northern Nigeria: Credit as Insurance in Rural Economy'. *The World Bank Economic Review*, 4 (3): 251–69.

Webster Leila, Randall Ripelle and Anne-Marie Chidzero (1996). 'World Bank Lending for Small Enterprises 1989–1993'. World Bank Technical Paper No. 311. Washington, DC: World Bank.

World Bank (1999). 'The World Bank Group's Microfinance Institutional Action Plan 1999'. Washington, DC: World Bank.

World Bank (2002). 'Private Sector Development Strategy – Directions for the World Bank Group'. Washington, DC: World Bank.

Yaron, Jacob (1994). 'What Makes Rural Financial Institutions Successful'. *The World Bank Research Observer*, 9: 49–70.

Zeller, Manfred, Getrud Schrieder, Joachim von Braun and Franz Heidhues (1997). 'Rural Finance for Food Security for the Poor: Implications for Research and Policy'. *Food Policy Review*, 4. Washington, DC: IFPRI.

6

Flow of Foreign Direct Investment in Developing Countries: A Two-part Econometric Modelling Approach

Oluyele Akinkugbe

1 Introduction

The developing countries of the world have in general been recipients of both official and private financial flows over the last four decades. Understandably so, since in most of these countries, the level of domestic savings is generally very low, the financial sector is widely underdeveloped and in most cases repressed, and therefore the capacity to harness domestic financial resources for sustainable development of the key sectors of the economy is quite limited. A wide body of literature has investigated the role that the flow of external financing could play in the development of recipient countries. The convergence of opinion seems to be that on the balance, there is a net positive relationship between external financial assistance and economic performance of countries, particularly if and when such assistance is accompanied by conducive policy environment (Burnside and Dollar 2000). This may have in some way informed the UN General Assembly, which after adopting the international development goals (IDG) in September 2000, also conceded that the mobilization of external financial resources is essential to the attainment of the goals. An important component of the IDG is the commitment of governments to reduce by one half, the incidence of absolute poverty, which is more pronounced in the developing countries of the world by 2015. According to UN (2002: 5),

> private international capital flows, particularly foreign direct investment... are vital components to national and international development efforts. Foreign direct investment contributes toward financing sustained economic growth over the long term. It is especially important for its potential to transfer knowledge and technology, create jobs, boost overall

productivity, enhance competitiveness and entrepreneurship, and ultimately eradicate poverty through economic growth and development.

A similar position was also taken by OECD (2002) which alluded to the fact that FDI could serve as a powerful engine for achieving poverty-reducing growth and development.

Therefore, in the last decade or so when the flow of official development assistance (ODA) seems to have declined in relative importance, the flow of private resources and, in particular, foreign direct investment (FDI) to developing countries has been on the increase. Whereas in the 1990s the annual global flows of multilateral and bilateral development aid (ODA) remained stagnant at US$54 billion, global FDI inflows in 2000 reached a total of about US$1.6 trillion.[1] A number of factors may have been responsible for this development. One of such is the end of the cold war and the relative increase in net official flows to the countries in transition in Eastern Europe and former Soviet republics. Other reasons include the growing importance of private flows, particularly in the developing countries themselves, reflecting the new wave of liberalization and globalization and therefore the flow of foreign investment to the telecommunications, financial services and other sectors in many of the countries.

What seems to have characterized this increased flow of FDI, moreover, is that it has not only been volatile, but has also been concentrated in a fairly small number of developing countries. These are the very large economies (e.g. China, Brazil, Indonesia) or in the fairly advanced economies (e.g. Hong Kong, Singapore, Korea). Many low-income countries of Africa and the Pacific region have not been able to attract significant flow of FDI as a complementary source of financing investments and may have therefore been left out in terms of the benefit derivable from the increased flows. The question then remains as to why international investors have not found these developing countries attractive, and what factors may reasonably explain the volatility of inflow to existing receiving ones. This chapter, therefore, constitutes a major step towards examining these all-important development policy questions, which are considered to be very relevant in the search for sustainable source of financing private sector development, particularly in the hitherto neglected developing countries.

What distinguish our present effort from earlier studies on this subject are two fold. In the first instance, we have tried to recapitulate the subject matter into two interdependent parts. The first part relates to issues as to why foreign investors may choose to or not to allocate FDI to previously neglected developing countries, that is, whether or not to overcome the inertia by venturing into these countries. The second part then relates to issues of the volume of FDI to allocate to existing FDI-receiving countries and why the volatility in flows to these countries as witnessed over the years. Most recent studies on the subject (Collier and Pattillo 2000;

Noorbakhsh and Paloni 2001; Obwona 2001; Addison and Heshmati 2002; Asiedu 2002) have addressed only the second part. They have sought to explain why foreign investors might decide to increase or decrease the volume of FDI flows to receiving countries.

Second, with the use of pooled multi-country data, this study has tried to explain the domestic and external, or 'pull and push', factors affecting aggregate investors in the two-part decision scenario as highlighted. In this regard, the analysis in this chapter is based on the two-part econometric modelling framework. This methodology, which follows from the one that has often been used in explaining the allocation of foreign aid by bilateral donors among developing countries (Dudley and Montmarquette 1976; McGillivray and Oczkowski 1991, 1992; Tarp *et al.* 1998) is yet to be explored in the FDI literature.

The remainder of the chapter is organized as follows. In Section 2 we examine the recent trend in FDI inflow to developing countries, highlighting the fact that the flow has been unevenly distributed. Section 3 contains a brief review of existing FDI literature, and the conceptual framework adopted is discussed in Section 4. Empirical analyses and results are presented in Section 5 and in Section 6 we examine what lies ahead for low-income developing countries in terms of attracting foreign financial resources. Summary and conclusions are given in Section 7.

2 Recent trend in FDI inflow to developing countries

In recent times and in response to the need to provide investor-friendly environment so as not to be left behind in the new wave of global integration, the attitude of many developing countries has changed significantly. They have become more willing to offer numerous financial and non-financial incentives to multinational corporations in order to encourage them to increase direct investment flows (UNCTAD 1998). Given the open door policies, and some external factors in the developed world such as low interest rates and appreciable growth rates, the flow of FDI to developing countries has witnessed a rising trend in the last decade. As shown in Table 6.1, FDI flows to developing countries increased from US$59.6 billion on average between 1989 and 1994 to US$241 billion in 2000. In the same light, the stock of FDI in developing countries (Table 6.2) increased from US$257 billion in 1990 to US$2032 billion in 2000.

In spite of the dramatic increases in the stock and inflow of foreign direct investment to developing countries in the last decade as revealed by Tables 6.1 and 6.2, the geography of the flows has been very uneven. Table 6.1 shows that between 1989 and 2000, two regions, Asia, Latin America and the Caribbean attracted 92.5 per cent (Latin America and the Caribbean 29.4 and Asia 63.1) of the total on average for the period 1989 to 1994. In 2000 these two regions together continued to dominate the other

Table 6.1 Foreign direct investment flows by host region, 1989–2000

	1989–94 (ann. avg)	1995	1996	1997	1998	1999	2000
Billions of US dollars							
World	200.14	331.10	385.00	478.00	692.54	1075.05	1270.76
Developed countries	137.06	202.22	218.87	267.56	482.60	828.31	1004.30
Developing countries	59.64	114.58	153.31	191.17	188.93	223.51	241.04
Africa	4.01	5.93	6.44	10.97	8.27	10.47	9.07
of which least developed countries	0.89	1.66	1.65	2.17	3.21	4.77	3.89
Latin America and the Caribbean	17.51	32.31	51.28	71.15	83.20	110.28	86.17
Developing Europe	0.23	0.47	1.08	1.70	1.61	2.72	2.03
Asia	37.66	75.30	94.35	107.21	95.60	99.73	143.48
The Pacific	0.23	0.56	0.15	0.14	0.25	0.30	0.28
Central and Eastern Europe	3.44	14.27	12.73	19.19	21.01	23.22	25.42
Share of global inflows of FDI (%)							
Developed countries	68.5	61.1	56.9	56.0	69.7	77.0	79.0
Developing countries	29.8	34.6	39.8	40.0	27.3	20.8	19.0
Africa	2.0	1.8	1.7	2.3	1.2	1.0	0.7
of which least developed countries	0.4	0.5	0.4	0.5	0.5	0.4	0.3
Latin America and the Caribbean	8.7	9.8	13.3	14.9	12.0	10.3	6.8
Developing Europe	0.1	0.1	0.3	0.4	0.2	0.3	0.2
Asia	18.8	22.7	24.5	22.4	13.8	9.3	11.3
The Pacific	0.1	0.2	0.0	0.0	0.0	0.0	0.0
Central and Eastern Europe	1.7	4.3	3.3	4.0	3.0	2.2	2.0
Share of FDI inflows to developing countries (%)							
Africa	6.7	5.2	4.2	5.7	4.4	4.7	3.8
of which least developed countries	1.5	1.4	1.1	1.1	1.7	2.1	1.6
Latin America and the Caribbean	29.4	28.2	33.4	37.2	44.0	49.3	35.7
Developing Europe	0.4	0.4	0.7	0.9	0.9	1.2	0.8
Asia	63.1	65.7	61.5	56.1	50.6	44.6	59.5
The Pacific	0.4	0.5	0.1	0.1	0.1	0.1	0.1
Share of FDI inflows to Africa (%)							
Least developed countries	22.2	28.0	25.7	19.8	38.8	45.6	42.9

Source: Basu and Srinivasan (2002).

Table 6.2   Foreign direct investment inward stock by host region, 1980–2000

	1980	1985	1990	1995	1999	2000
	Billions of US dollars					
World	615.81	893.66	1888.67	2937.54	5196.04	6314.27
Developed countries	358.45	537.26	1388.76	2036.72	3301.92	4157.64
Developing countries	257.36	356.26	496.92	864.40	1792.15	2031.92
Africa	32.74	33.85	48.65	75.91	140.55	148.03
Latin America and the Caribbean	49.96	79.67	116.68	201.62	520.30	606.91
Developing Europe	0.16	0.28	1.13	3.26	9.45	11.46
Asia	173.35	241.27	328.23	580.70	1118.42	1261.77
The Pacific	1.18	1.20	2.23	2.90	3.45	3.74
Central and Eastern Europe	0.0	0.0	2.99	36.42	101.97	124.72
	Share of global stock FDI (%)					
Developed countries	58.2	60.1	73.5	69.3	63.5	65.8
Developing countries[a]	41.8	39.9	26.3	29.4	34.5	32.2
Africa	5.3	3.8	2.6	2.6	2.7	2.3
Latin America and the Caribbean	8.1	8.9	6.2	6.9	10.0	9.6
Developing Europe	0.0	0.0	0.1	0.1	0.2	0.2
Asia	28.1	27.0	17.4	19.8	21.5	20.0
The Pacific	0.2	0.1	0.1	0.1	0.1	0.1
Central and Eastern Europe	0.0	0.0	0.2	1.2	2.0	2.0

Note: [a] includes South Africa.

Source: Basu and Srinivasan (2002).

developing regions by attracting 95.2 per cent of the total FDI flows. This implies therefore, that Africa – including the least developed countries and the Pacific region – attracted quite an insignificant proportion of between 7.5 and 4.8 per cent of FDI inflows to developing countries in the period 1989–94 and 2000.

Table 6.3 shows the top 10 recipients of FDI inflow amongst the developing countries. These are China, Brazil, Mexico, Argentina, Poland, Chile, Malaysia, Venezuela, Russian Federation and Thailand, all middle-income countries. They received close to 70 per cent of total FDI inflows between 1992 and 1998. World Bank (1999) classified these top 10 recipients as those that possess important advantages, which might have made them very attractive to foreign investors. These advantages included the market size and increased openness in the case of China, and improved policy and strong economic fundamentals in the case of Malaysia, Thailand and Chile. Table 6.3, therefore, reveals that about 93 per cent of total FDI flows to all developing countries went to the middle-income developing countries,

Table 6.3 Net FDI inflow to developing countries: top 10 recipients and regions, 1992–98

Country/country group	1992	1993	1994	1995	1996	1997	1998
Top 10 recipients							
China	11.2	27.5	33.8	35.8	40.2	44.2	42.0
Brazil	2.1	1.3	3.1	4.9	11.2	19.7	24.0
Mexico	4.4	4.4	11.0	9.5	9.2	12.5	10.0
Argentina	4.0	3.3	3.1	4.8	5.1	6.6	5.6
Poland	0.7	1.7	1.9	3.7	4.5	4.9	5.5
Chile	0.9	1.0	2.6	3.0	4.7	5.4	5.0
Malaysia	5.2	5.0	4.3	4.1	5.1	5.1	5.0
Venezuela	0.6	0.4	0.8	1.0	2.2	5.1	3.7
Russian Federation	0.0	0.0	0.6	2.0	2.5	6.2	3.0
Thailand	2.1	1.8	1.4	2.1	2.3	3.7	4.8
Share of total (%)							
Low-income countries	6.9	7.2	6.2	6.9	7.4	6.5	6.8
Middle-income countries	93.1	92.8	93.8	93.1	92.6	93.5	93.2
Top 10 countries	67.6	69.2	70.7	67.2	68.8	69.5	70.1
Transition economies	9.0	9.4	8.2	16.6	13.3	14.3	13.5

Source: World Bank (1999).

Table 6.4 FDI flows to developing countries: percentage of GDP, 1990–98

Country group	1990	1991	1992	1993	1994	1995	1996	1997	1998
Middle-income	0.6	0.8	1.1	1.5	1.9	2.0	2.2	2.7	2.6
Excluding China	0.6	0.8	0.9	1.0	1.3	1.5	1.7	2.3	2.2
Top 10 countries	0.7	1.0	1.4	2.0	2.5	2.5	2.7	3.3	3.1
Excluding China	0.7	1.0	1.1	1.0	1.4	1.6	2.0	2.7	2.7
China	1.0	1.2	2.7	6.4	6.2	5.1	4.9	4.9	4.2
Low-income (non-oil exporters)									
Mineral producers	0.5	1.1	1.1	1.7	1.5	2.0	2.4	2.6	2.4
Others	0.0	0.2	0.2	0.3	0.4	0.6	0.7	0.9	0.9
Low- and middle-income oil exporters	0.6	0.9	0.5	1.1	1.0	0.2	0.8	2.1	1.8

Source: World Bank (1999).

while their low-income counterpart attracted just about 7 per cent of inflow between 1992 and 1998. Table 6.4 also demonstrates the increasing importance of the transition economies of Eastern Europe and the former Soviet republics as alternative destinations of foreign direct investment flows.

To further reinforce this argument of uneven flows of FDI to developing countries, in Table 6.4, we show the ratio of FDI to GDP in the top ten recipient countries and country groups. As revealed by the table, in the middle-income countries, FDI/GDP ratio increased from 0.6 per cent in the early 1990s to an average of 2.5 per cent in the late 1990s. On the other hand, the FDI/GDP ratio in low-income developing countries increased from only 0.5 per cent in the early 1990s to about 1 per cent since 1995. For the low-income countries that are neither oil nor mineral producing, the ratio of FDI to GDP remained at less than 1 per cent in the last one decade.

An important point that derives from the pattern of concentration of FDI flows among developing countries described above is the fact that the ten countries highlighted as the most important FDI destinations constitute only about 38 per cent of the total population of all developing countries and territories (UNCTAD 2001c). This may mean that the remaining 62 per cent of developing countries' population were in receipt of only 30 per cent of FDI inflows in 1998 (Table 6.3). In other words, about two-thirds of the developing world was still virtually written off the map as far as any assumed benefit from FDI inflow was concerned during the greater part of the 1990s.

Turning to the sectoral or industrial composition of FDI inflow to developing countries, Table 6.5 reveals that as a proportion of total world FDI

Table 6.5   FDI inflows to developing countries by industry, 1988 and 1997 (US$ billions)

	1988			1997		
	Total	% share	% of world total	Total	% share	% of world total
Primary	1.78	6.7	17.2	7.47	4.6	46.5
Agriculture	0.57	2.1	99.8	1.80	1.1	82.8
Mining, quarry and petroleum	1.22	4.6	12.4	5.67	3.5	40.8
Manufacturing	17.80	66.8	33.7	81.20	50.1	53.6
Chemicals	3.37	12.7		14.40	8.9	
Machinery	1.02	3.8		4.51	2.8	
Electronics	2.07	7.7		5.40	6.6	
Transport and equipment	0.24	0.9		0.78	0.5	
Services	6.65	25.0	14.3	66.79	41.3	38.8
Trade	0.84	3.2		5.56	3.4	
Finance	0.86	3.2		7.26	4.5	
Real estate	0.68	2.5		7.43	4.6	
Communications	0.55	2.1		12.10	7.5	
Unspecified	0.42	1.6		6.45	4.0	
All industries	26.67	100.0	22.3	161.90	100.0	44.9

Source: UNCTAD (1999).

inflows, developing countries received only about US$26.7 billion or 22 per
cent in 1988. This, however, increased appreciably to about US$162 billion
or 45 per cent of world total in 1997. In terms of the industrial composition
of these flows, Table 6.5 shows the rapidly growing share of FDI flows to the
services sector of developing countries. From only about US$6.6 billion in
1988, FDI inflow to the services sector increased to US$66.8 billion in 1997.
This demonstrates the growing investment in the information, communications and technology (ICT) sectors in many developing countries in the
last decade, and particularly in the economies of the highlighted top ten FDI
recipients. Similarly, when compared with the rest of the world, the share of
inflow to the agriculture subsector in developing countries remained consistently very high. This again is an indication of the continuing concentration of activities in the primary producing subsectors in many developing
countries of Africa and the Pacific regions.

What seems to have emerged from this uneven distribution of FDI inflow
is the fact that it reflects, to a large extent, the concentration of economic
activities. Export performance and therefore the extent of openness to international trade, domestic investment levels and productive activities as well
as technology and payments are key to the capacity of regions and countries
to attract FDI inflows (UNCTAD 2001b). The richer and more competitive
economies of the world tend to possess these capacities and are therefore
able to receive more international direct investment than the poorer and
underdeveloped nations.

From the foregoing, the central question then remains as to what could
be done to ensure to rectify this lopsided distribution of FDI, particularly to
ensure that low-income developing countries have sustained access to this
form of external financial resources. Provision of some clues to this intriguing question is what constitutes the primary objective of this chapter.

3   Factors that determine FDI inflows: existing literature[2]

Earlier theoretical and empirical studies on FDI have adopted either one or
a combination of two approaches. The first or the 'pull-factor' approach
examines the relationship between host-country specific conditions and the
inflow of FDI. Under this approach FDI is either classified as (i) import-
substituting; (ii) export-increasing or (iii) government-initiated (Moosa
2002). The second or the 'push-factor' approach leans towards examining
the key factors that could influence or motivate multinational corporations
(MNCs) to want to expand their operations overseas. Under this second
approach, FDI is either classified as horizontal or market seeking, vertical or
conglomerate (Caves 1974; Moosa 2002).

Turning to the first approach, Akhter (1993) posited that host-country
specific conditions might encompass a number of socioeconomic and
political factors within a country where FDI is made. These factors tend to

determine available business opportunities and pending political threats within the host countries. Among others, the socioeconomic and political factors commonly cited in this strand of the FDI literature include infrastructure; market size, level of human capital development, distance from major markets, labour cost, openness of the economy to international trade, exchange rate, fiscal and other non-tax incentives, political stability, monetary policies and the extent of liberalization or otherwise of the financial sector. In addition to these socioeconomic and political variables are also the presence of natural resources such as mineral ores, petroleum and natural gas, coal and other raw materials, the availability of which may also act as location specific advantage in attracting FDI to host countries. Recent studies along this line include those by Asiedu (2002); Noorbakhsh and Paloni (2001); Collier and Pattillo (2000); Pigato (2000); and Obwona (2001).[3] Addison and Heshmati (2002) recently added a new dimension and therefore new determinants to this strand of the FDI literature. They examined recent changes in the global economy, termed the 'third wave of democratization' and the current spread of new economy in terms of new information and communication technology as likely determinants of a developing country's ability to attract FDI. The two variables capturing these developments were found to have positive effects on the inflow of FDI even though information, communication and technology was observed to be country specific in its effect on FDI inflows.

With regards to the exposition on factors that may or may not motivate MNCs to expand their operations overseas, researchers have focused on firm and market-related factors, using two interrelated hypotheses – the internationalization hypothesis and the monopolistic advantage hypothesis as summed up in the Dunning's eclectic theory (Dunning 1980; Moosa 2002). Except for a few, the majority of the previous empirical work based on the eclectic theory tend to also consider one or two host-country specific advantages as well as some indicators of uncertainty (Cleeve 2000; Donnenfeld and Weber 2000; Urata and Kawai 2000).[4]

Over the years, moreover, wide divergence and convergence of views and empirical results have characterized the FDI literature in so far as factors affecting the flow of FDI to developing countries are concerned. An attempt to streamline the issues and albeit provide some practical step towards resolving the diversity of views was made by Chakrabarti (2001). He employed the technique of extreme bound analysis (EBA) and the cumulative distribution function. The result of this recent effort provided some evidence on the sensitivity of earlier studies with regards to the determinants of FDI flows. It indicated a strong support for the explanatory power of market size of the host country, measured by per capita GDP as a major, if not the most significant, determinant of FDI inflow. Other factors, such as openness to international trade, wages, net exports, growth rate, tax regime, tariffs and exchange rate turned out to be less robust though not very fragile as determinants of FDI inflow. According to these findings, while openness to trade, growth rate and tax regime are likely to be positively correlated, wages, net exports and exchange rate are more likely to be negatively correlated with FDI. Finally another set of indicators such as inflation, budget deficit, domestic investment, external debt, government consumption, political stability, human capital, natural resources and infrastructure was found to be very fragile in their effect on FDI inflow and are highly sensitive to small alterations in the conditioning information set.

The objective of this chapter is not to contribute towards resolving the conflict in the literature as regards the fragility or otherwise of the respective factors so mentioned. We have rather attempted to examine which of these host countries' and external factors could well explain the policy relevant issues as to why a foreign investor in the first instance may choose to or not to locate FDI in a previously neglected developing country. Second, whether or not the same set of variables may be relevant in determining the volume of FDI to allocate to existing FDI-receiving countries.

4   Conceptual framework

Most of the previous studies that try to explain FDI inflow to developing countries have used the traditional cross-section or cross-country multiple regression and/or panel estimation methods. These studies have been more or less directed at establishing the empirical linkages between FDI inflow and a number of explanatory variables. This regression model could be written as:

$$Y_{it} = \alpha_0 + \alpha_1 X + \xi \tag{1}$$

Where Y_{it} is the FDI share of GDP for country i ($i = 1, 2, \ldots n, N$) and X a vector of independent variables viewed as possible host-country or external factors that may determine the flow of FDI. ξ is a random error term with the usual properties.

As mentioned above, this chapter sets out to examine two important issues. The first relates to why foreign investors may decide whether or not to venture into those countries that never received FDI before and the second has to do with how much to allocate to countries already receiving significant FDI inflow. This is more or less an aggregate foreign investors' behaviour analysis, which necessarily involves in the first case an eligibility decision and, second, a decision on volume to allocate. The ordinary multiple regression model (equation 1) used in previous studies has not been able to adequately address these two issues. Suffice is to say, that an appropriate methodology would be the two-part econometric approach which has been used to investigate the allocation of foreign aid by bilateral donors among developing countries.[5] We have therefore adopted the two-part methodology for the analyses in this chapter.

The two-part econometric model[6]

The first part of the two interdependent decisions modelled has to do with deciding on whether or not to locate investments in a hitherto neglected developing country. In this part the country selection process may be conceptualized as one in which foreign investors identify 'j' different developing countries. These countries are evaluated based on a number of relevant socioeconomic and country characteristic indicators, 'Z_j', depending on the motives of the investors, which in this case we assume to be purely, profit maximization.

Each of these indicators could be assigned different weights 'α' such that 'l' number of countries are chosen as FDI recipients among the evaluated 'j' countries. That is, as in Woodward and Rolfe (1993) and Urata and Kawai (2000) we can describe the profit (π) of multinational firm 'i' obtainable from undertaking FDI in country 'j' as:

$$\pi_{ij} = \beta' X_j + \xi_{ij} \tag{2}$$

X_j is a vector of observable characteristics of country j and ξ_{ij} is a random disturbance term reflecting measurement and/or specification error. The probability of selecting a specific country depends on the attributes of the selected country relative to the attributes of all other countries in the sample.

Given the profit equation (2) and on the assumption that ξ_{ij} are independently and identically distributed with Weibull density functions (McFadden 1974), then the probability of locating in country j will be given by:

$$P_j = \frac{\exp[\beta' X_j]}{\sum_{k=1}^{l} \exp[\beta' X_l]} \tag{3}$$

Estimates of β can be obtained by maximizing the likelihood function:

$$L(\beta) = \prod_{j=1}^{l} P_j \tag{4}$$

The second decision has to do with how much of FDI to allocate to the 'l' selected countries. Since it is reasonable to assume that this decision should be related to the first one, then the amount to invest in a chosen country should be non-zero. In this regard, a positive cut-off level, which distinguishes FDI receiving from non-FDI receiving developing countries, was set at an FDI/GDP ratio of 0.01. This threshold derives from Pigato (2000) who showed that on average, the FDI/GDP ratio for low- and middle-income developing countries between 1987 and 1998 was about 1.3 per cent. Similarly, Singh and Jun (1995) classified as a low FDI receiving country any developing country with an average FDI/GDP ratio of 1 per cent and as a high FDI receiving any country with an average above 1 per cent. For the purpose of the analysis in this chapter, an FDI receiving country is treated as one which, over the decade 1990 to 2000, received a gross inflow that is greater than this cut-off point.

From above if we denote as '*j*' the potential FDI recipient countries, the econometric model can be written as:

$$E_j^* = \alpha Z_j + \xi_j \qquad \xi_j \sim N(0, 1) \tag{5}$$

$$A_j^* = \beta X_j + \mu_{ij} \qquad A_j^* > 0, \mu_j \sim N(0, 1) \tag{6}$$

Z_j and X_j are regressors, α and β are parameters to be estimated. E_j^* according to McGillivray and Oczkowski (1991: 148) represents the difference of the indirect utilities between the events of allocating FDI or not and A_j^* denotes the potential positive or significant amount of FDI, that is, an amount which is greater than the cut-off point. Equations (5) and (6) above actually describe latent unobservable events of the two-part decision process. The events that can be observed and considered could then be conceptualized as the decision of whether or not to allocate FDI to a country I_j (a dummy endogenous indicator) and the potential or actual FDI allocated to any receiving country over and above the cut-off point A_j. The relationships defined by the two observable events can then be written as:

$$I_j = 1 \qquad \text{if } E_j^* > 0 \tag{7}$$

$$I_j = 0 \qquad \text{if } E_j^* \leq 0 \tag{8}$$

$$A_j = A_j^* \qquad \text{if } I_j = 1 \tag{9}$$

$$A_j = 0 \qquad \text{if } I_j = 0 \tag{10}$$

Equations (7) to (10) simply highlight the stylized facts of the two-part aggregate foreign investors' decision process. That is, if given the evaluation criteria, a country is chosen as an FDI recipient ($I_j = 1$), then the amount of FDI allocated to such a country will be equal to an amount designated as the significant flow of FDI ($A_j = A_j^*$). On the other hand, if a country is not chosen ($I_j = 0$), then FDI inflow to such a country will not be observed and as such, $A_j = 0$. This implies that such a country or countries will not feature in the second step of the analyses. The dependent variable in this first step is then a binary variable with a value 1 if FDI flows to a country *j* is greater than the cut-off point or threshold value and 0 if below the cut-off point. The parameters of the explanatory variables in this step could then be estimated using the one way random effects probit model.

In the second step, FDI as discussed above is allocated to only selected countries in the first step, or to those countries that by our definition in this chapter had received over the last decade significant inflow of FDI. This implies that A_j is only observed when $I_j \neq 0$. That is, step two is dependent on step one, such that the conventional multiple regression or panel estimation method could be undertaken to obtain the parameter estimates of the explanatory variables.

The equations for the two steps are as follows:

$$E_j^* = \alpha_0 + \alpha_1 X_j + \alpha_2 Y_j + \alpha_3 Z_j + \xi_j \tag{11}$$

$$A_j^* = \beta_0 + \beta_1 X_j + \beta_2 Y_j + \beta_3 Z_j + \mu_j \tag{12}$$

X's are some economic variables, Y's the country characteristic variables and Z's are variables representing any external indicator. α's and the β's are the parameters to be estimated. It is assumed as usual that the error components are normally distributed.

The model as elaborated above indicates that once a decision based on the selected indicators has been made in the first step as to whether or not to invest in a particular country, the decision-making problem changes in the second or subsequent step. Assuming that countries $k = 1, 2, \ldots l$ are selected in the first step as potential investment destinations, then, $l \leq j$ and foreign investors will allocate FDI to receiving country 'k' at subsequent periods also based on selected indicators. Accordingly, if we could hypothesize that the decisions of aggregate foreign investors are always consistent with their objectives in the two-part interdependent decision processes, then the same set of explanatory variables could be used in the two steps. In the empirical analysis that follows therefore, we investigated whether the impacts of the chosen explanatory variables are the same in the two steps.

Data and data sources

Variables

The dependent variable used in the two steps of our analyses is the net FDI/GDP ratio obtained from the World Bank *World Development Indicators* (WDI) online (2002a). The explanatory variables, on the other hand, derive essentially from the pull or host-country variables as had previously been considered in the FDI literature, and five external or push-factors. The push factors are:

- ECONCYCLE: The indicator of economic cycle in the developed world (OECD countries). This indicator (ECONCYCLE) is computed as the deviation from the long-term growth trend of the GDP in OECD countries. We expected this variable to have a positive sign since an upswing in the level of economic activities in advanced countries should generate a positive flow of FDI to developing countries.

- OECDGRATE: This is the annual growth rate in OECD countries, which is expected to have the same effect on FDI inflow to developing countries as ECONCYCLE.
- OECDDRATE: This is the weighted average of discount rate in OECD countries. This variable is used to proxy the EURO DOLLAR London rate and it is expected to have a negative effect of reducing FDI flows to developing countries.
- OECDGNS and OECDEBAL: These are the gross national savings and external balance in OECD countries, respectively. These two variables proxy the maximum volume of resources available for foreign resource transfers by both the private and public sectors in OECD countries. They are expected to have positive signs.

For the pull variables, we had relied on the results of the EBA analysis of Chakrabarti (2001), Asiedu (2002), Addison and Heshmati (2002), Noorbakhsh and Paloni (2001), Singh and Jun (1995) and other previous studies for the expected signs. The explanatory variables added to the push-factors are:

- Real per capita GDP (PINCOME) (+);
- Ratio of exports plus imports to GDP (OPEN) (+);
- Growth rate of real GDP (GROWTH) (+);
- Taxes on income, profits and capital gains (TAXES) (−);
- Import duties as percentage of imports (MDUT) (−);
- Wages and salaries as per cent of total expenditure (WAGES) (+);
- Commercial energy use (kg of oil equivalent per capita) (COMM) (+);
- Rate of change of consumer price index, inflation (INF) (−);
- Domestic credit to the private sector as per cent of GDP (CREDIT) (+);
- Fuel exports as percentage of total merchandise exports (FUEX) (+);
- Ores and metal exports as percentage of merchandise exports (ORES) (+);
- General government final consumption expenditure as percentage of GDP (GCOM) (+);
- Index of political freedom (POLT) (−);
- Index of government crises (CRISES) (−);
- Dummy variable to capture events of the 1990s, particularly opening up of Eastern European countries and countries of the former Soviet republics to the international trade and financial system which may be exerting a negative influence on the flow of FDI to developing countries (DUMMY90) (−);
- Real interest rate (per cent) (REINT) (+);
- Manufacturing value added as per cent of GDP (GDPMAN) (+).

Data sources

Pooled, cross-country, annual time series data for the period 1970–2000 for 89 developing countries[7] are used for the empirical analyses. Most of the macroeconomic and country characteristic or institutional variables are obtained from two World Bank sources, the *World Development Indicators* (online) and the *Global Development Network* growth database (online). Data on political freedom, which are a composite of two indices (political rights and civil liberty) are obtained from the Freedom House database (online). Data on legislative fractionalization and constitutional changes which may also proximate for political risk are obtained from the Polyarch dataset (Vanhanen 2001). FDI inflow and related data as shown in the different tables were obtained from various World Bank (*Global Development Finance*) and UNCTAD (*World Investment Report*) sources between 1992 and 2002 and the IMF's *International Financial Statistics* (online).

One major problem with the various dataset and particularly, data from the World Bank (2002a,b) is the issue of missing data points which is so acute. In this regard, such important variables as black market premium, rate of unemployment, exchange rate overvaluation, secondary school enrolment rate, or real effective exchange rate, tend to reduce the number of useable observations, the significance of parameter estimates as well as the goodness of fit of the equations when combined with other variables. This limited our use of these variables and some of the variables listed above.

Given the problem of missing data points and the assumption that on average, multinational corporations that undertake FDI in developing countries may face information lag, our estimations were based on non-overlapping five-year averages of all the variables. By so doing, we were able to reduce the problem of random fluctuations in the data and at the same time exploit the time-series variation in the dataset.

5   Empirical analyses and results

Equation (11) above describes step 1 of the analyses and was estimated using the probit model. Equation (12), on the other hand represents the second step and was estimated using the Heckman's sample selection-corrected two-stage method. This involved computing the Heckman's parameter ('λ' or the inverse Mill's ratio) for each observation on the basis of the first step probit estimation and including this in the second step regression as an explanatory variable. A second step estimation without the Heckman's parameter would only give unbiased estimates if the two error terms in the two steps were independent. This means that for a country, which receives FDI, eligibility would be independent of the amount of FDI received, a situation which may or may not be true (Tarp *et al.* 1998: 18; Heckman 1979). The estimations in the second step were based on the panel regression technique and the one way error component random effects model.[8]

Different combinations of the variables were tried for the two steps of the analyses. Only four variables: real per capita income (PINCOME), real interest rate (REINT) (proxy for rate of return on vestment as in Addison and Heshmati 2002), the indicator of openness (OPEN) and phones per 1000 people (an indicator of the level of infrastructure development adopted for our analysis) turned out to be significant and robust in the numerous combinations considered for the two steps. These four variables then constituted the control variables for our model such that the specification shown in column 1 of Tables 6.6A and 6.6B is the basic model. The final results are as shown in columns 1 to 5 of the two tables, Table 6.6A for the probit estimations of step one and Table 6.6B for the panel estimations in step two. The proportion of correct predictions in Table 6.6A and the R^2 in Table 6.6B indicate that to a large extent, the two models have strong explanatory power.

The results shown in column 1 of Tables 6.6A and 6.6B indicate that real per capita income (an indicator of market size, degree of affluence or command over commodities in a country), and the trade/GDP ratio (an indicator of the degree of openness of an economy to international trade), real interest rate (an indicator of the rate of return on investment), and the level of infrastructure development, which are statistically significant in the first step also have a statistically significant impact in the second step of the analyses. Similarly the signs of the parameter estimates of these variables are the same in the two steps. These imply that there is a very high degree of consistency in terms of the criteria which foreign investors may employ in deciding to choose whether or not to venture into a previously neglected developing country and the decision as to the volume of FDI to allocate to existing FDI-receiving developing countries. Table 6.6B also shows that the Heckman's parameter is significant, which may indicate that there is some correlation between step one and step two of the analyses.

The results reported in columns 2 to 5 of the two tables show that the basic model is to a large extent, robust to changes in specifications. Column 2 of Tables 6.6A and 6.6B indicate that when interacted with the control variables, the level of industrialization of a developing economy turned out to be important in the decision of MNCs to venture into such a country as well in deciding on the amount of further FDI to locate in the receiving countries. Similarly high levels of taxes on income, profits and capital gains may act as deterrent to MNCs that may want to venture into previously neglected developing countries. This may also negatively impact on the volume of FDI to further allocate to existing FDI-receiving countries (column 2, Table 6.6B). The level of government final consumption expenditure, as percentage of GDP, which may indicate the size of government in an economy, turned out to be insignificant at conventional levels and, therefore, may not be important in the two-part decision processes.

Column 3 of Table 6.6A seems to indicate that the presence of solid minerals, external balance situation in advanced (OECD) countries and the post-1990 dummy may also constitute, in addition to the control variables,

Table 6.6A   Probit estimations

	Estimates and *p*-values				
	(1)	**(2)**	**(3)**	**(4)**	**(5)**
Constant	3.681	0.996	3.742	−1.914	11.265
	(0.06)	(0.82)	(0.08)	(0.77)	(0.52)
Real per capita GDP (log)	0.691	0.545	0.726	1.351	1.334
	(0.03)	(0.02)	(0.03)	(0.09)	(0.10)
Trade (exports and imports)	0.009	0.027	0.009	0.034	0.030
(% of GDP)	(0.02)	(0.02)	(0.03)	(0.04)	(0.04)
Real interest rate (%) log	0.055	2.008	1.07	0.031	0.034
	(0.00)	(0.00)	(0.00)	(0.16)	(0.15)
Phones per 1000 people	0.739	0.843	0.750	1.241	1.175
(infrastructure)	(0.00)	(0.02)	(0.00)	(0.00)	(0.00)
Manufacturing value added	—	1.993	—	—	—
(% of GDP) (log)		(0.00)			
Indicator of economic cycle in	—	—	—	35.419	—
advanced (OECD) countries (log)				(0.07)	
OECD external balance	—	—	0.177	0.067	0.116
			(0.19)	(0.06)	(0.59)
Gross national savings in OECD	—	—	—	—	4.032
countries					(0.44)
Domestic credit to private sector	—	—	—	—	0.015
(% of GDP) (log)					(0.96)
Post-1990 dummy	—	—	−0.888	—	—
			(0.03)		
Ores and metal exports	—	—	0.893	—	—
(% of merchandise exports) (log)			(0.00)		
Fuel exports (% of merchandise	—	—	—	—	0.521
exports) (log)					(0.00)
General government final	—	−0.015	—	−0.179	—
consumption expenditure		(0.73)		(0.03)	
(% of GDP)					
Taxes on income, profits and	—	0.024	−0.016	—	—
capital gains (% of total taxes)		(0.07)	(0.04)		
Inflation, consumer prices	—	—	−0.019	−0.005	−0.002
(annual %) (log)			(0.38)	(0.83)	(0.94)
Political risk	—	—	−0.003	−0.181	−0.109
			(0.96)	(0.29)	(0.52)
Number of observations	206	117	201	115	111
Number of countries	89	89	89	89	89
Log likelihood	−76.168	−28.523	−38.55	−18.45	−18.676
P(n)	0.84	0.91	0.84	0.90	0.92

Notes: The numbers in parentheses below the parameter estimates are the *p*-values. A *p*-value that exceeds 0.10 indicates that the parameter estimate is not significant at 1%, 5% and 10% levels; P(n) refers to the proportion of correct predictions in each equation.

Source: UNCTAD (1999).

Table 6.6B   Panel estimations

	Estimates and *p*-values				
	(1)	**(2)**	**(3)**	**(4)**	**(5)**
Constant	6.781	0.996	7.481	6.398	5.778
	(0.14)	(0.82)	(0.00)	(0.22)	(0.27)
Real per capita GDP (log)	1.314	2.396	0.034	0.119	1.177
	(0.04)	(0.09)	(0.00)	(0.05)	(0.09)
Trade (exports and imports)	0.019	0.018	0.020	0.019	0.018
(% of GDP)	(0.00)	(0.02)	(0.00)	(0.00)	(0.00)
Real interest rate (%) log	0.032	2.345	0.034	0.053	0.025
	(0.07)	(0.09)	(0.10)	(0.00)	(0.00)
Phones per 1000 people	0.139	1.388	1.378	1.246	1.232
(infrastructure)	(0.00)	(0.03)	(0.02)	(0.00)	(0.00)
Manufacturing value added	—	2.379	—	—	—
(% of GDP) (log)		(0.09)			
Indicator of economic cycle in	—	—	—	24.615	—
advanced (OECD) countries (log)				(0.03)	
OECD external balance	—	—	0.545	0.120	0.109
			(0.00)	(0.35)	(0.39)
Gross national savings in OECD	—	—	—	—	5.000
countries					(0.10)
Domestic credit to private sector	—	—	—	—	0.263
(% of GDP) (log)					(0.57)
Post-1990 dummy	—	—	−1.787	—	—
			(0.00)		
Ores and metal exports	—	—	1.319	—	—
(% of merchandise exports) (log)			(0.02)		
Fuel exports (% of merchandise	—	—	—	—	0.118
exports) (log)					(0.41)
General government final	—	−0.080	—	−0.08	—
consumption expenditure		(0.28)		(0.17)	
(% of GDP)					
Taxes on income, profits and	—	0.024	−1.038	—	—
capital gains (% of total taxes)		(0.07)	(0.28)		
Inflation, consumer prices	—	—	−0.032	−0.021	−0.031
(annual %) (log)			(0.11)	(0.33)	(0.14)
Political risk	—	—	−0.051	−1.275	−0.151
			(0.76)	(0.11)	(0.39
Heckman's parameter	0.021	0.471	1.481	1.851	1.686
	(0.00)	(0.80)	(0.951)	(0.16)	(0.18)
Number of observations	120	94	97	94	97
Number of countries	71	71	71	71	71
R^2	0.75	0.84	0.83	0.79	0.76

Notes: The numbers in parentheses below the parameter estimates are the *p*-values. A *p*-value that exceeds 0.10 indicates that the parameter estimate is not significant at 1%, 5% and 10% levels.

Source: UNCTAD (1999).

dominant variables in the allocation criteria of foreign investors, when deciding on whether or not to venture into a previously neglected developing country. These variables also turned out to be significant in the second-round decision of the volume of FDI to allocate to receiving countries. The results reported in column 4 of Table 6.6A show that in addition to the control variables, the indicator of economic cycle, the external balance situation, in advanced (OECD) countries and the level of government final consumption expenditure as percentage of GDP are important in choosing which developing countries to venture into by foreign investors. On the other hand, the rate of inflation and political risk may not be as important. For the existing FDI-receiving countries moreover, these variables are weakly significant in the decision whether or not to locate more investments.

Finally, column 5 of Tables 6.6A and 6.6B show that besides the control variables, it is only the presence of petroleum resources that may constitute an important factor in deciding whether or not to venture into a previously neglected developing country. For the existing FDI-receiving countries, the volatility of FDI inflow may, on the other hand, be explained by the level of gross national savings in advanced (OECD) countries. Inflationary tendencies and political risk again turned out to be insignificant.

On the basis of the results of our empirical analyses, we are able to conclude that a combination of four variables – real per capita income, real interest rate, the indicator of openness and the level of infrastructure development – reasonably explain why previously neglected developing countries may have failed to attract foreign direct investment in the last three decades. This is an indication that not only is the level of per capita income or size of the market very important in the choice of investment location by foreign investors, it is also necessary that countries actively engage in international trade. Similarly, one may posit that since foreign investors have primarily commercial motives, they will only choose such countries where a high rate of return on their investments could be assured and where they will not have to commit so much of their initial investable resources to road construction, power generating equipment, water treatment plants and telecommunication facilities.

6   Flow of FDI to neglected low-income developing countries: what lies ahead?

In the last section we identified the factors that seem to be the major determinants of international investors' decision whether or not to locate FDI in neglected developing countries as well as the volatility of flows to existing FDI-receiving ones. These are the presence of local markets as proxied by the level of real per capita GDP, the degree of linkage of the host economy to the international trading system, the rate of return on investments and availability of infrastructure. All of these four factors may have resulted in the increasing concentration of FDI in middle-income developing countries and the industrialized countries. At the same time, they may have resulted in the declining competitiveness of low-income developing countries in attracting significant inflow of FDI. This is because per capita income continues to be very low (below US$800 on average) in the low-income countries, infrastructure is poorly developed in many of these countries and the ratio of exports plus imports to GDP, which measures the degree of openness falls significantly below appreciable level. Thus the situation of declining competitiveness of the low-income developing countries have prevailed despite quite favourable policy framework put in place for FDI inflow in many of these countries in recent years. This finding corroborates the results of a number of earlier quantitative studies, which have reached convergence on the major factors that determine FDI inflow. This similarly corroborates the findings of UNCTAD that the concentration of FDI seems to reflect the concentration of economic activity, and that richer and more competitive economies tend to receive more international direct investment than the poorer and less competitive ones (UNCTAD 2001b).

The foregoing may suggest that low-income countries and the least developed countries of the world may continue to be marginalized well into the coming decades in terms of the distribution of FDI inflow. This is because many of the economic reform programmes instituted in these countries are yet to transform into positive results in terms of increasing rates of growth, increasing level of economic activity, increasing participation in international trade and high per capita income levels. Similarly, most of the low-income countries continue to rely more on locational advantages to attract FDI inflow which, on the other hand, are based on cheap labour and natural resource endowments, factors that have turned out to be weakly significant in many earlier studies. This means that the concentration of FDI inflow in high- and middle-income countries may even intensify.

The question then arises as to whether the ability of the low-income countries to attract a substantial magnitude of FDI inflow from the conventional western sources can improve in the nearest future. More so, in the light of the fact that the attainment of the International Development Goals (IDG), particularly the goal of reducing by half the incidence of absolute poverty in developing countries, is based on the sustainability of external financial resource flows. One may be tempted to posit that the prospect does not look too bright. It is most unlikely that these countries could attain such a level of per capita income and integration into the global trading and financial systems that could make them internationally competitive in the next couple of years. This may suggest that even though the recent upsurge and expansion of FDI inflow into developing countries as a whole is a welcome development in itself, it may not be able to compensate for the declining levels of official development financial assistance, which will need to be directed to the poorer developing countries. In this regard, a critical re-examination of current donors' practices, their major instruments and channels of aid delivery for private sector development in low-income countries may be required. This is because if for the observable factors, an improved flow of FDI to the hitherto neglected developing countries may not be realized in the nearest future, then the flow of official development assistance for private sector development from donors may serve as a veritable option.[9]

Having said this, it is still important for the low-income developing countries to focus more on policy factors. These will include factors that could integrate them into the global trading system, fiscal and non-fiscal incentives, the improvement of infrastructure, human resources development, the creation and nurturing of local entrepreneurship. All of these will have to be consistent with the entrenchment of suitable political and legal framework and such other conditions for productive investment and private sector participation in order to set the stage for the process of growth and development.

In realization of these, many low-income developing countries have in recent times opened up their economies to foreign investment by eliminating or reducing various types of regulatory barriers. Many of these countries have designed policies to shift away from targeting specific sectors or specific foreign investors, and have sought to promote broad-based private sector participation in economic development. All of these efforts will need to be intensified and widespread in the low-income developing countries. Similarly the low-income countries will all need to strive to significantly reduce, if not completely abolish, the system of government equity participation in joint ventures. Government participation in joint ventures in many of these countries has continued to perpetuate the existence of under-performing and inefficient state-owned or state-managed enterprises, which in most cases account for a disproportionately high share of the GDP (Ramamurti 1999). The move towards privatization of these enterprises or free market orientation as being recently undertaken in a sizeable number of countries may result in renewed interest by foreign investors in the form of equity, joint venture or even sub-contracting.

Regional economic cooperation among low-income developing countries may also help. Since the size of host-country market has turned out to be an important determinant of FDI inflow, developing countries, and especially the smaller ones could improve their chances of attracting FDI inflow through participation in regional economic integration. These schemes have the potentials to enlarge the size of accessible markets and attract the attention of market-seeking FDI. Similarly, regional economic cooperation among low-income developing countries could pave the way for exploiting the potentials of intra-regional investments that may be substantial and prove useful for the restructuring of industries in participating countries for improved efficiency. Recent experiences in this regard could be found in the way in which many South African corporations have expanded into the member countries of the Southern African Customs Union (SACU) and are now expanding further afield into the other countries of the much wider Common Market for Eastern and Southern African Countries (COMESA).

Significant changes in the productive structures in many low-income developing countries may also have an impact in attracting FDI. An important facet of this structural shift could be in the form of greater foreign trade in manufactured inputs as opposed to the primary products and raw materials as is currently the case. Increased foreign trade in manufactured inputs may result in more FDI by the final users of these inputs and increased trade liberalization in both the host and home countries. Many countries, such as Mauritius, have been successful in their attempt in this regard by utilizing their low-wage workers in export processing zones in order to expand their exports of intermediate goods. Though others have not been too successful (Nigeria, Botswana), the fact remains that the more outward oriented an economy becomes, the more successful such economies tend to be in their attempt to encourage FDI inflow. Lucas's (1993) investigation of Southeast Asian countries provides some evidence of the relative importance of the outward-oriented policies. Specifically that FDI is relatively more elastic with respect to demand for exports than to aggregate domestic demand. This implies too that for low-income developing countries to be successful as export-oriented economies and be able to attract FDI, they have to put in place liberal trade policies, remove to a significant extent all forms of quantitative and barriers of equivalent effect to the free flow of goods, services, payments and labour. Not only could this attract export-increasing FDI, it could also attract import-substituting FDI.

As was noted in this study and in earlier ones, a high rate of return on investment could be an important determinant of FDI inflow to previously neglected low-income countries. The measure of rate of return adopted for this study is the real rate of interest, as previously used by Addison and Heshmati (2002). This implies that positive real rate of interest may signal positive return to domestic savings, an indicator which may be important to aggregate foreign investors. Moreover, a positive real rate of interest can only be ensured in an economy with a complement of monetary and fiscal policies that will guarantee monetary stability and low levels of inflation. This also implies that to a reasonable degree, the financial system will have to be liberalized, free of government controls and, therefore, free of repression. Liberalized financial markets in low-income developing countries will not only reduce the degree of fragmentation of the sector, it could also lead to a well-developed and diversified financial markets and instruments, all of which breed investor-friendly environment.

By way of summary, one may want to say that while a number of host-country factors may act as determinant of the decision by foreign investors to locate direct investment in previously neglected low-income countries, some are much more critical to the decision than others. Factors such as natural resource endowment and probably cheap labour may arouse investors' interest. More importantly, however, are macroeconomic fundamentals, openness of the economy to international trade and the availability of reasonably developed infrastructure. Similarly, the channelling of official development assistance towards private sector development in low-income countries may well complement the insufficient flow of FDI to these countries.

7 Summary and conclusions

In this chapter we have shown that the last decade or so has witnessed dramatic increases in the inflow of foreign direct investment to developing countries of the world as a whole, and at the same time recorded a declining volume of flow of official development assistance. FDI inflow however has been uneven. High- and middle-income developing countries, countries of Southeast Asia, Latin America and the Caribbean, have continued to receive larger share of the flows at the expense of lower income developing and least developed countries of the world. The sectoral distribution of the flow has followed exactly the same pattern, such that in the low-income developing countries, FDI inflow is concentrated in the primary sectors, particularly in agriculture and mining.

Multi-country panel data for 89 developing countries over the period 1970 to 2000 were employed to explore two complementary policy issues that relate to aggregate foreign investors' decisions in terms of FDI location in developing countries. These two issues are the factors that may influence aggregate investors' decision first in choosing to or not to allocate FDI to hitherto neglected countries and second, in determining the volume of FDI to allocate to existing FDI-receiving countries. The methodology adopted for this study departs radically from what received FDI literature seems to suggest. We adopted the two-part econometric approach. This approach entailed the use of a probit model to examine the binary issue of whether or not to locate FDI in a developing country as a first step. In the second step, a panel regression model was then used to examine the factors that explain the volume of FDI to further allocate and the volatility of flows to the existing FDI-receiving countries. Our analysis was based on a rather heroic assumption that foreign investor's decisions are always consistent in the two steps. Hence the same set of explanatory variables were used for the probit and the panel regression models.

The results of the first step analysis indicate that a combination of high per capita GDP, high rate of return on investment, outward-orientation to international trade and the level of infrastructure development are the significant and important decision parameters as to whether or not to locate investment in a developing country. The panel regressions of the second step seem to point to the fact that the volume of FDI to allocate to existing

FDI-receiving developing countries and the volatility of such inflow may be explained to a large extent by the same factors. Though in this second step, some other determinants of FDI inflow as previously reported by earlier researchers turned out to be marginally significant. These variables include political risk, taxes on income, profits and capital gains, the level of inflation, the level of financial sector development and the availability or otherwise of solid minerals and petroleum resources. We also had integrated a number of push factors into our analyses. These include the indicator of economic cycle, the gross national savings and the external balance situation in advanced (OECD) countries. However only the indicator of economic cycle turned out to be significant in the two steps.

What seems to have emerged from the analyses in this chapter is the fact that low-income developing countries may continue to be marginalized far into the distant future in terms of the inflow of FDI. This is because these countries are still characterized by low levels of per capita income, fragmented and underdeveloped financial system, low integration into the international trading and financial systems, poor infrastructural base and slow response of economic fundamentals to reforms that could arouse the level of investor confidence to an appreciable degree. One may be led to conclude, albeit with caution, given the nature of the data employed that a combination of mutually re-enforcing factors such as sound monetary, fiscal, trade and exchange rate policies, fewer records of political instability and macroeconomics crises, reforms tailored specifically at factors that hitherto hindered FDI inflow may all enable the previously neglected and the receiving countries to attract FDI inflow. Similarly, renewed donor efforts in terms of channelling substantial amount of official development assistance for private sector development may be an important component in the sustainability of external development financing for developing countries.

Notes

1. UNCTAD, *World Investment Report*, 2002.
2. To save space, studies cited in this section are, except in two cases, limited to those reported in 2000 and after. Earlier and more extensive literature citations are in Akinkugbe (2003).
3. For a recent comprehensive survey of literature on location specific advantage as host-country determinants of FDI inflows, see Moosa (2002); Asiedu (2002) and Chakrabarti (2001).
4. For a review of the hypotheses and studies based on such, see Moosa (2002); Urata and Kawai (2000) and the like.
5. For an elaborate exposition of the two-part methodology, see Dudley and Montmarquette (1976); McGillivray and Oczkwoski (1991, 1992); Tarp *et al.* (1998).
6. This sub-section derives substantially from Tarp *et al.* (1998).
7. The 89 developing countries and the countries eliminated after step one are as follows: Algeria, Angola, Argentina, Bangladesh, Benin, Bolivia, Botswana, Brazil, Burkina Faso, Burundi, Cameroon, Central Africa Republic, Chad, Chile, China,

Colombia, Congo, Dem. Rep., Congo Rep., Costa Rica, Côte d'Ivoire, Cyprus, Dominican Republic, Ecuador, Egypt, El Salvador, Ethiopia, Fiji, Gabon, Gambia, Ghana, Guatemala, Guinea, Guinea-Bissau, Guyana, Haiti, Honduras, India, Indonesia, Iran, Jamaica, Jordan, Kenya, Korea, Rep., Lesotho, Liberia, Madagascar, Malawi, Malaysia, Mali, Malta, Mauritania, Mauritius, Mexico, Morocco, Mozambique, Nepal, Nicaragua, Niger, Nigeria, Oman, Pakistan, Panama, Papua New Guinea, Paraguay, Peru, Philippines, Rwanda, Senegal, Seychelles, Sierra Leone, Singapore, Somalia, South Africa, Sri Lanka, Sudan, Swaziland, Syria, Tanzania, Thailand, Togo, Trinidad and Tobago, Tunisia, Turkey, Uganda, Uruguay, Vanuatu, Venezuela, Zambia, Zimbabwe.

Countries eliminated after step one: Algeria, Bangladesh, Botswana, Burundi, Cameroon, Central African Republic, Congo, Dem. Rep., Congo Rep., Haiti, India, Iran, Kenya, Liberia, Nepal, Niger, Rwanda, Sierra Leone, Turkey.

8. For a discussion of the econometric theory behind the one way error component model as well as the differences between the use of the fixed and random effects model, see Baltagi (1995) and Hsiao (1986).
9. This and related issues of the role of multilateral development banks in private sector financing have been extensively covered in Chapters 2 and 4 of this volume.

References

Addison, T. and A. Heshmati (2002). 'Democratization and New Communication Technologies as Determinants of Foreign Direct Investment in Developing Countries'. Paper presented at the WIDER Conference on 'The New Economy in Development', 10–11 May 2002. Helsinki.

Akhter, Saed H. (1993). 'Foreign Direct Investments in Developing Countries: The Openness Hypothesis and Policy Implications'. *The International Trade Journal*, 7: 655–72.

Akinkugbe, O. (2003). 'Flow of Foreign Direct Investment to Hitherto Neglected Developing Countries'. WIDER Discussion Paper No. 2003/02. Helsinki: UNU/WIDER.

Asiedu, E. (2002). 'On the Determinants of Foreign Direct Investment to Developing Countries. Is Africa Different?'. *World Development*, 30: 107–19.

Baltagi, Badi H. (1995). *Econometric Analysis of Panel Data*. West Sussex: John Wiley & Sons.

Basu, Anupam and Krishna Srinivasan (2002). 'Foreign Direct Investment in Africa – Some Case Studies'. IMF Working Paper WP/02/61. Washington, DC: IMF.

Burnside, C. and D. Dollar (2000). 'Aid, Policies and Growth'. *American Economic Review*, 90 (4): 847–68.

Caves, R. E. (1974). 'Causes of Direct Investment: Foreign Firms' Shares in Canadian and United States' Manufacturing Industries'. *Review of Economics and Statistics*, 56: 279–93.

Chakrabarti, A. (2001). 'The Determinants of Foreign Direct Investment: Sensitivity Analyses of Cross-Country Regressions'. *Kyklos*, 54: 89–114.

Cleeve, E. (2000). 'Why Do Japanese Firms Locate in Particular British Regions?' *Asia Pacific Journal of Economics and Business*, 4: 112–24.

Collier, P. and C. Pattillo (2000). *Investment and Risk in Africa*. New York: St. Martin's Press.

Donnenfeld, S. and A. Weber (2000). 'Exporting versus Foreign Direct Investment'. *Journal of Economic Integration*, 15: 100–26.

Dudley, L. and Claude Montmarquette (1970). 'A Model of the Supply of Bilateral Foreign Aid'. *The American Economic Review*, 66: 132–42.

Dunning, J. H. (1980). 'Toward an Eclectic Theory of International Production: Some Empirical Tests'. *Journal of International Business Studies*, 11: 9–31.

Heckman, J. A. (1979). 'Sample Bias as a Specification Error'. *Econometrica*, 17: 153–61.

Hsiao, Cheng (1986). *Analysis of Panel Data*. Cambridge and New York: Press Syndicate of the University of Cambridge.

IMF (online). *International Financial Statistics*. Washington, DC: IMF.

Lucas, R. B. (1993). 'On the Determinants of Foreign Direct Investment: Evidence from East and Southeast Asia'. *World Development*, 21: 396–406.

McFadden, D. (1974). 'Conditional Logit Analysis of Qualitative Choice Behaviour', in P. Zarembka (ed.), *Frontiers in Econometrics*. New York: Academic Press.

McGillivray, M. and E. Oczkowski (1991). 'Modelling the Allocation of Australian Bilateral Aid: A Two-Part Sample Selection Approach'. *The Economic Record*, 67 (197): 147–52.

McGillivray, M. and E. Oczkowski (1992). 'A Two Part Sample Selection Model of British Bilateral Foreign Aid Allocation'. *Applied Economics*, 24: 1311–19.

Moosa, Imad A. (2002). *Foreign Direct Investment: Theory, Evidence and Practice*. New York: Palgrave.

Noorbakhsh, F. and A. Paloni (2001). 'Human Capital and FDI Inflows to Developing Countries. New Empirical Evidence'. *World Development*, 29: 1593–610.

Obwona, M. B. (2001). 'Determinants of FDI and their Impact on Economic Growth in Uganda'. *African Development Review*, 13 (1): 46–81.

OECD (2002). *New Horizons for Foreign Direct Investment*. OECD Global Forum on International Investment. Paris.

Pigato, A. Maria (2000). 'Foreign Direct Investment in Africa: Old Tales and New Evidence'. ARWPS 8. Africa Region Working Paper Series. Washington, DC: World Bank.

Ramamurti, R. (1999). 'Why Haven't Developing Countries Privatized Deeper and Faster?' *World Development*, 27 (1): 137–55.

Singh, H. and K. Jun (1995). 'Some New Evidence on Determinants of Foreign Direct Investment in Developing Countries'. Policy Research Working Paper No. 1531. Washington, DC: World Bank.

Tarp, F., F. C. Bach, H. Hansen and S. Baunsgaard (1998). *Danish Aid Policy: Theory and Empirical Evidence*. Copenhagen: Institute of Economics, University of Copenhagen.

UN (2001). Recommendations of the High-level Panel on Financing for Development. United Nations General Assembly, A/55/1000, New York.

UN (2002). Final Outcome of the International Conference on Financing for Development. A/Conf/198, New York: United Nations.

UNCTAD (various years). *World Investment Report*. Geneva: UNCTAD.

UNCTAD (2001a). *FDI in Least Developed Countries at a Glance*. New York and Geneva: United Nations.

UNCTAD (2001b). *World Investment Report 2001, Promoting Linkages* (Internet edition). Geneva: UNCTAD.

UNCTAD (2001c). *Handbook of Statistics*. Geneva: UNCTAD.

Urata, S. and H. Kawai (2000). 'The Determinants of the Location of Foreign Direct Investment by Japanese Small and Medium-Sized Enterprises'. *Small Business Economics*, 15: 79–103.

Vanhanen T. (2001). *Measures of Democratization*, Introduction (online).

Woodward, D. P. and R. Rolfe (1993). 'The Location of Export-oriented Foreign Direct Investment in the Caribbean Basin'. *Journal of International Business Studies*, First Quarter: 121–44.

World Bank (1994). *Adjustment in Africa: Reforms, Results and Road Ahead*. New York: Oxford University Press.

World Bank (1999). *Global Development Finance. Analysis and Summary Tables*. Washington, DC: World Bank.

World Bank (2001). *Global Development Finance. Analysis and Summary Tables* (Internet edition). Washington, DC: World Bank.

World Bank (2002a).World Development Indicators (online).

World Bank (2002b). Global Development Network Growth database (online).

7
Flight Capital and its Reversal for Development Financing

*Niels Hermes, Robert Lensink and Victor Murinde**

1 Introduction

Capital flight remains one of the enigmatic policy and academic issues of the day. Although from the end of the 1980s and early 1990s the debt crisis appeared to be contained and attention to the capital flight phenomenon waned, capital flight still remains a serious problem in a number of countries. The most pronounced concern among policymakers, researchers and the key stakeholders in economic development is that in most developing countries which are riddled with heavy debt burdens, foreign exchange shortages, transient and chronic poverty, capital flight amounts to a substantial proportion of the very resources which are essential for financing economic growth and reversing the perverse economic trends.[1]

Most of the initial empirical studies on capital flight focused on Latin American economies. Capital flight from Latin America during the 1970s and early 1980s appeared to be voluminous in absolute terms. The sheer volume posed a threat to the viability of the domestic banking system, national solvency and economic stability. In addition, the flight of capital occurred at the same time that the countries were in desperate need for foreign exchange to amortize their outstanding debt to commercial banks in industrial countries. Later studies showed that capital flight was also an important issue for countries in other developing regions, however.

During the early 1990s the interest for the capital flight phenomenon waned, since most Latin American countries had reduced their external debt problems and capital started to flow back to many of the emerging economies in this region, as well as to East Asia. Yet, from the mid-1990s the international financial system was confronted with the outbreak of several major financial and economic crises. These crises contributed to large outflows of capital from several developing countries and led to renewed attention to the capital flight phenomenon. First, in 1994–95, Mexico and some Latin American countries experienced the Tequila crisis. Then, in 1997–98, several Asian countries experienced a deep financial and economic crisis, followed by Russia in 1998 and Brazil in 1999. These financial crises added an important dimension to the capital flight problem. For example, the mounting complexity of imbalances in the underlying economic fundamentals in the Asian economies culminated into a scenario of collapsing exchange rates and share prices, initially in Thailand and Indonesia, which provoked domestic and international investors to immediately withdraw their money, and thereby caused panic on the international financial markets. There were even fears of bank runs which, due to bandwagon and contagion effects, threatened the stability of the international banking system. In this context, the Asian financial crisis demonstrated how adverse domestic economic conditions influence the behaviour of domestic and international investors in accelerating capital flight.

This chapter aims to examine the key aspects of capital flight and highlight the prospects for reversing the flight of capital from developing countries. Several definitions of the term capital flight are isolated; it is shown that each definition offers an associated approach for measuring the magnitude of capital flight. Moreover, the chapter discusses the main determinants of capital flight, including variables that capture bank intermediation behaviour, political risk and policy uncertainty. One of the important conclusions of the chapter is that good policies may help reverse capital flight.

The remainder of this chapter is structured into four parts. Section 2 provides an overview of the definition of capital flight and the main methods used to measure capital flight. The magnitude of capital flight is discussed in Section 3. Section 4 presents an overview of the theoretical and empirical literature on the determinants of capital flight. Section 5 concludes and proposes policy measures that may help to reverse capital flight.

2   The measurement of capital flight

In the literature there is no consensus about the definition of capital flight. Several studies suggest capital flight should be distinguished from *normal* capital outflows. According to these studies, normal outflows are based on considerations of portfolio diversification of residents – for example, in terms of portfolio or direct investment and trade credit – and/or activities of domestic commercial banks aiming at acquiring or extending foreign deposit holdings. In their view, the phenomenon of capital flight is somehow related to the existence of extremely high uncertainty and risk with respect to returns on domestically held assets. Residents take their money and run in order to avoid extremely high losses on their domestic asset holdings. Authors like Deppler and Williamson (1987) argue that capital flight is motivated by the fear of losing wealth due to, for example, expropriation of wealth by the government, sudden exchange rate depreciation, non-repayment of government debts (changes in) capital controls and financial market regulations, and (changes in) tax policies. Walter (1987) and Kindleberger (1987) have a similar opinion. These authors suggest that capital flight should be related to the abnormal or illegal nature of certain capital outflows. Yet, in practice it is extremely difficult to empirically distinguish between normal and abnormal or illegal capital outflows (see also Gordon and Levine 1989). Therefore, several authors argue that capital flight should not be distinguished from normal capital outflows (see, for example, Erbe 1985; World Bank 1985; Morgan Guaranty 1986, 1988). It is argued that for countries struggling with (large) current account deficits and external debt payments – and which are thus in need of foreign capital – any capital outflow increases the problems of financing their net imports and debt payments.

The measurement of capital flight is not straightforward, given that there is no consensus on the definition of capital flight. Indeed, several capital flight measures are available in the literature. Not surprisingly, this leads to differences in capital flight estimates for different countries. In general, the following measures of capital flight can be distinguished in the literature (Claessens and Naudé 1993: 2–9): (i) the residual (or broad) method; (ii) the Dooley method; (iii) the hot money method; (iv) the trade misinvoicing method; and (v) the asset method. Below, we will briefly describe these different methods of measurement.

The residual method

This method measures capital flight indirectly by comparing the *sources* of capital inflows (i.e. net increases in external debt and the net inflow of foreign investment) with the *uses* of these inflows (i.e. the current account deficit and additions to foreign reserves). This approach starts from the standard balance of payments framework. In principle, if the balance of payments statistics were to be used (reported by the IMF Balance of Payments Statistics), the uses and sources of funds should be equal. However, since these statistics may not accurately measure flows, and in particular private capital flows, World Bank statistics on the change in the external debt are used instead. If the sources, calculated by using World Bank debt data, exceed the uses of capital inflows, the difference is termed as capital flight. The residual method acknowledges the difficulties of separating abnormal from normal capital outflows and, therefore, measures all unrecorded private capital outflows as being capital flight.

According to the residual method, capital flight is calculated as follows:

$$KF_r = \Delta ED + FI - CAD - \Delta FR \tag{1}$$

where KF_r is capital flight according to the residual method, Δ denotes change, ED is stock of gross external debt reported in the World Bank data, FI is the net foreign investment inflows, CAD is the current account deficit and FR is the stock of official foreign reserves.

In the literature, the residual method has been widely used, in some cases with (minor) modifications. The standard approach as described above has been used by, among others, the World Bank (1985) and Erbe (1985). Morgan Guaranty (1986) takes into account an additional item, that is, the change in the short-term foreign assets of the domestic banking system (ΔB). This modification is introduced to focus on non-bank capital flight. Thus, capital flight according to the Morgan Guaranty variant of the residual method (KF_m) can be calculated as:

$$KF_m = \Delta ED + FI - CAD - \Delta FR - \Delta B \tag{2}$$

Cline (1986; cited in Cumby and Levich 1987) also uses the residual method, but proposes to exclude the following items from the current account balances: travel (credit), reinvested earnings on direct investment abroad, reinvested earnings on direct investment domestically and other investment income (credit). He argues that income from tourism, border transactions and reinvested investment income should not be considered capital flight since these earnings are beyond the control of the authorities (Cumby and Levich 1987: 33–4). Claessens and Naudé (1993), in contrast to most others, take into account net acquisitions of corporate equities in their measure of foreign direct investment. Zedillo (1987) argues that the standard residual method should be modified with respect to the measurement of external debt and the current account deficit. First, instead of measuring changes in the stock of external debt, Zedillo proposes to look at flows, since this may more accurately report annual capital flows. Second, he proposes to adjust the current account for interest earned and retained abroad. This is estimated by taking the interest on identified deposits of residents held abroad. Brown (1990) and Vos (1992) propose to take into account the unrecorded remittances of workers abroad. These remittances tend to be understated in the balance of payments statistics of developing countries, leading to an overstatement of the current account deficits. This would then result in lower estimates of capital flight. Remittances of workers abroad are important sources of foreign exchange for several developing countries, including Egypt, Sudan and the Philippines. Finally, Morgan Guaranty (1988), Pastor (1990), Boyce and Ndikumana (2001) and Ndikumana and Boyce (2003) add interest earnings on the stock of assets held abroad, taking a representative international market interest rate to compute these earnings. This, of course, increases the estimates of capital flight based on the residual method.

The Dooley method

This method aims at distinguishing normal from abnormal, or illegal capital flows. Dooley (1986) sees capital flight as the total amount of externally held assets of the private sector that do not generate income recorded in the balance of payments statistics of a country. Or, stated otherwise, capital flight is all capital outflows based on the desire to place wealth beyond the control of the domestic authorities. The Dooley method of measuring capital flight starts by computing total capital outflows as reported in the balance of payments statistics, but then makes a number of modifications. First, errors and omissions are taken into account to measure total capital outflows. Second, the Dooley method takes into account the difference between the World Bank data on the change in the stock of external debt and the amount of external borrowing as reported in the balance of payments statistics. If the first is larger than the second, this difference is assumed to be part of capital flight. Third, the stock of external assets is computed that correspond to the reported interest rate earnings in the balance of payments by using a representative market interest rate (that is, the US deposit rate). The difference between total capital outflows and the change in the stock of external assets corresponding to reported interest income is measured as capital flight.

According to the Dooley method, capital flight is measured as follows. First, the amount of total capital outflows is calculated:

$$TKO = FB + FI - CAD - \Delta FR - EO - \Delta WBIMF \tag{3}$$

where *TKO* is total capital outflows, *FB* is foreign borrowing as reported in the balance of payments statistics, *EO* is net errors and omissions (debit entry) and *WBIMF* is the difference between the change in the stock of external debt reported by the World Bank and foreign borrowing reported in the balance of payments statistics published by the IMF.

The stock of external assets corresponding to reported interest earnings is:

$$ES = INTEAR/r_{us} \tag{4}$$

where *ES* is external assets, r_{us} is the US deposit rate (assumed to be a representative international market interest rate), and *INTEAR* is reported interest earnings. Capital flight according to the Dooley method is then measured as:

$$KF_d = TKO - \Delta ES \tag{5}$$

The Dooley method is conceptually different from the residual method. Yet, Claessens and Naudé (1993: 5–7) show that in practice capital flight measured according to the Dooley method and the residual method are fairly similar, since most of the data used for calculation are the same in both cases.

The hot money method

According to this method capital flight is measured by adding up net errors and omissions and non-bank private short-term capital outflows.

Cuddington (1986, 1987), Ketkar and Ketkar (1989) and Gibson and Tskalotos (1993) are examples of authors who have used this method of measuring capital flight. Like the Dooley method, this method corresponds to the idea that capital flight goes unrecorded, due to the illegal nature of these capital movements. The unrecorded capital movements are believed to appear in net errors and omissions. Moreover, by concentrating on short-term flows, medium- and long-term outflows are excluded, which are viewed as being normal in character (Gibson and Tskalotos 1993: 146). Thus, the hot money method (KF_h) can be calculated as follows:

$$KF_h = SKO + EO \tag{6}$$

where *SKO* is the total amount of short-term capital outflows.

The trade misinvoicing method

Some authors use the amount of trade misinvoicing as a measure of capital flight (Claessens and Naudé 1993). Trade misinvoicing is determined by comparing trade data from both the importing and exporting country. Importers are assumed to be involved in capital flight when they report higher values of imported goods as compared to the reported value of the same goods by exporters. In turn, exporters are involved in capital flight when they report lower values of exported goods as compared to the reported value of the same goods by importers. Proponents of this measure stress the fact that abnormal capital outflows of residents may be included in export underinvoicing and/or import overinvoicing, since both these malpractices provide channels to siphon domestically accumulated wealth outside the country. In some cases, those authors using the residual method argue that the measurement of capital flight in this way is inaccurate due to the poor quality of export and import figures resulting from trade misinvoicing. They, therefore, propose to adjust capital flight figures based on the residual method (Gulati 1987; Lessard and Williamson 1987; Vos 1992; Boyce 1993; Eggerstedt *et al.* 1995; Ajayi 1997; Collier *et al.* 2001; and Ndikumana and Boyce 2003).

The asset method

Some authors take the total stock of assets of non-bank residents held at foreign banks as a measure of capital flight. This is the so-called asset method (Hermes and Lensink 1992; Collier *et al.* 2001). The asset method is a short-cut measure of capital flight. This measure may be seen as an indication of the minimum amount of assets held abroad, since residents may hold their assets in other forms next to bank accounts, for example, in foreign equity holdings. The IMF provided data on these bank assets until 1994. For recent years, however, no information is available to apply this measure.

The methods and their drawbacks

The methods discussed above have important drawbacks. In our view, the Dooley method and hot money method are conceptually wrong. We would argue that the distinction between normal and abnormal or illegal capital outflows is not useful. What really matters is that a country confronted with a lack of financial resources to finance long-term development experiences an adverse impact on its future growth prospects when net capital outflows occur. With respect to the hot money it may be added that it is unclear why capital flight should consist of short-term capital movements only. Assets of residents held outside the home country based on a longer-term perspective should also be part of capital flight. The asset method may suffer from being too narrow a measure of total capital flight and may leave out potentially large parts of capital flight. Moreover, assets held at foreign banks are not always specified by ownership. Taking into account the inaccuracy of trade data due to misinvoicing may help to improve capital flight estimates. Yet, it has been argued that trade misinvoicing may also occur in the presence of trade taxes. Calculated trade misinvoicing may then be unrelated to the phenomenon of capital flight (Gibson and Tskalotos 1993: 150). Moreover, Chang and Cumby (1991: 167) in a study on the magnitude of capital flight in Sub-Saharan Africa point out that '...the systemic underreporting of trade figures in both directions to avoid trade barriers...seems to overwhelm any discernible capital flight through misinvoicing'. Since many developing countries make use of some form of trade barriers, we have every reason to assume that this finding will also apply in the case of other developing countries.

Taking into account the above mentioned drawbacks of the different methods of calculating capital flight, we would favour the use of the residual method when measuring capital flight.

3   The magnitude of capital flight

We estimate the magnitude of capital flight for four regions, namely East Asia, South Asia, Sub-Saharan Africa and Latin America, for the period 1983–98. The estimates are based on the residual measure: change in debt + net foreign investment − current account deficit + change in reserves. Only countries for which data were available for the entire sample period have been included in the estimations (see note to Table 7.1 for the complete list of countries on which we report capital flight data). We also report data on the 'burden' of capital flight, measured by the ratio of capital flight to national income. The data are described and reported in Table 7.1.

When looking at the figures presented in Table 7.1, we may conclude the following about the absolute and relative size of capital flight from the countries in our sample:

For East Asia, capital flight in absolute terms was most intense during the period 1990–93. The region also experienced the highest levels of capital

Table 7.1   Magnitude and burden of capital flight: flows for 1983–98

	East Asia		South Asia		Sub-Saharan Africa		Latin America	
	CF (US\$ bn)	CF to GDP (%)	CF (US\$ bn)	CF to GDP (%)	CF (US\$ bn)	CF to GDP (%)	CF (US\$ bn)	CF to GDP (%)
1983	5	1.1	5	1.7	−0.9	−2.4	4	0.9
1984	7	1.3	0.2	0.1	0.5	1.3	17	3.9
1985	3	0.5	3	0.8	5	11.4	9	2.0
1986	10	1.9	5	1.6	5	10.8	−8	−1.5
1987	37	6.4	6	1.7	6	12.1	15	2.8
1988	33	4.8	−4	−1.2	−2	−3.1	−3	−0.5
1989	17	2.2	8	2.1	2	4.4	5	0.8
1990	50	5.8	−0.1	−0.03	4	8.1	26	3.5
1991	51	5.4	7	2.0	1	2.3	19	2.5
1992	42	4.1	5	1.3	−0.4	−0.8	40	4.9
1993	46	4.1	10	2.7	−0.1	−0.3	16	1.8
1994	140	10.5	17	4.0	2	5.2	30	2.9
1995	113	6.9	−16	−3.3	4	6.9	28	2.3
1996	102	5.6	−6	−1.2	0.7	1.3	52	3.9
1997	103	5.6	−4	−0.7	−3	−5.6	33	2.3
1998	189	12.2	8	1.5	0.4	0.6	24	1.7

Notes: The table shows data for capital flight based on the residual measure (change in debt + net foreign investment − (current account deficit + change in reserves)). Data are taken from World Bank (2002). Change in reserves refers to: BN.RES.INCL.CD – Changes in net reserves (BoP, current US\$).

Debt refers to: DT.DOD.DECT.CD – External debt, total (DOD, current US\$).

Current account refers to: BN.CAB.XOKA.CD – Current account balance (BoP, current US\$).

Net foreign direct investment refers to BN.KLT.DINV.CD – Foreign direct investment, net (BoP, current US\$).

GDP refers to NY.GDP.MKTP.KD – GDP at market prices in US\$.

Only countries for which data were available for the entire sample period are included. The countries included in the sample are the following:

East Asia: China, Fiji, Indonesia, Korea, Papua New Guinea, Philippines, Samoa, Solomon Islands and Thailand.

South Asia: Bangladesh, Bhutan, India, Pakistan and Sri Lanka.

Sub-Saharan Africa: Botswana, Cameroon, Côte d'Ivoire, Ethiopia, Kenya, Mauritania, Mauritius, Mozambique, Swaziland and Uganda.

Latin America: Argentina, Barbados, Bolivia, Brazil, Chile, Colombia, Costa Rica, El Salvador, Jamaica, Nicaragua, Paraguay and Venezuela.

Data on capital flight of individual countries are available in Appendix Table A7.1.

flight as compared to the other developing regions, especially towards the end of the 1990s. The burden of capital flight was most severe in 1998, when total flows of capital flight amounted to 12 per cent of GDP of the countries in the sample.

For South Asia the table shows a mixed picture of capital flight as well as its reversal. Generally speaking, for this region capital flight has been rather modest as compared to East Asia, in absolute as well as in relative terms (relative to GDP). The highest flight of capital relative to GDP was experienced in 1993 and 1994, when it amounted to 2 to 4 per cent. Yet, in the year thereafter the reversal of capital flight was over 3 per cent and the reversal continued until 1998 when the Asian financial crisis broke out, leading to a flight of capital that amounted to 1.5 per cent of GDP.

According to the figures in Table 7.1 the sub-Saharan African countries included in our analysis experienced a high burden of capital flight. While in absolute terms capital flight from these countries was low during the entire period as compared to other regions, it was very high relative to GDP, especially during 1985–87 (between 11 and 12 per cent) and 1990 (8 per cent). The Sub-Saharan African countries seem not to have been affected by the Asian crisis in 1997–98: capital flight was low in 1998 and in 1997 the table even reports capital reversal for these countries.

The Latin American countries in our sample have experienced high levels of capital flight, at least in absolute terms, especially during the period 1990–98. However, the capital flight burden is not as high as in the East Asian or sub-Saharan African region. Then highest burden is reported for 1984 and 1996, when capital flight amounted to almost 4 and 5 per cent of GDP, respectively, of the countries in the sample.

Next to providing data on the flows of capital flight, we also report stocks of capital flight over the 1983–98 period. Table 7.2 shows that the East Asian countries in our sample have by far the highest stock of capital flight, amounting to 60 per cent of GDP in 1998. An important source of the high level of the stock has been the Asian crisis; as reported in Table 7.1, during 1998, the total stock of capital flight increased by 20 per cent for this region. Also for the Sub-Saharan African countries we report high stocks (40 per cent of GDP). The stocks are relatively low for the countries in South Asia (almost 8 per cent of GDP).

These figures show that there may be potentially large resources available for development financing if countries are able to conduct policies that contribute to the reversal of capital flight.

4   The determinants of capital flight[2]

Stated in a formal way, capital flight is directly related to the behaviour of a risk-averse individual who diversifies his wealth in order to maximize asset

Table 7.2   Stocks of capital flight, end of 1998

	Capital flight (US$ bn)	**Capital flight to GDP in 1998**
Latin America	309	22.0
Sub-Saharan Africa	25	41.3
South Asia	43	7.8
East Asia	947	60.9

Note: Stocks are found by adding up annual flows for 1983–98. See also note to Table 7.1.

returns. This emphasizes the decision to hold assets abroad as part of the process of portfolio diversification (Cuddington 1986; Gibson and Tskalotos 1993; Lensink *et al.* 1998). Differences in rates of return between domestic and foreign asset holdings, the amount of wealth, and risk and uncertainty aspects influence this decision. The following main determinants of capital flight are discussed here: (i) macroeconomic instability; (ii) political instability; (iii) rate of return differentials; (iv) capital inflows; (v) stock of capital flight; and (vi) public policy uncertainty. These determinants have a direct influence on portfolio decisions of individuals. As will be shown, in a number of cases the determinants are closely connected.

Macroeconomic instability

Macroeconomic instability occurs when aggregate domestic demand exceeds aggregate domestic supply on a structural basis. The causes of this instability may be manifold, for example, political tensions and instability, wrong or lacking incentive structures and institutions to let markets efficiently coordinate demand and supply and heavy government involvement, which may put markets at the sideline. Whatever the exact reasons, when a country experiences macroeconomic instability this may become manifest in a number of ways: budget deficits will rise, current account deficits increase, exchange rate overvaluation occurs and inflation is growing. Variables describing such factors are often found in studies on the determinants of capital flight.

Exchange rate overvaluation is often found to be an important variable in studies of capital flight and its underlying determinants. An overvalued exchange rate leads to increasing expectations of depreciation in the near future. This in turn will lead to rising prices of foreign goods relative to those of domestic goods and thus to loss of real income. To avoid welfare losses, residents hold at least part of their assets abroad. High inflation directly erodes the real value of domestic assets, stimulating residents to hold assets outside the country. Moreover, inflation rates and the exchange rate are closely connected, since high inflation may lead to increasing expectations of depreciation in the future. High current account deficits may have a similar impact on exchange rate expectations, and may thus be a stimulus for capital flight. Government budget deficit may stimulate capital flight, since it raises expectations of residents with respect to future tax increases or increases in inflation tax, since it is anticipated that the government needs to repay its debt. In both cases, the real value of domestic assets is eroded, leading to capital flight.

In all the cases discussed here, macroeconomic instability leads to (indirectly) increasing taxes and tax-like distortions. This will lower returns and increase risk and uncertainty of domestically held wealth (Collier *et al.* 2001). This will increase incentives for capital flight. The large outflows of capital at the beginning of the debt crisis in the early 1980s and at the outbreak of the

Asian crisis in 1997–98 support this view. The macroeconomic situation of these countries was highly unstable during these years.

Political instability

Whereas macroeconomic instability variables focus on the outcomes of public policies and their impact on capital flight, one may also look at the institutional context in which these policies have been carried out. The institutional context itself may give rise to capital flight. Public sector behaviour may have an impact on the risks and uncertainty regarding the policy environment and its outcomes More specifically, residents may decide to hold their assets abroad based on lack of confidence in the domestic political situation, perceived high levels of corruption and the consequences of these factors for the future value of the assets. In these cases, perceived political instability may generate capital flight. Models that illustrate the impact of political instability on capital flight can be found in Alesina and Tabellini (1989), Tornell and Velasco (1992) and Bhattacharya (1999). It is shown that when different governments with different interest groups supporting them come into office, uncertainty increases with respect to future fiscal policies. Such an unstable political situation may, for example, lead to a political business cycle. Political instability may also turn into political unrest, leading to strikes, riots, assassinations and so on. Finally, different forms of the regime type (democracy, autocracy, etc.) may have a different impact on the degree of uncertainty about future policy and their outcomes.

Political instability may thus have an influence on the possibility that the government may in one way or another erode the future value of asset holdings. The erosion of future wealth is based on the expectation that domestic political instability causes rising macroeconomic instability, leading to rising budget deficits, current account deficits, exchange rate uncertainty and high inflation. Several studies on the determinants of capital flight take into account one or more variables that measure the degree of political uncertainty.

Rate of return differentials

Of course, capital flight may occur simply because the returns on assets are higher abroad as compared to assets held domestically. Most studies on the determinants of capital flight take this into account by adding a variable that measures the (after tax) real interest rate differential.

Capital inflows

Several authors specifically emphasize the role played by foreign borrowing as a determinant of capital flight. The explanations for the relationship between foreign borrowing and capital flight are related to the issues discussed earlier with respect to macroeconomic and political instability. In the literature several models deal with the issue of the simultaneous occurrence of capital flight and capital inflows. Moreover, as we will show below, most empirical studies emphasize the role played by capital inflows in explaining capital flight.

Especially during the 1970s and early 1980s, developing countries experienced massive capital inflows and outflows at the same time. Eaton (1987) presents a theoretical model in which he explains why the increase of foreign borrowing may stimulate capital flight. According to the model, residents may borrow on international capital markets and then use the loans (plus potential domestically held assets) to buy foreign assets. This is advantageous if they expect their government to nationalize debt repayments at some point in time, which will release them from the obligation to repay, and if domestic taxes are high. These expectations reflect moral hazard behaviour of residents, who expect to be bailed out by their government. In the early 1980s the moral hazard behaviour of domestic borrowers was indeed rewarded when governments of several developing countries actually nationalized foreign debt repayments.

Under the above-mentioned assumptions, current foreign borrowing increases future repayment obligations of the government when it actually nationalizes debt repayments. If residents perceive that the government will pass the costs of these repayments on them, for example, by using the inflation tax, they may choose to convert their domestic assets into foreign assets. Boyce (1992, 1993) and Ndikumana and Boyce (2003) refer to this as the 'revolving door syndrome'. Moreover, the occurrence of capital flight itself stimulates others to hold money abroad, since now the future costs of debt repayment by the government have to be shared by a decreasing number of wealth holders. Similar models by Eaton and Gersovitz (1989) and Ize and Ortiz (1987) show that capital flight is stimulated when the public sector itself borrows in the international capital markets to finance its current expenditures. Fry (1993) stresses that growing government guaranteed foreign debt may increase expectations about exchange rate devaluations, which provides a stimulus to hold foreign assets.

Other authors stress the importance of differences in perceived risk of investing in the domestic economy to explain the simultaneous inflow and outflow of capital (Khan and Ul Haque 1985; Dooley 1988; Diwan 1989). Residents face a higher risk of a reduction in the value of their domestically held assets as compared to foreign investors. This may lead to a situation where domestic investors buy foreign assets while foreign investors buy domestic assets at the same time. Unlike domestic investors, foreign investors are not hurt by the inflation tax, since they lend in foreign currency. A similar asymmetry in perceived risks holds with respect to currency depreciation following the accumulation of debt obligations. Domestic investors will experience a reduction of the real value of their assets, whereas foreign investors are not hurt by such exchange rate changes.

It has also been argued that in practice the domestic debt obligations of the government are junior to foreign debt obligations (Ize and Ortiz 1987;

Kant 1996), which reduces the willingness of residents to lend to their own government. Foreigners, instead, are not reluctant to lend to the government due to the seniority of their claims.

Razin and Sadka (1991), Dooley and Kletzer (1994) and Bjerksund and Schjelderup (1995) present models that emphasize differences in tax treatments for domestic and foreign investors, leading to simultaneous capital inflows and capital outflows.

Finally, simultaneous capital inflow and outflow may also be due to asymmetric information about expected returns on domestic assets between domestic and foreign investors.

The stock of capital flight

Another determinant of capital flight is the stock of capital flight itself. The argument to take the stock of capital flight as a determinant of the flows of capital flight stresses the spillover effect of large assets holdings abroad on the expected losses on domestically held assets. When residents hold large amounts of foreign assets, the tax base is reduced considerably. Under these circumstances, the tax burden due to increased public expenditures and foreign borrowing has to be shared by a smaller tax base, increasing the burden per unit of domestically held asset. Consequently, this will further stimulate residents to take their money and run. Thus, the larger the stock of capital flight, the higher the incentives to flee (Collier *et al.* 2001). An entirely different argument to take the capital flight stock as a determinant is given by Vos (1992). He argues that the stock of capital flight reflects the desire of residents to hold foreign assets to satisfy their foreign consumption needs. In this spirit, flows of capital flight may reflect residents' behaviour in targeting a certain stock of foreign asset holdings.

Public policy uncertainty

As discussed above, public policy behaviour may be one of the main determinants and is related to both macroeconomic and political instability. If the content and direction of current and future public policies are uncertain and/or unstable, domestic investors will be uncertain about the impact of these policies on the real value of domestically held assets in the future. This uncertainty may stimulate investors to sell their domestic assets and buy foreign assets. One example of a theoretical analysis of policy uncertainty and its influence on capital flight is found in Sheets (1995). Sheets argues that the shock therapy implemented by some transition economies led to substantial capital flight, since the policy reforms initially generated increased uncertainty about policies and their outcomes.

Evaluating empirical studies of the determinants of capital flight

A large number of studies is available in which the determinants of capital flight are analysed empirically. Table 7.3 provides an overview of these

Table 7.3   Overview of empirical studies on the determinants of capital flight

Author(s)	Methodology	Countries	Sample period	Estimation technique	Main determinants tested
Cuddington (1986)	Hot money	Argentina, Brazil, Chile, Korea, Mexico, Peru, Uruguay and Venezuela	1974–82	OLS	$REER$ (+/−), $FINC$, $RINTR$, $RINTRF$, $INFL$ (+)
Cuddington (1987)	Hot money	Argentina, Mexico, Uruguay and Venezuela	1974–84	OLS	$REER$ (+), $RINTRF$, $INFL$
Dooley (1988)	Dooley	Argentina, Brazil, Chile, Mexico, Peru, Philippines and Venezuela	1977–84	OLS (pooled) with instruments	$INFL$ (+), $FINC$ (+), PR (−)
Ketkar and Ketkar (1989)	Hot money	Argentina, Brazil and Mexico	1977–86	OLS	$RINTR$, $RINTRF$, $INFL$ (+), $REER$ (+), $DUMG$ (+), $SPREAD$
Pastor (1990)	Residual	Argentina, Brazil, Chile, Colombia, Mexico, Peru, Uruguay and Venezuela	1973–87	OLS (pooled)	$INFL$, $FINC$ (+), $REER$ (+), $BUDDEF$ (+), YG (−), $TAXGDP$
Mikkelsen (1991)	Weighted average of residual and hot money	22 LDCs	1978–85	OLS (pooled)	YG (−), ΔE ($FINC$) (+), $\Delta BUDDEF$ (+)
	Weighted average of residual and hot money	Mexico	1976–85	OLS	ΔE ($FINC$) (+), $\Delta RINTR$, $DUMG$ (+)
Hermes and Lensink (1992)	Residual and asset	Côte d'Ivoire, Nigeria, Sudan, Tanzania,	1978–88	OLS (pooled)	$DEBTGDP$ (+), $REER$ (+) $FINC$, YG, $RINTRF$, $AIDGDP$, $SHDGDP$
Muscatelli and Hallet (1992)	Hybrid	4 Latin American countries + Philippines	1976–88	OLS	$INFL$ (+), YG (−), $BUDDEF$ (+), $RINTR$ (−), $REER$ (+)

Study	Method	Sample	Period	Estimation	Variables
Vos (1992)	Residual	Philippines	1971–88	OLS	*DEBTGDP* (+), *REER* (+) *CFS* (+), *SPREAD* (+)
Boyce (1992, 1993)	Residual	Philippines	1962–86	OLS	*DEBTGDP* (+), *RINTR* (+), *BUDDEF* (+), *YG*
Henry (1996)	Residual	Barbados, Jamaica and Trinidad and Tobago	1971–87	OLS	*BUDDEF, YG, TAXGDP, REER, INFL, DEBTGDP* (+), *SPREAD*
Murinde *et al.* (1996)	Residual	Côte d'Ivoire, Nigeria, Sudan, Tanzania, Uganda and Zaire	1976–91	SUR	*DEBTGDP* (+), *REER, FINC, INFL, YG, RINTRF, AIDGDP*
Lensink *et al.* (1998)	Residual	9 African countries	1970–91	SUR	*DEBTGDP* (+), *REER, FINC, INFL, YG, RINTRF, AIDGDP*
Hermes *et al.* (1999)	Residual	Hungary, Poland and Romania	1982–95	OLS	*DEBTGDP* (+), *REER, BUDDEF, FINC, AIDGDP*
Lensink *et al.* (2000)	Residual, hot money and Dooley	84 LDCs	1971–90	EBA and CDF	*BANKL* (+), *AIDGDP* (+), *FDI, PINSTAB, WAR, CIVLIB* (+), *PRIGHTS, PARCOM* (+)
Ng'eno (2000)	Residual	Kenya	1981–95	OLS	*YG, RINTR, REER*
Nyoni (2000)	Residual	Tanzania	1973–92	OLS	*YG, INFL, FINC, POLRISK*
Olopoenia (2000)	Residual	Uganda	1971–94	OLS	*YG, INFL, FINC*
Collier *et al.* (2001)	Residual	39 LDCs	1970–90	LAD	*DEBTGNP* (+), *REER* (+), *CFS* (+)
Hermes and Lensink (2001)	Residual	84 LDCs	1971–91	CDF	*BANKL* (+), *AIDGDP* (+), *PINSTAB* (+), *CIVLIB* (+), *EGOVC* (+), *ETAX* (+), *EBUD* (+), *EINFL* (+), *ERINTR* (+)

Table 7.3 Continued

Author(s)	Methodology	Countries	Sample period	Estimation technique	Main determinants tested
Ndikumana and Boyce (2003)	Residual	30 Sub-Saharan African countries	1970–96	OLS	*KF-1* (+), *KF-2* (+), *ΔDEBGDP* (+), *DEBST* (+), *INFL, BUDDEF* (−), *FINC, VOICE* (−), *FREE* (−), *CORR* (+), *GOVEFF, CONT*

Notes: In all studies listed in the table the dependent variable is capital flight, measured in different ways, however (see Column [2]).

The estimation techniques mentioned in column [5] are: ordinary least squares (OLS), seemingly unrelated regressions (SUR), quantile regressions using least absolute deviation estimation (LAD; see Collier *et al*. 2001), extreme bound analysis (EBA; see Levine and Renelt 1992), and estimation with cumulative distribution functions (CDF; see Sala-i-Martin 1997).

Column [6], indicating the 'main determinants tested', only shows those variables of interest to the study of capital flight and its determinants. In several cases the specification of the equations estimated also may contain control variables. These variables have been left out of the table. A(+) or (−) behind a variable in this column indicates that this variable is significantly positive (or negative) related to capital flight, i.e. t-values for this variable are above 1.7 in the majority of the equations estimated in the studies listed.

For abbreviations of variables used in the table, see Appendix A.

studies, specifying the measure of capital flight used, the determinants of capital flight, the countries or regions of which data have been used, the sample period and the estimation technique. The summary presented below will focus on discussing some of the most interesting features and findings of these studies. Due to limitations of space we cannot discuss the studies in detail. The interested reader is referred to the original articles.

Starting with the measure of capital flight used, the summary in Table 7.3 makes clear that most studies use a version of the residual method. Some studies empirically investigate the determinants of capital flight using the hot money method. In several cases, estimations are presented using different kinds of measures for capital flight to show the sensitivity of the estimation results to the specific measure used. In general, the table shows that estimation results differ, depending on the measure of capital flight used. This indicates the crucial importance of the issue of measurement of the capital flight phenomenon.

The studies summarized in Table 7.3 focus on developing countries. The Table shows that most studies focus on capital flight of Latin American countries. Only a few have focused on African countries. The emphasis on Latin America is due to the massive outflows these countries experienced during the 1980s following the debt crisis. As was shown in Section 3, in absolute terms capital flight of these countries, at least during the 1980s, was by far the largest. However, the relative burden of capital flight during this decade was higher for countries in Sub-Sahara, Africa, emphasizing the need for research with respect to the determinants of capital flight from this continent. In a number of cases estimations have been carried out using individual country data. This particularly holds for early attempts to investigate the capital flight phenomenon. More recently, two studies have investigated the determinants of capital flight using a large sample of developing countries (Lensink *et al.* 2000; Hermes and Lensink 2001).

In most cases the empirical studies on the determinants of capital flight implicitly use a portfolio model to decide which variables should be taken into account. Almost all studies estimate a reduced form equation. Consequently, this leads to equations of a rather *ad hoc* nature, which in a way is a shortcoming of the empirical literature on capital flight. Only Lensink *et al.* (1998) aim at estimating a full portfolio model, in which capital flight is taken into account as one of the assets, and which allows for investigating the simultaneity of different effects between different variables. Most studies estimating a reduced form equation apply OLS. In some cases the empirical studies deal with time series, in other cases they use pooled regressions.

As was already mentioned, in most cases empirical studies implicitly use a portfolio model to decide which variables should be taken into account. If we take the different categories of determinants of capital flight as discussed in the previous section, the following broad picture emerges.

With respect to *macroeconomic instability*, one or more variables such as exchange rate overvaluation, government deficits, the inflation rate and current account deficits appear in almost all studies. In particular, measures of the degree of exchange rate overvaluation are prominently present in these studies. The results of the empirical investigations indicate that macroeconomic instability causes capital flight. In most specifications variables measuring the extent of macroeconomic instability are statistically significant and positively related to capital flight.

Few studies focus on measures of *political instability* as determinants of capital flight. Several kinds of measures have been used. In some cases, the empirical investigations focus on the regime type as measure of political instability, using different dummy variables that proxy for the degree of democracy of a country. Other studies use dummy variables to measure issues related to the policy regime, such as indexes of civil rights and liberties. Still other studies use more direct measures for political instability, such as the number of assassinations and revolts, dummies for the fact that a country has been involved in a war situation. In general, the results of the empirical investigations support the view that political instability, measured in various ways and capital flight are positively related.

Proxies of the *interest rate differential* are used in some studies to measure the relative attractiveness of domestic as compared to foreign assets. In most cases, researchers have calculated some kind of exchange rate differential between the domestic interest rate on deposits and a foreign deposit rate, normally the US deposit rate. Another measure proxying for the attractiveness of different assets used is the growth rate of GDP or GNP. Measures of the interest rate differential do not always have a statistically significant relation to capital flight. This may indicate that other determinants, such as macroeconomic and political instability, are more important to explain capital flight.

In many studies, *capital inflow* variables are taken into account. In several cases these capital flows have been split into one or more forms of inflows. In particular, research has focused on investigating the impact of long-term versus short-term foreign debt. A few studies have also investigated the role played by aid flows. Among others, Bauer (1981) argues that development aid would be used to finance capital flight. The table shows that especially long-term debt inflows have a statistically significant influence on capital flight. The hypothesis put forward by Bauer on the relationship between aid and capital flight is supported in some of the studies surveyed.

To our knowledge only a few studies focus on *the stock of capital flight* as a determinant of capital flight (Collier *et al.* 2001). This study finds evidence for the positive relationship between capital flight and the stock of capital flight. Vos (1992) also finds a positive relationship, which he takes as evidence for his hypothesized stock-adjustment behaviour based on satisfying foreign consumption needs of residents.

Finally, one recent study has analysed the relationship between *public policy uncertainty* and capital flight by directly focusing on uncertainty with respect to government consumption expenditures, taxes, budget deficits, inflation and real interest rates (Hermes and Lensink 2001). The evidence from this study shows that public policy uncertainty indeed plays an important role in explaining capital flight.

In conclusion, it appears that foreign debt variables, exchange rate overvaluation and political risk variables do have a statistically significant impact on capital flight in all empirical studies summarized in Table 7.3. It should be added, however, that the studies also show quite diverse outcomes with respect to the determinants of capital flight at the individual country level. In several cases, other macroeconomic instability variables do have an impact on capital flight. The table only shows general results found.

5   Conclusions: policies for reversal of capital flight

This chapter has examined the key issues in the literature on capital flight, including the main measurement methods, magnitude and a discussion of its determinants. Our chapter first of all clearly shows that capital flight is still a serious issue. Many developing countries have suffered from large capital flight during the 1980s and 1990s. The potential for capital reversals seem to be quite substantial. In 1998, stocks of capital flight held abroad amounted to over 40 per cent of GDP on average for the Sub-Saharan African countries in our sample. For the East Asian countries such stocks were even 60 per cent of GDP. Even for the Latin American countries in our sample, capital flight was still over 20 per cent of GDP in 1998. These figures show that there may be potentially large resources available for development financing if countries are able to conduct policies that contribute to the reversal of capital flight.

The review of the theoretical and empirical literature on the determinants of capital flight provided insights into the factors that may possibly contribute to the return of capital flight. Based upon the insights from the review, we come to the following main conclusions about policies that may help to reverse capital flight in the near future.

Macroeconomic stability

Policymakers have to recognize the need for macroeconomic stability in order to stem continued capital flight and induce capital flight reversal. As discussed, the causes of this instability may be manifold, for example, political tensions and instability, wrong or lacking incentive structures and institutions to let markets efficiently coordinate demand and supply and heavy government involvement, which may put markets at the sideline. Whatever the exact reasons, when a country experiences macroeconomic instability this may become manifest in a number of ways: budget deficits will rise, current account deficits increase, exchange rate overvaluation occurs and inflation is growing.

In all these cases, macroeconomic instability leads to (indirectly) increasing taxes and tax-like distortions. This lowers returns and increases risk and uncertainty of domestically held wealth and increases incentives for capital flight. The large outflows of capital at the beginning of the debt crisis in the early 1980s and at the outbreak of the Asian crisis in 1997–98, when the macroeconomic fundamental in these countries were highly unstable, support this view.

In this context, it is necessary to adopt an appropriate exchange rate and positive real interest rates, as well as pay attention to budget deficits in order to increase the prospects for the reversal of capital flight. Reducing macroeconomic instability and carrying out sound macroeconomic policies will also reduce the uncertainty with respect to government policies.

Political stability

Policymakers also have to look at the institutional context in which good macroeconomic policies have been carried out. As we have seen, the institutional context itself may give rise to capital flight. Public sector behaviour may have an impact on the risks and uncertainty regarding the policy environment and its outcomes. More specifically, residents may decide to hold their assets abroad based on a lack of confidence in the domestic political situation and its consequences for the future value of their assets. Hence, political stability is important in order to stem continued capital flight and induce capital flight reversal.

Rate of return differentials

Consistent with economic theory and the empirical studies, capital flight may occur simply because the returns on assets are higher abroad as compared to assets held domestically. Indeed, most studies on the determinants of capital flight take this into account by adding a variable that measures the (after tax) real interest rate differential. In order to stem continued capital flight and induce capital flight reversal, policymakers have to pay attention not only to maintaining positive real interest rates but to ensure a competitive interest rate and to capture the covered and uncovered parity conditions. Yet, our review of the empirical evidence also showed that, in general, interest rate differentials were a less important determinant of capital flight. Therefore, maintaining a positive interest rate differential may be a necessary but not sufficient condition to secure capital reversals. For reversals to occur, macroeconomic and political stability seem to be more important.

Capital inflows

As discussed earlier, capital flows may be an important determinant of capital flight, mainly because high inflows may signal future payment problems for the government. If residents perceive that the government will pass the costs of these repayments to them, for example, by using the inflation tax, they may choose to convert their domestic assets into foreign assets. Moreover, the occurrence of capital flight itself stimulates agents to hold money abroad, since the future costs of debt repayment by the government have to be shared by a decreasing number of wealth holders. In this context, policymakers need to pay attention to external debt management. The empirical evidence is clear about the importance of the adverse incentives of large external debts on investment decisions of domestic wealth holders. For this matter, the international financial community may be advised to consider providing debt relief in a number of individual country cases. In the case of several Sub-Saharan African countries, for example, debt relief can have a strong positive effect on increasing resources available for policy reform: it reduces debt payment obligations, while at the same time it stimulates capital flight reversals.

Appendix A: List of abbreviations and variables used in modelling the determinants of capital flight

Δ	change in a variable
AIDGDP	development aid as a percentage of GDP
BANKL	bank and trade related lending as a percentage of GDP
BUDDEF	overall budget deficits, including grants as a percentage of GDP
CFS	stock of capital flight
CIVLIB	index measuring civil liberties
CONT	measure of risk of contract repudiation
CORR	index measuring the extent of corruption
CREDITPR	credit to the private sector as a percentage of GDP
DEBST	total stock of external debt service as a percentage of GDP
DEBTGDP	the external debt to GDP ratio
DEBTS	total external debt service as a percentage of GDP
DUMG	dummy variable for regime change
E(.)	expected value of a variable
EBUD	uncertainty with respect to government budget deficit
EGOVC	uncertainty with respect to government consumption expenditures
EINFL	uncertainty with respect to inflation
ERINTR	uncertainty with respect to real interest rate
ETAX	uncertainty with respect to taxes
FDI	foreign direct investment as a percentage of GDP
FINC	difference between domestic and foreign interest rate corrected for changes in the exchange rate
FREE	measure of political freedom
GOVEFF	measure of government effectiveness
INFL	annual domestic inflation rate
KF-1	capital flight one period lagged
KF-2	capital flight two periods lagged
LDCs	developing countries

PARCOM	extent to which non-elites are able to access institutional structures for political expression
PINSTAB	measure of political instability, calculated as 0.5 times the number of assassinations per million population per year plus 0.5 times the number of revolutions per year
POLRISK	measure of political risk
PR	political risk variable (specified in Dooley 1986)
PRIGHTS	index of political rights
REER	real (effective) exchange rate
RINTR	real interest rate (%)
RINTRF	foreign real interest rate (%)
SHDGDP	short term debt to GDP ratio
SPREAD	interest rate spread (i.e. foreign minus domestic real interest rate)
TAXGDP	total taxes as a percentage of GDP
VOICE	measure of voice and accountability
WAR	dummy variable (1 = country participated in at least one external war during 1960–85; 0 = no participation in external wars)
YG	rate of domestic economic growth

Table A7.1   Individual country data on capital flight, averages 1983–98

Country	Period	CF (US$ million)	CF/GDP (%)
East Asia			
China	1983–89	4 827	1.9
	1990–98	64 493	10.2
Fiji	1983–89	33	3.0
	1990–98	−33	−1.9
Indonesia	1983–89	2 864	3.4
	1990–98	9 389	6.7
Korea	1983–89	5 989	4.0
	1990–98	11 323	3.2
Papua New Guinea	1983–89	−5	0.2
	1990–98	402	8.9
Philippines	1983–89	115	0.6
	1990–98	1 978	3.3
Samoa	1983–89	16	15.4
	1990–98	8	3.1
Solomon Islands	1983–89	−2	−0.01
	1990–98	14	4.7
Thailand	1983–89	2 061	3.5
	1990–98	5 335	4.6
South Asia			
Bangladesh	1983–89	164	0.9
	1990–98	−160	−0.2
Bhutan	1983–89	−74	−33.8
	1990–98	−13	−4.5
India	1983–89	2 694	1.1
	1990–98	2 555	0.9

Table A7.1 Continued

Country	Period	CF (US$ million)	CF/GDP (%)
Pakistan	1983–89	2 761	0.9
	1990–98	−282	−0.2
Sri Lanka	1983–89	46	0.7
	1990–98	286	2.8
Latin America			
Argentina	1983–89	952	1.3
	1990–98	7 056	3.3
Barbados	1983–89	70	5.6
	1990–98	70	4.0
Bolivia	1983–89	−151	−0.8
	1990–98	241	2.8
Brazil	1983–89	3 719	1.4
	1990–98	12 667	2.5
Chile	1983–89	−323	−1.7
	1990–98	3 081	6.1
Colombia	1983–89	665	1.6
	1990–98	1 412	2.5
Costa Rica	1983–89	78	2.3
	1990–98	−32	−1.0
El Salvador	1983–89	146	3.9
	1990–98	329	2.9
Jamaica	1983–89	122	4.8
	1990–98	15	0.3
Nicaragua	1983–89	369	18.9
	1990–98	−847	−41.5
Paraguay	1983–89	44	1.1
	1990–98	−65	−1.2
Venezuela	1983–89	40	−0.7
	1990–98	5 068	7.9
Sub-Saharan Africa			
Botswana	1983–89	635	32.0
	1990–98	651	15.4
Cameroon	1983–89	480	4.6
	1990–98	460	4.9
Côte d'Ivoire	1983–89	296	3.0
	1990–98	−346	−3.9
Ethiopia	1983–89	268	4.0
	1990–98	−13	−0.1
Kenya	1983–89	153	2.5
	1990–98	32	1.3
Mauritania	1983–89	−16	−1.7
	1990–98	61	5.6
Mauritius	1983–89	134	7.3
	1990–98	193	5.4

Table A7.1   Continued

Country	Period	CF (US$ million)	CF/GDP (%)
Mozambique	1983–89	242	4.9
	1990–98	15	1.3
Swaziland	1983–89	50	7.5
	1990–98	43	4.2
Uganda	1983–89	57	1.4
	1990–98	−139	−3.3

Note: CF is capital flight; CF/GDP is the average level of CF/GDP over the entire period.

Notes

* We thank Léonce Ndikumana, Matthew Odedokun, George Mavrotas, Raghbendra Jha and participants at the UNU/WIDER Meeting on the Sustainability of External Development Financing held in Helsinki on 23–24 August 2002, for constructive comments on a preliminary version of this paper. However, the interpretations and conclusions expressed in this paper are entirely those of the authors and should not be attributed in any manner to UNU/WIDER.

1. The media has constantly spotlighted the capital flight phenomenon, remarkably arguing that precious resources from poor countries are being used to finance the egoistic consumerist habits of the world's richest people. For example, a respected *Financial Times* journalist, Martin Wolf, has argued that one of the most likely sources of unrecorded funding for the United States colossal US$392 billion current account deficit is capital flight from poor countries (see *Financial Times* 2002).
2. This section draws from Hermes *et al.* (2003).

References

Ajayi, I. S. (1997). 'An Analysis of External Debt and Capital Flight in the Severely Indebted Low Income Countries in Sub-Saharan Africa'. IMF Working Paper WP/97/68. Washington, DC: IMF.

Alesina, A. and G. Tabellini (1989). 'External Debt, Capital Flight and Political Risk'. *Journal of International Economics*, 27 (3–4): 199–220.

Bauer, P. T. (1981). *Equality, the Third World and Economic Delusion*. London: Weidenfeld and Nicolson.

Bhattacharya, R. (1999). 'Capital Flight under Uncertainty about Domestic Taxation and Trade Liberalization'. *Journal of Development Economics*, 59: 365–87.

Bjerksund, P. and G. Schjelderup (1995). 'Capital Controls and Capital Flight'. *FinanzArchiv*, 52 (1): 33–42.

Boyce, J. K. (1992). 'The Revolving Door? External Debt and Capital Flight: A Philippine Case Study'. *World Development*, 20 (3): 335–49.

Boyce, J. K. (1993). *The Philippines: The Political Economy of Growth and Impoverishment in the Marcos Era*. London: Macmillan Press.

Boyce, J. K. and L. Ndikumana (2001). 'Is Africa a Net Creditor? New Estimates of Capital Flight from Severely Indebted Sub-Saharan African Countries, 1970–1996'. *Journal of Development Studies*, 38 (2): 27–56.

Brown, R. (1990). 'Sudan's Other Economy: Migrants' Remittances, Capital Flight and their Policy Implications'. Sub-series on Money, Finance and Development Working Paper 31. The Hague: Institute of Social Studies.

Chang, P. H. K. and R. E. Cumby (1991). 'Capital Flight in Sub-Saharan African Countries', in I. Husain and J. M. Underwood (eds), *African External Finance in the 1990s*. Washington, DC: World Bank, 162–85.

Claessens, S. and D. Naudé (1993). 'Recent Estimates of Capital Flight'. Policy Research Working Papers, WPS 1186. Washington, DC: World Bank.

Collier, P., A. Hoeffler and C. Pattillo (2001). 'Flight Capital as a Portfolio Choice'. *World Bank Economic Review*, 15 (1): 55–80.

Cuddington, J. T. (1986). 'Capital Flight, Issues and Explanations'. *Princeton Studies in International Finance*, 58. Princeton, NJ: Princeton University.

Cuddington, J. T. (1987). 'Macroeconomic Determinants of Capital Flight: An Econometric Investigation', in D. R. Lessard and J. Williamson (eds), *Capital Flight and Third World Debt*. Washington, DC: Institute for International Economics, 85–96.

Cumby, R. and R. Levich (1987). 'Definitions and Magnitudes: On the Definition and Magnitude of Recent Capital Flight', in D. R. Lessard and J. Williamson (eds), *Capital Flight and Third World Debt*. Washington, DC: Institute for International Economics, 27–67.

Deppler, M. and M. Williamson (1987). 'Capital Flight: Concepts, Measurement, and Issues'. *Staff Papers for the World Economic Outlook*. Washington, DC: International Monetary Fund, 39–58.

Diwan, I. (1989). 'Foreign Debt, Crowding Out, and Capital Flight'. *Journal of International Money and Finance*, 8 (1): 121–36.

Dooley, M. P. (1986). 'Country-specific Risk Premiums, Capital Flight, and Net Investment Income Payments in Selected Developing Countries'. Washington, DC: IMF. Unpublished manuscript.

Dooley, M. P. (1988). 'Capital Flight: A Response to Differences in Risk'. *International Monetary Fund Staff Papers*, 35: 422–36.

Dooley, M. P. and K. M. Kletzer (1994). 'Capital Flight, External Debt and Domestic Policies'. NBER Working Paper 4793. Cambridge, MA: National Bureau of Economic Research.

Eaton, J. (1987). 'Public Debt Guarantees and Private Capital Flight'. *The World Bank Economic Review*, 1 (3): 377–95.

Eaton, J. and M. Gersovitz (1989). 'Country Risk and the Organization of the International Capital Transfer', in G. Calvo, R. Findlay, P. J. K. Kouri and J. Braga de Macedo (eds), *Debt Stabilization and Development: Essays in Memory of Carlos Diaz-Alejandro*. Oxford: Blackwell, 109–29.

Eggerstedt, H., R. Brideau Hall and S. van Wijnbergen (1995). 'Measuring Capital Flight: A Case Study of Mexico'. *World Development*, 23 (2): 211–32.

Erbe, S. (1985). 'The Flight of Capital from Developing Countries'. *Intereconomics*, 20: 268–75.

Financial Times (2002). 26 February.

Fry, M. J. (1993). 'Foreign Debt Accumulation: Financial and Fiscal Effects and Monetary Policy Reactions of Developing Countries'. *Journal of International Money and Finance*, 12 (4): 347–67.

Gibson, Heather D. and Euclid Tskalotos (1993). 'Testing a Flow Model of Capital Flight in Five European Countries'. *The Manchester School*, 61 (2): 144–66.

Gordon, David B. and Ross Levine (1989). 'The "Problem" of Capital Flight: A Cautionary Note'. *The World Economy*, 12 (2): 237–52.

Gulati, S. K. (1987). 'A Note on Trade Misinvoicing', in D. R. Lessard, and J. Williamson (eds), *Capital Flight and Third World Debt*. Washington, DC: Institute for International Economics, 68–78.

Henry, L. (1996). 'Capital Flight from Beautiful Places: The Case of Three Caribbean Countries'. *International Review of Applied Economics*, 10 (2): 263–72.

Hermes, N. and R. Lensink (1992). 'The Magnitude and Determinants of Capital Flight: The Case for Six Sub-Saharan African Countries'. *De Economist*, 140 (4): 515–30.

Hermes, N. and R. Lensink (2001). 'Capital Flight and the Uncertainty of Government Policies'. *Economics Letters*, 71 (3): 377–81.

Hermes, N., R. Lensink and V. Murinde (1999). 'The Magnitude and Determinants of Capital Flight in Eastern Europe', in A. W. Mullineux and C. J. Green (eds), *Economic Performance and Financial Sector Reform in Central and Eastern Europe*. Cheltenham: Edward Elgar, 243–55.

Hermes, N., R. Lensink and V. Murinde (2003). 'Capital Flight, Policy Uncertainty, and the Instability of the International Financial System', in A. Mullineux and V. Murinde (eds), *Handbook of International Banking*. Cheltenham: Edward Elgar.

Ize, Alain and Guillermo Ortiz (1987). 'Fiscal Rigidities, Public Debt, and Capital Flight'. *International Monetary Fund Staff Papers*, 34 (2): 311–32.

Kant, C. (1996). 'Foreign Direct Investment and Capital Flight'. *Princeton Studies in International Finance*, 80. Princeton, NJ: Princeton University.

Ketkar, S. L. and K. W. Ketkar (1989). 'Determinants of Capital Flight from Argentina, Brazil, and Mexico'. *Contemporary Policy Issues*, 7 (3): 11–29.

Khan, M. S. and N. Ul Haque (1985). 'Foreign Borrowing and Capital Flight: A Formal Analysis'. *International Monetary Fund Staff Papers*, 32 (4): 606–28.

Kindleberger, C. P. (1987). 'A Historical Perspective', in D. R. Lessard, and J. Williamson (eds), *Capital Flight and Third World Debt*. Washington, DC: Institute for International Economics, 7–26.

Lensink, R., N. Hermes and Victor Murinde (1998). 'The Effect of Financial Liberalization on Capital Flight in African Economies'. *World Development*, 26 (7): 1349–68.

Lensink, R., N. Hermes and V. Murinde (2000). 'Capital Flight and Political Risk'. *The Journal of International Money and Finance*, 19 (1): 73–92.

Lessard, D. R. and J. Williamson (eds) (1987). *Capital Flight and Third World Debt*. Washington, DC: Institute for International Economics.

Levine, R. and D. Renelt (1992). 'A Sensitivity Analysis of Cross-Country Growth Regressions'. *American Economic Review*, 82 (4): 942–63.

Mikkelsen, J. G. (1991). 'An Econometric Investigation of Capital Flight'. *Applied Economics*, 23: 73–85.

Morgan Guaranty (1986). 'LDC Capital Flight'. *World Financial Markets*, 2: 13–16.

Morgan Guaranty (1988). 'LDC Debt Reduction: A Critical Appraisal'. *World Financial Markets*, 7: 1–12.

Murinde, V., N. Hermes and R. Lensink (1996). 'Comparative Aspects of the Magnitude and Determinants of Capital Flight in Six Sub-Saharan African Countries'. *Savings and Development Quarterly Review*, 20 (1): 61–78.

Muscatelli, A. and A. H. Hallett (1992). 'How Successfully Do We Measure Capital Flight? Evidence from Five Developing Countries'. *Journal of Development Studies*, 28 (3): 538–56.

Ndikumana, L. and J. K. Boyce (2003). 'Public Debts and Private Assets: Explaining Capital Flight from Sub-Saharan African Countries'. *World Development*, 31 (1): 107–30.

Ng'eno, N. K. (2000). 'Capital Flight in Kenya', in I. Ajayi and M. S. Khan (eds), *External Debt and Capital Flight in Sub-Saharan Africa*. Washington, DC: The IMF Institute, 300–21.

Nyoni, T. (2000). 'Capital Flight from Tanzania', in I. Ajayi and M. S. Khan (eds), *External Debt and Capital Flight in Sub-Saharan Africa*. Washington, DC: The IMF Institute, 265–99.

Olopoenia, R. (2000). 'Capital Flight from Uganda', in I. Ajayi and M. S. Khan (eds), *External Debt and Capital Flight in Sub-Saharan Africa*. Washington, DC: The IMF Institute, 238–64.

Pastor, M. Jr. (1990). 'Capital Flight from Latin America'. *World Development*, 18 (1): 1–18.

Razin, A. and E. Sadka (1991). 'Efficient Investment Incentives in the Presence of Capital Flight'. *Journal of International Economics*, 31 (1–2): 171–81.

Sala-i-Martin, X. (1997). 'I Just Ran Two Million Regressions'. *American Economic Review*, 87 (2): 178–83.

Sheets, N. (1995). 'Capital Flight from the Countries in Transition: Some Theory and Empirical Evidence'. International Finance Discussion Papers, 514. Washington, DC: Board of Governors of the Federal Reserve System.

Tornell, A. and A. Velasco (1992). 'The Tragedy of the Commons and Economic Growth: Why Does Capital Flow from Poor to Rich Countries?'. *Journal of Political Economy*, 100 (6): 1208–31.

Vos, R. (1992). 'Private Foreign Asset Accumulation, Not Just Capital Flight: Evidence from the Philippines'. *Journal of Development Studies*, 28 (3): 500–37.

Walter, I. (1987). 'The Mechanisms of Capital Flight', in D. R. Lessard and J. Williamson (eds), *Capital Flight and Third World Debt*. Washington. DC: Institute for International Economics, 103–28.

World Bank (1985). *World Development Report 1985*. Washington, DC: World Bank.

World Bank (2002). *World Development Indicators*. Washington, DC: World Bank.

Zedillo, E. (1987). 'Mexico,' in D. R. Lessard and J. Williamson (eds), *Capital Flight and Third World Debt*. Washington, DC: Institute for International Economics, 174–85.

8
The 'Pull' and 'Push' Factors in North–South Private Capital Flows: Conceptual Issues and Empirical Estimates

Matthew Odedokun

1 Introduction

Attracting private capital, especially foreign direct investment (FDI), to developing countries has recently received much attention in international policy circles. For instance, it occupied a central place in various recent United Nations Summit on Finance for Development in Monterrey. From an essentially development perspective, it had earlier been considered the nexus of the OECD's Development Assistance Committee (DAC) which states in the *Development Cooperation* report (OECD 2001: 20):

> The time has therefore come to revisit development financing itself, to promote an overall coherent approach where each of the following aspects will have an important role: domestic resources; better distributed and guided expansion of private external flows for development in partner countries, including the poorest of them; and renewed role of development assistance, linked to increased efficiency and adequate volume.

Similarly, from a less developmental but largely financial policy perspective, FDI and portfolio capital flows (PCF) have featured prominently in proposals for the reform of international financial architecture (see Zedillo 2000). The reverse flows of private capital to Latin American countries in the early 1990s, coupled with the financial crisis in Mexico in 1994 and particularly in South-east Asia in 1997, gave impetus to this issue of north–south private capital flows.

The central place of cross-border private capital flows has given rise to a number of academic studies on the subject seeking to empirically determine the factors that influence such flows. Several models of capital flows have been suggested and a number of the empirical studies undertaken – as evidenced by the edited books that sprang up, particularly in the wake of the East Asian crisis (e.g. Armijo 1999; Edwards 2000; Ito and Krueger 2001; Chang *et al.* 2001; and Griffith-Jones *et al.* 2001). But despite this, not all the issues have been addressed and many that have been addressed are still far from being resolved.

In particular, most of the existing studies approach the matter from the perspective of the destination or host country (i.e. the south) and thus focus mainly on 'pull-factors', or characteristics of the destination countries. Related to this is the confusion that may arise in interpreting results of a model based on host-country perspective, as most studies understand the observed effects of the pull-factors to also mean those affecting foreign investors' aggregate supply responses, instead of merely those factors which affect allocation or distribution of (possibly, a given volume of) financial flows by northern investors to host countries in the south (see Oxfam America 2002). Also, the controversy still continues on the relative importance of pull- and push-factors (i.e. source country characteristics) on north–south capital flows. Many studies have addressed this issue (Hernandez and Rudolph 1995; Fernández-Arias 1996; Agenor 1998; Montiel and Reinhart 1999; Mody *et al.* 2001). While some studies (Fernández-Arias 1996) contend that push-factors are the major ones shaping the volume of capital flows, others (Hernandez and Rudolf 1995) argue differently.

Thus, many issues still need to be addressed, and the present chapter attempts to address these gaps in the literature. Particularly, we propose a model framework which identifies the effects of various pull-factors on the volume of private capital flows and which also permits testing for the effects of various source country-specific or push-factors as well as those relating to the generality of developed countries. The model is then estimated with annual panel data over 1970–2000 for about 20 DAC members. We report not only separate equations for total private flows, FDI and aggregate PCF but also for the various PCF components. Again, this is another feature not common in most earlier studies.

The rest of the chapter is organized as follows: Section 2 highlights some stylized facts on private capital flows while Section 3 presents a critique of the mainstream model framework and describes the framework adopted here. Operationalization of the suggested model framework is discussed in Section 4. The empirical results are given in Section 5 while Section 6 presents the summary and conclusion.

2   Some stylized facts

There has been a general upward trend (in nominal US dollar terms) in the volume of net capital flows from the developed to the developing countries in the past three decades (see Table 8.1 and Figure 8.1). Total net flows increased from an annual average of US$22.28 billion in the 1970s to

US$26.36 billion in the 1980s and finally to US$80.94 billion in the 1990s. FDI experienced a more rapid growth, increasing from just US$7.08 billion per annum in the 1970s to US$15.85 in the next decade and tripled in the 1990s to achieve US$49.95 billion annually. On the other hand, PCF during the same ten-year period decreased from US$15.20 per annum in the 1970s to just US$10.51 in the 1980s before it again rose, approximately at the same pace as FDI, in the 1990s to US$30.99 per year.

In relation to source country GDPs, however, total net capital flows have been declining, from 0.51 per cent of GDP in the 1970s to just 0.24 per cent in the 1980s before rising modestly to 0.39 per cent in the 1990s. But the FDI component actually recorded an upward trend to attain 0.24 per cent in the 1990s, after falling from 0.16 per cent of GDP in the 1970s to 0.14 per cent in the 1980s. PCF fell drastically from 0.35 per cent of GDP in the 1970s to a measly 0.09 per cent in the 1980s but compensated in the 1990s for some of this decline by rising to 0.15 per cent of GDP. Thus, private capital flows in relation to GDP were the lowest in the 1980s, and this trend applies to both FDI and PCF. Another remarkable feature of capital flows is the small magnitudes involved. After taking into account reverse transfers in the form of interest payments and profit remittances, amounts would probably be about the same as official development assistance (ODA) from the same DAC member countries. The latter averaged close to 0.30 per cent of donor GDP for the same decades.

The composition of capital flows, particularly PCF, is shown in Table 8.2. While non-bank and, hence, total export credits constituted in the 1975–84 decade a prominent component of PCF and of total capital flows, they have since become relatively insignificant. Instead, it is the securitized PCF that rose to prominence, particularly after 1995. As discussed above, PCF as a whole has been declining in relative importance, dropping from 69.39 per cent of total capital flows in 1975–84 to 24.57 per cent in 1985–94 before rising relatively to 37.05 per cent during 1995–2000 period.

Table 8.2 shows not only the flows in relation to source country GDPs but also in relation to the GDP of developing (or destination) countries. These accounted for 1.76 per cent of the GDP in destination countries in 1975–84 decade, fell by about half to just 0.95 per cent during the 1985–94 period, before rising to 2.44 per cent during the 1995–2000 period.

The trend movements in private capital flows from the US and other DAC member countries combined are shown separately in Figure 8.1, confirming the statistics given in Tables 8.1 and 8.2. In addition, Figure 8.1 shows that while net flows from the US are important, they have always (except for two isolated years) been less than flows from other developed countries combined, averaging about 70 per cent of the flows from other developed countries, or 40 per cent of the total (which includes the US itself). Thus, the almost exclusive attention and prominence given in the literature to flows from the US to developing countries seems to be unwarranted.

Table 8.1 Sources and volatility of foreign net capital flows to developing countries, 1970–2000

	Total private flows			Foreign direct investment (FDI)			Portfolio capital flows			Volatility index (coefficient of variation), 1970–2000		
	1970–80	1981–90	1991–2000	1970–80	1981–90	1991–2000	1970–80	1981–90	1991–2000	Total capital flows	FDI	Portfolio capital
	Amount (annual average, US$ billion, current values)											
Australia	0.16	−0.05	0.53	0.09	0.35	−0.49	0.07	−0.41	1.01	1.74	1.91	2.06
Belgium	0.82	0.28	0.61	0.11	0.18	0.54	0.71	0.10	0.08	4.97	1.59	9.21
Canada	0.74	0.62	3.51	0.21	0.25	3.48	0.53	0.38	0.03	1.20	1.47	2.49
Denmark	0.14	0.06	0.12	0.04	0.06	0.13	0.10	0.00	−0.01	1.69	1.39	4.46
Finland	0.03	0.08	0.28	0.01	0.04	0.11	0.03	0.04	0.17	1.91	1.87	2.86
France	2.53	2.35	3.61	0.36	0.82	3.07	2.17	1.53	0.54	1.09	1.14	2.13
Germany	2.10	2.88	9.84	0.78	0.97	3.32	1.31	1.91	6.52	0.91	1.03	0.91
Greece	—	—	—	—	—	—	—	—	—	—	—	—
Ireland	—	—	—	—	—	—	—	—	—	—	—	—
Italy	1.34	0.65	3.87	0.21	0.45	0.79	1.13	0.20	3.08	1.63	1.04	1.89
Japan	2.63	5.84	10.58	0.69	3.52	5.91	1.93	2.32	4.67	1.04	0.97	1.59
Luxembourg	—	—	—	—	—	—	—	—	—	—	—	—
Netherlands	0.60	0.42	3.86	0.24	0.41	3.19	0.36	0.00	0.66	1.30	1.51	1.95
New Zealand	0.01	0.03	—	0.01	0.03	0.02	0.00	0.00	—	0.93	0.83	1.46
Norway	0.13	−0.01	0.23	0.02	0.02	0.16	0.11	−0.03	0.07	1.47	1.70	2.27
Portugal	—	—	0.93	—	—	0.85	—	—	0.08	1.71	1.69	3.06
Spain	—	0.11	7.24	—	0.20	7.32	—	−0.09	−0.08	1.99	2.06	5.15
Sweden	0.30	0.38	0.63	0.08	0.15	0.39	0.22	0.23	0.24	1.07	1.34	1.43
Switzerland	1.18	1.16	0.64	0.18	0.74	0.89	1.00	0.42	−0.25	1.66	1.91	2.96
UK	4.52	3.52	8.45	0.77	2.67	6.62	3.75	0.85	1.83	0.84	1.00	1.65
USA	5.06	7.54	33.94	3.29	4.98	20.70	1.77	2.56	13.24	1.17	0.92	1.88
Total*	22.28	26.36	80.94	7.08	15.85	49.95	15.20	10.51	30.99	1.57	1.41	2.74
	Per cent of GDP											
Austria	0.14	0.23	−0.16	0.01	0.01	0.06	0.12	0.22	−0.22	NA	NA	NA
Australia	0.38	−0.05	0.26	0.22	0.36	−0.24	0.16	−0.42	0.50	NA	NA	NA
Belgium	1.23	0.23	0.26	0.16	0.15	0.22	1.07	0.08	0.03	NA	NA	NA

Table 8.1 Continued

	Total private flows			Foreign direct investment (FDI)			Portfolio capital flows			Volatility index (coefficient of variation), 1970–2000		
	1970–80	1981–90	1991–2000	1970–80	1981–90	1991–2000	1970–80	1981–90	1991–2000	Total capital flows	FDI	Portfolio capital
						Per cent of GDP						
Canada	0.43	0.16	0.59	0.12	0.06	0.58	0.31	0.09	0.00	NA	NA	NA
Denmark	0.35	0.08	0.08	0.09	0.07	0.08	0.25	0.01	−0.01	NA	NA	NA
Finland	0.12	0.10	0.24	0.02	0.06	0.10	0.11	0.05	0.14	NA	NA	NA
France	0.70	0.31	0.26	0.10	0.11	0.22	0.60	0.20	0.04	NA	NA	NA
Germany	0.40	0.28	0.47	0.15	0.09	0.16	0.25	0.18	0.31	NA	NA	NA
Greece	—	—	—	—	—	—	—	—	—	NA	NA	NA
Ireland	—	—	—	—	—	—	—	—	—	NA	NA	NA
Italy	0.59	0.10	0.34	0.09	0.07	0.07	0.50	0.03	0.27	NA	NA	NA
Japan	0.45	0.30	0.24	0.12	0.18	0.13	0.33	0.12	0.11	NA	NA	NA
Luxembourg	—	—	—	—	—	—	—	—	—	NA	NA	NA
Netherlands	0.62	0.22	1.05	0.25	0.22	0.87	0.37	0.00	0.18	NA	NA	NA
New Zealand	0.06	0.10	—	0.04	0.08	0.04	0.02	0.01	—	NA	NA	NA
Norway	0.40	−0.01	0.16	0.05	0.03	0.11	0.35	−0.04	0.05	NA	NA	NA
Portugal	—	—	0.92	—	—	0.84	—	—	0.08	NA	NA	NA
Spain	—	0.04	1.28	—	0.07	1.29	—	−0.03	−0.01	NA	NA	NA
Sweden	0.41	0.26	0.27	0.11	0.10	0.17	0.31	0.16	0.10	NA	NA	NA
Switzerland	1.98	0.83	0.25	0.30	0.53	0.34	1.67	0.30	−0.10	NA	NA	NA
UK	1.78	0.56	0.71	0.30	0.43	0.55	1.48	0.14	0.15	NA	NA	NA
USA	0.29	0.17	0.44	0.19	0.12	0.27	0.10	0.06	0.17	NA	NA	NA
Total	0.51	0.24	0.39	0.16	0.14	0.24	0.35	0.09	0.15	NA	NA	NA

Notes: * The numbers for the volatility index are averages (and not totals) across the 18 countries. (Australia's figure is excluded, being an outlier); — = non-availability of data; NA = non-applicable.

Source: Computed from DAC (online) and the World Bank's GDP figures from *International Development Statistics* (online).

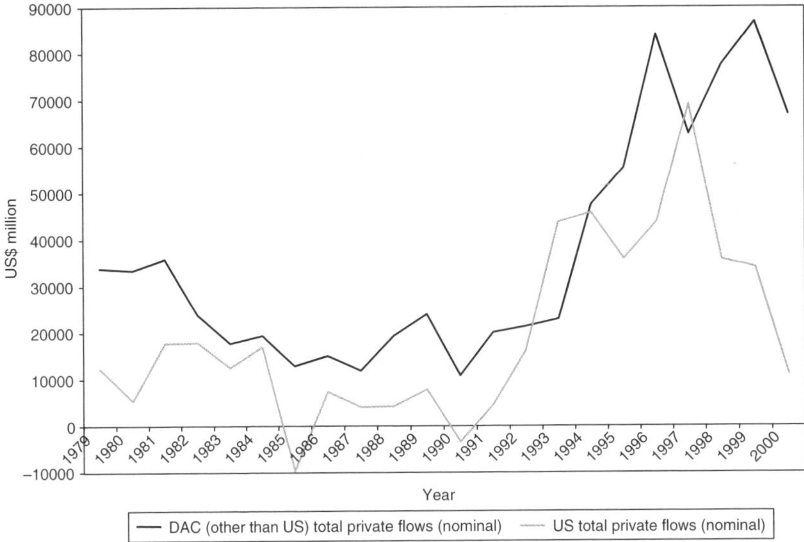

Figure 8.1 Total net capital flows from the US and DAC member countries, 1979–2000 (US$ million)

Source: DAC's *International Development Statistics* (online).

Table 8.1 also confirms the general notion that PCF is more volatile than the FDI. The coefficient of variation (a volatility indicator) is higher for PCF than for FDI for all source countries, except Germany.

3   Model framework

The existing or received framework: modelling from the perspective of destination countries

We start our exposition with the assumption that the developed countries are a single composite region called the 'north', which constitutes the source country of financial flows to the universe of m developing countries, collectively called the 'south'. The total – or envelope – of transferable resources (denoted by S) during each period from this composite north is, by definition, the country's excess saving over domestic investment spending which is also the same as its (current account) balance-of-payments (BOP) surplus.[1] This resource envelope S is to be allocated over its portfolio of potentially n foreign 'assets' or uses, as shown in Table 8.3. These could be net foreign direct investment, net portfolio investment, official loans, official unrequited transfers or grants, private unrequited transfers, autonomous reduction in foreign reserves held by developing countries and so on. We denote the amount allocated to each type i by F_i ($i = 1, \ldots n$). Also, for each category

Table 8.2   Indicators of structure and trends of commercial capital flows from developed to developing countries,* 1975–2000

	1975–84	1985–94	1995–2000	1975–84	1985–94	1995–2000
	Amount (US$ billion, annual average)			% of total private flows		
Total private flows	37.45	34.65	163.05	100.00	100.00	100.00
FDI	11.46	26.13	102.64	30.61	75.43	62.95
Portfolio capital: total	25.99	8.51	60.41	69.39	24.57	37.05
Portfolio capital: banks	—	—	23.74	—	—	14.56
of which: banks' net export credits	—	—	0.37	—	—	0.22
Portfolio capital: non-banks	—	—	35.48	—	—	21.76
of which: non-banks' net export credits	7.63	0.98	3.39	20.36	2.81	2.08
of which: non-banks' securities and other	1.24	4.26	31.66	3.31	12.30	19.42
Memo: Net export credits (total)	8.48	0.81	3.75	22.64	2.33	2.30
	% of source countries' GDP			% of destination countries' GDP		
Total private flows	0.54	0.22	0.71	1.76	0.95	2.44
FDI	0.17	0.17	0.45	0.54	0.72	1.54
Portfolio capital: total	0.38	0.05	0.26	1.22	0.23	0.90
Portfolio capital: banks	—	—	0.10	—	—	0.36
of which: banks' net export credits	—	—	0.00	—	—	0.01
Portfolio capital: non-banks	—	—	0.15	—	—	0.53
of which: non-banks' net export credits	0.11	0.01	0.01	0.36	0.03	0.05
of which: non-banks' securities and other	0.02	0.03	0.14	0.06	0.12	0.47
Memo: Net export credits (total)	0.12	0.01	0.02	0.40	0.02	0.06

Note: * The developing countries also include countries in transition.

Source: Computed from the DAC (online) and the World Bank's GDP figures from *International Development Statistics* (online).

of use, the source country has to decide on its allocation among m potential destination countries, each of which receives S_j $(j = 1, \dots m)$ in the form of a combination of n 'assets'. Ignoring the intra-destination countries' financial flows (which in real life are relatively few and small in amounts), the (current account) BOP deficit of each destination country j is the

Table 8.3   Hypothetical disaggregated BOP capital accounts for the developed country

	Destination country				Total for each type of resource transfer
	1	2	...	m	
Financial asset:					
1 (say, FDI)	y_{11}	y_{12}	...	y_{1m}	$\Sigma y_{1j} = F_1$
2 (say, portfolio investment)	y_{21}	y_{22}	...	y_{2m}	$\Sigma y_{2j} = F_2$
3 (say, foreign grants)	y_{31}	y_{32}	...	y_{3m}	$\Sigma y_{3j} = F_3$
.	.	.	...	.	.
.	.	.	...	.	.
.	.	.	...	.	.
n (say, decrease in foreign reserve holdings by destination countries)	y_{n1}	y_{n2}	...	y_{nm}	$\Sigma y_{nj} = F_n$
Total transfers to (or BOP deficitfor) each destination country	$\Sigma y_{i1} = S_1$	$\Sigma y_{i2} = S_2$	...	$\Sigma y_{im} = S_m$	$\Sigma\Sigma y_{ij} = \Sigma F_i = \Sigma S_j$

column total ($\Sigma y_{ij} = S_j$) for that country. The resulting m by n matrix of uses and destinations is shown in Table 8.3, which, therefore, constitutes a very disaggregated (mainly) capital account section of BOP record for the composite capital-exporting country. The relationship between the transferable resource envelope S and its uses is shown in equation (1) below, which is, in fact, an identity or BOP constraint.

$$S = \sum_{j=1}^{m} \sum_{i=1}^{n} y_{ij} = \sum_{i=1}^{n} F_i = \sum_{j=1}^{m} S_j \tag{1}$$

Previous econometric studies typically seek to explain, from the perspective of the south, the variation in just a single element y_{ij} of the above matrix, that is, net inflow to a given recipient country over time (or across countries at a point in time) of a particular category like foreign direct investment, portfolio investment or foreign aid. The typical equation specified, assuming a time-series approach, in the most elaborate studies takes the form:

$$y_{ijt} = f(x_{jt}, Z_t) \ (i = 1, 2, \ldots n; \quad j = 1, \ldots m; \quad t = 1, \ldots T) \tag{2}$$

where:

y_{ijt} = net financial inflow of type i that is being explained (say, portfolio investment) to the destination country j in period t;

x_{jt} = a representative element of the vector of specific characteristics or factors relating to the destination country j during period t, which are popularly referred to as the pull-factors in such studies; and

Z_t = a representative element of the vector of specific characteristics or factors relating to the international community, especially the source country (the north) at time t, which are popularly called the push-factors.

If the x_j is found to have a negative causal effect on y_{ij}, the inference would be that high value of x_j deters foreign financial inflow of type i to country j, so that policies aimed at attracting y_i to country j should aim at reducing that particular factor. The reverse holds if that factor is found to have a positive causal effect on y_{ij}.

This type of econometric analysis can highlight much about certain types of foreign financial allocation policies. For instance, it is sometimes desirable to target a given volume of north–south financial flows to a particular country j, in the form of a specific productive type i (like, say, foreign direct investment), irrespective of how this increased allocation is financed and whether any additionality exists. From this type of analysis, one can infer whether the pull-factor x_j has the effect of bringing this about. This would be satisfactory if the manner of financing the resulting increase in y_{ij} (or utilization of its induced decrease, if that is the case) is of no concern.

But this popular approach can also be defective or error prone in addressing other forms of allocation policies while it can fail woefully when it comes to additionality or crowding-out issues. The pull-factor induced increase in y_{ij} (i.e. x_j-induced) could have been at the expense of any combination of the remaining $nm - 1$ entries or cells of $y_{\kappa\tau}$'s ($\kappa = 1, \ldots -1$; $\tau = 1, \ldots m - 1$; $\forall\, \kappa \neq i$ and $\tau \neq j$) given in Table 8.3. In other words, it could have been financed by reducing other forms of inflow (i.e. some other elements of S_j, other than y_{ij}) to that particular country, as would have been the case if the increased FDI is partially or wholly financed by a corresponding decrease in foreign portfolio capital. It also means that the x_j-induced increase in y_{ij} could have been at the expense of a reduction in foreign resource flows (whether of the same type i or of any other types) to other destination countries. The existing approach is not equipped to shed much light here.

One important policy area is the allocation of a given volume of north–south financial flows – not to a particular country j as such, but to all or a combination of the m destinations countries – for a particular type i (say, FDI) from a combination of other types. This has to do with additionality or crowding-out effect of the pull-factors on a particular type i of north–south resource flow, viewed from the perspective of the totality of the destination countries. As a representative example of a practical and real life situation, competing for FDI through various fiscal or other incentives is often said to be a zero-sum game, where net inflows gained by the country providing the incentives equal the net inflows (of FDI and, probably, of other private investment) lost by other destination countries. This leads to cut-throat competition in the provision of such incentives. The approach has little light to shed on whether contentions like these are actually true, contrary to what previous studies often appear to claim.

The pull-factors identified through such studies indicate only the elements taken into consideration by source countries in allocating their net saving among the different types of foreign financial resource flows or among various potential destination countries. At best, they merely constitute the necessary conditions for changing the volume of a particular type of foreign transfer. The reason why they are necessary conditions is that, if the source country, in its allocation to the various types of financial flows and/or different destination countries, is observed not to have reckoned with a particular potential pull-factor, then this factor can be considered irrelevant in influencing the total volume of that specific type of financial flow to a particular country. Thus, the approach can be useful in screening the pull-factors which need further investigation. But a more reliable econometric approach is needed for identifying the genuine pull-factors which affect not only the allocation of a given volume of net saving between different types of foreign financial flows and destinations, but also entail an additionality of net financial flows. In other words, a potential pull-factor that does not actually affect the allocation of financial flows would also not affect the supply or total volume of such flows. But the converse is not true because certain factors, although not affecting total supply, can affect the allocation or 'rationing' of a given volume. Generally, in as much as the analysis is still confined to the specification of equations from the perspective of destination countries, there will be the inherent problem of conclusively inferring whether an identified pull-factor influences the source country's allocation decision only, or whether it also affects its overall supply or volume behaviour.

Distinctions between modelling financial flows from the source and destination perspectives

This distinction in the perspectives between destination and source countries needs to be elaborated further before we describe our modelling, which is based on the latter perspective. As already pointed out, in modelling the north–south financial flows from a source-country perspective, equations do not need to be specified for each destination country and, hence, for any of the nm matrix of y_{ij} or even S_j entries depicted in Table 8.3, but rather for the aggregate of these. This entails specifying an equation for each financial type i, that is, F_i in Table 8.2.[2]

Modelling equation for F_i is said to be from a source-country perspective. This is so because in this type of formulation (as further described in equation (5)), the z push-factor for individual source countries (i.e. if we relax the assumption of just a single composite source country) should now replace what in equation (2) constitute the composite Z push-factor for aggregate source country. Similarly, X, a composite aggregate for all the destination countries should now replace the *x* pull-factor for individual destination countries that features in equation (2). Otherwise, in principle, modelling from the source-country perspective does not necessarily entail a difference in the type of explanatory variables involved. But in practice, expediency often leads to testing for a different set of explanatory variables.[3]

Apart from this, a difference will also arise from normalizing or scaling the statistics used to estimate the model. Under the equation (2) format, the dependent variable is expected to be normalized or scaled by the price level (for the value, in real terms), by the population (for expressing it on a per capita basis) or by the GDP of the destination countries. But under the source-country perspective, it would now be normalized by similar source-country indicators.[4] And this introduces another serious flaw in specifying equations from the perspective of the destination countries. In modelling cross-border private financial flows, it is generally assumed, based on the presumption that destination countries are being rationed somewhat, that the observed flows stand for supply (at the initiative of investors in capital-exporting countries) as opposed to demand. Therefore attempts are made to model the behaviour or reaction of foreign investors. The objective is to explain (either the supply or allocation) response, effort or decision of the source country and not to describe the resource needs or requirements of the recipients. This means that the variables (price level, population, GDP, etc.) to be used in normalization should be those of the source country. But this becomes difficult, and sometimes impossible, if the destination country perspective is adopted.[5]

But the difference arising from scaling with the destination country variables can often be so substantial as to seriously affect the results of the model estimates. For example, when the normalization variable is the population, using this indicator for the recipient country underestimates the source-country's supply, allocation or effort over time because populations in destination countries often grow rapidly while typically the source-country population is almost stagnant. The converse may be true with price levels. Purchasing power parity does not always hold at every point in time – that is, if it holds at all. Generally in the recent past as a result of macroeconomic 'reforms' and so on nominal rates of foreign inflation-adjusted depreciation of domestic currency have been higher than domestic inflation rates. This means that a given amount of foreign resource flows, when converted into local currency and deflated by the price level, now appears larger, spuriously suggesting that the source country has become more 'generous'. Many destination countries (particularly the low-income ones) have been experiencing slower rates of real GDP expansion than the typical source country, so that using GDP as the normalization factor would have a similar effect. This problem becomes pronounced in cross-section and panel regression models, due to the usually great diversities among destination countries with regard to population growth, economic growth, inflation and currency depreciation. This problem, in conjunction with the low quality and scanty destination country data on GDP, population, prices and even BOP (or foreign resource receipts generally), suggests that the dependent variables in most existing studies are often not dependable, and the results should therefore be viewed with caution.[6]

Modelling from the perspective of source countries

To further describe the source country-based framework, we relax the earlier assumption of a single conglomerate country (called 'north') and replace it with the existence of q source countries that now comprise the north.[7] For a typical developed country k $(k = 1, \ldots q)$, its equivalent of Table 8.3 matrix would now look like Table 8.4, where the additional subscript k is added to indicate that the table is for the typical developed country k. The added element of Table 8.4 is the inclusion of financial flows $w_{\eta\tau}$ $(\eta = 1, \ldots n - 1;$ $\tau = 1, \ldots q - 1; \forall\, \eta \neq i$ and $\tau \neq k)$ between the typical country k and its other $q - 1$ developed country counterparts (with country k's financial flow with itself being shown to be zero). While financial flows among developing countries are few and often relatively negligible, this is not the case for intra-developed country flows, as their financial markets are highly integrated. Consequently, it is desirable to recognize this type of financial flow. So, with this assumption of many developed countries and the new notations, the utilization of the available transferable resource envelope (S_k) at the disposal of developed country k is described in equation (3). There, S_k is divided between transfers to all the developing countries, given by ΣF_{ik}, and the transfers to all the other $q - 1$ developed countries, given by ΣA_{ik} (where A_{ik} is the amount of financial transfer of type i from developed country k to all other developed countries).

$$S_k = \sum_{i=1}^{n} F_{ik} + \sum_{i=1}^{n} A_{ik} \tag{3}$$

Aggregating equation (3) over all the q developed countries yields equation (4), which corresponds (or should be equal in magnitude) to equation (1). By definition, the sum of the balances between developed countries $(\Sigma\Sigma A_{ik})$ should equal zero.

$$S = \sum_{k=1}^{q} S_k = \sum_{k=1}^{q} \sum_{i=1}^{n} F_{ik} + \sum_{k=1}^{q} \sum_{i=1}^{n} A_{ik} = \sum_{k=1}^{q} \sum_{i=1}^{n} F_{ik} + 0 \tag{4}$$

As mentioned earlier, the model specification from the perspective of the developed or source countries should be for the aggregate of each type of financial flow i, with the recipient developing countries' identity now no longer applicable. In other words, equations (assuming time-series approach) are now to be specified for F_{ik} so that for each developed country k, the supply function with respect to resource flow of type i is to be

Table 8.4 Hypothetical disaggregated BOP capital accounts for the representative developed country k

| | Net resource flows from the representative developed country k to each (and total) of the m developing countries | | | | | Net resource flows from the representative developed country k to each (and total) of the remaining $q-1$ *developed* countries | | | | | |
| | Developing country | | | | | Developed country | | | | | |
	1	2	...	m	Total	1	2	k	...	q	Total
Financial asset from country k											
1 (say, FDI)	y_{11k}	y_{12k}	...	y_{1mk}	$\Sigma y_{1jk}=F_{1k}$	w_{11k}	w_{12k}	$w_{1kk}=0$	...	w_{1qk}	$\Sigma w_{1jk}=A_{1k}$
2 (say, portfolio investment)	y_{21k}	y_{22k}	...	y_{2mk}	$\Sigma y_{2jk}=F_{2k}$	w_{21k}	w_{22k}	$w_{2kk}=0$	...	w_{2qk}	$\Sigma w_{2jk}=A_{2k}$
3 (say, foreign grants)	y_{31k}	y_{32k}	...	y_{3mk}	$\Sigma y_{3jk}=F_{3k}$	w_{31k}	w_{32k}	$w_{3kk}=0$	...	w_{3qk}	$\Sigma w_{3jk}=A_{3k}$
.	.	.	...	.	.	.	.	.	...	.	.
.	.	.	...	.	.	.	.	.	...	.	.
.	.	.	...	.	.	.	.	.	...	.	.
n (say, decrease in foreign reserve holdings in country k's currency)	y_{n1k}	y_{n2k}	...	y_{nmk}	$\Sigma y_{njk}=F_{nk}$	w_{n1k}	w_{n2k}	$w_{nkk}=0$	...	w_{nqk}	$\Sigma w_{njk}=A_{nk}$
Total transfers from or BOP (current account) bilateral deficit with country k	$\Sigma y_{i1k}=S_{1k}$	$\Sigma y_{i2k}=S_{2k}$	...	$\Sigma y_{imk}=S_{mk}$	$\Sigma\Sigma y_{ijk}=$ $\Sigma F_{ik}=\Sigma S_{jk}$						$\Sigma\Sigma w_{ijk}=\Sigma A_{ik}$

modelled, as shown in equation (5) below, which is equivalent to the earlier equation (2), that is, from a recipient-country perspective.

$$F_{ikt} = f(z_{kt}, X_t) \quad (i = 1, 2, \ldots n; \; k = 1, \ldots q; \; t = 1, \ldots T) \tag{5}$$

where:

F_{ikt} = net financial inflow of type i that is being examined (say, portfolio investment) from developed country k to all developing countries combined in period t;

z_{kt} = a representative element of the vector of specific factors relating to developed country k during period t, referred to as push-factors; and

X_t = a representative element of the vector of specific factors relating to the totality of developing countries (being measured as a composite or weighted average of the factor for all the developing countries), so that it constitutes a vector of some sort of composite pull-factors.

In the above formulation, the additionality (or lack of it) of the representative pull variable X should no longer be ambiguous. If the coefficient of X is zero (in practice, if it is statistically insignificant), it follows that the element could at best only affect the distribution of F_{ik} among the various recipient countries but not its total volume, so that no additionality is involved. But if the coefficient of that element is non-zero (and, presumably, of the expected sign), it would imply that its effect on various recipient countries does not cancel or crowd-out each other, so that there is additionality in its effect. It would also suggest that it does affect each of the m elements in the ith row (i.e. in the row for F_{ik}) in Table 8.5; that is, it could be deemed to have a similar effect on this type of flow to each of the m destination countries; consequently, there is little need for individually estimating equations for this particular type of transfer for each recipient country, as would have been the case in adopting a recipient-country perspective in the model specification. Both the necessary and sufficient conditions for the effect of that particular pull-factor in changing the volume of a specific type of financial flow to each developing country and the collectivity of developing countries would have been met.

As a practical illustration, let us assume that F_{ik} stands for total FDI flows from developed country k (say, Japan) and that X is the composite average of economic growth in all the developing countries. Also, let us assume that the coefficient of this composite economic growth is statistically insignificant in the FDI flow equation for Japan-to-developing countries. It means that even though economic growth in a particular developing country might be a potential pull-factor on FDI flows from Japan, this is entirely at the expense of its FDI flows to some other (presumably, non-growing) developing country. This follows from the observation that a simultaneous or average economic growth in all the developing countries does not affect

Table 8.5 Effects of per capita income levels and interest rates

	Total flows	FDI	Portfolio capital flows (PCF)					
			Total	Total for non-bank	Non-bank export credit	Non-bank securities	Total export credit	Total non-export credit
Per capita income (log)								
Specific donor	0.007	0.008	0.002	0.003	0.0004	0.001	0.001	0.001
under consideration	(1.6)	(2.2)	(0.6)	(0.7)	(0.3)	(0.4)	(0.9)	(0.3)
Average for other donors	−0.035	0.003	−0.036	−0.020	−0.014	−0.002	−0.009	−0.030
	(−3.6)	(0.9)	(−3.8)	(−2.9)	(−3.7)	(−0.4)	(−2.0)	(−3.6)
All developing countries	0.028	−0.009	0.033	0.017	0.011	0.003	0.005	0.031
	(2.6)	(−1.7)	(3.2)	(2.5)	(2.7)	(0.6)	(1.0)	(3.3)
Interest rate								
Specific donor	−0.032	−0.019	−0.017	−0.003	0.002	−0.012	0.004	−0.023
under consideration	(−3.0)	(−2.3)	(−2.3)	(−0.3)	(0.6)	(−2.1)	(1.1)	(−3.4)
Average for other donors	−0.080	−0.045	−0.029	−0.052	−0.032	−0.020	−0.040	0.010
	(−3.5)	(−3.9)	(−1.6)	(−3.0)	(−5.0)	(−1.2)	(−5.2)	(0.5)
Average for all	0.012	0.060	0.060	0.052	0.033	0.019	0.056	0.006
developing countries	(4.1)	(3.2)	(2.7)	(2.3)	(3.4)	(1.0)	(4.5)	(0.3)
Adjusted R^2	0.224	0.287	0.159	0.183	0.224	0.110	0.166	0.099
Total no. of observations	553	544	538	287	515	292	531	489

Notes: The dependent variables, indicated on top of each column, are fractions of source country's GDP; the numbers in parentheses are the t-values. A parameter estimate is statistically significant at 1%; 5%; and 10% levels if its t-value in absolute sense is not less than 2.6; 2.0; and 1.6, respectively.

Japan's FDI to these countries. But if the coefficient is positive and statistically significant, it follows that a simultaneous growth of all developing countries would induce a net addition to Japan's FDI inflow to developing countries. It also implies that Japanese FDI flow to each and every developing country is positively attracted or 'pulled' by the high growth performance in that country, making it conceptually superfluous to separately test for the effect of economic growth on Japan's FDI flows to each and every one of the countries.

But now if the effects of the push-factors (elements of vector Z_k) are to be properly determined, a different model specification problem has to be addressed. In equation (3) and Table 8.4, the presence of intra-developed country flows are highlighted so as to correspond to reality. It follows that there would be substitution between total financial flows from a particular developed country k to the m developing countries on one hand and to the rest of $q-1$ developed countries on the other. Thus, following from equation (3), the conditions in the $q-1$ developed countries, by affecting ΣA_{ik} (net inflow from developed country k to other developed countries combined), would also affect ΣF_{ik} (net inflow from developed country k to all developing countries), if the identity between fixed S_k (developed country k's balance of payment surplus or saving–investment balance) and $\Sigma F_{ik} + \Sigma A_{ik}$ is to hold. This means that the push-factors in the remaining $q-1$ developed countries, by affecting ΣA_{ik} in the particular developed country k, could have effects or, rather, cross-effects on financial flows from country k to the m developing countries, that is, in addition to the effects they would have on the direct flows from the $q-1$ developed countries to developing countries. For example, the flow from Japan of FDI (or even totality of financial flows) should depend not only on the economic growth in developing countries (i.e. pull-factor) or even in Japan (push-factor), but also on the economic growth in other developed countries outside Japan (namely, US, Germany, etc.). In other words, growth in these other developed countries has a direct effect on their respective bilateral FDI flows to developing countries, as well as an indirect effect through the volume of flows from Japan to the same developing countries. This arises from the complex interrelated cross-country flow-of-funds relationships, whereby events in one country have ripple effects on others.

Consequently, the model specification should take note of the ripple effect, and this can be accomplished within the framework of reduced-form equation (5) by including the composite push-factor equivalent of developed country k's z_k for other developed countries, (say, $\check{Z}_k$), as given in equation (6). This would be computed as weighted average of the factors for the $q-1$ developed countries (i.e. $\check{Z}_k = \Sigma_{h=1}^{q-1} \pi_h Z_h$, where π_h is the weight for or relative importance of country h so that $\Sigma_{h=1}^{q-1} \pi_h = 1, \forall\, h \neq k$).[8] By this, the cross-effects of z factor in the remaining developed countries on F_{ik} would be controlled for in estimating the effect of z_k. Except in some exceptional or rather uncommon circumstances (e.g. degree of openness of economy, as discussed later), we expect the coefficients of both z_k and $\check{Z}_k$ to have the same sign. Using the example above, by adding (and, hence, controlling for the 'cross-push' effect of) the weighted average of economic growth in all other developed countries as an additional regressor in the equation for the Japan-to-developing country FDI flow, the estimate of (own-push) effect of Japan's economic growth on its FDI flows to developing countries would be purged of this specification bias. And if high economic growth in Japan has the effect of, say, reducing its FDI inflows to developing countries by enhancing, for example, profitable domestic investment opportunities, so would also be the case of high economic growth in the remaining developed countries, as Japanese investors would see these as more profitable outlets for their FDI vis-à-vis the developing countries.

$$F_{ikt} = f(z_{kt}, X_t, \check{Z}_{kt}) \qquad (i = 1, 2, \ldots n; \ k = 1, \ldots q; \ t = 1, \ldots T) \tag{6}$$

Based on the above model description, most of the problems associated with modelling from the recipient's perspective have been addressed. Also, even though our discussion has so far been based on a time-series framework, the same applies equally to panel and cross-sectional frameworks, with one exception, however. In the case of cross-section framework, the composite pull-factor X in equations (5) and (6) is likely to be inapplicable since all developed countries are confronted by the same developing-country pull-factor at each point in time.

In this study, we operationalize the above model of equation (6) type, using panel regression framework to explain the flows of FDI and PCF from the developed to the developing countries. The operational model employed is described in the next section.

4   Operationalization of foreign financial flow modelling from the perspective of the source country

Model of developed–developing country flows of FDI and portfolio capital

Fernández-Arias (1996) and Fernández-Arias and Montiel (1996) proposed a generalized equation framework for estimating capital flow equations, which has since been adopted in subsequent studies in more specific forms. We also find this general equation suitable for the present study.

According to Fernández-Arias (1996), three broad factors are involved in the international portfolio allocation involving developing countries. One of these is the expected returns on the domestic 'project' in a potential destination country, D; the second is the opportunity cost represented by expected returns in the developed or source countries, R; and the third is the creditworthiness factor of (destination) country, C. Unlike in the conventional portfolio allocation models, the model assumes a non-arbitrage condition for mean returns adjusted by country default risk (DC), so as to highlight the role of the risk factor, as shown in equation (7).

$$DC = R \tag{7}$$

Next, the functional relationships for the expected return, D, and creditworthiness, C, are specified. F, the current flow of foreign debt (or foreign capital generally) in that country, is posited to enter negatively in the equation for D, because it is assumed that domestic project returns fall as foreign capital inflows increase due to the presence of diminishing returns. On the other hand, it is the existing or initial stock (S) of this foreign capital that enters the C equation negatively. These are expressed as follows:

$$D = D(d, F), \qquad D_1 > 0 \text{ and } D_2 < 0 \tag{8}$$

$$C = C(c, S), \qquad C_1 > 0 \text{ and } C_2 < 0 \tag{9}$$

where d and c are shift parameters, with the former reflecting the underlying economic climate regarding domestic investment returns and the latter reflecting the country's risk or ability to pay profile.

Through totally differentiating and then re-arranging the result of substituting equations (8) and (9) into (7), the author arrived at the reduced-form equation (10):

$$F = F(d, c, R, S), \qquad F_1, F_2 > 0 \text{ and } F_3, F_4 < 0 \tag{10}$$

Thus, the volume of capital flows positively depends on a positive investment climate (d) and ability to pay indicator (c) and negatively on foreign rate of return (R) and initial stock of foreign capital or external debt (S).

The above model by Fernández-Arias (1996) provides a good starting point for our study. Particularly, his departure from the orthodox arbitrage condition between domestic and foreign rates of return makes it adaptable to a development-oriented study, as opposed to just pure financial modelling exercise. The rationale given by Fernández-Arias (1996: 392) for the departure is as follows:

> In developing countries with substantial default risk and low creditworthiness the effect of shocks on mean returns is likely to be relatively more significant, and therefore dominate, the effect on variability. For these countries, first moments, as opposed to second moments, are likely to be a sufficient good approximation to describe changes in foreign investors'

choices between investing in these countries or elsewhere. The standard mean-variance portfolio models based on the trade-offs between first and second moments facing risk-averse investors is less relevant when default risk is not negligible and country creditworthiness is low.

What remains is the methodology for operationalizing it, particularly by finding appropriate measures of d, c, R and S in the above relationship. We discuss this issue next.

Measures of returns on investment and risk in destination countries, initial debt and international rates of return

Initial stock of debt

As indicated in equation (10), the stock of initial debt is expected to be negatively related to the volume of private capital flows. In the underlying structural equation (9), this is because a high stock of debt impacts negatively on the creditworthiness perception of investors. Although it is a pull-factor because of its relation to destination-country characteristics, it is also influenced (as rightly argued by Fernández-Arias (1996)), by international conditions beyond the control of individual destination countries. Therefore, it also constitutes a push-factor.

In the study, the initial debt stock is broken down into two items: private debt, and public and publicly guaranteed debt. High level of private debt could encourage further (though rather involuntary) private inflows to service existing debts. This is hardly the case with public and publicly guaranteed debts. Because of the source-country perspective adopted in the study, we utilize the aggregate stock of each debt category for all developing countries combined. We express each in relation to the aggregate GDP of the same developing countries.

Domestic and international rates of return in the source country

This factor is also expected to have a negative relationship on capital flows to developing countries. It is the opportunity cost of funds being invested in developing countries. If funds are cheap in the developed countries, more funds are expected to flow to developing countries as FDI and PCF.

Following on the source-country modelling perspective adopted here, we simultaneously test for the effect of the two interest rates, proxied by discount rates: interest rate in the specific source-country being analysed and domestic interest rates averaged over all other developed countries, except the one being examined. The former is expected to have a negative own-effect while the latter is expected to have negative cross-effect on capital flows to developing countries.

Similarly, we posit an anticipated economic growth (proxied by *ex post* growth) to enhance returns in the specific source country being examined and consequently to stem private flows to developing countries. A similar assumption is applied if the source economy is in a rising phase of its economic cycle. Economic growth in the remaining developed countries and the prevalence of a rising phase of their economic cycle are expected to have similar cross-effects on the specific source country's private flows because these other developed countries will now be host to more of the private flows that would have gone to developing countries. Anticipated economic growth should be particularly important in view of the inclusion of FDI in our private capital flows.

For the same reason, the level of per capita income in the source country should influence the volume of capital flows by affecting not only private net savings – with which net foreign flows are financed – but also by affecting returns on domestic investment opportunities. The two produce opposite-direction effects, and the overall impact on net private flows should be determined by an empirical study. The same applies to the cross-effect of the level of per capita income in other developed countries combined.

Returns on investments in the destination country

First, we consider the nominal rates of return on private debt flows to developing countries. This should have a positive effect on private capital flows, especially private debt flows. Second, we posit anticipated economic growth (proxied by actual or *ex post* growth) in developing countries also to be an indicator of expected returns, as also whether or not destination countries are going through a rising phase of economic cycle because expected returns might be less during economic depression than during an economic boom. The level of per capita income in the destination countries has often been posited in earlier studies to be a positive attraction of private capital flows, especially FDI; high income level is claimed to enhance returns on FDI. While we also maintain essentially the same position here, we are not oblivious to the theoretical possibility that high per capita income, by enhancing domestic net saving, could reduce demand for foreign finance which, if not supply-constrained, could lead to reduced private capital inflows.

Investment risks

Unlike the study by Fernández-Arias (1996), we do not limit our risk consideration to just creditworthiness, narrowly defined as the ability to pay. Instead, we broaden our concept of risk to include those elements which may, among others, impact on future rates of return. This is necessary especially since the present study is not limited to debt flows but also includes FDI. Also, unlike Fernández-Arias, we do not assume that investments outside developing countries are riskless. This follows from the broader definition of risks taken here. It is only if the risks are strictly limited to the ability to pay as assumed by Fernández-Arias, then it might be in order to assume absence of investment risks in the source countries.

One risk indicator we recognize here is the macroeconomic environment, particularly macroeconomic instability (alternatively proxied by inflation rate and monetary growth). This affects not only future repayment possibility (in the case of debts) but also the risks surrounding expected returns. We expect high inflation rate (or monetary growth) in the domestic economy of the specific source country under consideration to discourage domestic investment locally and thereby lead to enhanced capital flows to developing countries, just as the cross-effect of high inflation (or monetary growth) in other developed countries. High inflation (or monetary growth) in destination countries should have an opposite effect of retarding the volume of private capital flows received from developed countries.

Another indicator of risk is the existence of capital restrictions or controls (see Montiel and Reinhart 1999). These affect the prospect of capital repatriation, profit remittance and so on. The existence of capital controls in destination countries should have an unambiguous effect of reducing the volumes of private flows received. The effect of the existence of capital controls in a source country should similarly reduce capital flows to the destination countries. By reducing capital inflow and outflows to other countries, net inflows to developing countries can hardly be unaffected negatively. But the cross-effect of capital controls in other industrialized countries should, instead, have a positive effect on the flow from the particular source country under consideration to developing countries because the alternative of going to these other developed countries would be less attractive now. Instead of using qualitative capital control indicators as Montiel and Reinhart (1999) do, we proxy the lack of capital controls by the degree of openness in the BOPs capital account, measured as the sum of private inflows and outflows in relation to the GDP.

Specific model specification adopted in the study

We specify a regression equation of the form given in equation (6), reproduced as equation (11):

$$F_{ikt} = f(z_{kt}, X_t, \check{Z}_{kt}) \qquad (i = 1, 2, \ldots n; \; k = 1, \ldots q; \; t = 1, \ldots T) \qquad (11)$$

where:
F_{ikt} is the flow of ith type of private capital from source (developed) country k during year t to developing (destination) countries. Equations are estimated for different types and combinations of private capital flows, namely, total private capital flow; FDI; and PCF, with the latter decomposed, as determined by data availability, into non-bank PCF, non-bank securities, total export credit and non-export credit;
z_{kt} is the vector of source country k's specific or push-factors that make local investors seek cross-border investment opportunities (or desist from doing so, as the case may be);

$\check{Z}_{kt}$ is the average of corresponding elements of z_{kt} for all developed countries other than country k. The cross-effects of $\check{Z}_{kt}$ on net flows from country k to the developing countries are supposed to be broadly the same as those of z_{kt} (with the exception of the degree of openness of capital account), as already explained. Every element of this vector is in aggregate form, being a weighted average for all developed countries except the one under consideration;

X_t is the vector of destination (developing) countries' specific or pull-factors that attract or repel private capital flows from the developed countries. Every element of this vector is in aggregate form, being a weighted average for all developing countries.

Although not explicitly indicated, the above specification is for estimation with time-series data that are pooled across the countries to form a panel data. Specifically, annual data over the 1970 to 2000 period are pooled across the 19 donor countries with private capital flow statistics in Table 8.1.[9] But the resulting panel data are unbalanced in the sense that there are missing values for countries in a non-uniform manner with respect to both countries and variables. Also, because of this unbalanced nature of the data and due to the fact that some of the explanatory variables (e.g. inflation and monetary growth) are alternative proxies for essentially the same factor, we include only a few variables at a time. By doing so, not only is the incidence of multicollinearity minimized, but also the number of observations available to estimate the equation with fewer variables is maximized, as the inclusion of all or most explanatory variables in a particular equation would drastically reduce the usable data points. For each variable included for the source country, we also include the corresponding aggregate for all other source countries combined as well as for the destination countries. We employ a fixed-effect method that permits the intercept to vary across countries in the derivation of the panel data estimates.[10] Evidence on the existence (or lack) of stability of the parameter estimates is obtained indirectly: as pointed out above, the various equation estimates reported cover different periods, as dictated by data availability, with a number of regressors (such as per capita income and interest rates) featuring in many equations. By this, the temporal stability of parameter estimates of these regressors that feature in many equations can be inferred.

We expect some right-hand variables, particularly, interest rates and, possibly, the stock of external debt, to be endogenous. So, we use a form of instrumental variable method to cater for this. The 'instrument' is taken to be the fitted value of interest (discount) rate obtained by regressing the discount rate on its past value and past value of each of money market rate, economic growth and inflation. For the source countries, this is done on the basis of annual time-series regression for each source country before pooling the data and before aggregating the data into composite interest rate. But for all the destination countries, the fitted value used as the instrument is generated by regressing the composite interest rate on private debt to developing countries on similarly aggregated past value of each of external debt/GDP ratio, inflation rate and economic growth. Concerning the private debt/GDP and public debt/GDP ratios, their 'instruments' are simply taken to be their respective one-year lagged values. We take care of any existence of heteroscedasticity with covariance matrix correction method suggested by White (1980).

Data sources and how the variables are measured

Each of the dependent variables (from the DAC's *International Development Statistics*, online) referred to above is expressed as a fraction of the source country's GDP. Per capita income is the GDP per capita at the 1995 US dollar value; and the phase of economic cycle is computed as the residuals generated from regressing logarithm of real GDP index on a trend variable, so that the positive value of the residuals represents rising phase of the cycle. Degree of openness in the capital account is the sum of private capital inflows and outflows in relation to GDP. Public and private debt burden of developing countries is expressed in relation to GDP. Inflation rate is the growth of GDP implicit deflator. Domestic interest rate (obtained from IMF's *International Financial Statistics*, online) is the discount rate. All statistics, except where otherwise indicated, are from the World Bank's *World Development Indicators* (online) and *Global Development Finance* (online). All the aforementioned non-monetary figures are pure fractions, not percentages.

Concerning the composite variables, the average interest rate on current private lending to developing countries is available, already so computed, from the data source. The same applies to the following other composite variables for all developing countries: economic growth (real), degree of openness in the BOP capital account, private debt/GDP ratio, public debt/GDP ratio, inflation rate and monetary growth. While similar composite variables are also similarly published for the developed (source) countries, these could not be utilized, as we are interested in the composite for all developed countries except one. So, we compute these ourselves from the individual source country statistics and this requires choosing appropriate choice of weights in aggregating and averaging across the countries. For the rate of interest, we use the sum of exports and imports of goods and services as the weight (the sum of private capital inflows and outflows give practically the same results but they are dropped due to existence of missing values for some years). For per capita income, we use population while we use GDP as weight for all others.

5   Empirical results

The empirical results are reported in Tables 8.5 to 8.10. These show that the explanatory power of the equations is only modest, judging by the

Table 8.6 Effects of economic growth, per capita income levels and interest rates

	Total flows	FDI	Portfolio capital flows (PCF)					
			Total	Total for non-bank	Non-bank export credit	Non-bank securities	Total export credit	Total non-export credit
Per capita income (log)								
Specific source country	0.007	0.007	0.002	0.002	0.0003	0.0004	0.001	0.001
under consideration	(1.6)	(2.1)	(0.6)	(0.4)	(0.2)	(0.1)	(0.7)	(0.4)
Average for other source	−0.040	0.002	−0.040	−0.023	−0.015	−0.004	−0.010	−0.031
countries	(−3.8)	(0.4)	(−3.9)	(−3.1)	(−3.5)	(−0.9)	(−2.1)	(−3.6)
For all developing	0.032	−0.008	0.035	0.019	0.011	0.005	0.005	0.030
countries	(2.8)	(−1.2)	(3.3)	(2.7)	(2.6)	(1.1)	(1.0)	(3.4)
Interest rate								
Specific source country	−0.034	−0.019	−0.018	−0.004	0.002	−0.013	0.003	−0.023
under consideration	(−3.1)	(−2.2)	(−2.4)	(−0.5)	(0.6)	(−2.2)	(1.1)	(−3.5)
Average for all other	−0.097	−0.053	−0.036	−0.068	−0.038	−0.030	−0.048	0.011
source countries	(−3.8)	(−4.1)	(−1.6)	(−3.3)	(−5.3)	(−1.5)	(−5.3)	(0.5)
Average for all	0.117	0.060	0.056	0.051	0.035	0.016	0.057	0.001
destination (developing) countries	(3.7)	(2.8)	(2.4)	(2.2)	(3.4)	(0.9)	(4.5)	(0.03)
Economic growth								
Specific source country	0.002	0.011	−0.002	0.009	0.001	0.008	0.001	−0.003
under consideration	(0.2)	(1.8)	(−0.3)	(0.8)	(0.3)	(1.1)	(0.2)	(−0.3)
Average for other source	−0.014	−0.021	0.004	−0.018	−0.011	−0.011	−0.012	0.017
(developed) countries	(−0.8)	(−2.9)	(0.2)	(−1.7)	(−1.8)	(−1.4)	(−1.7)	(1.0)
Average for all	−0.030	−0.003	−0.025	−0.031	−0.003	−0.023	−0.006	−0.022
destination (developing) countries	(−1.2)	(−0.2)	(−1.3)	(−1.6)	(−0.4)	(−1.2)	(−0.7)	(−1.1)
Adjusted R^2	0.216	0.288	0.156	0.189	0.225	0.114	0.165	0.097
Total no. of observations	553	544	538	287	516	292	532	516

Notes: See Table 8.5.

Table 8.7 Effects of phase of economic cycle, interest rates and degree of capital account openness

	Total flows	FDI	Portfolio capital flows (PCF)						
			Total	Total for non-bank	Non-bank export credit	Non-bank securities	Total export credit	Total non-export credit
Rising phase of economic cycle								
Source country under consideration	0.007 (0.7)	0.018 (2.4)	−0.008 (−0.9)	−0.013 (−1.0)	0.001 (0.4)	−0.015 (−1.5)	0.002 (0.5)	−0.010 (−1.4)
Average for other source countries	0.044 (2.2)	0.009 (1.0)	0.041 (2.2)	0.059 (2.5)	0.020 (2.7)	0.036 (2.1)	0.018 (2.2)	0.025 (1.6)
For all developing countries	−0.007 (−0.3)	−0.013 (−1.0)	0.001 (0.1)	−0.004 (−0.3)	0.002 (0.3)	−0.001 (−0.1)	−0.005 (−0.6)	0.008 (0.4)
Interest rate								
Specific source country under consideration	−0.045 (−3.0)	−0.026 (−2.2)	−0.021 (−2.4)	0.013 (1.4)	0.000 (0.8)	−0.003 (−0.4)	0.004 (0.9)	−0.027 (−3.5)
Average for all other source countries	−0.141 (−4.0)	−0.008 (−0.5)	−0.128 (−3.9)	−0.124 (−4.6)	−0.070 (−5.5)	−0.031 (−1.8)	−0.073 (−4.5)	−0.059 (−2.2)
Average for all destination (developing) countries	0.226 (6.4)	0.035 (1.8)	0.189 (6.3)	0.127 (4.3)	0.090 (6.8)	0.021 (1.2)	0.102 (6.1)	0.090 (3.7)
Degree of capital account openness								
Source country under consideration	−00.002 (−1.2)	0.002 (1.3)	−0.004 (−1.4)	0.001 (0.1)	−0.002 (−2.0)	0.003 (0.7)	−0.001 (−1.0)	−0.003 (−1.1)
Average for other source countries	−0.024 (−2.7)	0.006 (0.9)	−0.030 (−4.4)	−0.028 (−4.2)	−0.015 (−5.3)	−0.012 (−2.4)	−0.014 (−4.7)	−0.018 (−2.8)
Average for all destination countries	0.039 (1.4)	0.002 (0.1)	0.031 (1.5)	0.057 (3.6)	0.021 (2.8)	0.038 (2.9)	0.018 (1.9)	0.018 (0.8)
Adjusted R^2	0.218	0.296	0.166	0.250	0.221	0.192	0.171	0.121
Total no. of observations	446	441	435	210	411	215	427	413

Notes: See Table 8.5.

Table 8.8 Effects of phase of economic cycle, degree of capital account openness and monetary expansion

	Total flows	FDI	Portfolio capital flows (PCF)						
			Total	Total for non-bank	Non-bank export credit	Non-bank securities	Total export credit	Total non-export credit
Rising phase of economic cycle								
Source country under consideration	0.001 (0.1)	0.013 (2.1)	−0.011 (−1.2)	−0.010 (−0.9)	0.002 (0.4)	−0.017 (−1.9)	0.002 (0.6)	−0.014 (−1.8)
Average for other source countries	0.021 (1.1)	0.006 (0.8)	0.020 (1.1)	0.038 (1.7)	0.007 (0.9)	0.036 (2.4)	−0.001 (−0.1)	0.024 (1.5)
Average for all developing countries	0.018 (1.1)	−0.013 (−1.7)	0.028 (2.0)	0.016 (1.7)	0.014 (3.0)	−0.005 (−0.9)	0.018 (3.1)	0.009 (0.6)
Degree of capital account openness								
Source country under consideration	−0.002 (−0.9)	0.002 (1.3)	−0.004 (−1.3)	0.001 (0.3)	−0.001 (−1.5)	0.003 (0.8)	−0.0001 (−0.1)	−0.003 (−1.0)
Average for other source countries	−0.003 (−0.4)	0.012 (1.9)	−0.016 (−2.4)	−0.018 (−2.6)	−0.007 (−3.0)	−0.007 (−1.4)	−0.007 (−2.7)	−0.010 (−1.5)
Average for all destination countries	0.087 (3.4)	0.017 (1.0)	0.066 (3.2)	0.077 (4.1)	0.035 (4.7)	0.045 (2.8)	0.036 (3.7)	0.035 (1.7)
Monetary growth								
Source country under consideration	0.001 (0.4)	0.001 (0.8)	0.001 (0.1)	0.001 (0.4)	0.002 (2.0)	−0.002 (−1.0)	0.002 (1.7)	−0.002 (−0.8)
Average for other source countries	0.056 (3.0)	0.019 (1.6)	0.035 (2.3)	0.014 (0.9)	0.014 (3.1)	0.013 (1.0)	0.013 (2.6)	0.026 (1.7)
Average for all destination countries	−0.010 (−2.4)	−0.001 (−0.1)	−0.010 (−3.0)	−0.004 (−1.2)	−0.004 (−3.0)	0.001 (0.4)	−0.003 (−2.4)	−0.007 (−2.0)
Adjusted R^2	0.204	0.282	0.158	0.215	0.193	0.195	0.126	0.124
Total no. of observations	447	441	427	210	410	215	426	394

Notes: See Table 8.5.

Table 8.9 Effects of per capita income and inflation rates

	Total flows	FDI	Portfolio capital flows (PCF)					
			Total	Total for non-bank	Non-bank export credit	Non-bank securities	Total export credit	Total non-export credit
Per capita income (log)								
Specific source country under consideration	0.007 (1.7)	0.008 (2.3)	0.003 (1.0)	0.001 (0.3)	0.001 (0.4)	0.0001 (0.1)	0.001 (0.7)	0.002 (0.6)
Average for other source countries	−0.032 (−3.7)	0.005 (1.2)	−0.037 (−4.4)	−0.010 (−1.5)	−0.011 (−3.4)	0.006 (1.5)	−0.012 (−2.9)	−0.025 (−3.3)
For all developing countries	0.034 (3.9)	−0.008 (−1.7)	0.037 (4.5)	0.013 (2.3)	0.011 (3.5)	−0.002 (−0.6)	0.012 (2.9)	0.026 (3.5)
Inflation rate								
Source country under consideration	0.004 (0.3)	−0.087 (−0.2)	0.005 (0.4)	0.002 (0.3)	0.005 (1.2)	−0.007 (−1.6)	0.005 (1.0)	0.0001 (0.01)
Average for other source countries	0.0002 (1.2)	0.009 (1.1)	0.015 (1.0)	0.019 (1.8)	0.007 (1.2)	0.015 (2.2)	0.005 (0.6)	0.012 (0.8)
Average for all destination countries	−0.009 (−4.7)	−0.005 (−4.0)	−0.004 (−2.7)	−0.005 (2.9)	−0.003 (−5.4)	−0.003 (−1.9)	−0.003 (−4.7)	−0.002 (−1.1)
Adjusted R^2	0.202	0.272	0.155	0.191	0.235	0.112	0.153	0.090
Total no. of observations	558	544	530	287	515	292	531	489

Notes: See Table 8.5.

Table 8.10   Effects of per capita income and initial external debt burden

	Total flows	FDI	Portfolio capital flows (PCF)					
			Total	Total for non-bank	Non-bank export credit	Non-bank securities	Total export credit	Total non-export credit
Per capita income (log)								
Specific source country under consideration	0.008 (1.5)	0.009 (2.3)	0.005 (1.4)	0.001 (0.3)	0.001 (0.8)	−0.0005 (−0.1)	0.001 (0.9)	0.003 (0.8)
Average for other source countries	−0.020 (−2.5)	0.008 (2.0)	−0.028 (−3.8)	0.004 (0.5)	−0.006 (−2.2)	0.012 (2.2)	−0.007 (−1.9)	−0.021 (−2.9)
For all developing countries	0.035 (4.7)	−0.009 (−2.4)	0.041 (6.1)	0.016 (3.5)	0.014 (5.4)	−0.002 (−0.6)	0.015 (4.5)	0.027 (4.2)
Public debt stock/GDP ratio								
Average for all destination countries	−0.042 (−4.2)	−0.013 (−2.6)	−0.032 (−3.4)	−0.038 (−4.7)	−0.020 (−6.6)	−0.014 (−2.2)	−0.020 (−4.7)	−0.015 (−1.6)
Private debt stock/GDP ratio								
Average for all destination countries	0.051 (2.4)	0.051 (3.0)	−0.004 (−0.3)	−0.008 (−0.4)	−0.007 (−1.3)	0.010 (0.5)	−0.004 (−0.6)	−0.002 (−0.1)
Adjusted R^2	0.234	0.302	0.172	0.234	0.265	0.116	0.178	0.098
Total no. of observations	536	528	514	275	498	280	514	474

Notes: See Table 8.5.

corresponding modest values of the adjusted R^2. Next we examine the effects of each explanatory variable on the different categories and various combinations of foreign capital flows.

Effects of per capita income levels

Per capita income of the specific source country
As reported in Tables 8.5, 8.6, 8.9 and 8.10, this has a positive and statistically significant coefficient in all equations (except that of non-bank securities in Table 8.10) but the coefficient is statistically significant in the FDI equation only. Since the dependent variables are expressed as fractions of the source country's GDP, the coefficients could plausibly take any sign. A negative coefficient (depending on its magnitude) could mean that capital flows, in monetary terms, increase with the source country's income but simply do not keep up proportionally. A zero or statistically insignificant coefficient would mean that capital flows simply rise in more or less strict proportionality to the per capita income level, suggesting that the average (income) propensity to invest abroad is constant. On the other hand, a positive and statistically significant coefficient, as observed here in the case of FDI, suggests that capital flows from the source country rise faster than the country's per capita income so that marginal (income) propensity to invest in developing countries is positive. Similar evidence seems to exist for PCF and its various components, but in a weak form due to statistical insignificance of the rather consistently positive coefficients. Thus, while there is strong evidence that source countries' FDI rise faster than their per capita income levels, the evidence of this effect for PCF and its various components is rather weak.

Per capita income (aggregate) of other developed countries
The coefficient of this is not significant in the FDI equation nor in the equation for non-bank securities, suggesting that a source country's investment in these two items is largely immune from the level of per capita income in other developed (or source) countries (see Tables 8.5, 8.6, 8.9 and 8.10). On the other hand, its coefficient is negative and statistically very significant in the equations for all other PCF components (and the equation for total PCF, as well). This evidence suggests that a capital-exporting developed country's PCFs (with the exception of non-bank security investment) to developing countries are diverted away by rising per capita income levels in other developed countries.

Per capita income (aggregate) of the destination countries
Its coefficient is not statistically significant in the equations for FDI (where it even has the rather implausible negative sign) nor for non-bank securities (see Tables 8.5, 8.6, 8.9 and 8.10). On the other hand, its coefficient is positive and statistically very significant in equations for all other components of PCF (and the equation for total PCF also). Thus, the evidence suggests that a rising level of per capita income in developing countries 'pulls' or attracts

all PCF components (except non-bank securities) but, surprisingly, no evidence of this effect is recorded for the FDI.

Effects of interest rates

Interest rate in the specific source country under consideration
The coefficient is not statistically significant in the equations for total and non-bank export credits and for non-bank PCF as a whole (see Tables 8.5 to 8.7). But it is consistently negative (as expected) and statistically significant in all FDI equations and those for the non-export credit and the non-bank security components of total PCF, as well as those for total PCF itself and, indeed, all private flow equations. Thus, except for export credits, all components of private capital flows tend to be 'pushed' to developing countries as a result of low interest rates in the specific capital-exporting country. This finding is in agreement with some earlier studies, for example, Montiel and Reinhart (1999) who report that interest rates in the US and Japan negatively affected the allocation of capital flows to the selected developing countries covered in their study. Conversely, Hernandez and Rudolph (1995), for example, find no evidence of statistically significant interest rate effect on long-term capital flows. The short span and a particular episode-specific coverage of most of the earlier studies could be a likely reason for their generally contradictory findings.

Interest rate (aggregate) in other developed countries
This exerts the same effect as the interest rate in the specific source country, as discussed above, except that its coefficient in the equations for non-bank and total export credits is now negative and statistically significant. Furthermore, the statistical significance of its coefficient in the total non-export credit and non-bank security equations is now less (see Tables 8.5 to 8.7). But on the whole, the same broad picture also emerges here of the deterring effects of high interest rates on private flows to developing countries, as discussed above. FDI and practically all PCF components from a particular capital-exporting developed country are found to be diverted away from developing countries by high interest rates in other developed countries.

Interest rate (aggregate) on private lending to developing countries
As expected, the coefficient of this variable is positive in all equations and also statistically significant in all, except in some of the equations for total non-export credit and non-bank securities (Tables 8.5 to 8.7). Thus, interest rate (as a proxy for returns on private capital flows) is a significant pull-factor for flows to developing countries.

Effects of economic growth

Economic growth in the specific source country under consideration
The coefficient of this factor is not statistically significant in any equation (Table 8.6). Hence, there is no evidence that economic growth in the capital-exporting country in fact affects net private capital flows.

Economic growth (aggregate) in other developed countries
The coefficient is negative (as expected) and statistically significant in the FDI equation, with marginal significance in the equations for both total and non-bank export credits and for the non-bank component of PCF (Table 8.6). But the coefficient is statistically insignificant in all other equations. Thus, high economic growth in other developed countries could be said to divert each capital-exporting developed country's FDI (and, to some extent, the export credit component of PCF) away from developing countries while other PCF components are hardly affected.

Economic growth (aggregate) in the destination countries
The coefficient of this factor is not statistically significant in any equation (Table 8.6). Hence, there is no evidence that economic growth in destination countries has any pull on net private capital flows.

Effects of phase of economic cycle

Phase of economic cycle prevailing in the specific source country under consideration
The positive coefficient of the rising phase of economic cycle in the FDI equation is the only one that is statistically significant (see Tables 8.7 and 8.8). Its coefficient in other equations are either significant (marginally) in only Table 8.8 or not significant at all in any of the tables. Thus, what can be inferred is that the rising phase of economic cycle in a capital-exporting developed economy appears to have 'pushed' FDI to developing countries. This rather unexpected effect on FDI is probably due to the fact that net savings – and hence domestic availability of funds – increase with an economic upswing. But there is no evidence that PCF or any of its components is affected by the phase of economic cycle.

Phase of (aggregate) economic cycle prevailing in other developed countries
The unexpectedly positive coefficient of the rising phase of economic cycle in the equation for the non-bank security component of PCF is the only one that is statistically significant in Tables 8.7 and 8.8. Its coefficient in other equations, while mostly positive and significant in Table 8.7, is not significant in Table 8.8, thereby making the evidence non-robust. The unexpectedly positive coefficient in non-bank securities equation is not unlikely to be caused by the fact that the sudden attraction to investors (especially, since 1995 as reviewed in Section 2) of this type of PCF merely coincides with the rising phase of economic cycles in major developed countries. The total picture emerging is that the phase of economic cycle prevailing in other developed countries does not have much influence on the magnitude of net private flows from a particular capital-exporting developed country.

Phase of (aggregate) economic cycle prevailing in the destination countries
The coefficient of this variable, although broadly positive (as expected) and statistically significant in most equations in Table 8.8, is not significant in

Table 8.7, thereby making the evidence non-robust. In totality, the picture seems to indicate that the phase of economic cycle collectively prevailing in the developing countries does not pull foreign private capital to them as such.

Effects of openness of the economy regarding BOP capital account transactions

Openness in the BOP capital account of the specific source country under consideration
The coefficient of this factor is not statistically significant in the equations (see Tables 8.7 and 8.8). Thus, the removal of capital controls in a capital-exporting developed country is observed not to have pushed net capital flows to developing countries.

Openness (aggregate) in the BOP capital account of other developed countries
The coefficient of this variable is not significant in the FDI equation. But it is negative, as earlier posited, in the equations for total private flows and PCF, as well as for all PCF components. It is also statistically significant in almost all these (Tables 8.7 and 8.8). This suggests that net flows of all PCF components from a particular capital-exporting developed country are being diverted away from developing countries as a result of the removal of capital controls (or increased BOP capital account openness) in other developed countries.

Openness (aggregate) in the BOP capital account of destination countries
As expected, the coefficient of this variable is positive in all equations. And although it is not statistically significant in the FDI ones, it is significant in almost all equations for PCF and its components (see Tables 8.7 and 8.8). This evidence suggests that the elimination of capital controls by developing countries is a significant pull-factor for foreign private flows, particularly, PCF.

Effects of unstable macroeconomic environment

Macroeconomic environment in the specific source country under consideration
Neither of the two alternative proxies of macroeconomic imbalances, inflation rate and monetary growth, has a coefficient that is statistically significant in any of the equations. This suggests that resident investors in a capital-exporting country do not see domestic macroeconomic imbalances as a major issue that would push them to invest in developing countries. Alternatively, it is possible that macroeconomics imbalances in each capital-exporting country were not sufficiently severe to make investors consider them a serious disincentive.

Macroeconomic environment (aggregate) in other developed countries
In line with expectations, the coefficients of both inflation rate and monetary growth, the two alternative proxies for macroeconomic imbalances, are

positive in all equations (see Tables 8.8 and 8.9). Although the coefficients are rather insignificant in the equations for FDI and some components of PCF, the broad evidence emerging is that net private flows, especially PCF, from a particular capital-exporting developed country are diverted to developing countries as a result of macroeconomic problems and imbalances in other developed countries.

Macroeconomic environment (aggregate) in the destination countries
As expected, the coefficients of the two alternative proxies of this factor, inflation rate and monetary growth, are negative and statistically significant in practically all the equations. It can therefore be inferred that stable macroeconomic environment, in the form of low inflation and low monetary expansion, is an important factor that pulls or attracts foreign private capital to developing countries.

Effects of existing level of external debt burden

The coefficient of the size of public and publicly guaranteed external debt in relation to GDP is, as expected, negative and statistically significant in all equations (see Table 8.10). Thus, foreign private investment of all categories appears to be consistently deterred from highly indebted developing countries. Foreign private investors seem to regard it as a high-risk indicator.

The coefficient of the size of private external debt in relation to GDP, on the other hand, is unexpectedly positive and statistically significant in the FDI equation while in the equations for PCF and its various components, it is not statistically significant (see Table 8.10). That the coefficient is positive in the FDI equation is probably a coincidence arising from the fact that countries with high private external debt are mostly in Latin America and also happen to be, for different reasons, among those receiving much FDI. Thus, on the balance of evidence, private debt seems to have little impact on net private capital flows in general. The opposing forces (including involuntary lending to re-finance maturing debts might neutralize the risk implied by high debt level) which could give rise to this were discussed earlier.

6   Summary and conclusion

The study reported in this chapter is an attempt to rectify some problems that characterize most earlier studies seeking to explain private capital flows to developing countries – or, at least to examine the subject from a different and complementary perspective. To accomplish this, we propose a model framework that approaches the issue from the perspective of a capital-exporting developed country and which also takes cognizance of developments in other developed countries that could be competing with developing countries for private capital flows from that source. The model is operationalized and estimated with annual panel data over the period

1970–2000 for 19 capital-exporting developed countries. Specifically, we estimated equations for total private flows, FDI, total PCF as well as the various categories of PCF. We tested for the effects of a number of factors, each of which has its own push- and pull-components. The main highlights of our findings include the following:

Effects of per capita income levels
First, while there is strong evidence that source countries' FDIs rise faster than their per capita income levels, the evidence of this effect on PCF and its various components is rather weak. Second, a capital-exporting developed country's PCF (with the exception of non-bank security investment) is diverted from developing countries by rising per capita income levels in other developed countries. And, third, rising level of per capita income in the developing countries pulls or attracts all PCF components (except non-bank securities) but, surprisingly, there is no evidence of this effect for the FDI.

Effects of interest rates
First, except for export credits, all components of private capital flows tend to be pushed to developing countries as a result of low interest rates in the specific capital-exporting developed country. Second, FDI and practically all PCF components from a particular capital-exporting country are noted to veer away from developing countries as a result of high interest rates in other developed countries. And, third, interest rate (as a proxy for return on private capital flows) is a significant pull-factor for flows to developing countries.

Effects of economic growth
First, there is no evidence that economic growth in the capital-exporting country truly affects net private capital flows. Second, high economic growth in other developed countries could be said to divert the FDI – and, to some extent, the export credit component of PCF – of each capital-exporting developed country away from developing countries while other PCF components are hardly affected. Finally, there is no evidence that economic growth in destination countries has any pull on net private capital flows.

Effects of phase of economic cycle
First, the rising phase of economic cycle in a capital-exporting developed economy appears to have 'pushed' FDI to developing countries, while there is no evidence that PCF or any of its components are affected by economic cycles. Second, the phase of economic cycle prevailing in other developed countries did not matter much in determining the magnitude of net private flows from a particular capital-exporting developed country to the developing countries. Finally, the phase of economic cycle collectively prevailing in developing countries did not pull foreign private capital to them as such.

Effects of openness of the economy regarding BOP capital account transactions

The removal of capital controls in a capital-exporting developed country is observed not to have pushed net capital flows to developing countries. But net flows of all PCF components of a particular capital-exporting developed country are being diverted away from developing countries by the removal of capital controls (or increased BOP capital account openness) in other developed countries. Also, elimination of capital controls by developing countries is a significant pull-factor for foreign private flows, particularly, PCF.

Effects of unstable macroeconomic environment

Resident investors in a capital-exporting country appear not to view domestic macroeconomic imbalance (as alternatively proxied by high inflation and monetary growth) as a major issue that would push them to invest in developing countries. But the net private flows, especially PCF, of a particular capital-exporting developed country are diverted to developing countries as a result of macroeconomic problems and imbalances in other developed countries. Also, stable macroeconomic environment in the form of low inflation and low monetary expansion is an important factor for attracting foreign private capital to developing countries.

Effects of existing level of external debt burden

Foreign private investments of all categories appear to be consistently deterred from highly indebted developing countries. Foreign private investors seem to regard severe indebtedness as a high-risk indicator, while private debt seems to have little effect on net private capital flows in general.

Despite measurement or data aggregation difficulties entailed by the adopted approach, it seems to have advantages in terms of conceptual clarity and policy relevance. Our findings corroborate those of a number of existing studies that have investigated the pull- versus push-factors in foreign private capital flows and also go beyond this to shed light on additional issues, including cross-effects of factors prevailing in the developed countries other than the one being studied.

Notes

1. The concept of saving can be thought of as gross national income less gross national expenditure, and before net unrequited transfers, which, in turn, are below the line' items in defining the BOP surplus as excess of exports over imports of goods and services. This BOP definition is to include grants (official unrequited transfers) in the north–south financial flows.
2. Information on F_i can be obtained by aggregating y_{ij} over the m destination countries, which can be tedious and, therefore, hardly adopted in reality. Given the manner in which statistics are normally made available, an easier approach is to obtain the information in 'ready made' form from the source country, since it is

simply the source country's transfer of type *i*, without concern about the receiving countries. For instance, statistics on FDI from a particular FDI-exporting country are more readily available at source than attempting to collate the same from several destination countries.

3. For example, information on some push-factors may now be available for each individual source country which may not be available (or feasible to compute) in composite form for all countries in estimating equation (2), just as some push-factors for individual destination countries in equation (2) may now cease to be available (or practicable to compute) in composite form for all.

4. Ordinarily, if market clearing exists in international financial markets, observations on the nominal value of each type of resource flow can be described either as transfers or receipts, just as the observed market quantity (in the absence of rationing) can be called demand or supply. In this sense, a researcher that describes the cup as being half-full would be equally as right as the one describing it as half-empty. So, it is what we do with it (including whether we normalize it with variables from source or destination countries) that determines whether we model it from the source or destination country perspectives.

5. For instance, in practice, in equation (2), y_{ij} flow to destination country *j* could have come from several source countries, so that the resulting normalization would become extremely tedious and painstaking. Probably because of this statistical expediency, the adoption of destination country perspective (as in equation (2)) and normalization in terms of the destination country variables have always been going together.

6. Some of the issues here have to do with the relative attractions of using the DRS (debtor reporting statistics) typified by World Bank publications and CRS (creditor reporting statistics) typified by the OECD and BIS (Bank for International Settlements) publications.

7. Henceforth, these are referred to as developed countries and destination countries as developing countries, so as to avoid confusion.

8. The variable to use in calculating the weights π_h's is an empirical issue.

9. This means Greece, Ireland and Luxembourg are excluded.

10. The random-effect alternative also gives practically the same results. But to save space, we do not report these.

References

Agenor, P. R. (1998). 'The Surge in Capital Flows: Analysis of "Pull" and "Push" Factors'. *International Journal of Finance and Economics*, 3 (1): 39–57.

Armijo, L. E. (ed.) (1999). *Financial Globalization and Democracy in Emerging Markets*. New York: Palgrave.

Chang, H., G. Palma and D. H. Whittaker (eds) (2001). *Financial Liberalization and the Asian Crisis*. New York: Palgrave.

Edwards, S. (ed.) (2000). *Capital Flows and Emerging Economies: Theory, Evidence and Controversies*. NBER Conference Report Series. Chicago and London: University of Chicago Press.

Fernández-Arias, E. (1996). 'The New Wave of Private Capital Inflows: Push or Pull?' *Journal of Development Economics*, 48 (2): 389–418.

Fernández-Arias, E. and P. J. Montiel (1996). 'The Surge in Capital Flows to Developing Countries: An Analytical Overview'. *The World Bank Economic Review*, 10 (1): 51–80.

Griffith-Jones, S., M. F. Montes and A. Nasution (eds) (2001). *Short-term Capital Flows and Economic Crisis*. Oxford and New York: Oxford University Press.

Hernandez, L. and H. Rudolph (1995). 'Sustainability of Private Capital Flows to Developing Countries: Is a Generalized Reversal Likely?' World Bank Working Paper Series 1518. Washington, DC: World Bank.

IMF (online). *International Financial Statistics*. Washington, DC: IMF.

Ito, T. and A. Krueger (eds) (2001). *Regional and Global Capital Flows: Macroeconomic Causes and Consequences*. NBER-East Asia Seminar on Economics, Vol. 10. Chicago and London: University of Chicago Press.

Mody, A., M. P. Taylor and J. Y. Kim (2001). 'Modelling Fundamentals for Forecasting Capital Flows to Emerging Markets'. *International Journal of Finance and Economics*, 6 (3): 201–16.

Montiel, P. and C. M. Reinhart (1999). 'Do Capital Controls and Macroeconomic Policies Influence the Volume and Composition of Capital Flows? Evidence from the 1990s'. *Journal of International Money and Finance*, 18: 619–35.

OECD (Organization for Economic Co-operation and Development) (online). *International Development Statistics, IDS*. Paris: OECD.

OECD (Organization for Economic Co-operation and Development) (2001) *Development Co-operation, The DAC Journal, 2000 Report*, 2 (1).

Oxfam America (2002). 'Global Finance Hurts the Poor: Analysis of the Impact of North–South Private Capital Flows on Growth, Inequality and Poverty'. An Oxfam Report. Boston: Oxfam America.

White, H. (1980). 'A Heteroscedasticity-consistent Covariance Matrix Estimator and Direct Test for Heteroscedasticity'. *Econometrica*, 48: 817–38.

World Bank (online). *Global Development Finance*. Washington, DC: World Bank.

World Bank (online). *World Development Indicators, 2001*. Washington, DC: World Bank.

Zedillo, Ernesto (2000). 'Report on the High-level Panel on Financing for Development'. Report commissioned by the Secretary-General of the United Nations. Available at: www.un.org/reports/financing/.

Index